D1576100

MARRIAGE
AND THE
FAMILY

*A Comparative Analysis
of Contemporary Problems*

Edited by
MEYER BARASH
HOFSTRA UNIVERSITY

ALICE SCOURBY
C. W. POST COLLEGE

HQ
728
.B36

Random House New York

POINT PARK COLLEGE LIBRARY

Copyright © 1970 by Random House, Inc.
All rights reserved under International and Pan-American Copyright Conventions. Published in the United States by Random House, Inc., New York, and simultaneously in Canada by Random House of Canada Limited, Toronto.

Library of Congress Catalog Card Number: 78–106974

Manufactured in the United States of America by H. Wolff Book Manufacturing Co., Inc., New York, N. Y.

Design by Saul Schnurman

FIRST PRINTING
98765432

ACKNOWLEDGMENTS

We will not attempt the impossible task of acknowledging the assistance of everyone who has been helpful to us at various stages in the preparation of this anthology, even though all have our gratitude. Nevertheless, specific mention must be made of a few key individuals. To Charles Page, of the University of Massachusetts, we express appreciation for the many provocative questions and suggestions that compelled response. Theodore Caris, of the College Department at Random House, helped us through many crises that might have posed serious obstacles to the felicitous completion of this book. Muriel Smith, of Random House, edited our manuscript with painstaking care and with a creativity that went far beyond the usual expertise associated with the editorial function.

If this work has anything to contribute beyond the offerings of other anthologies in the field, it is in no small measure due to our classes and the opportunities they afforded us to test many of the ideas contained herein.

M.B.
A.S.

CONTENTS

MARRIAGE AND THE FAMILY

INTRODUCTION

This anthology was undertaken with the undergraduate student in mind. The selections represent some of the substantive problems found in the field of marriage and the family. They provide an interdisciplinary approach with emphasis upon role behavior and the relation of the individual to the social world in which he lives.

The central focus of this book is to examine family change within its social milieu. We do not view any change in family life as isolated phenomena but, rather, as integrated aspects of family life modified in their expression by the social context in which this change occurs. For this reason we have included numerous cross-cultural studies as well as articles relating to interclass family behavior.

The readings have been selected and organized around the basic assumption that family behavior is a matter of social roles that are inseparable from the roles one plays in other contexts. In emphasizing crucial aspects of social change and the consequences these have for the family, we have called into question the accepted tenets of authoritarian, patriarchal, and traditional family patterns.

Our point of view is institutional rather than guidance-oriented. As a result we have omitted selections dealing with adjustment, child care, mate selection, and therapy even though there have been significant recent contributions in all these areas. Instead, we believe that every selection included has substantive as well as theoretical value within an institutional and cross-cultural context. Moreover, all the readings have been written within the past decade.

The material selected for this book focuses on several major problems in the order outlined in the following questions:

1. Is the dominance of the nuclear family of western Europe and the United States a functional consequence of urbanization and the Industrial Revolution?

2. Is secularization of human values positively associated with urbanization and industrialization?

3. What is the relationship between normative and behavioral aspects of authority and power?

4. What role reversals take place within the multigenerational family network?

5. What major trends in American life have encouraged withdrawal among large segments of Negroes, women, and middle-class youth in our society?

These are broad, substantive questions that purport to systematically relate phenomena often left disconnected. In order to avoid ethnocentrism and to delineate the traditional system of family life in high relief, it is necessary to expose the reader to family systems very different from his own, where change has not obscured traditional patterns to the same degree it has in America. We start from the basic premise that the family almost everywhere has been traditionally structured in terms of patriarchal norms reinforced by a double standard of morality. Although other forms have always existed, monogamy has been the rule for obvious social and economic reasons. Technically, monogamy remains the prevalent form even when the individual marries more than once. However, this does not make monogamy more "natural" than any other form of marriage.

Another concept basic to our approach is that sex roles are verifiably social roles and are not to be reduced to a biological level of explanation. Indeed, the prevalence of such reductionism would seem to reflect aspects of the current "folk lore of sex"—to borrow Albert Ellis' phrase—in that patriarchal norms can be easily rationalized by assuming that social roles are natural roles and that, therefore, the subordination of the female is regarded as biologically justified. It may very well be that the major justification of a cross-cultural approach to familial institutions may lie in demonstrating the numerous permutations and combinations that the sexual division of labor may entail.

Although it is easy to posit a single standard of morality as a logical alternative to the traditional double standard and to substitute an equalitarian trend for the patriarchal norm, especially in a modern context, we believe that such an evolution is not likely. A single standard of sex behavior cannot be maintained unless the rest of the social system supports it.

There is a tendency to avoid discussion of causation by taking refuge in unspecified connotations of the concept "functional." Our view is that in such areas as marriage and the family, criminology, and delinquency a commitment to the positive approach of causation is methodologically crucial. In the field covered by this anthology, for example, we may posit the following formula of a causal nature: Marriage is the cause of certain behavior patterns whether defined by the group as normal or deviant. In our society, marriage, which is a vehicle for cultural continuity, also causes prostitution and divorce. The fact that the majority of the clients of prostitutes are not unattached males but married men is causally significant. Men are freer than women to deviate from traditional cultural expectations regarding fidelity. In addition, women are more frequently prosecuted for sex offenses, even though men, by definition, create the social demand for such behavior. This is especially true of middle-class males in our society. Cross-culturally, concubinage, in the traditional Asiatic context, is the counterpart of prostitution in modern urban society. Prostitution, like concubinage, may be either a stabilizing or a disruptive social force, depending upon ideology, social class, and whether or not the society is undergoing modernization or other forms of rapid social change.

Role reversal may be our most significant single clue to social change both within the family and in the larger social system. In the rural society of early nineteenth-century America, one cultural expectation was that children would assume responsibility for the care of their parents. In contemporary American urban middle-class contexts, roles are reversed, and parents assume financial and related obligations of a continuing nature even after their children are adults. Marriage as a passage rite no longer connotes adulthood in the sense of independence. Role reversal may also give us a clue to understanding some of the problems of alienation and lack of commitment of the young alluded to in the selections by June Bingham and Kenneth Keniston. An illustration of role reversal is found in modern urban industrial society where the multigenerational family network is dysfunctional to the activities and sentiments of its members. If family members accept the legitimacy of social institutions outside the family and experience varying degrees of commitment to them, then interference with and weakening of family solidarity is to be expected. (For example, the middle-class married woman is in conflict with economic, not domestic, responsibilities.) In traditional family systems, role reversal is least likely to occur. This poses an important problem for societies undergoing basic changes in their social structure as well as those societies that are experiencing rapid social change— a challenge to which industrial as well as preindustrial societies must respond in ways appropriate to their respective cultural backgrounds.

Minority group family behavior in the United States can be scaled on a continuum between the opposite poles of rebellion and withdrawal, which indicates that alienation is not a monopoly of any one social class. Somewhere toward the middle of the continuum would be family behavior and ideology reflecting "the American dream," namely aspiring to emulate or to identify with the norms of the dominant middle class. During periods of rapid social change, family behavior in the same groups tends to have a higher incidence of polarization. At one extreme would be those in rebellion against the dominant group norms who pursue a goal of changing from a double standard to a single standard and thus accelerating the trend from patriarchal to equalitarian patterns. At the opposite end would be those who have accepted withdrawal or retreatism as a consequence of alienation or disenchantment. Their view is the possibility of adapting to or changing the family system. The black bourgeoisie, as E. Franklin Frazier conceived them, in identifying with the norms of their white middle-class counterparts comprise one mode of adaptation (see his *Black Bourgeoisie*, 1957). Women, as a sex fighting for equal rights, are another. The hippie counterculture and the advocates of black power and segregationism are contemporary illustrations of withdrawal and retreatism.

Those writers on marriage and the family who as liberals identify with an egalitarian, single-standard, romantic ideology in contrast to the traditional patriarchal norms, are sometimes unaware of the cultural inconsistencies that characterize this historic evolution. No man is an island, and no family exists in a sociocultural vacuum. As a result the price a man and woman pay for commit-

ment to a romantic ideology includes such symptoms as role conflict, role confusion, anomie, and alienation because the surround-
ing economic, political, religious, and related institutions that
have an impact on the family reflect a double standard.

For many centuries there has been an awareness of the differences between institutional conformity to societal goals and the
distraction from such goals caused by deviation from cultural expectations. Ever since the fifteenth and sixteenth centuries, when
the Calvinist ethos began to take form, a new rationale for conformity to institutional requirements began to make itself felt.
This rationale maintained that even though sacrifices of individual
freedom were inevitable as a result of institutional ties, advantages nevertheless accrued in terms of relative immunity to distraction from efficiency in performing God's work on this earth.

If a person is married and leads a life that is predictable, he is
ready to take on the economic challenges of the next day (or at
any rate, he is readier than if he had spent the previous night
pursuing some will-o'-the-wisp). However, Max Weber claimed
that this very process of adaptation to institutional requirements
in the interest of a stable social order results in the "routinization
of charisma"—the loss of a sense of novelty and spontaneity (*Essays in Sociology*, 1946). In twentieth-century terms this means
that any marriage has a potentially built-in risk of incompatibil-
ity. Our view is that charisma may be equated with the search for
novelty, whereas routinization, whatever its advantages, may correspond in time to habit, jaded appetites, and lack of challenge.
Even for a couple able to recognize and articulate this problem,
there is the stumbling block of the Protestant Ethic, with its emphasis on day-to-day duties and responsibilities that take priority
over occasions for spontaneity.

It may well be asked why this introduction is climaxed by the
problem of loss of novelty and spontaneity. If the dilemmas of
contemporary marital relationships are at issue, it is our view that
a romantic, single-standard, interpersonal relationship has to
reconcile the spontaneous and the routine. Such a reconciliation
seems almost inherently contradictory—at least for the middle-
class American who is sensitized to articulate but is nevertheless
unable to solve this problem. These dilemmas would have no
functional relevance for traditional societies, but family systems in
nations undergoing modernization feel the impact in varying degrees.

One concluding point we would like to make about this reader is that although it is conventional for editors of anthologies to preface each selection or group of selections with what is essentially a summary, we have chosen the alternative path of providing comments at the ends of selections. This has been done for several reasons. First, we have noted too many cases in our teaching experience in which students have read the editorial summaries and ignored the selections themselves. Even more important is the conviction that this volume will have greater pedagogical value if the readings precede our editorial comments. This procedure leaves the reader's mind relatively unstructured and therefore more receptive to the impact of the selections themselves. Finally, the editorial comments do not attempt to summarize the readings directly but rather to make evaluations designed to provoke thought on the part of the students. With this goal in mind we have not hesitated to be controversial, open-ended, ambiguous (on occasion), and even elliptical in our comments.

1

INDUSTRIALIZATION
AND THE FAMILY
IN SOCIOLOGICAL THEORY

SIDNEY M. GREENFIELD

The small nuclear family found in western Europe and the United States is generally viewed in sociological theory as a consequence of the urban-industrial revolution. The present paper questions the hypothesis and suggests alternative lines of thinking.[1]

As Western society continues to disseminate its distinctive technology to the remainder of the world, both theoretical and practical consideration must be given to the changes in social organization that accompany the introduction of the machine and the market-exchange economic system. The specific task of the sociologist and cultural anthropologist here is to seek empirically founded generalizations about cultural process, causality, and functional interdependence. For policy-makers and administrators in foreign affairs and international relations have been applying ill-founded generalizations uncritically: they reason that, if certain types of social organization and urban-industrial technology and the market-exchange economic system are interrelated, they must inevitably accompany Western technology, and as consequence, they support action programs designed to establish and foster these forms.

The dominant sociological hypothesis relating technology and

From American Journal of Sociology, 67 (November 1961), 312–322. Reprinted by permission of University of Chicago Press.

social organization postulates a functional interdependence between industrialization and urbanization, the techno-economic system, with the small nuclear family as the unit of social organization. Hypotheses of functional interdependence, however, take several forms, each with different implications. As Nagel has pointed out, statements phrased in functional terms are the equivalent of those phrased in nonfunctional terms and any statement in one terminology can be translated into the other: "The difference between a functional and a nonfunctional formulation," he states, "is one of selective emphasis; it is quite comparable to the difference between saying that B is the effect of A, and saying that A is the condition (or cause) of B." [2]

There are, however, two contrasting ways of conceptualizing sociocultural phenomena that result in significantly different meanings for statements of functional relationships. In one formulation the functional statements have approximately the same meaning as conventional causal statements while, in the other, a special type of causal implication is rendered. The most widely adopted formulation of functionalism found in social science is based upon the organic analogy. Sociocultural systems are likened to living organisms in being goal-directed, self-righting systems in which all of the parts "function" to maintain the whole in a state of equilibrium. As phrased by Radcliffe-Brown:

> The concept of function involves the notion of a *structure* consisting of a *set of relations* amongst *unit entities*, the continuity of the structure being maintained by a *life process* made up of the *activities* of the constituent units.
> Such a view implies that a social system (the total structure of a society together with the totality of social usages in which the structure appears and on which it depends for its continued existence) has a certain kind of unity, which we may speak of as functional unity. We may define it as a condition in which all parts of the social system work together with a sufficient degree of harmony or internal consistency, i.e., without producing persistent conflicts which can neither be resolved nor regulated. [3]

Maintenance of the state of equilibrium, then, is likened to the continuance of life in the organism; the destruction of the equilibrium is analogous to death. The system is closed, and change in the total configuration is ruled out by the basic assumptions. The state of equilibrium is based upon the efficient integration of all of the parts, each of which functions to maintain the continuing existence of the whole. As long as the system continues, then, each part is necessarily functional and its relationship vis-à-vis any other part is one of functional interdependence—all of the parts operating to achieve the goal or purpose of the whole: maintenance of the state of equilibrium. Given this self-maintaining system, we can say that both parts and whole are functionally interrelated and interdependent. By varying our perspective, however, we may view each as a functional consequence of the other, that is, any part is a functional consequence of the operation of the total system, or the whole is a functional consequence of the operation of all the parts.

In the terminology of cause and effect there may also be two perspectives: Starting from the parts, we may say that they are the cause of the whole, which is the effect of their activity, since they maintain the totality in a given state. On the other hand, however, the whole is also the cause of the parts, since the latter operate in accord with the pattern of the former, thereby becoming its effect. In this formulation, however, no causal statements can be made about relations among the parts themselves; that is, one part cannot be the cause of any other since all, taken cumulatively, are either the cause of, or are caused by, the whole. The only relationship that can exist among the parts of a self-regulating, functionally integrated, equilibrium system is that of functional interdependence.[4]

The alternative formulation of functional theory in social science modifies the assumption of equilibrium and discards the organic analogy. To those who hold this position, the empirical evidence suggests the conclusion that sociocultural systems are never in a state of complete equilibrium. They are always changing and, consequently, equilibrium is a state relative to a given period of time and, at best, only approximated. In the long run, all sociocultural systems appear to be in continuous flux and both the parts and the whole can and do change. Adherents of this opinion, then, do not generally conceptualize sociocultural systems as self-regulating and goal-directed; consequently, the specialized set of functional statements used to analyze self-regulating systems are not necessary. Functional statements in this formulation are thus the direct equivalent of causal statements, and a causal relationship is implied whether the terms "functional consequence" or "functional interdependence" are used. The term "functional consequence," however, may be read as necessary and sufficient cause while "functional interdependence" is the equivalent of sufficient cause alone.

In accord with this view the possible relationships between part and whole and part and part differ from those possible in the prior formulation. Since equilibrium is not assumed, the cause of the total system being maintained in its given state is not the functioning of the parts, nor is the cause of the operations of the units taken to be the achievement of the goal of the whole. Here the total system tends to be viewed as resulting from a process of change and adjustment among the parts. Thus, one part can and does, as the interpretation is made, exert a causal effect on the other parts and by implication on the whole. It is only after the parts have had their effect on the other units that the parts may be thought of as being functionally interrelated—the term being taken to mean operating in a state of harmony with each other for a given time. So conceptualized, the locus of the causal nexus is the part-part relationship rather than the part-whole relationship, as is the case in the alternative formulation.

Many students in both Europe and the United States have studied the historical conditions that have produced the distinctive modern form of the family. We select Ogburn and Nimkoff because they present the generally accepted point of view. They distinguish three basic types—the consanguineous, the stem, and the conjugal family in that temporal order. "The consanguine family and the clan," they state, "tended to break up in the course of time. . . . The family [then] took on the pattern found in historical Europe and colonial America. The consanguine family tended to disappear, especially in the western world, and the conjugal family became the predominant type." The stem family is seen as a transitional form. "With increasing industrialization," however, it "tends to be superseded by the conjugal family." [5]

For the United States, the base line used in the study of the family is the nineteenth century and the focal type is the rural farm family.

The American family is not a European institution transplanted to a new environment and slightly changed by this transferring. Instead it represents an original development which so reconstructed the contributions of European culture as to bring forth a family type in its characteristics clearly distinctive from the original European institution. [6]

The industrial revolution, starting in the nineteenth and going into the twentieth century, is seen as the force that changed the farm family and is basically responsible for the "modern American family." Industrialization had several immediate consequences:

Industrial organization eventually outgrew the family. The trend was in this direction as the inventions used in handicrafts manufacture multiplied and the use of windmills increased. But with cheaper iron and steel, and the use of streams as a source of power applied to tools, more space was needed and more workers were required than were to be found in the household. The steam boiler was too big for the home and the power generator required more space for the machine. The factory instead of the homestead became the unit of production. The factory was too large to be manned even by a very large family.[7]

Thus, the adoption of the machine resulted in sweeping changes in social organization: factories needed laborers who could be more readily obtained in cities than on farms; urbanism and industrialization worked hand in hand to change the structure of American society; industry needed laborers and the cities grew to provide them.

In addition to ecological and demographic changes, there were significant structural-functional changes in the social system, primary among them being the expansion of the industrial factory system to assume most of the tasks formerly handled by the isolated farm family. At first, industry was only a new techno-economic system transforming methods of production. But along with the new technology there developed a set of social relations with its own specific principles of organization and stratification, and its own way of patterning interaction between individuals, into which rural people were assimilated as they moved into the cities to work.[8] One aspect of all this was the small nuclear family with its distinctive form and means of social articulation.

The argument here is concerned with social and cultural change, and a state of equilibrium is therefore not assumed. In fact, it precludes the existence of a self-regulating system since the family is being analyzed in terms of change occurring in it, in the total system, and in the other parts of the system. In formal terms the argument is that the small nuclear family found in the United States takes its present form because of the national industrialization and urbanization. Within a system in a state of change then, one part is the cause of the new form taken by another part.

Once the change is completed, however, and all of the causal factors achieve their effects, a new equilibrium in the total system is commonly assumed. For the present scholars tend to view the small nuclear family as being in a state of functional interdependence with industry and the other parts of what may be loosely called the American form of Western civilization. The family now is functional in that it operates to maintain the new equilibrium.

In Europe, the best example of this line of thinking is presented by Max Weber who, in his *General Economic History,* for example, states the reasons for viewing the changes in the family as a function of its changing economic position that, in turn, is a function of the changes in the total society that stemmed from the industrial revolution. The concluding paragraph of Part I of the book summarizes a part of the argument:

With the dissolution of the manors and of the remains of the earlier agrarian communism through consolidation, separation, etc., private property in land has been completely established. In the meantime, in the course of the centuries, the organization of society has changed in the direction described above, the household community shrinking, until now the father with his wife and children functions as the unit in property relations. Formerly, this was simply impossible for physical reasons. The household has at the same time undergone an extensive internal transformation, and this in two ways; its function has become restricted to the fields of consumption, and its management placed on an accounting basis. To an increasing extent, the development of inheritance law in place of the original complete communism has led to a separation between the property of the men and the women, with a separate accounting. This two-fold transformation was bound up with the development of industry and trade.[9]

A fuller reading of this and his other works completes the presentation which, though more scholarly and sophisticated, is the same in theory as is argued in the United States. Though Weber seems to imply functional interdependence of the small family and industrialization, the conceptual formulation he uses in explaining the changes in the family is the one in which parts in a dynamic system may be construed to have a causal impact on other parts. It is only after industrialization is accomplished and the new whole is created that he postulates an equilibrium in which the causal nexus is between part and whole and the parts are only interdependent.

In a recent paper Erwin H. Johnson questioned the hypothesis that the small nuclear family is caused by industrialization and urbanization. After examining the data from modern Japan, he concludes that the stable stem family, which is at least four hundred years old there, "is sufficiently generalized in its nature to conform to the needs of the changing technology of Japan." He then goes on to say that the traditional family, in fact, had not and "does not have to give way under . . . urban or industrial influences."[10]

Modern Japan, then, provides us with a case of both urbanization and industrialization with a family other than the small nuclear form. Garigue reports extensive kinship networks among urbanized, industrialized French-Canadians in Montreal. These extended networks of "urban French-Canadian kinship," he writes, "are no new development, but seem to have been in existence since the period of New France." He concludes:

The collected evidence indicates no trend toward transformation of the present French-Canadian urban kinship system into the more restricted system reported for the United States. While difficulties were reported in maintaining a united domestic family or an integral kin group, there is no reason to suppose that these difficulties were caused primarily by urban living. Moreover, many cases were reported where the kin group re-formed after a period of disunity. There are many reasons for believing that the present system will continue. Far from being incompatible, kinship and urbanism among French-Canadians seem to have become functionally related.[11]

In a recent paper on Luso-Brazilian kinship patterns, Wagley, after examining data on the *parentela*—a bilateral kindred—from seven Brazilian communities, writes: "It is evident from the data provided . . . that kinship plays an important role in social, economic and even political affairs." [12] The *parentela*, he adds, operates in both rural and urban areas. In the cities, kinsmen tend to purchase apartments in the same building to facilitate the working out of kinship obligations. The studies by Firth, Young, Shaw, and Townsend in London show further evidence of the extension of kinship in urbanized, industrialized areas.[13]

Additional evidence is presented here to question the hypothesis of functional interdependence and implied causality between urban-industrial technology and the small nuclear family, challenging that part of the generally accepted hypothesis in which the diachronic formulation of sociocultural events is used. The position which assumes a static equilibrium in which functional interdependence within a closed, stable system is assumed a priori will not be argued other than to stress that even here there may be a range of family forms that can serve as functional alternatives to the small nuclear family in urbanized, industrialized systems. The additional evidence is found in an analysis of the family on the island of Barbados where the small nuclear family and fragmented kindred are present in the same form and functionally articulated with the larger society in the same way as in industrialized Western society, but without industry and machines.

We shall, then, have examples from the ethnographic record in which urbanization and industrialization are present without the small nuclear family and fragmented kindred, and the nuclear family is found in the same form and with the same functions as in industrialized Western society but without industrialization and urbanization. Taken together, these combinations seriously question a hypothesis that has received general acceptance in sociological theory before being tested by the comparative evidence.

Barbados is a small, densely populated island, twenty-one miles long and fourteen miles wide, located in the Caribbean Sea at the eastern rim of the Lesser Antilles. It was first colonized by Great Britain at the beginning of the seventeenth century, and, in contrast with her other Caribbean possessions, has remained a British colony from the time of its settlement until 1956, when, with nine other English Caribbean dependencies, it became part of the Federation of the West Indies. [In 1966 Barbados became independent.]

Today, Barbados is not a folk or peasant society. On the other hand, it is not highly mechanized and industrialized. Its economy, which is based upon agriculture, is best not considered underdeveloped since the application of additional capital has not, and, at present, cannot lead to a profitable expansion of productivity and employment opportunities for its very large population.

At present, Barbados—only 166.3 square miles in area—is one of the most densely populated areas in the world: its inhabitants numbered approximately 230,000 at the end of 1956—a density of almost 1,380 persons per square mile—and were increasing at a rate of about 2 per cent per year. Overpopulation has long been recognized as a major problem on the island.

How is this myriad of human beings supported? While its economy is based upon agriculture, in contrast with most of the world's densely populated rural areas where subsistence as well as cash crops are raised, Barbados is almost exclusively dependent upon a single cash crop—sugar. As emphasized in a recent national accounts study of the economy of Barbados,[14] agriculture, in which the growing of sugar cane predominates over all other forms of agricultural activity, is the most important contributor to the island's gross domestic product in which the processing of sugar and molasses accounts for more than half the total contribution of manufacturing. Sugar, to quote the authors of Barbados' ten-year development plan, is truly "the blood of the island." [15]

Barbadians, then, are not subsistence farmers. The island's agricultural activities are organized around the production of sugar, which is cultivated because it provides more revenue per acre than any other crop which could be grown on the island and for which a world market exists.[16] Individuals earn their livelihood in the form of wages; they produce very little for their own consumption.

Barbados, as has already been mentioned, is not an industrialized society in the general sense of the term. The concept of industrialization, however, as it is used in sociological discussions is ambiguous. The specific referent is technological—machines and factories. In general, however, it refers also to the system of social relations that organize human populations in the management of the machines. The use of one term to refer to both the technology and the social structure is regrettable since it leads to thinking of the two as inseparable: that is, the student finds it difficult to think of machine technology without the specific social patterns that have developed in Western civilization. This double referent, however, reveals more of the causal assumptions made by the early students of industrialization: the causal impact of machine technology was considered to be so great that the social relations governing the use of the machines was conceptualized as a necessary consequence of it. Both referents of industrialization must be considered independently, at least until some evidence is presented to demonstrate that there is only one way to organize a population in the use of machines.

This inadequate conceptualization is crucial, however, in the analysis of the data from Barbados since many of its social structural forms are those generally associated with machine technology in North America and Europe, although there are few factories and machines are little used except for a handful of instances in the sugar industry. This situation, itself, however, provides an additional challenge to the hypothesis which claims that industrialization—which at the beginning, at least, was purely technological—is the cause of social organization, since the consequence is present without the cause.

The elementary family in Barbados, as in most of the islands of the West Indies, takes two basic forms—one conjugal or nuclear, the other subnuclear and generally matrifocal. As used here, matrifocality refers to the form of the family in which the mother-child relationship is stronger and more durable than the conjugal (husband-wife) bond. It is characterized by (1) a marginal role for the husband-father; (2) high percentages of female heads of households; (3) easy adoption and high ratios of children per household; (4) high rates of illegitimacy (by European and American standards); and (5) low rates of "legal" marriages. The conjugal or nuclear family, on the other hand, is based upon the husband-wife relationship and is characterized by the converse of the features of the matrifocal family.

The household, which generally contains at least one of the elementary kinship units, is variable. Ideally, it is composed of an isolated nuclear family which lives in a separate shelter, usually provided by the adult male. This, however, is rarely achieved by most of the population. When not composed of an isolated nuclear family, the household may consist of a number of alternative forms. The first is a nuclear family in which a mature child, invariably a daughter, has begun to have a family—often she is unmarried—before establishing a firm conjugal relationship in a separate dwelling. This extended family group, or "multi-family" household, is of three generations and is composed of one nuclear family plus one or more matrifocal units of unwed mother and children, all sharing the same house. An alternative appears when a woman and her children become established in an independent dwelling unit without an adult male. This occurs either when the members of the conjugal group separate—the male leaving—or when a woman obtains a dwelling, usually through inheritance, and occupies it with her children but without a mate. An infrequent variant of this denuded family occurs when a man is left alone with his children in a household without an adult female. These denuded family households can become extended when the children mature and begin to have offspring while they are still living at home. Here we find a three-generation unit which, generally, is composed of a woman and her children, including mature daughters and their offspring. This form, which is found throughout the Caribbean, is usually referred to as the "grandmother family." A household then, can consist of one of four alternative forms which are found distributed in the same frequencies in both the rural and urban areas: (1) a nuclear family, (2) a nuclear extended family, (3) a denuded or subnuclear family (male or female, but usually female-centered), and (4) a denuded or subnuclear extended family (male or female but again usually female-centered).

In form and functional integration with the total society—an at least temporary state of equilibrium is assumed for the purpose of analysis—the ideal nuclear group found in Barbados is very similar to the nuclear family found in the United States and described by Parsons.[17] The tendency toward structural and spatial isolation appears in both places; the importance of the mother in the process of the child's socialization and in the development of his personality are similar; the role of the adult male within the family as "breadwinner," responsible for supporting the entire group, is likewise analogous. More significantly, even the relationship between the individual and the larger society is the same. Individuals are all members of families linked to the larger society through the adult male who occupies a place in the local occupational system, and in both cases, the position of the latter member in the occupational system is a primary determinant of the position of the others in the social hierarchy.

Other similarities can be found in patterns of descent: Both systems are bilateral. In Barbados, illegitimacy is common, it is usual for parents to leave wills bequeathing their property to all of their children.[18] Relations with ascending and descending generations show no tendency toward structural bias in favor of any one line of descent. Both Barbados and the United States, therefore, can be described as symmetrically multilineal.

In both cases, the tendency toward structural isolation is reinforced by the relationship between the family and the occupational system, particularly with reference to social mobility. Each nuclear family is ascribed a place in the system of stratification which is based upon the social class of the family of orientation of its adult male subject to the mobility he may achieve in his occupational pursuits. Mobility is a driving force in both societies. Kinship relationships are generally divorced from the occupational system, thus permitting conjugal units to be socially mobile, independent of kinship ties. Nuclear families striving for mobility are often best able to do so by almost total denial of kinship claims, which, of course, leads to the isolation of the conjugal family. In Parsons' terms, then, both the Barbadian and American nuclear families can be characterized as "bilateral, structurally isolated, open, multilineal, conjugal systems." [19] The alternative forms of the household discussed above are all variants of the isolated nuclear unit produced by factors relating directly to the integration of family and society.

The primary functions of Barbadian society are performed through a highly stratified system of occupational statuses; the hierarchically ranked positions, however, provide their occupants with wages that vary considerably. The insular system of social stratification is tied directly to these ranked occupational positions since they are the primary determinant of an individual's social class. Families are articulated with the larger society through adult males who are members of both a family and the occupational system simultaneously: the male role is defined in terms of supporting women and children; he is also expected to hold a position in the occupational system. In the latter system he holds one of a series of ranked positions from which he receives money and prestige; in the family he holds a position that calls for the contribution of income obtained in the occupational world. Women and children, who, in the ideal, are outside the dominant institutional complex, are linked to it through reciprocal role obligations to a male within the family. Satisfactory performance of the adult male role within the family requires an individual to hold a position in the occupational system that provides him with income sufficient to support a family.

The occupational system in Barbados, however, is so constituted that many, if not most, of the positions at the lower end of the hierarchy provide neither the prestige nor the income necessary for the support of a family. The occupants of these low-ranked positions are not able to fulfil the role expectations of adult male within the family, and if they cannot improve their occupational status after a period of time they tend to leave the household, thereby creating a denuded, subnuclear, matrifocal or mother-oriented group. The extended family households, both nuclear and denuded, appear when the fathers of the children born to girls living in parental households have not been able to attain an occupational position with rewards sufficient to purchase a house and to establish the new family as an isolated nuclear group.

The importance of a man to his family and his relationship to the others, therefore, will vary directly with the income and status he earns in the occupational world. Consequently, we may expect both the family and the household to take different forms of varying socioeconomic levels. Whether the unit is nuclear or matrifocal is, therefore, a function of the system of social stratification and the way in which adult males link the family to society. Where adult males hold positions that provide rewards sufficient for the support of a nuclear family, the nuclear group is isolated in a separate household; where not, a subnuclear, matrifocal group appears, causing the household to take one of the forms outlined above.

On the tiny sugar-growing island of Barbados, then, we find the same small nuclear family, articulated with the larger society in precisely the same way as we find in industrialized Western society, but without urbanization and industrialization. The industrial revolution, in fact, has not yet come to the island.

The existence of an industrialized and urbanized society in Brazil, French Canada, England, and Japan with an extended family, and the small nuclear family—identical in form and function to the nuclear family of industrialized Western society—in Barbados without industrialization or urbanization provides evidence to question the hypothesized causal relationship between urban-industrial technology and the family. The explanation for the similarity in family form and function in Barbados and in industrialized Western society, however, may provide us with a new perspective with which to re-analyze the historical data used to support the old hypothesis.

Barbados was settled by colonists who came in family groups from Great Britain. Though African slaves were later introduced to work on the sugar plantations, significant numbers of English and Irish families remained and their descendents are still there today. The institutionalized form of family now found in Barbados was brought to the island by the first settlers and later, adopted by the Negroes when integrated into the larger society through the occupational system immediately following Emancipation.[20]

The small nuclear family, the *famille particulariste* of Le Play, which is native to North Europe,[21] is known to have existed in England in the seventeenth century, prior to the colonization of the New World. Specialists in the culture of the Old World (Europe, Mediterranean, Middle East), in fact, believe it to be much older, "as old as the Vikings or older" according to Arensberg.[22] If this is the case, it antedates both urbanism and machine technology in England and the United States. Perhaps its contemporary place in modern, urban, industrialized society is related to its temporal priority to machine technology.

If, at the very beginning of the urban-industrial revolution, the inventors of machine technology already lived in small nuclear families, it is no small wonder that this form became functionally integrated with industrial technology as a new equilibrium was achieved. As North European man developed the social forms to go with the machine, it is quite probable that he reworked the social institutions with which he was already familiar. If so, the relationship between the small nuclear family and industrialization is better interpreted as one of the temporal priority of the former and not a necessary functional consequence or cause and effect in which the latter is the determinant. Further investigation of the historical material, then, may indicate that the two are related because the small nuclear family was there first. Subsequent social institutions, such as the occupational system, that went with the machine were probably adapted to, and therefore fitted with, a society organized in small families. One wonders what organizational forms urban-industrialized society might have today if these early North Europeans lived in extended families.

Some might argue that wage labor more than machine technology is the cause of the distinctive Western family. If one uses the equilibrium formulation, there is no doubt that wage labor and the small family are functionally interrelated and interdependent. The question, however, is whether a system of wage labor is a necessary and sufficient cause for the small family when an entire sociocultural system is in the process of change.

The crucial relationship between wage labor and the form of the family concerns the scale of remunerations. In the systems of North America, Europe, and Barbados, with the exception of the relative few who hold positions at the top of the hierarchy, workers earn only enough for the support of a nuclear group. While variability in wages is considerable, we rarely find a job paying enough to support more than one nuclear family. Since men are the principal wage-earners—this probably being based upon a prior cultural definition of the sexual division of labor in North Europe—they are expected to provide money for the kinship unit. The degree of possible extension of the kin group is thus related to the income earned by men. Since each nuclear unit also is expected to have its own wage-earner, it is economically independent, which brings about a weakening of reciprocal relations between members and kinsmen outside the group. Within the nuclear family, however, there is relative equality, each member having a right to a share of the income of the adult male or the goods or services it can buy.

Were the occupational system so organized as to pay one individual enough to support a larger group or to enable him to provide employment for such a unit, extended families might arise to engulf or submerge the nuclear group. Perhaps, if extended families had existed in England when the complex took its present form, the remuneration scale of modern industrial society would be very different.

In the United States, industrialization started in the Northeast, a section appropriately called New England. With reference to the family in New England, Arensberg writes, "The brittle, easily split 'nuclear' or 'democratic' ('Eskimoan') family, . . . came with [the] Yankees from England and fitted well with their egalitarian, unstratified farmer-artisan towns." [23] The small nuclear family, then, was brought to the United States from Great Britain by its earliest settlers. Therefore, it was present before the industrial revolution began in the United States. We suggest that it was reworked, as it had been several centuries earlier, in England, to provide the foundation for the new system of social organization that developed and spread with the industrial revolution. Here again, it was not the industrial revolution that produced the small nuclear family; in fact, the opposite may be true. The prior existence of the small nuclear family as the basic kinship unit of the people who industrialized both Great Britain and the United States may have been responsible for the very forms of social organization that developed along with the machines.

Furthermore, the data from Barbados demonstrates that the small nuclear family can diffuse without urbanization and industrialization just as the latter seems to be able to diffuse without the small nuclear family.

In conclusion, then, an examination of both the comparative and historical evidence indicates that, developmentally, there is no necessary and sufficient causal relationship, whether expressed in terms of necessary functional interdependence or consequence, between the small nuclear family and urbanization and industrialization. Any relationship that exists most probably results from the presence of the small family in North Europe prior to the industrial revolution.

Notes

1. A portion of this paper was presented under another title at the annual meeting of the American Anthropological Association, Minneapolis, Minnesota, November, 1960.

2. Ernest Nagel, "A Formulation of Functionalism," in *Logic without Metaphysics,* Glencoe, Ill.: Free Press, 1956, p. 251.

3. A. R. Radcliffe-Brown, *Structure and Function in Primitive Society,* Glencoe, Ill.: Free Press, 1952, pp. 180, 181.

4. Associated with the notion of functional interdependence of parts is that of functional alternatives. This refers to a limited range of parts that can perform the same function as the given part in the total system and consequently may be considered as substitutes for the given part since the equilibrium will still be maintained after the exchange.

5. William Ogburn and Meyer F. Nimkoff, *Sociology,* Boston: Houghton Mifflin Co., 1950, p. 469.

6. Ernest Groves and Gladys Groves, *The Contemporary Family,* Philadelphia: J. B. Lippincott Co., 1947, p. 140.

7. Ogburn and Nimkoff, *op. cit.,* p. 473.

8. Wirth, in his "Urbanism as a Way of Life," *American Journal of Sociology,* XL (July, 1938), pp. 1–24, argues that the modern small nuclear family is a function of city living.

9. Trans. Frank H. Knight, Glencoe, Ill.: Free Press, 1950, p. 111.

10. "The Stem Family and Its Extensions in Modern Japan" (paper presented at the Annual Meeting of the American Anthropological Association, Minneapolis, Minnesota, 1960), p. 13.

11. Philip Garigue, "French Canadian Kinship and Urban Life," *American Anthropologist,* LVIII (December, 1956), pp. 1098–1099.

12. Charles Wagley, "Luso-Brazilian Kinship Patterns" (unpublished manuscript, 1960).

13. Raymond Firth, *Two Studies of Kinship in London,* London: Athlone Press, 1957; Michael Young, "Kinship and Family in East London," *Man,* LIV, No. 210 (September, 1954), pp. 137–139; L. A. Shaw, "Impression of Family Life in a London Suburb," *Sociological Review,* III (December, 1955), pp. 175–195.

14. Jeanette Bethel, "A National Accounts Study of the Economy of Barbados," *Social and Economic Studies,* IX, Special No. (June, 1960), pp. 127–128.

15. *A Ten Year Development Plan for Barbados, 1946–56,* Bridgetown, Barbados: Advocate Press, n.d., p. 11.

16. Lord Simon of Wythenshawe, *Population and Resources of Barbados,* Bloomcroft: Disbury, 1954, pp. 1–2.

17. Talcott Parsons, "The Kinship System in the Contemporary United States," *American Anthropologist,* XLV (January, 1943), pp. 22–38. See also Talcott Parsons and Robert Bales, *Family, Socialization and Interaction Process,* Glencoe, Ill.: Free Press, 1955.

18. Sidney M. Greenfield, "Land Tenure and Transmission in Rural

Barbados," *Anthropological Quarterly*, XXXIII (October, 1960), pp. 165–176.

19. The most significant difference between the Barbadian and the American nuclear family is size. This difference, however, most critically effects the socialization and personality development of the children and not the form of the family or its articulation with the larger society (Parsons and Bales, *op. cit.*, p. 18). It is, therefore, excluded from the present comparison.

20. It is significant to note that the family form has remained the same even though it has been transferred from one ethnic group to another.

21. Frederic Le Play, Focillon, and DeLaire, *L'Organisation de la famille*, (Tours, 1884) (see also Edmond Demolins, *Comment la Route Crée de type social*, Paris: F. Didet, n.d., 1890?, 2 vols.; and Carle C. Zimmermann and Merle Frampton, *Family and Society*, New York: D. Van Nostrand & Co., 1937, pp. 97 ff.).

22. Conrad M. Arensberg, "Discussion of Methods of Community Analysis in the Caribbean by Robert Manners," *Caribbean Studies: A Symposium*, Mona, Jamaica: Institute of Social and Economic Studies, 1957, p. 97. An example of what might have happened in the total society is found at the upper end of the occupational ladder where a given individual can earn enough to support more than one family.

With the acquisition of great wealth and property, we find the development of extended families, with the income-earning property accumulated by one generation providing support and prestige for several other generations. These extended families, usually patrilineages in Europe, North America, and the West Indies, develop around family property that provides income and status to all who can establish a valid genealogical connection therein.

At the lower end of the occupational scale, jobs do not provide sufficient income for a man to support even one family and the prestige rating is so low as to deny status either for himself or his family. It is here that women and children must enter the labor force to help out. The jobs available to them, however, are also at the bottom of the hierarchy. As the primary feature of the division of labor is destroyed, so is the strength of the conjugal bond. It is then that the subnuclear, matrifocal family appears.

The close functional adjustment between the isolated nuclear family and this form of stratified occupational system is related to the organization of the latter system. Since most jobs pay enough to support one family, the total system functions best when one wage-earner links one family to the social system through his wage contribution. His income and status are identified with the members of the nuclear group until the children are old enough to establish their own nuclear families, each with its own adult male wage-earner.

23. Conrad M. Arensberg, "American Communities," *American Anthropologist*, LVII (December, 1955), p. 1149.

Commentary: *The Dominance of the Nuclear Family*

In his comprehensive analysis of the relationship between the nuclear family and the processes of industrialization and urbanization, Sidney M. Greenfield goes into considerable detail on both theoretical and cross-cultural levels. He points out that the mere existence of the nuclear family is not dependent upon, or a necessary consequence of, industrialization and urbanization. His conclusion is valid because if by nuclear family we mean the immediate family of procreation as a distinguishable unit, it has always existed. However, if we are concerned not with existence but with dominance, *the same literature that Greenfield examines, which shows that the nuclear family cannot become dominant over the clan or stem types until there has been an industrial revolution, also shows that urbanization alone is not enough. Ancient Rome and ancient Babylon were urban societies in which the nuclear family existed but was not dominant.*

On another level the cross-cultural evidence is equally striking. If, in oversimplified fashion, we say that urbanization means the presence of large cities, all we need note are the teeming millions of urbanites living in such cities as Bombay, Calcutta, and Dacca, all of which are both preindustrial and dominated by joint or extended types of families. Until an urban society anywhere undergoes an industrial revolution, the nuclear family cannot become dominant. In the course of half a lifetime, Max Weber demonstrated this historically and comparatively in his many works on the sociology of religion. William F. Ogburn demonstrated it for contemporary American society (Social Change, 1922).

Because Greenfield has a very instructive analysis of the stem family in urban Japan, the reader may find that an immediate comparison with Ezra F. Vogel's article, "The Decline of the Ie *Ideal," would be relevant.* (*Vogel's article begins on page 96.*)

Because of the above considerations, Greenfield's conclusion that the alleged relationship between the small nuclear family and urbanization and industrialization "probably results from the presence of the small family in North Europe prior to the industrial revolution" can be reinterpreted from a new perspective. The new perspective poses the following question: Is mere existence of a family type more important or is dominance the key to the problem? Unless the nuclear family is dominant and unless this occurs as a result of industrialization and urbanization, romantic equalitarian and single-standard norms do not emerge. An American-educated professor at the University of Dacca in East Pakistan who lives with his family in an apartment in the heart of the city is obviously proof of the existence of the nuclear family. However, when it is realized that his marriage was arranged and that if any relatives, no matter how far removed, visit from his ancestral village they take priority for living space in terms of their traditional seniority, the dominance of the extended family is manifest.

2

AN HISTORIAN'S VIEW
OF THE
CHINESE FAMILY SYSTEM

PING-TI HO

Ever since the opening of China in the 1840s, Chinese society has been regarded by Western people as a "familistic" society par excellence. Until recently, we could point to no other civilized society in which the family, together with its kinship superstructure, held so strategic a position in the total society. Yet, today, nowhere else do the family's chances for survival appear slimmer than on the Chinese mainland. While in the West many religious and secular organizations can count on society's moral support in their search for means to strengthen the family, which forces of continual industrialism have weakened, in the Chinese mainland today no one dares to defend the family without running the risk of being publicly condemned as a person of reactionary or "feudalistic" views. If the family on the Chinese mainland is to survive, it will have to withstand not only the impact of similar forces of industrialism but also the onslaught of the monolithic, omnipotent, and omnipresent state. It seems appropriate, therefore, that in a symposium on "The Family's Search for Survival" there should be a paper devoted exclusively to China.

But it is not easily conceivable why such a paper should be

From Man and Civilization: The Family's Search for Survival *by Farber, Mustacchi & Wilson. Copyright © 1965 by McGraw-Hill, Inc. Used by permission of McGraw-Hill Book Company.*

presented by an historian of early modern China who, as far as the Chinese family is concerned, is at best an interested layman. Indeed, not until I had found a justification in the words of a prominent British anthropologist, Dr. Maurice Freedman of the London School of Economics and Political Science, did I dare to accept the honor to address this gathering of distinguished scholars and experts on family affairs. After paying due tribute to those well-known writers on the Chinese family, Dr. Freedman remarks:

> But it is no disrespect to these scholars to assert now that their work is incomplete. It is in fact incomplete over the whole historical range. . . . In other words, it is not merely the Chinese family since 1949 that we are ignorant about. Political and emotional barriers separate us from the Chinese mainland at the present; . . . there are other barriers between us and the China of the past.[1]

From an historian's point of view, I should like to make the following general observations on existing works on the Chinese family. First, chronologically, most of them deal with the period after 1920, and even those few dealing with the traditional family and kinship system do not go back much further than the late imperial age. The result is that very little has been said about the historical evolution of this venerable Chinese institution throughout the past two thousand years. Second, geographically, those well-known works on the Chinese family revolution in pre-Communist times usually skip over the vast rural hinterland and deal mainly with changes in family structure in or near urban centers. Third, the picture of the traditional Chinese family drawn by modern writers is based largely on legal and ethical principles; seldom if ever is it based on the voluminous and wide-ranging historical material in which the researcher naturally finds discrepancies between ideals and realities. Last, since modern writers concern themselves mostly with the disintegration of the old family and the emergence of the new, they tend to overemphasize, sometimes frankly out of necessity, "the harsh and tyrannical features of the traditional family and its internal tensions and conflicts." [2]

Within the time allowed, I shall confine myself to a brief critical analysis of the following: (1) the size of the historical and modern Chinese family; (2) the different types of kinship organization and the net relationship between the modern-type patrilineal clan and the family; (3) the question as to whether the traditional Chinese family was as patriarchal as is usually believed; and (4) forces of change in the twentieth century and the present state of the Chinese mainland family.

The most economical way to summarize the historical evolution of the Chinese family is to study its average sizes during those few periods of history which yield relatively useful statistical data. The common impression that China has been a land of large families is due primarily to the inability of nineteenth-century Western writers on China to differentiate the family from the clan and to distinguish the high-status families from those of lower social orders. In fact, ever since the impending collapse of the feudal system during the fourth century B.C., China has been a land of small families.

One of the main reforms carried out by statesmen of various contending states during the fourth century B.C. was to sweep away remnants of the feudal land system, transforming feudal serfs into independent small holders and encouraging the setting up of small families. The most successful of these statesmen was the Lord of Shang of the northwestern state of Ch'in, which, as a consequence of his reforms, eventually conquered all other states and founded the first unified empire in Chinese history. Shortly after 346 B.C. the Lord of Shang passed a law by which adult brothers, if they lived under the same roof, were liable to double taxation and *corvée* duties.[3] That this law did have its expected long-range effects on the family structure is best testified to by Chia I (200–162 B.C.), a brilliant and unusually observant scholar-official of early Han:

Forsaking propriety, righteousness, benevolence, and grace, the Lord of Shang devoted himself only to making his state powerful. After his law was enforced for two years, social customs of the Ch'in people already began to deteriorate. Consequently, an adult son of a rich household usually moved out of his father's family and set up his own, and an adult son of a poor household often moved into his wife's family and took up her surname. The son would lend a harrow or hoe to his father as if he were conferring a favor. The wife would immediately curse if her mother-in-law occasionally used her basket or broom. . . . Such sons and their wives loved only their own children and knew of only self-interest. How little difference there is between such people and the beasts.[4]

Shorn of its Confucian moral bias, the above passage may well be an apt description of the worst father-son and in-law relationships in the modern industrial society. Chu-fu Yen, who rose from obscurity to high power and died in 127 B.C., recalled his relations with his family during his long struggling years: "My father would not treat me as a son, [and] my brothers refused to have anything to do with me." [5] We have ample evidence showing the high incidence of infanticide and the reluctance of the nation, including the ruling class, to observe the twenty-seven-month mourning for a deceased parent—the most important symbol of the later Confucian pseudo-religion of filial duty.[6] It does not seem an exaggeration to say that the Chinese family during the early empires was as small, self-centered, and atomistic as that of modern industrial society. In any case, the respectable census of A.D. 2 yields 12,233,062 households and 59,594,978 mouths, giving an average of 4.87 persons per household.[7] It should be noted that by definition and in practice a household was always somewhat larger than a family.

We need to mention only a few more comparatively useful historical figures to show that the average Chinese family has been persistently small in size. The average numbers of persons per household for A.D. 755, 1393, and 1812 are 5.95, 5.68, and 5.33, respectively.[8] Most pre-1949 sample surveys show that the average Chinese family in the twentieth century comprised about five persons. The historical and modern figures all testify, therefore, to the elemental fact that the size of the Chinese peasant family was determined primarily by its basic economic needs and by the fiscal burden it bore.

While from the standpoint of size, the family has undergone comparatively little change during the past two thousand years, there have been significant developments in the family superstructure, which is called *tsu* in Chinese and which literally means "clan." Historically there are three different types of *tsu*, of which modern writers on the Chinese family system know only the third and latest. The *tsu* of the ancient feudal nobility, which was patrilineal and based strictly on primogeniture and which petered out by the third century B.C., should not concern us here. It seems pertinent, however, to review briefly the effect of the second type of *tsu* on the revival of family-orientated values and mores.

As has been pointed out earlier, the Chinese family ties were weak during the Ch'in and former Han period (221 B.C.–A.D. 8). Being apprehensive of the possible correlation between weak family ties and social instability, the rulers of former and later Han repeatedly exhorted the nation to practice the Confucian teaching of filial duty. By later Han times (A.D. 25–220), when the imperial authority progressively declined, powerful officials and landed magnates found in these imperial exhortations a most useful pretext for self-aggrandizement. For as long as a man was able to expand his property and to share it with his forebears, brothers, and close and remote collaterals, he could justify himself by the much-distorted and hypocritized theory of filial duty so typical of later Han times.[9] Consequently, men of political and economic influence established their *tsu*, which usually had a large number of retainers, warriors, tenants, and other kinds of social dependents of various surnames appended to the relatively small core of patrilineal kin. Structurally, therefore, these *tsu* differ from the *tsu* of ancient feudal nobility, based strictly on consanguinity and primogeniture, and from the modern type of kinship so well known to us.

During the subsequent period of barbarian invasions and political division, which lasted roughly from A.D. 300 to 600, the most powerful of these *tsu*, numbering a few dozens, dominated the state and became a self-perpetuating aristocracy. They began to decline from the seventh century onward when China was reunited under the centralized T'ang Empire and when the permanently institutionalized competitive civil service examination system broke up their political monopoly.

Since these *tsu* were by nature aristocratic houses, they had little effect, structurally and functionally, on the modern type of patrilineal clan. But they nevertheless fulfilled an important historical mission by disseminating and perpetuating a central Confucian doctrine which through distortion and hypocritization suited their selfish interests so well. In fact, ever since their rise in later Han times members of these *tsu* led the nation in reviving the twenty-seven-month mourning for deceased parents, in sharing wealth and property with brothers and collaterals, and in transforming the doctrine of filial duty into a pseudo-religion.[10] In due course of time these family-oriented values and mores permeated the lower social strata. This, in the last analysis, is the permanent legacy left by the aristocratic *tsu*, a typical product of the long period of political decentralization. It is worth mentioning in passing that for about thirteen centuries since the founding of the first empire, Chinese commoners in general had no kinship organization.

The third or modern type of *tsu* dates back to the middle of the eleventh century, when the hereditary aristocratic houses had become extinct and the society much more mobile under the combined impact of the examination system and the rise of a variegated economy. Recalling the abject poverty of his orphanhood, the famous early Sung statesman Fan Chung-yen (989–1052) in 1050 donated most of his life savings to setting up a charitable estate for his patrilineal kin in the hope that they and their descendants might not suffer destitution in an increasingly competitive society.[11] Since Fan's charitable estate answered a basic social need, it was immediately hailed as a model, from which patrilineal clans of varying strengths and resources have been evolved. The most successfully and elaborately organized clan usually had a permanent fund and property for the maintenance of the ancestral hall, the relief of poor kin, the operation of the clan school, the periodic compilation of clan genealogy, and even subsidy for kin who sought their higher academic degrees at provincial and national capitals. Besides, such a highly organized clan had its head and elected officers who administered common clan affairs, arbitrated intraclan disputes, and served as a cushion between kinsmen and local authorities. It thus performed many of the functions which in other societies would have been performed by various social and religious organizations.

The structure and functions of the post-Sung patrilineal clan being well known, I shall restrict myself to an assessment of the extent to which it has affected the life of the Chinese. In the first place, the kinship system is likely to have been less extensively distributed geographically than is usually imagined. In general, it has been well developed in lower and central Yangtze provinces and in the two southernmost coastal provinces of Fukien and Kwangtung, but distinctly underdeveloped and thinly spread in the northern half of China. This uneven geographic distribution of patrilineal clans may have been due to the fact that the south, particularly the lower Yangtze, has been economically more advanced and academically more successful. To say that the kinship system is common to all parts of China is therefore incorrect.

In the second place, from its very inception in the middle of the eleventh century the kinship system has always had its organizational weakness because its creation and expansion depend primarily on donations by its most successful members.[12] Few donors were as generous as Fan Chung-yen, who gave most of his life savings to his clan as common property. The economic and social milieu in post-Sung China was such that few families could perpetuate their academic and economic success and retain their wealth for more than a limited number of generations. Unless a clan could renew its socioacademic success from time to time, it was bound to become progressively incapable of performing its original functions. Since at any given time bureaucratically and economically successful men constituted a small fraction of the population, well-endowed clans which could function efficiently as corporate units of social structure must have been statistically rather insignificant.[13]

Third, it is important to analyze the relationship between the family and the clan. Even when a clan was well endowed and highly organized, the natural family, which consisted of the husband, wife, immature children, and occasionally one or both of the husband's aging parents, constituted a unit of common consumption. The family rather than the clan has always been basic to economic life. There were, of course, clans in which several generations shared property and lived together, but such clans must have been rather rare at any given time, hence invariably extolled by rulers and members of the elite as models. From genealogies, biographies, local histories, and individual literary works it is quite clear that the property owned by the clan, if any, was usually rather small in proportion to the total amount of property separately owned by its various component branches and families: and this despite the fact that the clan property was in principle inalienable because of the necessity to perform certain common clan functions, while the family properties were periodically divided by male heirs who set up their own families. In terms of the most important economic function, therefore, the clan was at best marginal to the average Chinese, whose life was lived within his own small family.

All this does not, however, mean that the patrilineal clan has played no significant role in the life of the Chinese. Politically, a well-organized clan served as a useful intermediary between its members and local authorities. By maintaining the ancestral hall, observing ancestral worship, compiling genealogy, and disseminating Neo-Confucian ethical ideals, the clan certainly helped, at least sentimentally, to strengthen the family and kinship ties. I suspect that it is chiefly by studying these noneconomic and peripheral functions rather than the bookkeeping of highly organized clans, which are statistically insignificant, that modern students have acquired the impression that the Chinese society is familistic and clannish.

To conclude our discussion on the kinship system, I should like to point out its one legacy that has not been noticed. As has been mentioned, the clan was an important instrument for the dissemination of the Neo-Confucian teaching of sharing one's wealth with one's kin. The permeation of this teaching, together with the general insecurity of property and the constant working of social and economic leveling forces, has diluted the concept of property and accounted for the typically Chinese fatalist view that property is inconstant. In this connection, it seems a historical irony that the kinship system, which has been condemned for so long by modern Chinese radicals as "feudalistic," has in fact facilitated the revolution in property ownership in the present Chinese mainland.

The problem as to whether the Chinese family was truly patriarchal may conveniently be examined from two angles: the authority of the family head, who normally the father, and the status of women.

The authority of the father reflected in traditional Chinese law and ethical precepts is well summarized by a modern writer:

> The Chinese family was patriarchal. The grandfather or father was the ruling head and had authority over all the members of the family, including his wife and concubines, his sons and grandsons, their wives and children, his unmarried daughters, his collateral relatives who were junior to him and who shared his domicile, his slaves and servants. His control of the family economy and his power to make financial decisions strengthened his authority. In addition, since the concept of ancestor worship was central to the perpetuation and solidarity of the family, the authority of the family head, who was also the family priest, was further enhanced. Finally, his authority was recognized and supported by the law.[14]

If we scratch the dynastic codes deeper, we find in those clauses defining the so-called father's authority that the father is invariably mentioned together with the mother. The authority was therefore not the father's alone but that jointly held by the parents, which by definition included more senior direct patrilineal ascendants. For the basic legal and ethical principle regulating the traditional Chinese family was based not so much on sexes as on senior-junior relationships. This being the case, juniors owed their filial duty to seniors of both sexes. "This elementary consideration alone," writes a British expert on Chinese law, "marks off a clear distinction from the unitary *patria potestas* of the Romans." [15] This is why throughout Chinese history there have been a number of female rulers, and even down to the early years of the Republic there were still many matriarchs in high-status families.[16]

Moreover, although it is a common belief that the Chinese family head had an unrestricted authority to control and dispose of family property, various types of Chinese historical literature and modern Japanese surveys of Chinese customary law reveal a far different picture. Numerous cases can be culled from genealogies and biographies to show that although legally an adult son succeeded his father as the family head, he could not dispose of the family property without the authorization of his widowed mother, who, according to Neo-Confucian precepts, should obey her son. Japanese field surveys of customary law carried out in North China during the last war further reveal that "in many places people would at any rate not buy land from a father unless his sons joined in the conveyance." [17] Historical literature also shows that in many cases the family property, which was legally in the possession of the family head, was virtually held under a sort of father-son co-ownership or family joint ownership.

Concerning the status of Chinese women, the late Dr. Hu Shih (1891–1962), the greatest scholar of twentieth-century China, had the following to say:

> At the outset, it is necessary to point out that the position of women in the old family was never so low as many superficial observers have led us to believe. On the contrary, woman has always been the despot of the family. The authority of the mother and the mother-in-law is very well known. Even the wife is always the terror of the husband; no other country in the world can compete with China for the distinction of being the nation of hen-pecked husbands. Certainly, no other country has produced so many stories of hen-pecked husbands. The wife built up her strong position sometimes upon love, sometimes upon beauty or personality, but in most cases upon the fact that she could not be dislodged from her position: she could not be divorced! It is true that there was no law forbidding divorce; and that the Classics laid down seven conditions for divorcing a wife. Jealousy, or failure to bear sons, or even talking too much, would be sufficient to divorce her. But the same Classics also gave three conditions under which she could not be sent away: (1) if she has shared with the husband a three-year mourning for one of his parents; (2) if the husband has become rich or attained high official positions since marriage; or (3) if she has no home to go back to. These conditions were very common and almost made divorce absolutely impossible. [18]

In spite of the very considerable truth in Dr. Hu Shih's observation, it is likely somewhat one-sided; nonetheless, it is invaluable as a corrective to an equally one-sided view that Chinese women have always been cruelly subjected to men.

To get a more balanced view, we have to differentiate the families of higher and lower social orders. Only a high-status family could afford to be large, and hence it would be more prone to have intergenerational and in-law tensions and conflicts, which, shown in legal and ethical precepts on which much of modern scholarship is based, are necessarily exaggerated. In fact, much of the harsh authoritarian character of the Chinese family reflected in law was often mellowed by social customs, human nature, and traditional teachings to curb one's own desires and to consider others' interests. When high-status families are not treated as an abstract theoretical model but as concrete historical examples, cases of tyrannical "patriarchs" must have been rather rare in any period of Chinese history. The low-status family usually was structurally simple and numerically small. Life at this social level depended primarily on the husband's labor, which not even his father could exploit. He thus usually set up his own small family, apart from his brothers and parents. Since he had to toil together with his wife to make ends meet, he did not have even the faintest resemblance to the august head of a high-status family. His wife, if she did not have the material comfort and security of the wife of a high-status family, had more strength as an individual and was much less likely to have an in-law problem. In fact, even the mores and norms of low-status families differed from those of high-status families. To give only one example, the Neo-Confucian taboo on widow's remarriage has seldom if ever applied to women of lower social orders.

Now we shall assess the changes in the family and kinship system in modern times. Prior to the founding of the People's Republic of China in October, 1949, the family and kinship system had already been weakened by forces and factors such as, for example, the beginnings of industrialization along the eastern seaboard and inland river ports, the improved means of transportation and the more diversified professional opportunities which brought many peasants and intellectuals from their ancestral homes to large urban centers, the new schools and universities which exposed the young to Western ideas and culture, and the so-called renaissance movement from the late 1910s onward which engendered among the intelligentsia a revolt against traditional institutions and family-oriented values.

In the last analysis, it was members of the intelligentsia who were the standard-bearers of the so-called family revolution, which demanded, among other things, the adoption of a single sex standard, the emancipation of women, free choice of mate, and greater freedom for the young. Some of them went so far as to attack even filial duty, which had accounted so much for the family-mindedness of the Chinese. Since the intellectuals came usually from families of higher social orders, in the cities as well as in the country, the movement gradually brought about a liberalization of high-status families throughout the country. But the vast majority of families of the rural hinterland remained little changed. What was most adversely affected by these new forces and ideas was the clan, which was always marginal to economic life and which always depended on the support of its successful members. Since successful men were now mostly urban dwellers susceptible to new ideas, clans in general suffered. In retrospect, perhaps the most striking change in social institutions in pre-1949 China was not the so-called family revolution, because most families were able to hold on, but the fairly rapid decline and disintegration of the kinship system.

One interesting product of this period of change was the Civil Code of 1931, which was partly a crystallization of the ideas of Western-trained intellectuals, partly a compromise with tradition, and partly for foreign consumption because ever since the Washington Conference of 1921–1922 the successive Chinese governments had been working on modern codes in the hope the extraterritoriality might soon be abolished. Such a curious mixture defies precise analysis, but it is a landmark in the history of Chinese law for having established the principle of monogamy, though not without exceptions, and of women's improved status in terms of marriage, divorce, and property. There is no evidence, however, that this code was ever seriously enforced by the Nationalist government.

But there can be no doubt that from its promulgation in May, 1950, to about the end of 1953 the Marriage Law of the People's Republic of China was energetically enforced. Despite its narrow title, it actually amounts to an abbreviated code regulating a wide range of family affairs. It reaffirms or establishes the principle of monogamy; of free choice of partner; of completely equal rights for both sexes as to the management and inheritance of property, choice of occupation, and rearing and educating of children; of divorce upon mutual consent or upon insistence of one party; and of protection of children's interests. So perfect is the symmetry of rights for both sexes that it is high fashion for a married woman to retain her own family name. The law makes a significant concession to tradition by providing that parents and children have the duty to assist each other and to inherit each other's property. Thus the family may, in addition to husband, wife, and immature children, consist of one or both aging parents. In terms of membership, therefore, the law is by no means revolutionary since the majority of families have always been small and only occasionally three-generational.

But functionally the present family is truly revolutionary. As Dr. Freedman ably puts it:

> The whole range of activities once covered by the family is now reduced to a narrow field in which husband, wife and children associate together in the interstices, so to speak, of large institutions—the work group, the dining hall, the nursery—which have taken over the functions of economic coordination, housekeeping, and the rearing and educating of children. The family has become an institution for producing babies and enjoying the leisure time left over from the major pursuits of everyday life.[19]

What is left to the Chinese family is precious little. We want to ask: can that precious little survive?

Much of the reporting in our press on Chinese family life in the communes is secondhand and too biased to be worth mentioning. Fortunately, there is a firsthand report by a highly trained Canadian child psychiatrist, entitled "The Cheerful Children of Red China's Communes," which says:

> I was particularly interested in observing the effects of communal living, a way of life that now involves some eighty percent of all Chinese families. The mother . . . delivers her child to a crèche or nursery in the morning and picks him up at night. In larger towns, members of the family eat all meals in communal dining rooms; sewing, washing, ironing and other household chores are performed by communal service stores. Most Western writers have concluded that this shift in responsibility has disrupted family life to an alarming degree. From my own observations, I don't share this alarm. The old-style patriarchal home is certainly being replaced, especially in the cities, but I don't think the new kind of Chinese home has appreciably weakened family ties. . . . I was impressed by the relaxed, happy relationship of parents and children in the evenings. In the country, the children played or rested nearby as the parents gossiped with relatives and neighbors. In the city, they went together to beautiful public parks that provide outdoor plays, movies, operas, concerts, acrobatics, puppet shows and art exhibits. It seemed to me that these relaxing hours made up, to a large extent, for the lack of contact with the mother during the day. . . . I couldn't help thinking that the day-to-day routine of the Chinese family has much to commend it, compared to that of the family of a Canadian working mother. . . . In some respects, there is greater warmth in Chinese children-parent relationship than there is in Canada.[20]

I would not have believed the above report had I not had opportunities to hear similar observations from the ex-cultural attachés of the British and Swedish embassies in Peking, from a French sinologist and his Chinese wife, and from my own relatives.

In my final conclusion, I should like to point out that one of the geniuses of the Chinese people has been their ability to reduce complex things to bare essentials. Well over a thousand years ago they had reduced the thirty or so heavens and the eighteen or so hells of Indian Buddhism into little more than a system of metaphysics and mental hygiene. Today, after more than two thousand years, they have stripped the family of all its functions except one, namely, to procreate, nurture, and educate children with understanding and love, a function which no other human agency can perform. If they have so far succeeded in making this one function work under circumstances many times more difficult than those which confront the Western family, we may perhaps end on a note of guarded optimism: the family will survive.

Notes

1. Maurice Freedman, "The Family in China, Past and Present," *Pacific Affairs*, 31(4):334, Winter, 1961–1962. This article is, in my opinion, the best analysis of the Chinese family in any language. I am deeply indebted to it for having helped me to better focus my accumulated historical data, which lead to conclusions similar to Dr. Freedman's. The other well-known works on the subject are: Marion J. Levy, Jr., *The Family Revolution in Modern China*, Cambridge, Mass., Harvard University Press, 1949; C. K. Yang, *The Chinese Family in the Communist Revolution*, Cambridge, Mass., The Technology Press of the Massachusetts Institute of Technology, 1959; Francis L. K. Hsu, *Under the Ancestor's Shadow: Chinese Culture and Personality*, New York, Columbia University Press, 1948; Morton H. Fried, *Fabric of Chinese Society: A Study of the Social Life of a County Seat*, New York, Frederick A. Praeger, Inc., 1953; and Olga Lang, *Chinese Family and Society*, New Haven, Conn., Yale University Press, 1946. The two useful works on the Chinese kinship system are: Hsien-chin Hu, *The Common Descent Group in China and Its Functions*, New York, Viking Fund, 1948; and Hui-chen Wang Liu, *The Traditional Chinese Clan Rules*, New York, Association for Asian Studies, 1959.

2. C. K. Yang, *op. cit.*, pp. 20–21.
3. Ssu-ma Ch'ien, *Shih-chi*, Palace ed., Chap. 68.
4. Pan Ku, *Han-shu*, with additional commentaries by Wang Hsien-ch'ien, 1902 ed., Chap. 48, pp. 18b–19a.
5. Ssu-ma Ch'ien, *Shih-chi*, translated by Burton Watson under the title *Records of the Grand Historian of China*, New York, Columbia University Press, 1961, Vol. II, p. 236.
6. Lei Hai-tsung, "Chung-kuo ti chia-tsu chih-tu" (The Family System in Chinese History), *She-hui k'e hsueh* (The Social Sciences, Tsing-hua University), 2:4, July, 1937.
7. Pan Ku, *op. cit.*, Chap. 28, Parts 1–5, *passim*.
8. The figures for A.D. 755 are from Tu Yu, *Tung-tien*, Commercial Press reprint, Chap. 7, p. 41. Figures for 1393 and 1812 are from Ping-ti Ho, *Studies on the Population of China, 1368–1953*, Cambridge, Mass., Harvard University Press, 1959, pp. 55–57. It should be noted that the figure for 1812 covered only fourteen provinces.
9. Since filial duty had by later Han times been generally accepted as the most important yardstick with which to assess one's moral character, many people purposely extended the twenty-seven-month mourning to fantastic lengths—six or more years. Some even observed similar mourning for former official superiors or teachers. The hypocritization of filial duty may best be illustrated by the commoner Chao Hsuan of Ch'ing-chou in central Shantung, who observed mourning for his parents for over twenty years and consequently was hailed by people of his locality as a man of great virtue. However, Ch'en Fan, one of the officials of real integrity, sentenced Chao to prison on the ground that the latter, instead of practicing continence as a genuine practitioner of filial duty, had, during the period of mourning, sired five children. Shortly before the fall of later Han in A.D. 220, K'ung Jung, a descendant of Confucius serving as governor of Tung-hai in modern Hopei, so revolted against the social hypocrisy of his time that he executed a social aspirant because the latter, while wailing full-lunged at his father's burial, showed no real grief. Some members of the ruling class and many more social climbers would relinquish their own shares of family property for their brothers and near kin in order to win social recognition as men of fraternal love. For examples of genuine and false practices during this period of revival of filial duty and family ties, see Chao I, *Nien-erh-shih tsa chi* (Notes on Twenty-two Dynastic Histories), Shih-chieh shu-chu ed., pp. 61–62; and Ch'ien Mu, *Kuo-shih ta-kang* (An Outline of Chinese History), Ch'ang-sha, 1940, Vol. I, pp. 132–36.
10. Lei Hai-tsung, *op. cit.*, and Yang Lien-sheng, "Tung-Han ti hao-

tsu" (The Powerful Houses of Later Han), *Ch'ing-hua hsueh-pao* (Tsing-hua Journal), 9:4, October, 1936.

11. For the life and career of Fan Chung-yen, see James T. C. Liu, "An Early Sung Reformer: Fan Chung-yen," in J. K. Fairbank (ed.), *Chinese Thought and Institutions*, Chicago, The University of Chicago Press, 1957. For Fan's pioneering clan organization and its historical evolution, see Denis C. Twichett, "The Fan Clan's Charitable Estate, 1050–1760," in David S. Nivison and Arthur F. Wright (eds.), *Confucianism in Action*, Stanford, Calif., Stanford University Press, 1959.

12. In fact, Fan's later contemporaries, especially the famous Neo-Confucian philosophers Ch'eng Hao and Ch'eng I, understood the basic weakness of the patrilineal kin better than most modern writers. In order to prevent patrilineal kin from suffering an almost inevitable long-range social and economic leveling, they advocated the revival of the ancient feudal type of clan based strictly on primogeniture. Only by so doing, they argued, could the clan property remain locked in the hand of the *tsung-tzu*, i.e., the eldest heir of the eldest legitimate line. But social customs and economic conditions from Sung times onward made the adoption of this proposal impractical.

13. From my own sampling of scores of clan genealogies I have the impression that really well-endowed clans which could perform efficiently their multiple functions were rather few. Genealogies usually list more functions than the mere maintenance of the ancestral hall, but it may be conjectured that only clans of above-average economic means could periodically print their genealogies. The majority of clans do not seem to have been able to manage much more than maintenance of the ancestral hall and observance of ancestor worship. It is interesting to note that in North China few clans had even an ancestral hall or any property. Sidney D. Gamble, in *North China Villages: Social, Political, and Economic Activities before 1933*, Berkeley, Calif., University of California Press, 1963, p. 15, states: "In most villages even the largest family groups were hardly large enough or wealthy enough to have clan halls or clan land. So far as we could observe, such properties were not part of the general pattern in North China."

14. T'ung-tsu Ch'u, *Law and Society in Traditional China*, Paris, 1961, p. 20.

15. H. McAleavy, "Certain Aspects of Chinese Customary Law in the Light of Japanese Scholarship," *Bulletin of the School of Oriental and African Studies, University of London*, 17 (3):544, 1955.

16. Lien-sheng Yang, "Female Rulers in Imperial China," *Harvard Journal of Asiatic Studies*, 23:61(esp.), 1960–1961.

17. McAleavy, *op. cit.*, p. 544.

18. Hu Shih, *The Chinese Renaissance,* Chicago, The University of Chicago Press, 1934, pp. 104–105. Copyright (1934) by The University of Chicago Press.
19. Freedman, *op. cit.,* pp. 332–333.
20. Denis Lazure, "The Cheerful Children of Red China's Communes," *MacLean's Magazine,* Mar. 11, 1961.

Commentary: *Chinese "National Character"*

Ever since race as an explanatory concept was discarded by social scientists, there has been a tendency to substitute a less lethal kind of portmanteau concept—even at the risk of vast oversimplification. We allude here to the concept of national character or its many analogues.

Ping-ti Ho mars an otherwise excellent analysis of the Chinese family system by his reference to "the genius" of the Chinese people as "explaining" their ability to reduce complex things to bare essentials.

We suggest that it is not the Chinese people but the concept of genius that is guilty of the reductionism. To reduce complex things to bare essentials is the kind of distortion belied by the rest of the article. We rather doubt that viewing Buddhism as "little more than a system of metaphysics and mental hygiene" is ethnocentric oversimplification. Similarly, we doubt that the Chinese family has been stripped of all its functions except the procreation, nurturing, and education of children with understanding and love.

Historically speaking, it is important to realize two things. Buddhism broke with Hinduism because of its opposition to the caste system in India. In addition, the Buddhists felt that a religion should center about ethical precepts as a basis for its rituals rather than provide a sanction for a particular system of social differentiation and privilege. Interestingly enough, as Buddhism moved southeastward the same dilemmas were encountered in different contexts. For example, Buddhism was able to gain inroads to China because Confucianism was the monopoly of the gentry. Civil service examinations for entry into the ranks of the governing elite were based on knowledge of the analects of Confucius. This requirement effectively excluded the commercial classes, and these classes seized upon Buddhism to compensate for their exclusion from the closed society of Confucianism. Generally, in Southeast Asia Buddhism has adapted in various ways, including, on occasion, the incorporation of aspects of caste foreign to its origins. For example, the French anthropologist Paul Mus pointed out in an informal address presented to a Columbia University seminar on South and Southeast Asia in 1968 that there is evidence in Vietnam that Confucianism has been associated with family and social stability and Buddhism with periods of social unrest. Therefore, to say that Buddhism can be equated with metaphysics and mental hygiene is, in a sense, to confine one's view of the religion to certain cultist aspects that are by no means typical.

Although the Chinese family has tended to lose many of its functions to outside institutions and agencies as a result of recent social changes (just as the American family had done much earlier but for different reasons), we object to Ho's rather extreme judgment that all of the functions have been lost. In any event, for obvious political reasons a crucial empirical test by a qualified social scientist is impossible in mainland China, at least for some time to come, especially because modern China is so geographically and sociologically complex.

3

THE NEW DUBLINERS

ALEXANDER J. HUMPHREYS

If you come into Dublin on a train out of the West, as the average immigrant from the countryside does, the confluence of railroads and highways from all over the country, the compacted houses, factories and ornate public buildings that slide by your window, the activities in the harbour and on the Liffey River and the incessant traffic in the streets overwhelmingly impress upon you the fact that here life is organized on quite a different basis than in the small, quiet, rural community you have left. All of these things make for a very palpable realization of what the incoming countryman has known only in an abstract way: that it is in its organization that Dublin differs most from the countryside. For Dublin is truly a modern metropolis where the great organizations of government, industry, commerce, education, communication, art and entertainment are centred and mesh.

Actually, of course, Dublin appreciably differs from the countryside in other, less tangible respects of which the incoming countryman initially, perhaps, is not so aware. Just because it is the capital and the one major metropolis in the Irish Republic,

From Alexander J. Humphreys, New Dubliners: Urbanization and the Irish Family, 1966 (*New York: Fordham University Press, 1966*), *Chap. 1. Copyright Alexander J. Humphreys, 1966. Reprinted by permission of Fordham University Press.*

Dublin is much more in contact with the world outside of Ireland. As a result it has been penetrated much more deeply than the countryside by that world and has become much more intimately engaged with ideas and values that stem from that world. These ideological currents that wash into Dublin through diverse channels are many and varied. But the current whose force has been most strongly felt in modern Dublin is that of rationalistic secularism which has been associated with the modernization of Dublin itself.[1] For Dublin's recent development has been directly influenced by the growth of industrialization in Europe and particularly in England in the last one hundred years. Thus it has occurred at a time when English society, having already passed through the several phases of religious thought associated with the earlier stages of the Industrial Revolution, has given wide acceptance to secularism. In Dublin conflict between basic systems of value is now mainly between traditional Irish Catholic views and secularistic views rather than traditional Protestant conceptions.

The major values which secularism embodies are the supremacy of human nature, reason and action, and the sufficiency of human nature to perfect itself by its own unaided powers. This necessarily entails a rejection of any supernatural dimension in life, and therefore of the notion of original sin and of redemption by God through Christ, as well as of the existence, let alone the efficacy, of any supernatural influence such as grace. It likewise includes the repudiation of a transcendent, yet personal and provident God; or if it concedes the possibility of the existence of such a Being, it doubts God's involvement in man's life or, at any rate, man's capacity to know how and in what direction God may influence human affairs. Man's destiny, in consequence, resides entirely within himself and must be achieved without reference to any putative moral law originating with a personal and concerned God. As a result, secularism assesses religion as having only therapeutic value, whether sublimational or opiate, whereby it may contribute to organizational efficiency by insuring, for those who happen to need it, mental and emotional health and by promoting effective morale. But it discounts religious knowledge as being in any way valid knowledge of objective reality and so, except for purely therapeutic purposes, it tends to isolate religion from the political, economic and educational spheres of life and, more and more, from the family and the community altogether. Finally, although man is to achieve his destiny alone, probably the more prevalent secularistic view of man is mechanistic rather than humanistic. Man does not carve out his niche in the universe by the force of his will which asserts his inalienable self, but by finding through the good offices of reason the laws inherent within him which determine the proper equilibrium of his native forces that will yield the healthy personality and the good society.

Of the major forms of secularism the one that, up to the moment, has had the greatest impact on Dublin has been the individualistic variety which has grown out of the classical liberalism of nineteenth-century England rather than the socialism which stems largely from Marx and which has had wider acceptance on the continent. Dublin has not been impervious to socialist influence particularly through the agency of the labour union movement and especially during the first quarter of the century. But generally speaking conservative liberal forces have made greater headway than socialistic movements in the Irish capital. Consequently, the more current species of secularism in Dublin makes the primary agent of naturalistic perfection, both of the human person and of the human community, the human individual rather than the human group. As a result, in theory at least, it tends to subordinate the group—government, business, the family—to the individual.

Merely to describe this complex of ideas is to indicate how forcefully it clashes with the Irishman's system of Catholic ideas and values. The fact that these secularistic values are given much more effective voice in Dublin than in the countryside means that the conflict between the two sets of values is much sharper in Dublin than in rural Ireland and we shall eventually have to appraise the effects of this conflict upon the New Dubliners.

But the countryman entering Dublin undoubtedly is not as aware of this conflict as he is of the more tangible difference between Dublin and the rural community which lies in the organizational structure of the city. For in Dublin the primary influence upon community life and affairs is no longer exerted by the family and groups that are kindred to the family to which the countryman is accustomed, but by large, impersonal and non-familistic organizations, particularly of business and of government.

Whether they be governmental or economic, these large-scale organizations in Dublin have for their goal the production of goods and services according to a specific rational code of efficiency.[2] Both the economic concerns which are motivated by profit, and the governmental agencies which, theoretically at least, are not so motivated, have in common the express aim of producing the maximum of quality goods or services at a minimum of cost and labour. This is judged by a complex set of standards that are determined by objective analysis of the facts of experience. Although this goal is never perfectly realized, its legitimacy is as commonly accepted in Dublin as it is elsewhere in modern industrial society and with the same result. As a consequence, the ascendancy of power and control over community organization and affairs has shifted from private families linked together by ties of kinship and common residence to foster familial ideals and interests, and has passed into the hands of a comparatively small number of large impersonal organizations which are interlocked for quite a different purpose. The manner in which these large-scale corporations are internally organized, as well as the manner in which they are mutually interrelated, are central factors in producing the differences that are to be found between the family of the countryman and the New Dubliner.

The clearest indication of this shift in power is to be found in the ownership and control of property devoted to production and service. There are in Dublin, perhaps more than in any other comparable city in Great Britain or the United States, shops and stores that are family owned and operated, but even in Dublin the number of these are relatively few. In the course of time, productive property and its administration has almost wholly passed out of the hands of private families and has come under the control of a relatively small group of large corporations, public and private.

Internally, these corporations are organized on the basis of a formal rational analysis of the most effective way of relating to one another material, machines, men and their operations in order to reach the end of the greatest practicable productivity and service. The criterion whereby this effectiveness is judged is the pragmatic crucible of observable qualities and experience. It is no argument against this to note that many a concern in Dublin, especially newly founded concerns, simply try to ape the patterns of organization which have been successful elsewhere and so tend to accept them on traditional grounds, for the industrial tradition embodies the need to adhere to this formal code of efficiency. Neither is the fact that in every case, especially in Dublin, a host of other factors—and principally familial factors—are at work to modify these central organizational principles so that they are never realized in all their abstract perfection. Despite these limitations, in each case this set of principles has the primacy in fixing the general structure of these organizations and their relationships to one another.

All of this is simply saying that in the main the business concerns and governmental bodies of Dublin organize themselves according to established principles of economic organization and of public administration current in the industrial nations of the West. But it is worth spelling this out in order later to appreciate in detail the transforming impact these principles have on the family of the New Dubliners. Each public or private corporation, even the quite modest one, divides its jobs and their interrelationships, and especially its offices of authority and their hierarchy, on the basis of an empirically tested analysis of the pattern logically most likely to achieve its purpose. The same rule is applied to the choice of persons who are to fill these offices and perform these tasks. As a result, the corporation rarely employs an already established group and almost never a family. Rather, it selects individuals who are assigned to their position, given their rank in the company and promoted according to their individual ability as established by objective, impersonal tests and records of achievement.

In such circumstances, the force of age and sex as the grounds for the division of labour and authority sharply declines. Seniority remains important, but more as an evidence of proven competence and ability than as a claim on the corporation's gratitude for loyal services that can no longer be as effectively tendered as before. On the other hand, because it tends impersonally to select the competent individual, the corporation in Dublin has opened up jobs and occupational careers for women on a hitherto unprecedented scale, and employment and promotional policies that are still discriminatory against women stem less from any internal principle of organization within the corporation than from the requirements of outside groups, and especially of the family.

The same general principles of efficiency largely determine the relationships between the various corporations in Dublin, and these in turn profoundly affect the structure of the entire Dublin community. It is more economical in every sense of the word for corporations which are constantly dealing with each other—governmental as well as private—to set themselves up near each other in one central locale. And it is precisely this geographic centralization of productive and service facilities and of labour that has made Dublin the economic and political capital of Ireland and the large metropolis that it is.

However, as we have already noted, these principles of efficient organization are affected in many ways by the needs of familial organization and by familial values. The combination of these two produces another striking feature that distinguishes Dublin from the rural community. On the one hand, the bureaucratic system of ranks within the corporation establishes between the people who occupy them a complex set of differentials in income, prestige and power. On the other hand, principles of family organization require that these differentials be shared by the families of the individuals employed by the corporation. Because the levels of rank in Dublin corporations are many, the result is that the class levels in the community also become more numerous and heterogeneous. Thus the class structure of Dublin is more complex than that of the rural community.[3] At the same time, because the system of ranks within the corporation is open and the corporation fosters the promotion of capable individuals, there is considerable movement of families from one class level to another; and in the Dublin community at large the amount of social mobility, which usually involves residential mobility, is very great by contrast to the relative class rigidity of the countryside.

On the whole, then, the manner in which the large corporations of Dublin organize themselves and their mutual relationships has, by comparison with the rural community, changed the fundamental form of community solidarity. Where the solidarity of the rural community is pre-eminently inter-familial and rests on intense interaction between families which is particularistic and diffuse, the structure of Dublin promotes the co-operation of specialized individuals who interact in a universalistic, specific, impersonal and segmental way.[4] This does not, of course, mean that inter-familial solidarity ceases in Dublin altogether. But it does mean that inter-familial solidarity declines sharply and that the most extensive relationship in the city becomes the interaction of specialized individuals.

Geared to this world, the New Dubliner's family differs significantly from that of the countryman in its internal structure. The most glaring difference is that typically the New Dubliner's family does not own and operate property productive of income and as a result it not only has lost central control over such productive activities, but has ceased to be a collective domestic unit of production. The activities of its members upon which its livelihood depends are not, as in the countryman's family, performed together at home but are dispersed and performed individually outside the home. Because of this elemental change among the New Dubliners, the wife in the usual case no longer participates in activity which produces income, while the husband is taken out of the home and away from the family for the major portion of the working day. This economic mutation radically transforms the balance of labour and responsibility between family members which is so characteristic of the countryman's family. On the marital axis, the New Dubliner husband and wife no longer share direct domestic responsibility in roughly equal fashion, but the major portion of these now falls upon the wife's shoulders.

Despite the fact that the New Dubliner wife no longer engages in productive activity, she must perforce assume the major portion of the total economic load. Unlike the rural wife whose husband divides these activities with her, the New Dubliner wife with few exceptions is responsible for virtually all of the exchange and service activities so important for the family. She manages the budget, does nearly all the buying, is responsible not only for the cooking and cleaning, but also for the household repairs and entertainment, and for the most part is the actual representative of the family to the immediate local community. More significantly, the wife carries the greater responsibility in the matter of raising the children. In the actual exercise of authority and discipline, it is she who has to watch, admonish, give orders and apply the sanctions which usually must be administered here and now—for she alone is here to do it now. She also has the greater responsibility in providing the children with adult example and, in regard to her sons, this presents her with an especially harassing problem. The association of mother and daughter that we have noted in the rural family remains much the same and the New Dubliner mother can be an effective role model for her girls. But her sons, as they grow into adolescence, cannot look to her as an adult model for the simple reason that she is a woman and they are going to be men. Within the normal New Dubliner household, where the husband comes home tired from an exhausting day, there is no adequate model of manhood for the sons to contemplate and to imitate and they must, often without complete success, look outside of the home for substitute guides as to what a man should be.

Inevitably, in this situation the wife's authority over family affairs increases considerably and her relationship to her husband changes significantly. Where the rural wife is generally subordinate to her spouse, the New Dubliner wife has equal authority with her husband and, though technically he is still the "head of the house," both husband and wife feel, act and speak of themselves as "partners." This very fact modifies the delicate set of affectional relationships between parents and children. Because he no longer exerts constant daily authority over his sons in the rural fashion, the New Dubliner father, while maintaining essentially the same relationship with his daughters, is much more companionable with his sons in their late adolescence and they in turn are much more relaxed, open and frank with him. But in regard to all of her children, and especially her sons, the New Dubliner wife is in an ambivalent position. By position and by cultural definition she, above all, is supposed to be the source of warmth, affection and intimate, friendly relations, and she strives to maintain this role especially, like the rural mother, with her sons. Yet force of circumstance puts her in the central position of authority and this tends to reduce intimacy between her and her children and to beget restraint and even, under certain conditions, resentment.

But the increased responsibilities which devolve upon the New Dubliner wife do not result in a corresponding increase in her status as such in the community. On the contrary, since the primary grounds for status in Dublin, as in all the industrial nations of the West, normally lies in income-producing activity which she no longer shares with her husband, the status of wife and mother is generally lower in Dublin than it is in the countryside. As a result, as we shall see, there is a tendency among New Dubliner women to attempt to redress the balance by activities which are often in conflict with the traditional role of mother and wife in much the same fashion as women do elsewhere in the industrial West.

Internally, then, the New Dubliner's family by comparison with the family of the countryman is unbalanced in the distribution of direct family responsibilities in the sphere of economic activity, and consequently in the spheres of parental authority and example, of affectional relationships between family members, and of the individual status of husband and wife. The most notable consequences of this transformation in Ireland are the decline in the range of parental control and the power of the older generation, and in the earlier age at which children reach full social adulthood.

Under urban conditions where the family no longer controls and operates a productive holding, the patterns of inheritance change appreciably because there is no longer any need to transfer the family holding intact to one son, or to dower the daughters in the rural fashion. At the same time, the family economy ordinarily requires that the sons before marriage work outside the home and not at home under the direction of their father, and the Dublin community normally supplies enough occupational opportunities that they can do so without having to leave the city. As a result, the marriage of the inheriting son, so central in the cycle of the rural family, simply ceases to be as crucial a factor in the lives of the New Dubliners as it is for the country family. Without having to leave Dublin, all the sons can and generally do enter an occupational field in late adolescence, achieve occupational adulthood in early manhood and in many cases can climb to a higher occupational and social level than that of their father. Simultaneously, they are able to marry earlier without jeopardizing the family's interests and usually are in an independent economic position to do so. The daughters likewise, save in exceptional circumstances, no longer depend upon a dowry, find ample occupational openings in Dublin, and can marry earlier than the girls of the countryside. Often they have the opportunity, particularly through occupational contacts, to improve their social position by marriage. In short, New Dubliners of both sexes can and, as a rule, do achieve full social adulthood at an earlier age than the country people, and have better chances for social advancement to boot.

In preparing their children for this world, parents must inevitably yield to outside agencies a far greater measure of influence than rural parents. Having ceased to be a collective unit of production, the New Dubliner family tends to become less of a collective unit in certain other respects. As productive activities, so educational, recreational and courtship activities tend to become more individualized and dispersed throughout the Dublin community. The school, the shop or office where the young people learn their trades and skills, and the peer groups in which they recreate and meet their mates and which are no longer, as in the country, based on inter-familial ties—all of these are much more vital factors in moulding the children's attitudes, values and standards of behaviour than in the rural community.

The greater range, and the greater importance, of relationships that family members have with large, impersonal organizations and with groups that are not familial in character signalize another major change which accompanies the internal alterations in the structure of the family which urbanization produces. This is the decline and the weakening of the inter-familial solidarity on the basis of kinship and neighbourliness. City life not only affects the inner equilibrium of the family; it also tends to isolate the family from those families that are neighbours and kin, with which the rural family has such deep and crucial ties.[5]

This is evident from the fact that on every class level and with few exceptions almost every form of co-operation between neighbours and kin found in the rural community has diminished among the New Dubliners and in some cases has disappeared entirely. The major forms of co-operation between New Dubliner families are regular visiting and recreation, recurrent exchanges of gifts, help in times of crisis such as sickness and death, financial aid in periods of distress, and assistance in getting a relative a job. New Dubliner families, especially those related by kinship, may also jointly impose sanctions upon a miscreant member, particularly one who neglects his obligations to his family, but the social pressure neighbours or kin are able to bring to bear is considerably weaker than in the rural community. But the regular and extensive co-operation in economic activities, the exchange of goods and services, the channelling of trade along familial lines so widespread between rural kin and neighbours have virtually disappeared among the New Dubliners. Finally, while the older men in a neighbourhood may still gather of an evening in the local pub, their meetings are largely recreational and their discussions and decisions have nowhere near the influence of the old men's cliques in the countryside upon the affairs of the neighbourhood, much less the larger community. This decline in inter-familial solidarity lessens the support the nuclear family can receive on a familistic basis and therefore forces the family to rely the more for such support upon non-familistic groups and agencies in Dublin.

These profound organizational changes in the inner structure of the family and in its relations with both familial and non-familial groups in the community inevitably result in far-reaching modifications in the sentiments and values which are directly connected with the organization of life. The New Dubliner is not, like the countryman, concerned about land and the continuity of his family on a homestead, nor content with the acceptance of acquired status. Rather he is concerned with wage security and with the achievement of status by means of occupational advancement and hypergamy. Consequently, filial piety—that set of sentiments and values that bind parents and children together—changes significantly in Dublin. While children there have a solid respect for their parents, there is among the New Dubliners considerably less veneration and glorification of the aged than among the country people. Generally speaking, as there are greater equality and *camaraderie* between husband and wife, so children are less fearful of their parents and are less dominated by them. Both parents and children attach a much higher premium than the countryman to the ambitions and the earlier emancipation of youth from parental control. New Dubliners consider it right and proper that children should enjoy freedom and assume adult responsibilities in respect to occupation, marriage and indeed the whole range of life many years earlier than the rural community would allow. As a consequence among New Dubliners the juvenile attitudes towards sex and women, the sense of inferiority and submissiveness characteristic of the countryman are notably less pronounced and tend to disappear altogether.

The shift from the countryside to Dublin also has had important repercussions upon those values and attitudes which are not directly connected with organization at the family level. The New Dubliners retain the traditional Irish respect for the professions, but this has been tempered by their increasing appreciation of business as a career and their growing esteem of the role of business in the nation's welfare. As a people who have had political independence and the freedom to make their own way for little over a quarter of a century, the New Dubliners still frequently take as models of class behaviour the norms of the old Anglo-Irish Ascendancy. But the influence of a more open and flexible occupational and class structure has seriously altered these values and the New Dubliners are in the process of evolving their own somewhat distinctive class norms. In like fashion, while the New Dubliner is still quite sceptical of government and politics in general, he is far less suspicious of this sphere of life than his country cousin, perhaps because in the capital he has much wider contacts with government agencies and personnel in action.

Of all the countryman's values, the most notable fatality in the move to the city is superstition. Although their immigrant parents may have brought the rural "wee people" and pishogues with them into the city, the New Dubliners, except to a moderate extent those living in the slums, have lost these eccentric creatures and their ways. This is almost certainly due to the direct and indirect influence of the greater education which prevails in Dublin and to contact with a more reasoned and analytical way of life.

But what is perhaps most striking of all is that the basic set of religious values which the countryman accepts survives the transition to the city and persists among the New Dubliners. The New Dubliner entertains the same supernatural view of the universe as the countryman and like him considers that activities that merit and preserve supernatural grace are paramount in life. And he has much the same tendency to be wary and suspicious of human nature and its inclination towards evil. Both in regard to his bodily appetites and the power of reason he is inclined to think, as one Dubliner put it, that man has been given a "double dose of original sin." This is abundantly clear, as we shall see, from the religious sentiments and attitudes which New Dubliners of every class express. It is also evident from their religious practice and observance. Urbanization has not produced a significant decline in devotion, in the reception of the sacraments and in the fulfilment of religious duties. If anything, city life has facilitated and increased such behaviour by bringing the New Dubliner into closer physical proximity to the Church which is its centre. In short, in spite of his many points of contact with modern secularism and his involvement with a modern industrial economy, the New Dubliner has not become secularized.

There is, then, essential religious continuity between the countryman and the New Dubliner. Nevertheless, many of the religious attitudes and sentiments characteristic of the Irish are tempered and modified by city life. In general, the New Dubliner tends to be less traditionalistic and more intelligent and reasoned in his approach to religion. Thus, points of religious doctrine are much more frequently matters of discussion among the New Dubliners than among the country folk. The New Dubliner also feels much freer to criticize the clergy and to seek convincing reasons from them for the standards of behaviour they hold up and the policies they advocate. At the same time he is more open and frank than the countryman in discussing sex and the problems of sexual instruction and morality, and he tends to take a more reasoned, rather than a sheer authoritarian, approach to the religious instruction of his children.

It is difficult to sort out and assess the independent influence of ideological factors on the one hand, and of the organization of city life on the other, in producing these variations in the religious attitudes of the New Dubliners. Probably these changes are the result of the combined influence of both. Undoubtedly, the rationalism of the secular view of life challenges the New Dubliner to become more informed about his religious beliefs and to seek the grounds which make them intellectually acceptable. At the same time, he is daily confronted with an economy organized in such a way as to put heavy premiums on rational analysis and decision. One therefore reinforces the other in stimulating him to take a more inquiring and critical approach to life in general and to religion in particular, as well as to his familial situation and its problems.

The effects of urbanization on the family in Ireland, then, are extensive and quite swift. Despite certain radical continuities between the farm family and the family in Dublin, by the time the children of the immigrants from rural areas have reached full adulthood and founded their families the total round of change has reached the point where the distinctive pattern of the family life of the countryman is no more. The countryman has been transformed literally into a citizen.

Notes

1. I use the word "secularism" here because of its appropriateness in designating the substance of the views and values to which I refer. These conceive the temporal process of the observable cosmos as the only reality extant or, at least, knowable and therefore of relevance to human life and society. Consequently, "secularization" here means the process whereby such a set of views becomes accepted on a widening scale. Such usage has precedent in sociological and anthropological literature. For instance, "secularization" is used in this sense by Robert Redfield in *The Folk Culture of the Yucatán* (Chicago, 1941), esp. ch. ix. So is "secularism" by Harry Elmer Barnes as edited by Becker in Howard Becker and Harry Elmer Barnes, *Social Thought from Lore to Science* (2nd ed., 2 vols.; Washington, D.C., 1952), I, 540. But we should note that the term "secular" has a wider meaning as used in the sacred-secular theory of Becker, Hill and others where it signifies "readiness to accept or initiate social change." See Becker in ch. 6, "Current Sacred Theory and Its Development," in Howard Becker and Alvin Boskoff (eds.), *Modern Sociological Theory in Continuity and Change* (New York, 1957), p. 142. I am sure that secularism as I have defined it is included in Becker's formulation. But I use it in this restricted sense only and not in the expanded sense which identifies secular society with rapidly changing society, as opposed to "sacred" society which is traditionalistic and relatively impervious to change.

2. By "rational" I here refer to what Max Weber defines as a course

of action based on consciously reasoned "expectations as 'conditions' or 'means'" for the ends chosen by an individual or a group. There often seems to be a tendency in modern sociological literature to limit the term "rational" to this meaning which Weber called *zweckrational.* But this does not exhaust the meaning of the word. In addition, action may also be called rational "in terms of rational orientation to an absolute value . . . involving a conscious belief in the absolute value of some ethical, aesthetic, religious, or other form of behaviour, entirely for its own sake and independently of any prospects of external success." This Weber called *wertrational,* and I shall use "rational" in this sense later when discussing the approach of New Dubliners to religious ideas and values. *v.* Max Weber, *The Theory of Social and Economic Organization,* trans. A. M. Henderson and Talcott Parsons (New York, 1947), pp. 115–18; 184–6; 337–9.

3. The process of stratifying people into a complex class structure and the expansion of the bases of co-operation between individuals to grounds other than kinship and friendliness begins in towns much smaller and less differentiated than Dublin. *v.* Kimball, *op. cit.,* pp. iv–v, 253.

4. The concepts signified by the terms "particularistic" and "universalistic" are those of Talcott Parsons and are familiar to the professional sociologist. For the benefit of the general reader, a particularistic relationship is one that is based upon who a particular person is relative to another particular person or object, such as, for example, the relationship expressed when a man says: "I must help him because he is my brother." On the other hand, relationships that are independent of such particular, personal considerations and are based upon objective, impersonal characteristics and norms such as those between doctor and patient, employer and employee, etc., are universalistic. *v.* Talcott Parsons, *Essays in Sociological Theory Pure and Applied* (Glencoe, Ill., 1949), pp. 192, 195–7; and *The Social System,* pp. 61–5.

5. Parsons, *Essays in Sociological Theory,* pp. 237–8, has pointed out this phenomenon of the isolation of the conjugal family in urban America.

Commentary: *Secularization of Values*

A generally accepted formulation is that secularization of human values is positively associated with urbanization and industrialization. However, social scientists such as Sidney M.

Greenfield have assumed that urbanization and industrialization do not necessarily have the same implications for the nuclear family. Dublin is urban but preindustrial. New York is urban and industrial. Timbuktu is neither industrial nor part of an urban society. It is merely a primitive city in which neither urban nor industrial values are dominant. It is a cultural enclave in a society that is still quite close to its tribal roots.

On the subcontinent of Asia, even the families of the urban native elite are still dominated by traditional, extended, or joint family patterns. More specifically, the dominance of the nuclear family is a functional consequence of industrialization and not so much of urbanization. Alexander J. Humphreys, the author of the preceding article, finds, in an intensive study of twenty-nine families in Dublin, that although there have been significant changes in the organizational structure of the family, no parallel changes have taken place in their ideological commitments to ultimate religious ideas and values.

In our view this must be the case until Dublin becomes an industrial city. If the Dubliners are matricentric, as described in the selection, their preindustrial matricentrism differs radically from the matricentrism of two American family types: white middle-class suburban dweller or the Negro lower class urban dweller.

The matricentrism of the Dubliners is due in large part to the conditioning of traditional Catholicism, which exalts the role of the mother. If one were interested in speculating about origins, the focus upon the Virgin Mary might be mentioned. As a matter of fact, Roman Catholic missionaries scored their greatest successes with the Indians of South America after the Marian year was proclaimed. This was, syncretistically speaking, consistent with the earlier matricentric types of worship in these areas. It is interesting to note that the peasant origins of the Dubliners can be correlated with strength of traditional Church controls over behavior. The Dubliner is urban, but his family type has to be congenial to the matricentric type that was typical of peasant Ireland and sanctioned by the Church. We are implying that a cultural parallel exists between matricentric South American Indians and matricentric Dublin families in that the power of the Church might be weakened if it, too, were not in a sense Marian in central focus. In Dublin, therefore, a religious dimension exists that does not include such characteristics as demasculinization resulting from the absence of the father that one finds in mid-

dle-class white families or lower class Negro families in the United States.

The New Dubliners, although preindustrial and of peasant origin, have nevertheless been somewhat acculturated to the dominant values of the more industrialized and northern Protestant counties. Ever since the Easter Rebellion of 1916, there has been a migration from southern to northern Ireland paralleling, to some degree, the rural urban migration in the United States following the Civil War. From this, one may conclude that although the Dubliners are preindustrial, they are closer to industrialization than urban Africans or Asiatics. Or, stated more graphically and dramatically, one can say that Dublin is closer to Belfast than any Eastern city is to an industrial revolution.

4

THE SUBSTRUCTURE
OF POWER
AND AUTHORITY

AILEEN D. ROSS

Even in such a small intimate group as a family, responsibilities and rights must be distributed in order that the group may function smoothly and efficiently, and a hierarchy of authority be established to direct and co-ordinate the activity. Weber never specifically mentions the family in his discussion of authority, but his analysis of the "traditional" authority of corporate groups is applicable to the family unit. The family's authority is "traditional" in the sense that, as its rules are traditionally received, they are much more difficult to change than those of "rational-legal authority." Moreover:

The order underlying a system of traditional authority always defines a system of statuses of persons who can legitimately exercise authority. Such a status is different from an "office." It does not involve specifically defined powers with the presumption that everything not legitimized in terms of the order is outside its scope. It is rather defined in terms of three things. There are, first, the concrete traditional prescriptions of the traditional order, which are held to be binding on the person in authority as well as the others. There is, secondly, the authority of other persons above the particular status in a hierarchy, or in different spheres . . . and finally . . . there is a sphere of arbitrary free "grace" open to the incumbent.[1]

From The Hindu Family in its Urban Setting (*Toronto: University of Toronto Press, 1961*), *pp. 91–121. Reprinted by permission.*

Traditional family authority is usually accepted by children as easily and naturally as other types of family training. It does not always need naked power to enforce it, but uses persuasion to entice the individual to follow the dictates of those in control. This kind of power can be called "indirect authority" for the recipient is not always aware of its existence. A child may become so used to obeying the family mores that he may even experience feelings of deep guilt if he transgresses them long after he has been separated from his family, or even after his parents are dead.[2]

On the other hand, "direct" authority is usually felt to be compulsive and is, therefore, often distasteful to the recipient and may call out resentment and resistance. This type of authority is usually employed by an insecure person, such as a father who, in changing times, is not sure of what his relationship to his children should be. However, in all groups which exist for any length of time, authority will become an integral part of each status.

Every person fills a variety of authority positions during his lifetime. He may even have to occupy several different positions at the same time. For instance, as well as filling the position of father, he may also be son to the grandfather of the house, brother to a sister, uncle to a nephew or niece, and husband to his wife. His authority will vary in all these positions. It is only when the complexity of an individual's adjustment to others in his different roles is understood that the amazing flexibility of the human animal, and the delicacy of the balance of each social system is fully appreciated. These positions become even more difficult to fill when family relationships are changing. A more detailed description of the structure of authority of the joint family will emphasize the areas of strain in this substructure when the family grows smaller.

The Authority of Different Relationships

Head of the Household

The eldest male, whether grandfather or father, was the acknowledged head of the family.[3] He may never have had the power of life and death over family members as was common in ancient Roman families, but his authority was theoretically complete.[4] Moreover, the hierarchy of authority of the joint family has al-

ways been supported by caste and religion, and was formerly absolute and predictable. Particularly in isolated villages it is still
upheld by attitudes of respect and fear, and acts of deference.

One of the clearest descriptions of the hierarchy of authority of
the traditional Hindu family is given by Beals in his study of the
six main families of a village near Mysore. Each family had more
than thirty members:

. . . each formed an economic unit, and each was under the leadership of a single headman. The functions of family leadership were, to
some extent, shared by the brothers of the family head. The family
head was in charge of finances. He sat on the village panchayat, or
council, and represented the family in dealings with consanguineal and
affinal relatives living outside the village. Of the brothers of the family
head, one was usually in charge of dry-land agriculture; another managed the garden lands, the cattle, or the family industry. Such a division of labour persisted in large families even in 1953, although the
largest families of 1953 could count only twelve to fifteen members.
Allied with each of the six large families in 1900 were a number of
small households composed of distant relatives and dependents, such
as widows and impoverished brothers in law, as well as servants and
debtors of other castes. In this manner, the six large families included
many other families within their respective spheres of influence.[5]

The grandfather was theoretically the head of the family until
his death. This gave him power over his wife and children, his
younger brothers, and his sisters until they were married. Even
those who moved away to distant cities, or overseas, were theoretically still members of the family and therefore under his control
although he could not supervise their day-to-day affairs. On his
death, the authority passed to the next eldest male.[6]

Interviews showed that the grandfather's authority in fact
varied in the different families studied. At times it was strong and
his role was much like that of a dictator; at other times it was
weak and the family relationships were more equalitarian. But on
the whole, case studies tended to show at least one dominant
grandparent in most large joint families. They did not show, however, that grandparents were as influential in the life of the joint
family as had been expected, for the short life span in India
means that one or both of the grandparents usually die at a comparatively early age.

Only a few of the grandfathers mentioned in interviews had
had personal characteristics which had prevented them from carrying out their traditional roles. In one family the grandfather had
been so reckless with money that the control of the family finances

had been handed over to his son before his death. Apart from these few exceptions it was clear that control over important family decisions is still maintained by the older generation in large joint families.

The following interview indicates the rather typical way in which authority is handled in a family of several generations. It shows that the authority of the head, or grandfather, is in effect only over the major matters which affect the whole family life, whereas the grandmother holds authority in her own domain and can control the minute details of household life. Not all grandparents, however, exerted influence over their son's family. Nor were they necessarily stern in their discipline; a grandfather was quite often pictured as a loving, gentle person.

All the important decisions at home were made by Grandfather and Father. Grandmother was the authority in the domestic side, but she and Mother had no voice in outside matters. Mother did not even have the right to purchase her own saris. Grandmother was responsible for the children's training and behaviour. She taught us eating manners and caste duties. Grandmother, and sometimes Father punished us, not Mother. Grandfather never punished us. When he got angry, he used one or two abusive words, but nothing beyond.

On the other hand, the position of head of the family entails so much potential power that a harsh incumbent can disrupt family relationships. In one family, both grandfather and father had been extremely severe.

My father was terribly afraid of his father. And when Grandfather died and Father became head of the family he in turn made us all afraid of him. He made my uncles obey him implicitly. He beat Mother when she didn't carry out his orders. He harassed and punished all of us children. But Father felt guilty after he had punished us, and had terrible nightmares about Grandfather coming back and threatening him with a stick, because Mother was Grandfather's favourite daughter-in-law.

This extreme kind of discipline sometimes had unexpected results and it is quite likely that many sons rebelled against it. The following case study is an illustration of an unsuccessful rebel.

My great-grandfather was a dictator and believed in the strictest discipline. He used to give Grandfather and his brothers, five rupees for pocket money a month and they had to write accounts of every pie they spent. Grandfather had an independent spirit and resented this discipline; so he went off with friends and spent a lot of time with them. He used his school money and got into bad company and evil ways. When Great-Grandfather heard he stopped his allowance. Grandfather was desperate; so he started borrowing. Then he got in with a famous actress who promised him 500 rupees if he would drive in a chariot with her in a big procession—as he was the son of a famous man. Grandfather wanted to hurt his father for the way he had treated him so he went with her. Great-Grandfather was furious, his anger knew no bounds. He beat Grandfather mercilessly, and sent him and his wife to live in another town. Finally he disinherited him and left all his properties to his grandson—my father. Grandfather then had to live under the authority of his son, who had all rights over him.

The changing attitudes to such strict authority was shown in several interviews in which the grandfather who "wanted everybody under his thumb" was called a very old-fashioned man.

In the traditional joint family women were theoretically allotted a subordinate position to men. Even today they do not have controlling positions before the law, or in many economic or social matters. However, a closer analysis of joint family life shows that, in fact, women did have important positions in their own sphere. The wife of the eldest male member, usually the grandmother, had a clear position of authority as head of the domestic side of the household. Important household matters were theoretically controlled by the grandfather, but day-to-day routine matters were completely under her control. She administered the household, supervised or did the cooking, organized the work of the women of the household, and saw that the children were properly cared for. In the close confinement of the house, from which women rarely escaped, her main task must also have been that of mediator although this element of her role is never mentioned. If she had exceptional qualities, she could even wield great influence over the male head "behind the scene." If the grandfather died before her, as he often did, she might inherit his mantle of authority over all family affairs since her influence over her sons was usually so strong that she could dominate the family. The many facets of her duties and power are shown in the following description of a Hindu widow.

The widowed mother does nothing, but she manages everything. She has absolute rule over the family members. She sees that the daughters-in-law behave, that the house-father [the oldest son] receives the respect due to him from other family members, that servants of the household are well behaved and orderly, that the community thinks well of the house, that the family priest is respected and honoured, that enough money is contributed for feeding the Brahmans, that gods are venerated properly, and that there is some substantial saving in the house every month.[7]

In spite of her theoretical control different arrangements of authority between the grandmother and her sons were revealed in case studies. In one case, a grandmother had authority over all general family matters, while her two sons controlled their own immediate family affairs. In most families a son would continue to consult his mother on all important matters. The following case study shows how extensive a grandmother's influence can be in her son's household.

When I was growing up, Father was the chief authority in the home in all official and financial matters. He was a district commissioner and practically ruled the district like a king, and yet he would always go to his mother, who was nearly illiterate, for her final decision in any important family matter. Grandmother was the authority too in all household matters, and Father left everything to her. In such matters as settling weddings Father and Mother did the preliminary choosing, then Father would ask Grandmother for her final approval. I still remember how my brother's marriage was arranged. After all the preliminary arrangements had been gone through, the girl's parents came to visit us. Grandmother was cutting vegetables in the kitchen; so Father went to her and said: "The girl's father has come to enquire about our final decision. The girl is good looking, and the boy has given his consent. The family seems to be decent and of a good class. What is your opinion?" Then Grandmother said: "As the girl is liked by the boy, and comes from a good family the wedding can be set." If Grandmother had said that she didn't like the match, then Father would never have gone ahead with the wedding.

A situation which is becoming increasingly typical is that in which a son moves away from his paternal home with his wife and children, and later takes his mother to live with him when her husband dies. This new pattern usually causes strain, for technically speaking the grandmother is now living in someone else's home, and therefore the strict traditional definition of her position of authority does not apply. For instance, the wife of the house now seems to feel that instead of dealing with a revered "grandmother" she is rather coping with a "mother-in-law." It is a situation in which the lines of authority are less well-defined, and it is likely that a daughter-in-law feels more frustration and aggression towards a mother-in-law who attempts to exert her authority in her son's home than she would if she were still living in her mother-in-law's home where her dominance would be expected.

This situation is aggravated if the daughter-in-law was not the grandmother's choice, or if she had not been trained to the family ways, as in the days of child marriage. There would be especial tension if the daughter-in-law had more education than the mother-in-law, or was from another region or caste. For, the rigidity of caste and regional customs increases the areas of possible conflict for the women of the household when they come from different milieus. Peaceful co-operation between the two would further depend on whether the grandmother was from the maternal or paternal side, and whether the wife had been married as a child or an adult.

Case studies showed more grandmothers living with the families interviewed than grandfathers. This would be due to the earlier age of girls on marriage and the longer female life span. It seemed too that grandmothers were more often mentioned as strong authoritarians than were grandfathers. This may be because her two roles of grandmother and mother-in-law are played concurrently. It is useful to remember here that a "beloved" grandmother to the children and a "revered" mother to a son may be a "nagging" mother-in-law to the wife. If a grandmother had a strong personality, the grandfather would allow her much say in family matters. On the other hand, the grandmothers mentioned in case studies sometimes had personalities quite different from that expected of their position. One was referred to as a "very quiet, timid person." Such unexpected characteristics might mean that the grandmother would be unable to fill her role in the expected way, and thus might cause just as much conflict and tension as a person who had a particularly overbearing personality. If a grandmother carried out her role in an authoritarian way and was also a grumbler, the family often found her hard to endure. "Grandmother was always finding fault. She nagged a lot. She was the chief authority over the family until her death, which was a relief to us all."

The close mother-son tie in the joint family meant that the person who could handle the grandmother best was her son. If he had a domineering personality, she would be no trouble in the household.

The grandmother tended to exert most authority and influence over her daughters and daughters-in-law, even though the grandfather was theoretically head of all members of the household. Her control even extended to daughters-in-law living in separate households, for the social separation of men and women means that women are still somewhat confined to spending most of their leisure time with other relatives, even when they live in nuclear family units.

The position of the grandmother in the large joint family has been shown to be one of considerable importance. In it she had much power—explicit in her control of the other women, implicit through her influence over her husband, and through her close affectional relationship with her son. When the traditional joint family changes to a nuclear type, the power of the grandmother dwindles until she may only have symbolic or ritual influence and authority over her children and grandchildren.

Father

Many of the laws of Manu deal with the sovereignty of the head of the family, and prescribe his conduct towards subordinate members, always recommending forebearance and patience.[8] His position of authority is not out of line with his duties, for he is responsible for the well-being of all under his roof, particularly the women. Among other things he must preserve their chastity in order to secure pure-blood progeny.[9] The great authority of his position in the joint family meant that a man of strong personality could exert his personal preferences over the whole household. In former days little could happen without his consent, and he made all decisions even down to such matters as when babies should be ceremonially named.

A father of a family only has this position of complete authority if he is the head of a joint family. A man who was merely the father of a family unit within the joint family, and not the senior male member, did not appear to have much power. Very little is, in fact, recorded of his actual authority, but a few hints of it appeared in interviews. They showed that his power was fairly well confined to the day-to-day affairs of his own wife and children. In other words, his own small family unit was merely part of the large whole.

However, his actual relationship with his father was determined largely by their different personalities, for in several families the grandparents were merely the formal authorities, and the sons took much of the initiative in family matters. Most heads of houses were wise enough to consult their sons on important family matters when they were adults. This meant that even younger sons might have a good deal of power.

In nuclear family units a father's power is extensive over his children when they are growing up, and may extend over into their adolescence. But consultations with sons and daughters normally begin early, and the children are fairly independent as adolescents. As adults they are, theoretically, completely independent of their father's control, particularly when they are married, but in the nuclear Hindu families studied many sons and daughters continued to consult their fathers when adults, and most still regarded them with piety and respect.

The change in authority from father to son over the practical aspects of family life in the joint family was so institutionalized that it seldom caused strain or conflict between them. The eldest son's initiation into his responsible position would begin early, and even though the father would retain the reins of power in his own hands, the son would be gradually assuming control through consultation. The strict discipline of the father over him as a child would thus gradually change until the son became the real authority in the household. "When Grandfather was old, Father still held him in great esteem, and Grandfather always looked to him for advice on important decisions such as weddings or buying property. Grandfather was always told of Father's decisions, but as he hero-worshipped his son, Father's ideas always seemed best to him."

When the family structure changes from the joint pattern to the nuclear type, the problem of adjustment to new patterns of authority are probably greatest for father and son, husband and wife, and mother-in-law and daughter-in-law. All these relationships become more equalitarian, and before the adjustments are institutionalized there may be attempts on the part of the older generation to carry over the old patterns of domination. Levy believes that the two most crucial areas in family change will be found in the attempt of the son to emancipate himself from the dominance of his parents, and in women to change from their subordinate positions.[10] One case study shows the conflict which occurred between father and son before the son freed himself from his father's close supervision by leaving home.

It is no exaggeration to say that Father completely dominated us when we were children. He even dominated Mother. We never used to discuss things with him at home, and he never reasoned with us. When I was young, I just accepted his attitude, but later I felt great tension over some of the restrictions he wanted to impose, such as my going out at night, or going with certain friends.

My father and I did not agree, either, on my career. I wanted to go in for a professional course, but he wanted me to remain at home and teach; so I decided to leave home, and went to Bombay. I got a job there and cut off all contact with my home. Father was very annoyed at this. He sent one of my cousins to fetch me, and this man finally persuaded me to return. At home I tried to get a seat in a medical college, but when I failed to I had nothing to do. I led a very idle and rather loose life. Father began to grumble, and tried to persuade me again to go into teaching, which I hated. Mother was very worried because she thought that the situation would develop into a real fight between us; so she persuaded him to give me some money and I returned again to Bombay.

I have not gone home since then; so I have almost completely extricated myself from the clutches of Father's rigorous discipline. Now I do things according to the dictates of my conscience.

Not all young men, however, are able to emancipate themselves from their father's authority. In fact his control over his sons is still such an integral part of Hindu thinking that even at college young men will threaten or tease each other by saying "suppose your father knew what you had done!"

Case studies showed that fathers sometimes beat their sons up to sixteen or seventeen years of age. After that age there is no physical way of dealing with indiscipline, and a father who has not gained the confidence and respect of his children is at a loss. His only resort is to "nagging," which often turns his children still more against him.

In several cases fear seemed to be the dominant feeling towards the father, and when this was so it was such an effective deterrent that little or no punishment was necessary. "Father never had to cane us as we were all afraid of him. We never dared disobey him." On the other hand, the father's affection for his children often served to control their behaviour as effectively as fear.

On the whole the relationship between father and children is seldom completely free and easy, for as the main family disciplinarian the father tends to maintain distance from his children. Several interviews with older men indicated that they were often bewildered about how they should treat their sons.[11] "Fathers insist on their children studying, but how can they make them when they are adolescents? They tell them to, but the boy will be reading a novel under his books. The father can beat or thrash him when he is young, but this is harder when he grows older. It is finally impossible when he gets to be nineteen or twenty years of age; so the father gets desperate."

The father's main problem in a changing society is to gradually relinquish his position of dominant authority as his children grow older. This is most difficult for a father who has only ruled by virtue of his position, and has not gained the co-operation and real respect of his children. It is still more difficult when the traditional respect to older people weakens, and fathers no longer have the esteem of their children. Conflict between them will be most likely to occur if the father tries to maintain his power while the son insists on his freedom.

One father's dilemma in trying to handle his son and daughter after they had gained some independence is shown in the following interview:

I have serious disagreements with my daughter and son. My daughter is in her last year at college. She is a wild girl with the modern ideas of the day. She sings well, is good at sports, and always wants to be in the limelight. I don't like this; I don't like my daughter singing in a public auditorium or dashing about like a tomboy. We don't seem to be able to settle our differences of opinion. I don't want to oppose her too firmly in case she does something foolish, like running away. I do my best to keep up to the times and change my attitudes about the new things that have taken place, but I feel they are for the worse. I can't reconcile myself to them, although lately I have been quieter about my feelings.

My quarrels with my son are about his spending more time on college activities, such as sports and cadet corps, than on his studies. He hasn't actually failed any of his examinations, but merely passing them won't get him anywhere. He smokes, sees many movies, never is home early, and seldom studies hard.

Mother

A woman's authority in the joint family household was determined by the length of time she had spent in it, and the position of her husband in relation to his brothers. She entered her husband's home in a completely subordinate role, particularly if she married as a child. Her position improved when she became the mother of children and when she gave birth to a son she was given some "esteem in the family, a greater degree of independence, and the right to have her voice heard in the women's quarters." [12] If she was the wife of the eldest brother, she would eventually be expected to assume complete authority in the domestic sphere.[13] Occasionally if her husband's mother was dead, she might have to assume authority immediately. In one case a young bride had to run her husband's household from the moment she entered it, for she was the oldest woman, even though a child bride. Later, as grandmother, should her husband die, although theoretically subordinate to her eldest son, she might have to take over the complete authority of the whole joint family.

The traditional attitude is that Hindu women get influence through their relationships with men; their positions as "mothers of sons" gives them their authority in the household. Moreover, their traditionally close relationships with their sons meant that they could dominate them through affection and love. It might even mean that a son would be so overpowered by his mother that he would not develop leadership qualities, and would, therefore, be dependent on her when he became head of the family. Many older Hindu men still lean heavily on their mother's decisions. Bachmann says that she has often heard a man, when taking an important step, say: " 'It was the wish of my mother.' . . . In all circumstances, even when a mother urges a resisting son to go to battle, there is no way for him but obedience." [14]

In the cases studied, the position of the mother varied from that of being the chief authority of the family to that of being completely subjected to her husband. But in the majority of families, and particularly in those of the more traditional type, the mother had a position between these extremes. Her traditional role of dominance in the domestic aspects of family life has not been as publicized in literature and lore as the father's position as head of the family. But her position as consultant meant in reality that in most families she shared the responsibility of making the major family decisions with the father. These responsibilities increase in importance to the extent that her family unit is separated from the paternal or maternal stem. The mother is well qualified to act as adviser to the head of the house, for as she is the pivot around which the family revolves she is in a strategic position in relation to the whole gamut of household intrigue. Through her relationships with the women of the household and larger kin group she knows all the intimate details of the lives of family members and is thus in a position to advise her husband and later her son, and so control their decisions. Interviews also showed that she often influenced her husband's decisions by acting in the role of mediator between him and the children. She is closer to her children than he is and often they are afraid to go to him directly for what they want. In one family in which the father was hot-tempered, "Mother often intervened for us and shielded us from his wrath." In this way, "mothers," may have great power although the traditional picture of the Hindu woman shows her in a state of submission to husbands and elders. Several interviewees told of mothers who had played exceptionally authoritative roles even when their husbands were alive. "Mother was so authoritative and domineering that no relative tried to interfere with us, it would have been simply impossible."

In nineteen of the families interviewed, mothers were said to have complete authority in the family. These were mainly families in which the father was dead, and the mother had taken over control of affairs. But in one or two, the mother seemed to be the one who dominated the husband and could even stand up to her mother-in-law.

Mother was the complete authority in our home when I was young. She made the important decisions. She consulted Father, but she had the final say, and she always overlooked and ignored Father's opinions. Now, Mother is still the authority. She has a strong hold over everyone in the house. Father is insignificant. I don't want to obey her because I want to be completely independent. But this is impossible for Mother is too domineering and I am very much afraid of her. Grandmother is still alive, but she and my uncles have absolutely no authority over my parents.

At the other extreme were the families in which the wife had a mild personality and did little to influence family decisions. "Father dominated Mother. At first she used to make suggestions, but Father thought he was better informed and had had experience— in the end Mother just kept quiet."

If the families of this sample are indicative of Hindu families in general, there is no doubt that the father is still the most influential person in the Hindu home from the point of view of authority. In ten of the homes of the 168 interviewees who spoke of discipline the grandfather had been the chief authority, in ninety-three the father and in nineteen the mother. Besides this, grandfathers had had some authority in ten families, fathers in seventeen and mothers in thirty-nine. In fifteen families uncles were said to have had some authority, and aunts in nine. In only a few cases in which a father's personality interfered with his assuming his traditional role was he said to have no authority over the family.

A father's authority continues to be important when the children have grown up, for in ten of the families of married interviewees, the father was still the chief authority, and the mother in three. This implies that parents continue to exert influence over their married children, particularly when the young couple still live in the joint family. However, as some children marry they gradually pull away from the influence of parents, for nineteen interviewees said that the husbands were now the chief authority, and sixteen that the wife had more authority than either of the parents-in-law. Older brothers were also said to have had some authority in thirteen families.

Other relatives were seldom mentioned as having any authority or influence over immediate families except when some crisis had caused the withdrawal of one of the main supporting family members, such as the father or mother.

Very little has been written of the mother-daughter relationship, for when the daughter was married as a child she usually lived so far away that the occasional visit was their only contact after the daughter left for her husband's home. Now that daughters tend to marry at a much later age, the relationship between mother and daughter is changing. This change is not yet well enough established to permit full description, but some light was thrown on it in interviews. It would appear that even daughters who seemed to have broken away from many of the family controls still wanted help and advice from their mothers. In fact, this reliance will probably increase, for daughters who set up single families on marriage cannot count on guidance from their mothers-in-law or other older women, and so are more likely to turn to their own mothers for help.

One interviewee whose family had gone through the rigours of partition, and in which the father had died at an early age, had developed such a close relationship with her mother that they were more like sisters than mother and daughter. In another family, a very domineering mother supported her married daughter when she left her husband. These cases emphasize the point that even daughters who have achieved the mature state of married women may still depend very much on their mother's support. This adult dependence on mothers is understandable in the light of the strict training still given most daughters even in nuclear families. "Our girls are not allowed to go out alone after dark. Even in daytime they are expected to have some company when they stir out of the home. In any case parents must know where they go, when they expect to be back, what they intend to do, and whom they are likely to meet." However, the modern daughter tends to resent her mother's dominance, for she has learnt to become more independent, particularly if she has gone to college.

Now that I am going to the university Mother ought to treat me more like an adult and not expect me to obey her in everything. But she still treats me as though I didn't know anything, and wants me to live a sheltered existence; so I often rebel against her and do things which I know she will not like, such as reading "realistic" books, dressing in the very latest style, wearing heavy make-up, or going out with friends to pictures or restaurants without telling her of it. I don't feel guilty about this, because it's her fault for being over strict with me.

This desire for more independence will probably cause a greater amount of friction between mother and daughter, particularly when daughters are influenced by their growing outside contacts at college or work. On the other hand, the fact that they remain longer at home before marriage, may tend to develop a more companionate relationship between the two. If this latter trend develops, it may compensate a mother for her loss of control over her daughters when they marry. However, the strain in her relationship with her son may become more intense, particularly in the period of transition from one family type to another, for she not only loses her power to sway his decisions when he moves to a household of his own on marriage, but also has to accept a less important position in his affection.

Husband and Wife

In customary thought and before the law, the wife was on a level with servants, slaves and other members of the lower social classes in the traditional Hindu family.[15] The attitude of Hindu women to this subordinate position has not often been understood by Western observers, for they have seldom seen it in the context of the total family setting. Bachmann interprets the satisfactions which the Hindu woman did, in fact, derive from her seemingly "lowly" position:

To us "I am the servant of your feet" is humiliating, but later Hinduism so deeply impressed the ideal of a wife's complete devotion and self-denying service to her lord and master, whether he be human or God, as the only means of attaining bliss . . . that there is no humiliation in the expression to them. . . . With religious enthusiasm the wife took up her "Dharma"—not the Dharma of Brahmins which had to be fulfilled through knowledge, sacrificial worship and contemplation—but the Dharma of the slave who demanded complete devotion, obedience and service to her lord and master. . . . So the bride, in blissful joy, allowed bangles to be put on her wrists even though they were the symbols of slavery.[16]

Bachmann also illustrates this feeling when she writes about Gandhi's wife: "Whoever knows her is bound to believe that the self-surrender of the widow which led to the custom of self-immolation on the funeral pyre, must in certain cases have been quite voluntary." [17]

Thus, the term "obedience" as related to the husband and wife does not mean the same thing in India as it does in Western countries, for it does not imply external compulsion, but rather is seen as "the natural wifely desire and duty to please him, to serve him." [18] It is in this sense that the subordinate position of the Hindu wife cannot necessarily be said to be restricting, for, as it is accepted as "natural," she has a sense of freedom in her relationship to her husband which Western wives would not have.

The power of the husband over the wife was shown in several cases which cited husbands who had slapped or beaten their wives. The fact that the interviewees were not particularly disturbed by these instances implies that it is not an unusual practice for husbands to punish their wives in this way.

It has already been noted that a wife's authority in the household depended on her husband's position. If she was the wife of the oldest son, she might have power in household matters above an older sister-in-law. Any power she had over her husband depended on her personality, and on her ability to influence him to her views. It is quite possible that this influence was often considerable, and in some circumstances so great that she literally became the "power behind the throne." Such cases are found in literature and also in families interviewed for this study. In one family the mother of the interviewee had been so beautiful that the father worshipped her and became her complete slave. In a number of other families the wife dominated through her personality.

Father has never dominated anyone. He was very tolerant. But Mother tried to dominate everyone. It was in her blood to rule. When Father married her he made the blunder of going to stay with her in her ancestral home; so Mother felt that she was providing his shelter. This caused a lot of quarrels between them.

When I was growing up, I used to hear my parents constantly quarrelling and abusing each other. Mother always thought she had a higher social position than Father, and she used to abuse his ancestors. These quarrels reached a height when Father's business failed and he retired and depended on his properties for support. Sometimes the quarrels reached such extremes that Father would leave the house, and live separately for a long time.

However, not every woman attains a controlling position in the household, and even in old age some may still have "junior" status. Urquhart speaks of the docility of gray-headed "juniors" in a large household, who never lost a certain childishness of demeanour.[19]

The frequently made statement that the power of women was supreme in the domestic sphere, in so far as it is true, applies chiefly to women who were wives of the head of the household. In a large household a number of the wives would never obtain any power at all except over their children, and their husbands—if they were susceptible to their wives' persuasions.

Another factor which determined the authority between husband and wife was their respective ages. The wife was generally a number of years younger than her husband, probably had less education and certainly had less experience in the ways of the world because of her close confinement to the house. Thus the husband's greater experience and age put him more in the relationship of an adult to her than in that of an equal. This would be particularly true when widowers married second wives, who were often very young girls, a forty-year-old man sometimes marrying a girl of twelve.

However, it should be noted that, even in the joint family system there is usually a gradual change in the relations of power between husband and wife with time. According to an informant, "The husband is at first completely in control of his wife. But as they live together, and especially after children are born, they develop binding interests; so their relationship will gradually work out to a more even basis, where they share responsibilities and authority."

When industrialization affects the structure of the joint family and it breaks down into a single family unit, the relationship between husband and wife undergoes a major change. The wife gains a position of more importance because she is older when married, typically has more education, and there are no longer elder relatives in positions of authority over her. Moreover, if the wife grows up in a nuclear family she will be more accustomed to equalitarian relations between husbands and wives, and will tend to expect them in her own marriage.

On the whole, however, the traditional outlook on the husband-wife relationship is still so strong in India that it may be long before the more equalitarian ideal becomes part of the "natural" expectations of marriage. In a recent study, Desai found that although some Hindu women objected strongly to the complete obedience expected of them by their husbands, the large majority accepted the older concept of their subordinate position.[20]

Material from interviews supported Desai's study in that the majority of wives still accept their subordinate position to their husbands as natural, and look up to his superior knowledge and judgment. But the data also showed that many wives are consciously and unconsciously now wielding more authority. One interviewee illustrated the wife's position today by saying that in former days husbands would be seen striding along the street with their wives following behind carrying the bags and children, but nowadays the man carries both and his wife walks beside him. However, the new conception of their relationship is not yet clear, and the more modern husbands and wives often do not know exactly how the role of authority between them should be carried out. An older woman said:

When we were married, our husbands took so much responsibility on their own shoulders that we women did not have very much to worry about. Nowadays men are not so courageous. For instance, my son-in-law asks my daughter for her advice. But if anything goes wrong, he blames her for making the decisions, and this means a lot of quarrelling between them.

Brother-Brother

In the traditional joint family the authority of brothers followed their age sequence, with the eldest brother holding a particularly powerful position, for not only did he have the highest position of prestige next to the father, but also, as he passed through the usual experiences of life before his younger siblings, he was in a position to lead and guide them. Another factor which bolstered the eldest brother's position of authority was that new privileges accompanied the ability to handle new situations, and as the eldest son normally attained these privileges before the others, his position always entailed more prestige than theirs.

A great deal of responsibility fell on the eldest son's shoulders when he replaced his father, for he took on economic responsibility for family members as well as moral and ceremonial leadership. His economic obligations included marrying his sisters, in the higher castes, and seeing that his brothers were educated and well settled in life. Nowadays he is often also expected to see that his sisters get higher education. A consideration of these heavy responsibilities shows why his position had to be one of considerable power, even before his father died. Normally this power increased with age until he was supposedly in control of younger brothers, even when they were adults. The continuation of such control was shown by one young man who had lived by himself in Bombay for a number of years yet still obeyed his distant elder brother.

The death of a father could bring about a crucial situation if brothers did not get on. Jealousy could also be the cause of conflicts between them, particularly if aggravated by wives who feared they were not getting as much attention or family goods as other wives. When the joint family breaks up, and brothers move into their own separate homes, day-to-day frictions are avoided. But they may not be separated from each other's authority, or responsibility for each other's families. And these responsibilities may become irksome as interests and ways of life tend to differ. All these factors show why the brother-brother relationship was one of potential conflict. The eldest brother's gradual increase in authority means that his relationship with his father changes as well as that with his siblings. Ordinarily their relative positions of power slowly equalize, and the son may finally wield authority over his father in all areas of family life except ceremonial rituals, for the father remains the symbolic head of the house even when he has relinquished all other prestige and power positions.

The eldest brother may have difficulty in taking over his position of leadership when he is not sure of his power, or in families in which a younger brother has a more forceful personality. If he is not sure of his authority, he may develop bullying techniques. Several elder brothers were reported to have beaten their younger brothers for small misdemeanours, and several interviewees said they had been completely cowed at home by their elder brothers. On the whole, however, the elder brother enforces his will by building up attitudes of respect and fear in those who should obey him. This can best be done by keeping himself somewhat apart from his younger siblings.

The strict discipline which elder brothers were often able to maintain over younger ones in the joint family gives way to a relationship of more equality in nuclear families. In the transitional stage, elder brothers may consult their younger brothers more frequently, and, particularly when younger brothers move away from the ancestral roof, may find that they have little if any actual power over them. However, as in other changing family relationships, the notion of respect and obedience to elders will still carry over for some time, and younger brothers will probably not transgress their elder brother's wishes without some sense of guilt. On the other hand, the elder brother will be conscious of a loss of prestige or of failure if they so do.

Brother-Sister

In the traditional Hindu family, the brother-sister relationship was an extremely close one. Their companionship began in early childhood, particularly if they were close in age. If the brother was older, he assumed the expected pattern of male dominance. If the sister was older, the relationship was more equal, as the respect due her age tended to balance the respect due his sex. However, in most instances the sister's authority over younger brothers depended as much on her personal ability to dominate them as on their relative ages.

Strain could arise in their relationship if the sister became jealous of the privileged position of the eldest son. But tension of this sort was not a threat to the family stability, for the sister normally left the house at an early age. Her power ended with her marriage unless she married a wealthy or powerful man who might influence her former family's affairs.

A girl's training for her subordinate position to men began early, and at the same time her brothers would be being trained for their more authoritarian roles.

Mothers and grandmothers conscientiously watch over young girls and train them into complete submission and see that they also learn to worship males. In games, sisters must defer to brothers and be self-sacrificing. Even as little girls they see their brothers served first at meals. They see the mark of respect that the mother shows to brothers, which they do not get. They are therefore brought up in an environment where nothing special or great is either promised to them or expected of them.[21]

After a girl married and moved away to her husband's home, her brother's authority over her was theoretically at an end, for she then came under the authority of the men of her husband's house. However, a brother might be called in to protect his sister from her husband and in-laws, and to the extent that he looked after her, to that extent he would reassume his authority over her. If she was widowed and went to live in his household, she would assume the same subordinate relationship to her brother that all the women of the household had to him. If, on the other hand, she had money of her own, or had married a wealthy man, she might retain a very honoured place in her brother's family, and be able to exert more authority in his household than was generally expected of a widow. One interviewee said: "My aunt inherited 10,000 rupees when her husband died. She invested the money and bought property; so she always had an honoured place in our household. She had a lot of authority in the family too, and ordered us all about and scolded us. When she died, her four brothers performed her obsequies in a very grand style."

Brothers and sisters are on a much more equal basis of authority in nuclear families, particularly when the sister is the elder. In fact, unless the father dies at an early age and the eldest son becomes head of the house, no obedience is expected of sisters to brothers. However, in the transitional stage from one family form to another, sisters will normally still consult their brothers on important decisions, for the latter's wider experience in the outside world will make their guidance desirable.

Sister-Sister

The authority of sister over sister also followed an age sequence in the joint family, and the eldest sister's power over younger sisters was clearly defined and seldom questioned. She had an important position in the family in regard to the supervision of her younger siblings, and this gave her prestige as chief assistant to the mother. This task, along with a little housework, was her chief responsibility, but the change in age of marriage has given her heavier duties, and with these has come the possibility of assuming greater power in the household.

The death of a mother was a contingency which gave an elder daughter a much more important position, for then she might have to take over the organization of the household work.

In nuclear families sisters tend to maintain contact with each other and other family members to a much greater extent than in the traditional joint family. However, as the relationships within the nuclear family tend to be more equalitarian, older sisters are not as likely to maintain positions of authority over younger ones.

Uncles

If an uncle is older than the father, he may eventually become head of the joint family. In that case his role would be similar to that of the grandfather when holding the same position. But if the uncle is the father's younger brother his role is more that of consultant and adviser. An uncle's authority over his brother's or sister's family increased if the father died, for he then theoretically took over the father's responsibilities. In the families studied, this seemed to be particularly true of maternal uncles who on the whole seemed to have more influence and closer ties with the families than paternal uncles. However, this may have been due to influences carried over from the former matrilineal family system of South India.

The few families who mentioned that uncles and aunts had had much say in their family affairs were those in which: the uncle was head of the joint family; one or more of the parents had died and the children had been adopted by an uncle and aunt; children had been sent to live with an uncle and aunt in the city for their education; or childless uncles and aunts had grown so fond of nieces and/or nephews that they had taken almost complete control over them. In the last case the actual authority of the uncle and aunt over the children would depend on whether they were living in joint or separate family units. Sometimes they would be able to check a parent's authority over their own children when living in joint families. "When Grandfather died, Father became the chief authority of the family. But when I was punished, my uncle or aunt would object and speak highly of me to Father. On the other hand, if my cousins were punished, my father would remonstrate with my uncle, and tell him that his children were the best children in the world."

Unmarried uncles living with a family would sometimes have some power over nephews and nieces. One interviewee mentioned an uncle who was not only living with the family but also working in the father's business. This appeared to give him a lot of influence in family affairs. Another interviewee said that he hated his uncles and aunts because they spanked him when he was young, even against his father's wishes.

In spite of some of the above instances in which uncles played prominent roles in the control of nieces and nephews, their main role seemed to be that of family adviser. Maternal uncles were more likely to play this role for mothers, paternal uncles for fathers. However, if the father died, the mother would consult paternal uncles as well. Several interviews also showed that in important family matters, such as weddings uncles had to be consulted, and their consent obtained before the important event could take place.

In nuclear families uncles theoretically have no authority unless appealed to by family members. Moreover, the gradual separation of household units, and the decline in expectation of mutual responsibility, are usually accompanied by a weakening of control over relatives living outside the household unit.

Aunts

The authority of an aunt over nieces and nephews is not nearly as extensive in the joint family as that of the uncle, and theoretically would only last while they were children. As little is said of this relationship in Hindu literature, all that can be done is to describe it in the light of the data collected for this study.

The aunts mentioned in interviews were often widowed sisters who had returned to the family on the death of their husbands, with or without their children. Such an aunt might have a good deal of influence in the family if her bond with her brother was close, or if she had wealth of her own. Otherwise she might play a very subordinate role. Very little was said in interviews of the relation of the aunt to the mother, except when the mother was a young bride. It is probable that, as the mother was the chief authority over the domestic side of the household, the aunt, even if older, had to conform to her wishes. It is also possible that, as the dependent member of the family, she was relegated the hardest and least attractive household tasks. On the other hand, if she had been the eldest sister of the husband, or very close to him, she might be able to dominate the wife.

Nuclear families are not expected to look after widowed aunts, and they theoretically have no influence over nieces or nephews. However, the closer contact of sisters in such families may mean that they will continue to have some indirect influence through the mother. But their formal authority would certainly not be recognized. Thus both the direct and the indirect authority of aunts, as well as that of uncles, lessens when family units become spatially separated.

Father-in-Law–Daughter-in-Law

The authority entailed in the father-in-law–daughter-in-law relationship is not as clear in literature and legend as that of the position of the mother-in-law in relation to her daughter-in-law. Moreover, the only time the relationship was mentioned by interviewees was when a mother-in-law had died and a father-in-law was living with his son, and his family; or when the couple were living in a father-in-law's house, and he was domineering.

Still less is known of the husband–father-in-law relationship. A few remarks in interviews indicated that it was a very formal one, except when the wife's father came to live in the young couple's home. Ordinarily a father-in-law would be expected to live with his sons when his wife died, or in his old age.

His relationship with his daughter-in-law as a young bride in the joint family was supposed to be a very formal one. The mother-in-law was her custodian and the young bride would not see much of him because of the customary distance maintained between males and females. However, just as the head of the house can be considerate and gentle to his own children, the father-in-law can play the same role with his daughters-in-law.

> In our house Father-in-law was the authority, but he was very sweet in some ways. He knew the dishes liked by each one of us. He used to say: "This vegetable is a favourite of daughter-in-law number one and so we will have something that the second daughter-in-law likes tomorrow"; so not one of us felt left out or uncared for. He bore his authority so well that we never felt that it was authority.
>
> When he bought saris for us and clothes for our children he used to bring the same colour and pattern for all of us. Even for the children he used to buy one single bale of cloth from which everyone cut his requirements. Not one evening did he forget to bring us flowers for pooja for our hair and pan-supari. He looked after all our comforts very well. He never punished us, but preached sermons instead to make us obey, which in a way were punishment enough! There was no unpleasantness in the family. Father-in-law saw to it that every member was satisfied and happy.

In nuclear family systems the father-in-law will not have any authority over his daughter-in-law, and control over his son-in-law only if the latter becomes dependent on him.

Mother-in-Law—Daughter-in-Law

It is perhaps the potential drama entailed in the mother-in-law–daughter-in-law relationship that has caused it to be one of the most publicized of all family relationships. Traditionally, a mother-in-law was able to wield more "naked" power over her daughter-in-law than could be exerted in any other family relationship except that between parents and children. However, although children are in completely subordinate positions to their parents, they are trained into family discipline gradually, whereas a daughter-in-law comes into her new home suddenly, and has no one but her husband to protect her. Moreover, a mother-in-law's position of authority over the women of the household enables her to abuse her power over her daughter-in-law more than is possible in any other family relationship.

In the traditional joint family a daughter-in-law entered her husband's home to a position of very low prestige, because of her age and the fact that she was a stranger. Her lowly position only changed when she became the mother of sons, but even then her control extended only to trifling matters, and sometimes even the care of her children was taken out of her hands by the older women.

However, a young bride would be at least partially aware of her future position and so would be somewhat prepared for her new role. First of all, the model daughter-in-law was pictured in folk-lore and religious writings, and was well known to all young girls. One of the model wives was a heroine called Sakhu, who lived in the eighteenth century, and is still worshipped because of her heroic toleration and silent suffering in her husband's home. She was, moreover, a good-looking, modest and docile girl.[22] Moreover, down through the centuries Hindu girls have been carefully trained for the daughter-in-law role. Urquhart quotes from the *Gava Halud,* a book which was written for young wives to advise them on their conduct as brides: "No matter what is being said about you, you must behave like a Siddhapurusha [Holy Man]. You must not give any sign of being hurt or annoyed. You should not even smile at the remarks. You must keep your eyes fixed on the ground." [23]

In the second place, the young bride had seen the treatment of daughters-in-law about her, and had also had many warnings from her parents. If they were loving parents they would probably advise her carefully about her conduct in her new home, for they knew the problems she would face.

Her exact position within the new household was strictly defined. If she was the wife of the eldest son, she had an important place, second only to the mother-in-law, and would eventually replace her as head of the household. The mother-in-law's direct and complete authority over the young bride was due to the necessity of integrating the new wife into the female side of the family.[24] The new wife's obedience to her parents-in-law came first, and her husband was not expected to interfere in their treatment of her. The only members of his family who were expected to treat her with respect were her husband's younger brothers, but she could not count on their support. She had no one to whom she could appeal to if the discipline was too severe.

If she was attractive enough to elicit her husband's support, her position might become even more difficult. If he sided with her, the delicate balance of family relationships was upset, and tensions created which might react back on her. Her supervision was not given over to her husband for this might have developed a warm, personal relation between them, which again might have caused strain to the joint family system.

Karve says that Hindu folk literature singles out certain relationships as being those of natural enemies. One of these is the mother-in-law–daughter-in-law relationship which seems to have been almost universally harsh, or at least strict in extended family systems.[25] Mandelbaum thinks that there is a tendency to institutionalize the strictness of the mother-in-law in the Hindu family so that they are *expected* to be harsh.[26] He quotes a poem to show the ambivalence of the mother-in-law's attitude to the new bride:

> Joy at the prospect of her coming
> But from you your son she's stealing
> Gape your dismayed mouth at the heavens.[27]

For although it is essential for her to have grandchildren, the daughter-in-law challenges her authority as well as her close affectionate relationship with her son. Srinivas believes that the mother-in-law is strict because her house is her kingdom and she does not want her daughter-in-law to rival her power.[28] The actual transfer of authority from one to the other must eventually take place, and it is institutionalized and expected. But it is not easy for the mother-in-law to reconcile the growing independence of her daughter-in-law. Her watchfulness over her daughter-in-law is at first so constant that many songs talk of the "ever-wakeful" mother-in-law who would interfere even if the bride goes to her own husband at night.[29]

Another reason for their conflict is that, as wives often outlive husbands, the mother-in-law is apt to be longer with the young couple. Moreover, as they live in the same house they cannot avoid each other, and the two women may spend most of their time together in cramped quarters. As their leisure time is also spent largely in each other's company they have fewer outside interests on which to release frustrations and aggressions.

In one case both mother-in-law and daughter-in-law had no escape from each other.

I have a lot of problems with my mother-in-law. While my father-in-law was alive she was busy, so did not have too much time to criticize me, but now she has a lot of time on her hands.

She has very few near relatives and as my husband is her only son, she hasn't any other place to go, but stays with us all the time. The same is true for me. My parents are dead and I have cut off all connections with my only brother; so I have no place to go for a visit or a change. Day in and day out all through the year we have to be together. We have a lot of fights about my children for among other things she teaches them to disobey me.

Srinivas says that conflict between the two women may last until one dies or gives up: "But in some cases the struggle goes on, ending only with either separation of the pair from the joint family, or death of one of the fighters. Sometimes the mother-in-law might succeed in having the daughter-in-law driven out of the family." [30]

However, even living in separate houses does not always protect the daughter-in-law, for mothers-in-law can still exert a great deal of control over their sons from a distance or pay them long visits. "My mother-in-law comes to visit us for two or three months every year. Then the trouble begins." In another family, the daughter-in-law had to visit her mother-in-law two or three times a week, the son every day.

So many current proverbs stress the cruel mother-in-law that she must have been a fairly common phenomenon. Interviewees claimed that she could be utterly merciless, and the daughter-in-law could only escape her tyranny through suicide. Interviews showed that, out of thirty cases mentioning the relationship, thirteen had entailed a great deal of conflict, eight a good deal, and nine had been amicable. In several of these the conflict was specifically related to the question of authority between the two women, particularly in families in which the mother-in-law never relinquished her authority while alive. The worst conflict between mother-in-law and daughter-in-law for the leadership of the household probably occurs when the father-in-law dies, and the daughter-in-law theoretically becomes the wife of the head of the house.

A daughter-in-law may have a very difficult position in the joint family if her husband is absent from home for long periods of time, and so cannot protect her from the cruelty of the mother-in-law. "Grandfather lost his wife and immediately remarried a young woman. She became ruler of the family and Father suffered untold miseries from her. When he was married, his wife was also cruelly treated by the step-mother. Father was a doctor, and enlisted and sailed away when Mother was pregnant. He didn't come back for seven years, and Mother had to stay with her in-laws all that time. She was very badly treated by all of them and was unhappy the whole time."

In one or two cases the mother-in-law–daughter-in-law position of dominance was reversed, and the courage or aggression of the daughter-in-law enabled her to dictate to her mother-in-law. In one instance, a young bride of thirteen years of age "had the courage to speak up to her father-in-law and mother-in-law." This woman showed great aggression all her life, and completely dominated her own daughters. In one extreme case the daughter-in-law treated her mother-in-law so badly that they finally severed all connections.

The break over the mother-in-law's power is a point at which the old and the new come into serious conflict. Once the problem is posed in a family, the young couple can either submit or revolt. If they revolt, they break the old family entirely, for its interlocking solidarities permit little compromise. If the son refuses to enforce his mother's wishes, she can ask his father to order him to do so; if the son defies his father, the old family structure is finished. Thus the break of the mother-in-law's power almost inevitably involves other crucial aspects of family structure.[31]

The dominance of the mother-in-law would be expected to decline as family structures change from large joint families to nuclear units, first of all, because they will be spatially separated and each will be in charge of her own household. Conflict might arise, however, when the father-in-law dies and the mother-in-law must live with her son and daughter-in-law. In the second place, the later age of marriage means that the daughter-in-law has her first contact with her mother-in-law as an adult, and so the relationship between them is more equal from the start. It will be even more equal if the daughters-in-law have more education. On the other hand, interviews showed that unequal education often caused friction between the two. Moreover, the factors which now enable a daughter-in-law to be more independent are precisely those which make her a stronger rival to the mother-son bond. "From the beginning of my marriage I couldn't get on with my husband and mother-in-law, for they had very narrow ideas. They couldn't understand modern ways. Their idea was that women should stay at home and cook and have children. Finally I separated from my husband and went back to live with my mother."

This relationship, then, is one which does not change easily. For although friction between the two may be lessened by separation, older women tend to try to maintain some supervision of their children's lives even after marriage; so that, even though the daughter-in-law escapes her mother-in-law's tutelage in some matters, in others, such as the care of her children, she may still find her interference. Finally, it should be noted that the picture of the mother-in-law as a disrupting factor in family life is still prevalent in Western countries, where nuclear families have been established for a much longer period than in the East.

Other Relationships

Just enough information was obtained on the authority entailed in the following relationships to make a few comments about them.

BROTHER-IN-LAW TO WIFE. Formality usually existed between the wife and her husband's eldest brother in the joint family, but her relationship with her younger brothers-in-law was normally friendly. Should her husband die, her brother-in-law theoretically took over the position of authority over her. In the transitional stage of family change, brothers-in-law usually become the wives' chief advisers rather than their controllers. "After my husband's death I was the authority in the family, but I left the important decisions, such as the marriage of my daughters, the education of my son, and buying property to my brother-in-law. Now that my son and I have moved away to another city I consult my son on important decisions. However, if they are very important I still write to my brother-in-law. He will be the head of the family while he is alive."

BROTHER-IN-LAW OF HUSBAND (WIFE'S BROTHER). Occasionally, in both joint and nuclear families, a husband will go to his brother-in-law for advice or assistance, but on the other hand he may be too proud to take help from him. In one family a husband was not as well educated, nor as financially well off, as his brothers-in-law, and would not accept anything from them.

Considering that in the joint family the husband's brother-in-law normally had a close brother-sister relationship with the wife, it may be that jealousies sometimes existed between him and the husband. If this is so, it cannot have been very disruptive, for little is written of this relationship in Hindu literature, and it was very seldom mentioned by interviewees. Jealousy might particularly occur in families where there is still a "psychological" trace of the matrilineal line, and in which the sister relies on her brother as chief adviser and protector.

SISTER-IN-LAW. A new bride coming into a joint family household, particularly in the days of child marriage, was in a subordinate position to her sisters-in-law unless they were a great deal younger, for the sisters-in-law would be in established positions in the household when she arrived as a stranger.

Conflict between them has not been as widely publicized as that between mother-in-law and daughter-in-law, but writers show that it often occurred in the joint family. "The girl has no harmonious relations with her husband's sisters. . . . Her sisters-in-law take sides with their mother and wage a ruthless war against her. The only persons to support her are her husband and her father-in-law. . . . The males support her, and the women are against her. But the men will be absent from home most of the day. And the women will always be there ever ready to get at her. Hence many daughters-in-law have jumped into tanks to end their lives." [32]

Srinivas goes on to tell of how the sisters tend to get the best of everything in the home, while the new wife may be insulted. They often combine against her and report any of her misdemeanors to the mother-in-law. Even after many years there may be trouble when the sister returns to visit her family.

In several of the cases studied sisters-in-law were the chief cause of trouble for their brothers' wives.

My sisters-in-law were the chief mischief-makers in my home. They overheard our conversations, opened our letters, and sometimes even destroyed them. They carried tales to my mother-in-law. Whenever she was away from home, she put one of them in charge; so we were never free.

They never considered it worth while discussing things with us because we weren't thought of as human beings. I might be standing right in front of my mother-in-law and yet be ignored. But the daughters of the house had a very important place in the family council. We were always treated like outsiders. We had to ask about our work, but the daughters of the house did theirs the way they wanted to. We even had to ask our mother-in-law's permission about how much of the provisions we should measure out for the cooking.

The relationship was saved from too much strain by the fact that the sisters-in-law normally left home at a fairly early age for their husbands' homes.

The husband had very little contact with his wife's sisters, and consequently they were almost strangers. If the vicissitudes of family life brought them together, their relationship would follow the usual pattern of the subordinate position of women to men.

The gradual emancipation of the brother's wife comes as she replaces her mother-in-law in the hierarchy of household authority, and as her sisters-in-law are married and leave for their husbands' homes. A quicker way of accomplishing her independence from them is to persuade her husband to live in a separate house.

HUSBAND TO HIS IN-LAWS: Normally this relationship was very distant in the joint family, for, although the wife might return home for visits and for her pregnancies, she would not always be accompanied by her husband. If a family crisis arose in which the wife was forced to return to her own home with her husband and children, strain might occur in working out the authority arrangements between the husband and his father-in-law. The balance of power in this case would probably be determined by the personalities concerned, and the relative social and financial position of the husband and his male in-laws.

In nuclear families the influence of all the above relationships will depend on the intimacy of the different separate family units. However, little control over in-laws will be expected, and normally the families will depend more on close-by friends for advice.

Summary

The structure of authority, as the family moves from the joint to the nuclear form, weakens, and, as the small family units become separated from the large extended family group, comes to reside in each separate family unit. Moreover, the relationships within the small nuclear unit become much more equalitarian in character. These trends are in keeping with the general need for children to be brought up to be more independent in a world in which they may have to move far away from the original family stem, for, when separated from the control and advice of the extended family group, they will have to handle their problems and responsibilities by themselves.

Notes

1. Talcott Parsons and A. M. Henderson, *Max Weber: The Theory of Social and Economic Organization* (New York: Oxford University Press, 1947), pp. 60–1.
2. David Riesman, *The Lonely Crowd* (New Haven: Yale University Press, 1950), pp. 11–16. In this study Riesman gives a very good analysis of "tradition-directed" "other-directed" persons.
3. E. Kathleen Gough, "The Social Structure of a Tanjore Village," in McKim Marriott, *Village India* (Chicago: University of Chicago Press, 1955), p. 44. "Within each patrilineal extended family all submit to the oldest man."
4. E. W. Burgess and H. J. Locke, *The Family* (New York: American Book Co., 1945), p. 20; also Olga Lang, *Chinese Family and Society*, published under the auspices of the International Secretariat, Institute of Pacific Relations, and the Institute of Social Research (New Haven: Yale University Press, 1946), p. 54, for a description of the patriarchal family in China.
5. Alan R. Beals, "Interplay among Factors of Change in a Mysore Village," in *Village India*, McKim Marriott, ed. (Chicago: University of Chicago Press, 1955), p. 87.
6. David Mandelbaum, "The Family in India," in *The Family: Its Function and Destiny*, Ruth N. Anshen, ed. (New York: Harper and Brothers, 1949), p. 94. The traditional authority has passed down without too much change and with only slight deviations for some nine centuries and was prescribed in the *Mitakshara* which outlines the rights and duties of all family members.
7. Burgess and Locke, *The Family*, p. 19.
8. Hedwig Bachmann, *On the Soul of the Indian Woman: As Reflected in the Folklore of the Konkan* (Bastoria, India Portuguesa: Typografia Rangel, 1942), p. 82.
9. *Ibid.*, p. 104.
10. Marion J. Levy, Jr., *The Family Revolution in Modern China* (London: Oxford University Press, 1949) p. 175.
11. An informant who had spent several years in the United States thought that fathers were surer of their authority in that country, and therefore did not have to assert themselves by physically punishing their children as much as did Indian fathers. In other words, the relationships of the nuclear family are more firmly established on the North American continent.
12. Mandelbaum, "Family in India," p. 103.
13. *Ibid.*, p. 101. "The mother of the eldest male in the family is in the position of authority. After her death the wife of the eldest male succeeds to her position; if she should become a widow before

her sons are mature men, then the wife of the next eldest brother becomes head of the household."

14. Bachmann, *On the Soul of the Indian Woman*, p. 25.
15. *Ibid.*, p. 60.
16. *Ibid.*, pp. 57, 148, 150.
17. *Ibid.*, p. 156.
18. Margaret Cormack, *The Hindu Woman*, Teachers College Studies in Education, (New York: Bureau of Publications, Teachers College, Columbia University, 1953), p. 133.
19. Margaret Urquhart, *Women of Bengal* (Mysore: Wesleyan Mission Press, 2nd ed., 1926) p. 43.
20. Mrs. G. B. Desai, "Women in Modern Gujerati Life," Unpublished Master's Thesis, University of Bombay, Bombay, 1945, pp. 162–6.
21. Bachmann, *On the Soul of the Indian Woman*, vol. 2, p. 1.
22. *Ibid.*, p. 122.
23. Urquhart, *Women of Bengal*, p. 42.
24. Levy, *Family Revolution in Modern China*, pp. 106–8. From the point of view of the family: "The daughter entered an unfamiliar family, and from the point of view of her new family, she posed the problem of the integration of a stranger into a tightly knit disciplined group."
25. Irawati Karve, *Kinship Organisation in India*, Deccan College Monograph Series, 11 (Poona: Deccan College Post-Graduate and Research Institute, 1953), pp. 129–30.
26. Mandelbaum, "Family in India," p. 101.
27. *Ibid.*, p. 101.
28. M. N. Srinivas, *Marriage and Family in Mysore* (Bombay: New Book Co., 1942), pp. 191–8.
29. Karve, *Kinship Organisation*, p. 130.
30. Srinivas, *Marriage and Family*, p. 198.
31. Levy, *Family Revolution in Modern China*, p. 316.
32. Srinivas, *Marriage and Family*, p. 194.

Commentary: *On Authority*

Power relationships are difficult to assess in literature about the family. The terms referring to power relationships tend to be descriptive or anecdotal or both. A distinction must be made between deference, which is readily measurable, and power, which tends to be more subtle and elusive. Deference is regarded as any act that tends to put one in a subordinate position to someone else. Overt acts such as bowing, hand-kissing, and not speaking in another's presence are examples of this. There may or may not be any stigma attached to submissiveness—the point is that privileges and rights are measurable. Attitudinal conformity is another matter and may be the key to understanding power relationships within the family. These differences in the relations between role sets alert us to more subtle distributions of power and authority.

In the case of the subcontinent of Asia, power relationships are further complicated by the background of colonialism and the more subtle carry-over of British influence in the period after independence and partition. The Hindu and Moslem families of India and Pakistan share this heritage to varying degrees. But both structurally and functionally, these family types must be differentiated from the Japanese. India and Pakistan, despite their progress toward modernization, are still preindustrial, whereas Japan is industrial. A family in Tokyo, therefore, faces different problems from a family in New Delhi or Dacca. Deference in Japan is ceremonial because the substratum of the family does not involve any significant challenge to the power of the male. However, ceremonial deference in India and Pakistan masks role ambivalence in the male to this very day. For example, the Hindu male within the nuclear family is subordinate to the joint family. The Moslem male has less power within his nuclear family because it is subordinate to his extended family. Both the Hindu and Moslem families are subordinate to the weight of tradition and the principle of seniority, or gerontocracy.

Another reason for ambivalence with regard to both power and deference in Asia is that westerners on the subcontinent have nuclear family relationships that are dominant. When consideration is given to the heritage of colonialism and the ethnocentric assumptions by resident westerners that the nuclear family is superior to indigenous joint and extended types, the ambivalence of the South Asiatic male is more easily understood.

Much of the extant anthropological literature on India and Pakistan confuses the Hindu joint family with the Moslem extended family. This is true despite the fact that there are important differences between the two, especially regarding the law of inheritance. In the Hindu joint family, death is no reason for dividing the property, which continues to be held jointly from generation to generation. In the Moslem extended family, inheritance reflects a pattern more familiar in the West, where property is divided among the surviving heirs. This difference has had revolutionary historic repercussions for communal relation-

ships between Hindus and Moslems ever since the end of the Mogul period when the Moslem domination of India ended. Hindu families became richer while Moslem families, with each generation, became poorer as the average land holding decreased.

Another element that must be considered before power relationships can be understood in the context of South Asiatic culture is the fact that Hindu and Moslem families are adult-centered whereas modern western types, at least in the middle-class sector, tend to be youth-centered. This attitude reinforces respect for and submission to authority. It does so not merely because it is traditional but also because of the positive correlation in the validity of a point of view, the legitimacy of an order, and the age of the family member.

Because a preindustrial community, even if urban, is more uncritically patriarchal than an industrial society, whatever "freedom" a South Asiatic parent will tolerate in his children will apply to male, rather than female, progeny. For example, sons of the Moslem native elite in East Pakistan will be allowed to frequent clubs and homes where they can freely intermingle with the daughters of westerners. But the same Moslems will not permit their daughters to be exposed to unsupervised association with the sons of westerners. The teacher in this same context stands in loco parentis, *being accorded the same authority as the father.* Consequently, students will rarely, if ever, raise any questions in class. Isolated instances of rebellion against parental or educational authority are blamed on such western influences as the cinema. Even though antiwestern attitudes are present for a variety of reasons, western films are more popular with urban youth in India and Pakistan than the more traditional films of their native film industry. It is worthy of mention that the audiences at these films are almost exclusively male, thus increasing their value for scapegoating purposes (fathers use the films to explain away the rebellion of their sons).

5

THE DECLINE OF TRADITIONAL PATTERNS OF JAPANESE FAMILY AUTHORITY*

EZRA F. VOGEL

THE DECLINE OF THE *IE* DEAL

The Concept of *Ie*

Until the end of World War II, the Japanese government saw that all its citizens, through school and mass media, learned in great detail about "the family system." As a whole the government was amazingly successful. Not only did everyone learn about the ideal family, but many attempted to model their family on this ideal. Even today, Mamachi residents, like other Japanese, remember clearly the main outlines of what they were taught about the ideal family and the model of the *ie*[1] still has an important impact on family behavior. At the heart of the system was the *ie*, the single unbroken family line, including both living and dead, and the concept of filial piety. The basic goal of *ie* members was to care properly for departed ancestors and to preserve the continuity and prosperity of their *ie*. Selling land, for example, was considered a grave misfortune, both because it was a disgrace to the ancestors and because it might seriously affect the family's fortune for generations to come. Family members sacrificed personal pleasures and wants for the *ie*, not only to gain respect or rewards in this life, but to attain immortality, for the idea of after life was contingent on the continuation of the *ie*.[2]

From Japan's New Middle Class (*Berkeley: University of California Press,* *1963*), *pp. 165–180 and 194–207. Reprinted by permission.*
* This title includes the following two articles.

Small children belonged to their parents' *ie*. When the children of a family attained maturity, one son, usually the first, was given the honor and the responsibility for preserving the *ie*. The other children had to find another *ie* or, if given permission, they could start a new branch to the main *ie* into which they were born. When a daughter married, her name was crossed off her *ie*'s register and entered into the register of her husband's family. The *ie* gave daughters sizeable dowries and assisted younger sons in starting out in life, but the bulk of the family land and treasures was given to the son who had the responsibility for looking after the family line.[3] In theory, the family head did not own the property, but was merely the trustee[4] in the present generation who looked after the property of the *ie*, past, present, and future. If the head of the household died, normally his son would inherit the headship. If no son were available, a younger brother of the deceased might become head if he had not yet gone to another *ie,* or a wife might take over the headship until an heir was selected.

When a bride entered a new family, she was expected to learn her new family's customs (*kafuu*) and by hard work, automatic obedience, and enthusiastic submission to prove that she was sufficiently loyal to deserve family membership. If she failed, she was returned to her original home.[5] An adopted son-in-law had to go through the same process.

The bride was not simply a bride of her husband but of his *ie,* and his *ie* referred to her as *uchi no yome* (our bride). In many ways she was regarded as an adopted daughter, and she referred to her parents-in-law as mother and father.[6] She was chosen not by her husband but by his *ie,* on the basis of her willingness and ability to work hard and transfer her loyalty to her new family, and of her having the health, vigor, and wisdom necessary to produce and rear a desirable heir. Similarly, an adopted son was selected on the basis of his ability to continue the family line. Often it was more important for him to have skills necessary to operate the family farm or business enterprise than the attributes necessary for a good husband.

The son or adopted son who became the family head theoretically had absolute legal authority over the other family members. Just as children were to obey their parents, so the wife was to obey her husband, and when her son became family head, she was to obey him. Younger brothers were to obey the elder brother. The Japanese government held the family head responsible for the behavior of family members, and he was expected to use his authority to ensure that all members behaved properly.

Just as his authority was the greatest, so was his responsibility greatest. In addition to supervising the family enterprise, he had the onus of deciding on marriage and work arrangements for his children or younger siblings. He was responsible for the health and welfare of *ie* members, living and dead. He provided for his parents in their retirement. If his sisters or daughters were divorced and sent back because they were not acceptable to the new *ie* or if sons or brothers lost their jobs, he provided temporary food and housing and assisted them in finding a new opening. As preserver of the *ie*, he supervised the care of family shrines and graveyards and made certain that each summer, at the O-bon festival, lanterns were lighted so that the spirits of departed ancestors could find their way from the grave to the ancestral home.

A prosperous family might boast of a family genealogy and a family graveyard dating back several hundred years, although some families candidly admit doubt about the authenticity of some of the early part of the record. Yet the living members of an *ie* were usually limited to a stem family of father, mother, unmarried children, a married son, his wife, and their children. In a certain stage of the life cycle, if the grandparents died before the eldest son married, the household might consist only of parents and children. If a family were prosperous and wanted to expand, then a second son would be allowed to form a branch family (*bunke*) which would remain within the *ie*, but be subordinated to the original family (*honke*). In a farm family, the second son might be given a small plot of land, or, in a business family, he might be given a small part of the business or a branch office to provide support for his family. One of his children would be selected as his heir and would become head of the branch line. Theoretically, a main family could have many branches, and branches could have branches. Officially, there was a clear hierarchy of power, the branch family being subordinated to the main family. In fact, except for communities in which the main and branch families had close contact, these relationships had little significance beyond two or three generations. Usually the branch family which migrated to the city obtained virtual autonomy over its own sphere. Sometimes a second son who set up a family of his own did not even go through the formal procedures of setting up a branch family. This son officially retained membership in his original *ie,* but once he had a wife and children, he was granted virtual autonomy.

The Branch

The concept of *ie* continues to provide an important model for family behavior, but it is no longer imperative to sacrifice one's self for the *ie,* and some families without children are even willing to go without an heir. The desire to continue the *ie* is particularly weak in branch families, and in Mamachi, as in other urban areas, the overwhelming majority of families are branch families.[7] Because the main family (except for new main families formed by second sons who became independent) has a much longer tradition, it is natural that more effort will be put into its preservation than into the attempt to preserve the branch. The second son who migrates to the city has no responsibility to his *ie.* When he moves, he brings with him virtually no family treasures, he has no family graveyard or ancestral tablets and no family business to look after. Not only does he himself have no *ie* responsibility, but when he dies, his heir has a very shallow lineage heritage since it began only a generation before.

Even if the son in the city does not leave an heir or if his heir leaves no heir, it is not considered a tragedy. The main family from which the branch split off will not only continue to look after the ancestors and the prosperity of the *ie,* but they will look after the tablets and graves of the abortive branch family. Most branch families would like to have an heir, but it is difficult to get a satisfactory heir if parents do not give birth to a male child. Some families with only daughters still adopt sons-in-law, but a family can find a more desirable husband for their daughter if they do not require him to become an adopted son-in-law. Most Mamachi branch families consider a good son-in-law more important than the continuation of their branch line. Similarly, Mamachi salaryman families with no children have no family enterprise to offer an attractive young man in return for becoming their adopted son, so many branch families, rather than accept a successor who might lower the quality of their branch line, prefer to be buried at the place of their ancestors with the knowledge that their graves will be cared for by the main family.

In some businesses and crafts, an economic bond joins the

branch family to the main family. If a drug business expands, for example, a second son might be given financial support in setting up a branch shop, and the heirs of the branch family would continue to operate a branch shop of the larger shop directed by the main family. In such situations, the economic bond between the main family and the branch family would bring them close together, extending far beyond the business ties. No such economic interest binds the rural family attached to the land and the salary man in the city, nor is there any economic bond between an employee of a large corporation and his son, who is likely to be working in a different corporation or government office. In times of great need, the main and branch families may help each other and, if amiable, they may visit each other occasionally, but typically the tie between the main family in the country and the branch family in the city is little more than a sentimental attachment.

Main and branch families may disagree about how much to help each other, but the feelings of independence of each other have now become so strong that they rarely ask each other for aid, even in need. A more critical problem confronts the branch family if the head of the main family dies leaving no heir.[8] Family fortunes can be dissipated quickly in such instances, and the branch family is expected to see that family property is protected and the main family line continued. Sometimes a second son who is not yet firmly established in the city is called back to take over the family line after the death of his elder brother. However, we have heard of no cases in recent years where a man already established in the city has returned to take over the family line in the country. Life in the city is considered more attractive, and the urban wife and children are reluctant to go back to the rural areas under any circumstances. In two families in which an older brother died leaving small children in the country, the younger brother remained in Mamachi but assisted his brother's children until one could take over the duties of the heir. In one instance, a man got permission from his company to take his full vacation time during the busiest rice-harvesting seasons to return to his rural home and help with physical labor as well as finances. In effect, he temporarily shared the family headship with his deceased brother's wife until the children were in their mid-teens and old enough to carry out the farm work themselves. But in fulfilling this responsibility to his *ie* he created serious strains for his own wife and children who were reluctant for him to spend so much time, energy, and money looking after the *ie* in the country with which they did not feel identified. The husband felt caught between the pressures from the *ie* on the one hand and his wife and children on the other and unsuccessfully tried to resolve the conflict by remaining faithful to both.

In another case, in which the main family in the country owned no land and the heir to the family died, the branch family in Mamachi became the main family with all its responsibilities, but the location of the main family was shifted from the country to Mamachi. It was possible to remove the family heirlooms, tablets, and other property, and to preserve some of the family traditions in the city, although not to the satisfaction of all the relatives. Arrangements were made so that the family grave plot in the country could remain there and be cared for. In this event, the branch family was forced to assume the responsibility of the main family, and the concept of *ie* could not be dismissed so lightly.

Many people in Mamachi not only find little positive value in the *ie*, but they object to concern with ancestors and family lines. They regard the family system, especially the arbitrary rule of the family head, the domination of the branch family by the main family, and the emphasis on family tradition as remnants from the feudalistic past which should be done away with as quickly as possible. But part of the desire to forget tradition comes especially from families of humble origin who now enjoy higher positions. A rich family with a long history still draws respect, but families which have entered the middle class only in the last generation are usually anxious to overlook their humble backgrounds. They seem to acknowledge the importance of the family line as a basis for respect, for they not uncommonly exaggerate the length of time their family has lived in the city or the status of their ancestors, and are eager to tell of a rich or famous relative of theirs. Not only do humble families have shorter family genealogies and fewer family treasures to preserve, but their family tree gives them little to point to with pride. It is not surprising that many of them show so little interest in ancestors.

POINT PARK COLLEGE LIBRARY

The Decline of the *Ie*
Authority and Welfare

In many respects, the *ie* has been like a corporation. Traditionally, it had a set of offices under the direction of a head, a definite membership with set relationships to each other, and regular rules of procedure. Some of the larger or more prominent families actually had written rules, which the *ie* followed to the letter of the law. One of the responsibilities of the head of the main family of the *ie* was to provide for the welfare of all its members. As long as the major wealth of the *ie* was held by the main family and could be allocated or at least controlled by the head, the system worked well. Quarrels or a shortage of funds may have existed, but the family head clearly had the power and responsibility to see that family members gave assistance to needy members. As the power of the *ie* has become weaker, however, the head of the main family finds it difficult to control the allocation of funds to needy members. The power of the main family has been especially weakened by the urban branch families' becoming richer than the main family. As it became harder for the family head in the rural areas to request assistance from the richer branch family in the city, it also became more difficult for the branch family to obtain help from the main family in time of need. The bitter feelings between relatives who sought or gave aid immediately after World War II is adequate testimony to the collapse of the *ie* welfare system.[9] Some, of course, still help needy relatives, but this is no longer common and is usually limited to close relatives. Furthermore, whether help is given no longer depends so much on whether a relative is an *ie* member but on whether he is liked and judged needy and worthy.[10] The decision is controlled by sentiment, not duty to the *ie*.

Under the old system the family may have been dominated by an autocratic head but there was clarity and integrity to the system. The main family inherited the major share of family property and accepted the responsibility of providing for needy members. The eldest son, the trustee of family property, naturally cared for the elderly parents. According to the postwar revisions of the Civil Code, responsibility is to be shared by all children. Precisely how the responsibility should be shared is sufficiently debatable to cause considerable ill-will between siblings. Many still feel the first son should bear most of the burden.[11] Even if inheritance is divided equally, the responsibility for caring for parents cannot be divided equally. In a family of three children, for example, it is not easy for retired parents to spend four months living with each child. It is expected that financial help from the children will be based partly on their ability to pay, but there is no standard formula for deciding how much ability each child has. Furthermore, regardless of a married daughter's desire to help out, her husband may refuse to help support her parents. Even if the children can come to an agreement about the care of elderly parents, those providing the assistance feel it as a burden which the other siblings might have lightened.[12] And even if the children provide plentifully, the parents often feel that they are imposing on the younger couple; and the spouse who is not the child of the elderly persons is likely to make them especially uncomfortable. The prevalence of this problem was made clear to us because one of the most common questions we were asked about family life in America concerned the provision made for older people. The pattern of single inheritance and care for elders was a stable system; the pattern of elderly parents having enough means to support themselves might be a stable system but the area between, where parents require support from various children, appears to lead to inevitable difficulties.

Parents in their forties face a difficult decision about what to do in their old age. Although they recognize the problems of living with children in their old age and want to avoid difficulties, many are afraid that if they live alone they will be lonely and unable to make ends meet. Some bravely assert that they will live alone trying to convince themselves that such a life may not be lonely. Others admit they would be pleased if their children asked them to live together. Despite the problems in the new system of multiple inheritance and weakened *ie,* no one expects the power of the household head to be revived. Furthermore, the problem of supporting aged parents is mitigated by the father's membership in a large organization. Because the company will provide a pension or at least a large lump sum on retirement, the elderly couple need not be such a financial burden on their children. Having parents live with the younger couple is considered as more natural and less of an imposition than in the United States, and now that the *ie* has declined, increasingly large numbers of parents are able to depart from the traditional *ie* pattern and live with a daughter where there is sufficient positive feeling between the women at home to avoid the conflicts commonly found between mothers-in-law and daughters-in-law.

As the capacity of the family head to control welfare activities has declined, and as the branch family has grown in wealth, security, and prestige, the main family's sanctions have lost their force. No longer is the threat of expulsion from formal *ie* membership so frightening. The family head is especially weak in Mamachi salary families because of the combination of loss of *ie* consciousness in the branch family and the feeling of independence which comes from the economic security offered by the husband's firm.

The power of a household head above his power as a husband and father now are so insignificant that the transfer of position of household head is virtually meaningless.[13] In the local community an elderly father will simply continue to be listed as head of household if he lives with a son. Similarly, the distinction between the heir and other sons has been lessened, not only in matters of inheritance, but with respect to the position of children within the family. In the past, the elder son, as heir apparent, was treated with considerable respect by other members of his family, even before he assumed the position. Not only did parents give preferential treatment to the child who would become the heir, but grandparents openly preferred *uchi mago* (children of their heir) to *soto mago* (children of their other children). While the oldest child still may exert considerable authority over younger siblings, especially in a large family, authority today is derived more from relative age than from the prospect of becoming the heir. An older sister ordinarily has more authority than a younger first-born son.

Formerly the *ie* had considerable power in arranging marriages and jobs for the young. Since marriage was viewed as a change of *ie* for a girl or an adopted son-in-law, it was considered appropriate that the decision be made both by the *ie* receiving the member and the *ie* giving up the member. This attitude has not entirely disappeared, and wedding negotiations, arrangements, gift exchanges, and even the formal ceremonies still distinguish between the *ageru hoo* (the family which is "giving up" a person) and the *morau hoo* (the family which is "receiving" a person).

The investigations and negotiations leading to marriage, generally were carried out by a go-between (sometimes one for each side), who performed his services at the request of the *ie*. The view and temperament of the young man and young lady were considered, but it was expected that their wishes should be subordinated to the *ie*. This was not without some reason, for in the case of the first son, the young bride, after all, was coming to live with her husband's family, and might spend more time with her mother-in-law than with her husband. Even in the marriage of a second son, over which the family exercised less supervision, the family had to bear the responsibility for marital difficulties. Hence, the parents felt that their children (who until the time of marriage had virtually no opportunity for meeting with members of the opposite sex) required their help in selecting a spouse.

The young people of Mamachi now regard such marriage arrangements as remnants of antiquated feudalistic society whereby the *ie* imposes its will on the young people who must sacrifice themselves for the good of the *ie*. While the Mamachi young people no longer are expected to conform to the wishes of their *ie* as such, their parents still retain influence in deciding whom the children should marry. The residents of Mamachi differentiate between two kinds of marriage: the *miai* (arranged marriage) and the *renai* (love marriage). In the *miai*, typically the parents, and sometimes relatives and family friends, have more influence, and in *renai* the young people themselves have more say.[14] While only about half of the recent marriages are officially arranged, in the overwhelming majority parents take an active role, checking on details of the other family. Some families will engage friends or private detectives to investigate the other family. Families frequently argue about the degree of independence that young people should have in selecting a spouse, but the range of freedom subject to dispute is relatively narrow if one considers the overwhelming power of the family in the Japan of an earlier era or the much broader freedom given most young people in the United States.

Yet, compared to the previous age, siblings and friends increasingly are replacing parents as sources of introductions, and coeducational schools and places of work provide limited opportunities which did not exist a few decades ago for respectable middle-class children to meet on their own. Nevertheless, there are few acceptable ways for young people to meet without some kind of introduction. Too much freedom is still suspect. A girl who has had dates with more than two or three men before marriage is still considered a bit free and worldly, and some will wonder whether she will make a good wife. What is emerging to some extent is a combination of *miai* and *renai*—a combination considered desirable by most parents. Under this combination, an appropriate person whom the family already has investigated thoroughly and found acceptable is introduced to the young person. The young people are permitted a few meetings (preferably not too many) to fall in love and make a decision. Under such arrangements they feel they have the best of two worlds: responsible arrangements and romantic love. If a child were given freedom to make his own decision, few discussions with his parents would be necessary, but in Mamachi where the decision is typically shared between the child and his parents, the selection of a spouse may dominate family discussions for years. Certainly both parents and the older children will be included, and sometimes knowledgeable or thoughtful friends. These discussions (or arguments) turn on such questions as what kind of person is desirable, who can help locate a promising candidate, what are the relative assets and weak points of various candidates, how can they get a desirable candidate to agree, what kind of arrangements can be worked out for the marriage and living arrangements afterward. Particularly if the child is a daughter, these items are discussed, rediscussed, investigated, and reinvestigated. A family tries to arrive at a consensus on each minor step along the way. Indeed, they must arrive at a consensus if arrangements are to proceed smoothly. These discussions give the parents, and especially the mother, a purpose and function which they do not enjoy in many Western countries.

Considering how vehemently some adolescents insist on the freedom to find their own spouses, a surprisingly large number later acquiesce to arrangements or suggestions made by their parents. Many young people, especially the overprotected, the bashful, the cautious, those with high standards, those with a proud family history, the undesirable *urenokori* (leftovers) who did not find a spouse on their own, find the *miai* their best opportunity to get married and accept this pattern even if opposed to it ideologically. The willingness of children to let parents take an active part in the decision is undoubtedly related also to the close mother-child relationship and the fact that mothers have sacrificed so much for the children.[15] Furthermore, because children have had little opportunity to meet contemporaries of the opposite sex, they have little confidence in their own ability to make a proper decision. The modern parent of Mamachi does not object in principle to a child's selecting his own spouse; nor does a parent insist that the child follow his parents' choice out of duty to them and their *ie*, but by questioning the wisdom of the child's choice or questioning what the child would do if something went wrong, they can instill sufficient doubt so that he is willing to accede to the parents' advice.

A daughter is especially responsive to her parents' feelings because she would have to turn to them for help in case of marital difficulty. A generation ago divorce was not simply a separation of man and wife, but the husband's *ie* returning her to her parents' *ie*. It was necessary for the divorced woman to have the support of her *ie* if she were to have a source of livelihood and a reasonable chance of finding another spouse. Even today, because a widow or a divorcee has few chances for earning a living or finding a new spouse, the wife generally is reluctant to get a divorce. The rate of divorce among residents of Mamachi is still very low.[16] Even today a wife with marital difficulty, in effect, puts her case before her family and secures their approval before she decides to divorce, no matter how serious the trouble.

The Mamachi family has less direct control over occupational choice than over marital choice. Indeed, it has little reason to interfere with the son's occupational choice as long as it fits with the family's standard of respectability. Farmers and members of lower socio-economic groups placing a son in a small business concern still have considerable responsibility for making the necessary personal contacts. In the salary-man family, because hiring is largely determined by examinations or introductions, the child requires parental support only for preparing him for admission to a good academic institution. Once admitted, even if the boy does need financial help from his parents, his career plans are essentially outside the scope of his parents' planning. An academic degree and school contacts give a boy security so that he will not have to call on his parents for assistance in finding a new job if something should go wrong in his present place of work. Thus, even the first son in the salaried family has gained considerable freedom from his parents' domination without the necessity of rebelling against his parents, a situation in striking contrast to the first sons of farmers, owners of small businesses, and independent professionals.

Symbolic Remnants

Despite the massive inroads into the authority and economic significance of the *ie* in salaried families, there still is a strong attachment to this concept. Even branch families have a strong desire to continue the family line and an overwhelming hope that the family have at least one son to continue the family name. In fact, most families say they would like two sons and one daughter, so that if something should happen to one son they would still have one to continue the family line. The feeling remains that an *ie* has a tradition and that the person becoming a member of the *ie* should learn the family's customs and share the feeling of belonging to a long line of ancestors.

As much as they would like to adopt a son or son-in-law, few are willing to accept the problems this raises.[17] But there is a common compromise solution in Mamachi to the problem of having no heir: a family finding someone who accepts no other family responsibility than that of taking on the family name and looking after the family ancestral plots and plaques. If a family has only a daughter, at the time of her marriage they may work out an arrangement with her husband whereby she would enter her husband's *ie* and take on his name and family line, providing that one male child of theirs be given her maiden name to continue the *ie* into which she was born. According to another arrangement, if a man has no children to continue his name, he may ask a second son of one of his brothers or other near relatives to take on his family name. In some main families with no children, a child of relatives may still be adopted, but increasingly among salaried families agreements are reached whereby someone will continue the family name without being required to change residence.

Even the branch families often have a feeling of attachment to their ancestral home, although separated from it by generations. Many modern salary men, when asked where their home (*kuni*) is, will answer not their birthplace or their father's birthplace but the rural village where their grandfather or even great-grandfather was born. They may not expect to visit there, although if necessary they usually will be willing to help look after the family graves and ancestral tablets, but they retain a feeling of sentimental attachment which helps define their place in the world for now and ages yet to come.

The Decline of Family Principles

The *ie* was not simply a companionship family as in the West. It was a set of rules about how members were to behave and how the organization was to operate regardless of the sentiment or the convenience of the family members. One person had to be chosen as family head and all other members were to relate to each other depending on their position within the *ie*. It was a set of principles that governed the relationship of family members to each other.

Family relationships are now less governed by principles than by sentiment, power, and convenience. If the branch family has more wealth and power than a main family, it no longer is obliged to subordinate itself to the main family simply because it is the branch. A young man looking for a job or a marital partner may listen to his parents because of their authority, because he is fond of them, or because he respects their judgment. He is no longer obliged to follow his father's or his elder brother's wishes simply because of an obligation to obey the head of the *ie*. A person seeking financial assistance may go to his relatives for help, but he does not necessarily go to the family head, nor is the family head necessarily responsible for looking after the welfare of all members of the *ie*. He goes to relatives for assistance, not because of their position in the *ie* but because he feels close to them or because they are in a position to offer assistance.[18] If one visits the main family, it is not because it is part of a required formality. If the oldest son has the major responsibility of looking after the parents, it is likely to be because he has the kind of job and housing situation that make him most able to bear this burden.

The power of *ie* principles has given way under the impact of new ideology: of forming branch families with a shallow sense of tradition and the growth of large firms providing security and welfare services. The weakening of *ie* principles has not led to chaos, because a new familial order has arisen based on sentiment and a sharp division of labor and authority.

Notes

1. The same word, *ie,* is also used to mean simply home or a family, but in this chapter it is used only in its meaning as a family line. For a brief but authoritative account of the *ie,* see Kizaemon

Ariga, "The Family in Japan," *Marriage and Family Living*, 1954, 16:362–368. The term *dozoku* is used to denote a locality kin group comprising main and branch families sharing the same work. The main and branch families were sometimes linked not by blood but by fictitious kin ties. Cf. Michio Nagai, "Dōzoku: A Preliminary Study of the Japanese 'Extended Family' Group and Its Social and Economic Functions," Report No. 7, Project 483, Ohio State University (mimeographed).

2. Cf. Nobushige Hozumi, *Ancestor Worship and Japanese Law*, Tokyo: The Hokuseido Press, 1912.

3. It may be suggested incidentally that this practice played a crucial role in capital formation which was necessary for modernization. Many characteristics of modern developments (thrift, hard work, and even economic rationality) were often intimately associated with the attempt to develop and preserve the *ie*. Hozumi, *op. cit.*, notes that formerly rules existed against the *ie* giving too much away since this might interfere with family continuity.

4. Cf. the works of Carle Zimmerman.

5. Returning a bride was very common, especially in certain areas of northern Honshu, and it was this practice which made such a high divorce rate in the Meiji Period. The rate was even higher than statistics indicate because many brides were returned in the first months after the marriage before it was officially registered.

6. In Tokugawa census registers, a young wife is often listed as daughter without being distinguished from a true daughter of the household. For this information I am indebted to Robert J. Smith.

7. My survey data indicate that of 63 salary-man families, 86 percent were branch families; of 81 small shopkeeping families, 75 percent were branch families; of 172 farm families, 54 percent were branch families. Unfortunately, the designation of branch family does not indicate how many generations ago the branch split off from the main family. One may suspect that in many farm families this happened many generations ago.

8. This problem, although not so common now, was an acute issue in families where a son died during World War II and was in general more common in the previous era when the death rate was higher.

9. See the polls in Yoshiharu Scott Matsumoto, *Contemporary Japan: The Individual and His Group*, Philadelphia: The American Philosophical Society, 1960.

10. Even before World War II, the old *ie* system was under severe attack by those who supported the democratic principles of family equality. The sections in the postwar Constitution dealing with family law represented a clear-cut victory for those who believed in equality of inheritance. The new law accelerated the dispersal of family wealth; among salary men, where no attempts are made

to get around multiple inheritance, it has marked an end to the *ie*'s ability to control family money and provide for the assistance of needy members. Cf. Kurt Steiner, "The Revision of the Civil Code of Japan: Provisions Affecting the Family," *Far Eastern Quarterly,* 1950, 9:169–184.

11. In a study conducted in modern Tokyo apartments as many as 20 percent feel that the eldest son should have the main responsibility in caring for the support of needy family members, and 40 percent still feel the eldest son should inherit the majority of the property. In a nearby farming area, where the idea of *ie* is still much stronger, 74 percent felt the eldest son should have the major responsibility, and 84 percent felt the eldest son should receive the majority of the inheritance. Takashi Koyama, *Gendai Kazoku no Kenkyuu* (An Investigation of the Contemporary Family), Tokyo: Koobundoo, 1960.

12. One Japanese movie which we saw centered on the theme of siblings deciding how to care for their aged widow mother. The most touching scene was when the mother overheard the children arguing that not one but the other should be responsible for her care.

13. Formerly, in rural areas, at a certain time the household head stepped down and passed on the position of family head to his son. From this day on the father was officially retired and the responsibility was officially in the hands of the son. In some cases the elderly couple moved on the day of retirement to a small separate dwelling on the same land or to a separate room, passing on their own home to their son. See John Embree, *Suye Mura,* Chicago, University of Chicago Press, 1939.

14. Regarding these two forms of marriage, see Ezra F. Vogel, "The Go-Between in a Developing Society," *Human Organization,* 1961, 20:112–120. The distinction between these two types of marriage will be explored more fully in a forthcoming work by Professor Robert Blood.

15. Evidence for this, based on projective test material given to Japanese, is presented in George De Vos, "The Relation of Guilt to Achievement and Arranged Marriage among the Japanese," *Psychiatry,* 1960, 23:287–301. Judging from De Vos's work, even in rural Japan the willingness to follow the mother's wishes has less to do with the concept of duty to *ie* than with the emotional bond between mother and child.

16. Though I do not have adequate survey data, my impression is that it would be somewhat lower than the national average, which is about 10 percent.

17. This conforms to Professor Koyama's findings that only 21.8 percent of the dwellers of an urban apartment project (largely salary

men) would be willing to adopt a son-in-law if they had only daughters, while as many as 90.1 percent of farmers living in a community within commuting distance of Tokyo would adopt a son-in-law. If a family had no children, 35.6 percent of the city apartment dwellers think it necessary to provide for an heir, but 89.4 percent of the farmers think so. Koyama, *op. cit.*

18. Evidence from historical materials indicates that Japanese kinship terminology does not distinguish between relatives of one's father and one's mother. Cf. Robert Smith in Robert J. Smith and Richard K. Beardsley, eds., *Japanese Culture*, New York: The Viking Fund, 1962. With the decline of jural relationships between *ie* members, there appears to be no clear predominance of relationships with one side of the family as opposed to the other.

AUTHORITY IN THE FAMILY

The Tradition of "Male Dominance"

In the official ideology of "traditional Japan," the wife not only obeyed her husband, but showed that she enjoyed obeying him. According to traditional guidebooks on women's behavior, a woman's pleasure and freedom came not from asserting her independence, but from learning to want to do what she was required to do. She had no conception of rights, only of duties, and the only way to change her life was by attuning her character to the position she was expected to occupy.

However, when one asks concrete questions in Mamachi about a person's own parents and grandparents, one is often told that in their case the stereotype was not nearly so absolute, that the woman in fact had considerable say in how the house was run. In practice as well as in theory, the woman did show respect to her husband in public, but not necessarily at home. Even in traditional Japan, the husband often took little part in directing household affairs, and if the wife was supervised, it was usually by the mother-in-law rather than the husband. Even a generation ago, there was often a sizeable gap between the "beautiful virtue" of absolute obedience and actual practice.

Although the male dominance never approached the ideal, unquestionably male dominance has declined. As the popular saying goes, "since the war, stockings and women have grown stronger." Even the traditional saying, "fushoo fuzui," ("when the husband calls out, the wife jumps," the same pronunciation "fu" meaning either man or woman) is now sometimes interpreted by punsters as meaning "The wife sings out and the husband jumps." Others jokingly comment that even husbands who give orders to their wives in public now apologize to their wives when they return home. While the power of the Japanese woman within the family has unquestionably increased with the growth of democratic ideology and women's political rights, these jokes, like wartime American cartoons showing rich ladies rushing to obey their maids, should not be taken to mean that the power balance has completely changed.

The contemporary Mamachi wife does have more freedom and power than the wife a generation ago. Because she receives the largest portion of the husband's regular salary without daily pleading, she controls the family budget. With new electrical equipment she has free time to use as she wishes. The increased possibilities open to her in shopping, in outside activities, and in friendships have broadened her range of personal choice. Because the Mamachi wife has no commitments outside the household, and is usually free of direction from her mother-in-law and other relatives, she has effective control over her own sphere of activities.

Maintenance of Decentralized Authority

Farmers, small shopkeepers, and even independent professionals do not have a sharp separation between family activities and business activities. Since the father conducts his business in the home and the wife helps him in his work, she is constantly subjected to his authority. In those homes the father's centralized authority remains effective even though it is increasingly resented.

In the Mamachi salaried family, however, authority is decentralized, with the wife managing the home and the husband managing his work and recreation. In general, this principle of separate spheres of authority has been highly successful in maintaining harmony and satisfying the desires of both husband and wife.

The husband's sphere presents no problem. The wife knows little about the husband's work and therefore has virtually no opportunity to exert influence over his activities, nor does she have to help him with his work.

There is, however, a problem in the wife's maintaining authority over her sphere. As the husband has more free time to spend at home, and as the relative isolation of the nuclear family from relatives permits a closer relationship between husband and wife, the wife has more difficulty retaining exclusive power over the household. The impact of democratic ideals has raised her status in relation to her husband's, but, paradoxically, by encouraging the husband's participation in the home, she restricts her own sphere of free activity. The husband still has more authority than the wife, and while he must also be sensitive to her wishes and may try to refrain from giving her orders at home, he finds it hard to avoid it entirely. And as much as the wife wants to please her husband by being gentle and obedient, she resents her husband's interference. The Mamachi wife's real concern about power is not about women's rights in political and economic affairs, or even equality within the home, but about protecting her right to manage the household without the husband's interference.

Major family issues, like the children's schooling and choice of marital partner, usually pose no jurisdictional difficulties. Such issues are considered legitimate concerns of both husband and wife, and discussions begin before either has a firm opinion and continue until a consensus is achieved. A couple may passionately disagree on the content of these issues, but there is no disagreement about the process of reaching a decision.

Often the minor issues lead to serious marital disagreements because they most clearly raise the question of who has the authority to make household decisions. Even minor queries from the husband about the method of food preparation or about the allocation of money for children's clothes can arouse a wife to a vigorous defense of her autonomy.

Eventually, if the trend toward husband-wife closeness and mutual understanding increases, it might be possible to arrive at a new principle of allocation of authority: the co-operative sharing of decisions on issues now resolved separately by either husband or wife. Such a principle, however, would require much more intimacy and mutual discussion than now exists in most Mamachi families, and a conviction on the part of the wives that they can achieve as much by open expressions of opinion as they can by subtle manipulations. This seems unlikely in the near future because Mamachi families solidly dislike extended mutual exploration of emotion, particularly the more primitive sentiments of love and hate, and consider it best for each to control his feelings and to limit his expression of personal demands. The principle of shared authority may be possible at some time in the future, but, at present, the families' efforts are directed at maintaining the principle of decentralized authority. The wife in particular has developed subtle means of preserving her autonomy. If, for example, the husband raises questions about her household methods, she is likely to act so surprised by his intrusion that she must pause and think for a minute. Then she gives either a noncommital answer that indicates she does not quite understand the question, or a brief factual answer. In either case her reply is polite but rather stiff so that the husband does not feel comfortable in probing further. She prefers to avoid questions altogether, and to this end she practises concealment and evasion. Just as the husband does not inform his wife about his work, so she omits many details of household events in their conversations. She values preserving a desired type of relationship with her husband more than reporting carefully on household affairs. Most wives would even prefer that their husbands not give any help, rather than risk raising questions that might threaten their autonomy.

A good illustration of wifely technique of putting aside *hesokurigane* (literally navel money, i.e., secret savings) to preserve independent management of household finances is the case of one clever wife who decided that sizeable house repairs were necessary and in due time broached the subject to her husband. When he learned the estimated cost, he said it was too high and they could not afford the repairs. When the wife wondered what he would consider a reasonable price, he announced his estimate. A few days later the wife happily reported that she had found a place which would do the repairs for slightly lower than the husband's estimate, and he consented to the work. In fact, the wife had not found a cheaper firm, but she had been saving regularly in a private account and used her own money to make up the difference between her husband's figures and the cost of repairs.

The husband's increasing participation in home life does constitute a threat to decentralization of authority and requires the wife to use such clever techniques to prevent interference. The wife's eternal vigilance in preventing the husband's intrusions and his conscious restraint in expressing views about problems of household management are the price of her autonomy in the home.

The Nature and Exercise of the Husband's Authority

The fact that the husband's status is superior to his wife's is reflected in a variety of ways. Although he may call her by her first name, it is not proper for her to reciprocate but she may call him *anata* (a term used between spouses), or a term indicating parenthood, like *otoochan* (father).[1] A group of Mamachi mothers went into gales of laughter when talking about an American wife calling her husband's name from across the room and the husband calmly responding to her call. They explained that a Japanese wife would neither use her husband's first name nor call across a room to him, although a Japanese man could do both. When the husband arrives home, he expects and receives the family's attention. His wife and children hustle about getting his pipe and paper and if he wants anything else they are prepared to fetch and carry for him. If he wants an evening in town at the movies or at a bar, this is his privilege. But it is not a privilege which extends to the wife. Today both husband and wife laugh at the old tradition of a woman walking three paces behind the man, but in public women still defer to men. In mixed gatherings a woman speaks when spoken to, and then she often simply agrees with others rather than adding ideas or opinions of her own. When guests visit, the wife is more of a servant than a hostess. Of course the wife's deference and demeanor do not mean that she submits to all her husband's whims, but in a showdown, if the husband is insistent, the wife yields.

The average husband is most likely to express his arbitrary authority on matters of his personal pleasure or his wife's handling of the children. He is quick to anger if his comforts are not properly attended to at home and, lacking a clear conception of the work involved in housekeeping, he may become furious if the wife seems to spend more time cleaning or caring for the small children than attending to his pleasures. At the same time he wants the children to receive adequate maternal attention, and if a favorite child complains to the father that the mother has been harsh or that she was not home when the child returned from school, the father is likely to explode and demand that the wife provide proper care for the children. Often he lays down the rules which the mother must enforce concerning the children's discipline, their friends, and their social functions. On such matters, and sometimes even on various idiosyncratic matters, he can express his rights even if the rest of the family considers him arbitrary. Although they may not be aware of how much he must yield to his superiors at work, some wives have suspected that the husband's arbitrary outbursts might have more to do with problems in the office than with problems at home.

Since the husband's superior authority is no longer supported by the democratic ideals espoused by many husbands and wives, it is noteworthy that she accords him so much prestige and so many privileges. What most wives fear in their husband is not some kind of ultimate sanction like cruelty or divorce but his more immediate flashes of anger. Few wives have experienced physical violence, but since men are considered by nature more volatile, more explosive, and less able to endure hardships and sacrifices than women, wives feel they must be cautious not to arouse this anger. Aside from the fear of the husband's explosions, the continued subservience of the wife is undoubtedly related to the lack of alternatives for her in case of divorce or separation. But it is not simply the economic dependence of the woman on her husband, as emphasized by Marx and Engels, that gives the husband superior authority; it is the lack of socially acceptable alternatives that makes her more dependent on him than vice versa. Even if the wife is not consciously aware of these ultimate sanctions, they do serve to support the customs which give the husband his superior authority.

Despite his occasional explosions and more frequent dogmatic pronouncements, the typical husband thinks of himself as considerate and most of the time he is. While he wants to be sufficiently forceful to command the respect of his family, generally he is genuinely fond of his wife and children and wants to enjoy their love and admiration. He feels unhappy if his children regard him as frightening and he tries, not always successfully, to overcome their fears. Not only does the husband want to behave as a kindly father and husband, but he also feels sympathetic and sometimes even guilty about the sacrifices they make for his pleasures. It is precisely his sympathetic human feeling toward his wife and children and his desire to be liked by them which constitute the most effective curbs on the arbitrary exercise of his authority. Many a salary man is slow to demand what he considers his rights, out of consideration for the family's conveniences.

The Art of Husband Management

Because the husband is accorded a superior position, he can be direct in stating his wishes. Wives can be direct in stating their children's needs and basic household requirements, but most are reluctant in stating their own personal desires. However, some modern young wives enjoy frank discourse with their husbands, and in some older families the woman runs the household either because she has higher social status or stronger temperament.

Still, most Mamachi wives attain their wishes by subtle strategy rather than open request. The strategy is not always conscious, for in many ways a woman deals with her husband as she deals with anyone: by keeping a harmonious relationship and avoiding any show of unpleasantness. But this often requires such planning that it takes on the quality of an art—the art of husband management.

The Mamachi wife's arts for managing the husband are similar to those of an experienced American secretary in dealing with her boss. She studies his character and knows his moods. She knows when he must be left alone, when he can be humored, when she can take advantage of his "good days." She knows what issues she can decide on her own, what issues she can discuss openly, what issues she can discuss providing she hides certain facts and exaggerates others. In face of his anger, she knows how to plead innocence or misunderstanding and how to lighten the anger by criticizing her own stupidity, ignorance, or inattentiveness, or by simply waiting until the anger has dissipated.

But the Mamachi wife works much harder to please her husband than a secretary does to please her superior, and in some ways she treats her husband as her eldest child. As in dealing with her child, she tries to keep him continuously happy and satisfied, because then he will respond automatically to her wishes.

A young bride searches out every little indication and listens carefully to every phrase to discover what things please her husband. She tries to avoid any direct criticism of his behavior and any assaults on his masculine ego. At most, within the hearing of her own husband she might give him a hint indirectly by complimenting another wife on something that wife's husband had done. If the husband presents a view as fact, she will not offer contrary evidence even if she is convinced he is wrong. When she wants something, she makes vague suggestions that appeal to his desires rather than to logic or her own desires. If she wants an item for the home, she is not likely to talk about its use or cost, but about how beautiful it would look or how magnificent an important friend thought it was. These hints and vague suggestions do not require the disapproving husband to make a definite refusal, a refusal that might be embarrassing for him to change later.

Yet, many a wife who is reserved and self-effacing is amazingly persistent over time, continuing to find new examples, or new authorities, or new ways to point up the advantage of her plan. Some husbands yield not because they have been sold on the advantages or have been taken in by the cleverness of the wife's strategy but because they are not strongly enough convinced of the disadvantages to be able to withstand the wife's persistent efforts.

A persistent campaign may be illustrated by the woman who decided that it was time for their family to have a television set. One day she commented to her husband that a neighbor had just bought a nice-looking Hitachi television set through a dealer friend for only 48,000 yen. A few days later she incidentally told her husband that she had heard of another family who bought a television set at a different place for even less money, but that it did not look quite as nice as the first set. Since the husband still showed no interest, she dropped the topic. But a few nights later she called his attention to an article about a special educational television program being run and she openly wondered whether such programs really helped the children's studying. In the meantime, she and the children talked about how nice it would be if the father would buy a television set and the children began asking him for one. It was not long before the father announced that he had decided it was time to buy a television set.

It is usually difficult for the father to refuse his children directly, and it is not unusual for a mother to coach a child on how and when to make a request of the father or to stimulate the child's desire so much that he will ask the father for it without the mother's urging.

Not all husband management is positive, for there are times when the wife must cope with ill temper and anger. When a man is critical of his wife she suggests, but does not openly state, her self-sacrifice to the husband by working harder, paying more attention to the husband's desires than usual, heaving an extra sigh or two, or by looking haggard, tired, and harassed. Other wives respond to anger or criticism with somber quiet, or great surprise and innocence at the husband's criticism, or with self-accusations of inadequacy. Rarely does a Mamachi wife stand up directly against her husband to defend herself.

Some housewives are so skilled at husband management that the household runs smoothly. The husband feels flattered by his wife's hard work and devotion, retains his superior status, and yet the wife is, with proper subtlety, able to manage the household. In other cases, the wife, unable to charm him, deal with his rages, or get permission to buy things she wants, will run to her friends for help in interpreting her husband's behavior or in devising a more suitable strategy.

To some extent the skill is acquired as she gets to know her husband. Although some modern couples try to have frank discussions in their meetings before marriage, these discussions are often theoretical and do not fully cover all the aspects of the couple's actual attitudes. Even today, newly wedded couples often meet only three or four times before their wedding. Some brides try to follow their modern beliefs and express their views openly, but many are still reserved for the first months or even years of marriage until they feel it safe to begin expressing opinions or making personal requests. Some cautiously test their husbands' attitudes by dropping hints or talking about a neighbor family in which the wife has certain privileges or possessions. Many wives, after several years of marriage, recall how frightened and pitiful they were shortly after their wedding, afraid to make any requests, worried that they would not be able to satisfy their husbands. As they become more familiar with their husbands, prove their faithfulness, and produce a child (particularly a male), they acquire more confidence in their wifely ability.

The art of husband management is essentially an adjustment of the wife to the superior position of the husband. Because household affairs are more important to her and she has less authority than her husband, she spends more time trying to understand him than he does trying to understand her. She acquires more information relevant to the management of the household and spends more time devising plans to achieve her aims. The art of husband management, which is the outgrowth of these efforts, increases the likelihood that her wishes will be realized. It is an art which helps equalize the power of husband and wife without upsetting the superior position of the husband. In some ways, despite her lower status, she has more power over the activities of the home than the middle-class American wife who consults more closely with her husband.

The Mother-in-Law and Daughter-in-Law

Most homes in Mamachi do not include a mother-in-law and a daughter-in-law, but if they do, the difficulties between them are almost certain to dominate the family scene. In private conversations and in newspaper columns, the relationship between mother-in-law and daughter-in-law is commonly recognized as the most serious problem facing the modern family.[2] Some girls agree to marriage on the condition that the husband make arrangements for his mother to live elsewhere. Some wives have pleaded with their husbands to prevent the mother-in-law from moving in. Some wives and mothers-in-law have tried to adjust to each other, but the arguments have been so vicious that they have been forced to separate. Some wives, who might otherwise be unhappy, console themselves with the thought that at least they do not live with their mothers-in-law. Yet, as much as they both try to avoid living together, the cost of setting up separate households combined with the limited financial resources, the filial feeling toward parents, and the lack of other satisfactory arrangements for elderly people sometimes leaves no acceptable alternative, especially when the young couple is just getting started or after the mother-in-law is widowed.[3]

In traditional Japan, the only hope of the daughter-in-law for success was to prove her loyalty to the mother-in-law by learning how to satisfy her every wish. Not only was it virtuous for a young bride to obey her mother-in-law, but it paid off in the long run. Only after proving her devotion could she hope to have the freedom to do things on her own. If she failed badly, she was sent back to her original home in disgrace. Divorces were commonly initiated not by the husband but by the mother-in-law. Some Japanese have observed that in America relations with the mother-in-law are a *kigeki* (comedy), in Japan a *higeki* (tragedy).

Compared to the problem of the mother-in-law, the problem of the father-in-law seems almost inconsequential. Because the salary man has no business connection with his father-in-law, there is no serious authority problem between them. The daughter-in-law generally has little problem with her father-in-law because he takes little interest in the home. Often there is a positive attraction between daughter-in-law and father-in-law, which is not entirely dissipated even though it is often dealt with by avoiding any situation where the two of them would be alone. Even when the father-in-law is harsh and demands that the daughter-in-law cater to his wishes, she generally finds this much easier to adjust to than the harassment of the mother-in-law.

Although the wife would prefer to live with her mother than with her mother-in-law, if they live together the husband may have a power struggle with her mother, especially if the wife and mother give each other mutual support in resisting the husband's wishes or in making demands on him.[4] But the fact that he spends so little time at home restricts the scope of this conflict. Although the wife's mother usually has considerable authority and the wife sometimes resents being dominated, the positive feelings between mother and daughter are strong enough to bind their negative feelings. Especially if the wife has never lived apart from her mother, she feels dependent on the mother for advice and therefore readily follows her suggestions.

But there is no such positive bond to control the wife's feeling of annoyance with her mother-in-law. If the daughter-in-law does make a serious effort to serve the mother-in-law and is able and loyal, she may at times be treated almost as if she were a daughter instead of a daughter-in-law. But if she is not very competent or comes from a family of lower status than the husband, she may still be treated more like a servant. But even the best relationships are strained, and the strain is likely to be especially severe if the mother-in-law is a widow and lives with her only son.

Unlike the situation in traditional Japan, the critical problem in present-day Mamachi is not the harsh work load required of the daughter-in-law, but the lack of clarity of lines of authority. The mother-in-law has legitimate bases for arguing that the daughter-in-law obey, and the daughter-in-law has legitimate bases for expecting certain privileges. The ideal daughter-in-law is supposed to yield to the mother-in-law, but the ideal mother-in-law should not be harsh with the wife. In contrast to the situation in the United States, where the wife has primary authority, or to the situation in traditional Japan, where the mother-in-law had primary authority, there is no clear guiding principle. The object of the husband's primary loyalty is equally unclear. The answer to the traditional question, "Whom should a husband save if his wife and mother were drowning?" was "His mother" because he could always get another wife. Now the wife and mother are much more on equal grounds in competing for the husband's loyalty, and since there is no clear solution, the situation is one of continuing competition.

Although the mother-in-law occasionally goes out, most of the day both she and the daughter-in-law are at home. The latter generally does the heavy work and the mother-in-law often performs the more complicated tasks of cooking and sewing. But there is no such clear way for dividing up authority. If, for example, the mother-in-law has no income of her own, it is not clear who should decide how much spending money the mother-in-law should have. Since each typically has few interests outside the home, it is hard for the mother-in-law to refrain completely from supervising her daughter-in-law. The latter, in order to avoid the mother-in-law's disapproval, is cautious about going out of the home, buying things for the home, preparing food, and cleaning the house. Even a mere question from the mother-in-law sometimes makes the wife anxious. It is not only the actual commands of the mother-in-law which create the difficulties but the daughter-in-law's feeling of being unable to run the house as she wishes. As some wives put it, they feel as if they are forced to live with an enemy in their home.

The mother-in-law sometimes acts out her annoyance by being more critical and less willing to let the wife go out to visit friends, attend PTA meetings, or buy clothes for herself. The daughter-in-law may act out her annoyance by following the letter of the law laid down by the mother-in-law while defeating the spirit of the mother-in-law's wishes.

The battleground for the dispute is often the children. The grandmother tries to enforce her wishes on the children and to encourage them to resist their mother. The mother tries to win the children to her side and subtly encourages them to disobey their grandmother.

The wife fortifies herself for the struggle by keeping up with the latest information from newspapers, magazines, and books. She tries to keep up with the modern advice, and in discussions with the grandmother she relies heavily on "modern scientific information" to support her point of view and show that the grandmother is old-fashioned and superstitious. The grandmother typically respects scientific information, but sometimes suspects the daughter-in-law of manufacturing the thing which she "read in a recent magazine." The mother-in-law relies on her superior experience and her moral conviction that because the daughter-in-law is joining her family, she should learn the family's custom (*kafuu*). The mother-in-law, after all, knows her son's likes and knows what it means to rear children. Many a daughter-in-law, not confident of her own ability to please her husband or handle the children's problems, reluctantly yields to the mother-in-law's experience.

If the husband supports either his mother or his wife against the other, his opinion is decisive, and in one way or another, the wife and mother frequently appeal to him for his support against the other. The husband, however, ordinarily tries to stay out of the dispute. He tries to play down the seriousness of the dispute, and to encourage each to be more sympathetic to the other. Only when the husband regards the situation as unbearable or judges one side as being particularly unreasonable does he take the initiative in settling the dispute by encouraging his mother to accept modern ways or the wife to be kind to the aged.

The most commonly suggested solution to the conflict between the two women is for both to show reserve, and to contain themselves even when angry. Many advice columns include hints for how the two could adjust to each other, but the crux of the advice is usually another way for humoring the other one or a way for containing one's own feelings of annoyance.

But the problem involves fundamental attitudes and status relationships. Like the Negro in the American South, the daughter-in-law no longer feels compelled to accept a subservient position. But the price of her emerging freedom is a breakdown of the old social order and an uncontrolled competition between her and her mother-in-law. The Mamachi daughter-in-law has not yet been granted complete freedom even in the most modern family, and a stable new order of relationships has not yet been established except for avoidance, a solution which is not always possible.

Notes

1. Cf. Takashi Koyama, *Gendai Kazoku no Kenkyuu* (An Investigation of the Contemporary Family), Tokyo: Koobundoo, 1960. The fact that differences in kinship terminology continue to reflect differences in relationships is indicated by the fact that more modern than traditional couples use first names and Western terms like "papa" and "mama."

2. The common American stereotype is that the Japanese wife is rebelling against her husband, but it would be more accurate to say that the focus of rebellion, if present at all, is not the husband but the mother-in-law.

3. On the average, husbands are about three or four years older than

their wives, and women live about five years longer than men. Hence, in the average family, a woman lives about eight or nine years as a widow. During this time she is likely to live at the home of one of her children.

4. In two or three families where the mother-in-law and daughter-in-law got along relatively well, they likewise gave each other mutual support and sympathy in trying to get the husband to be more diligent in fulfilling family responsibilities.

Commentary: *The New Middle Class*

Ezra F. Vogel's research on the Japanese middle-class family is conducted in "Mamachi," a fictitious name for a suburban neighborhood that is regarded by Japanese social scientists as typically middle class. Vogel used anthropological field methods, that is, he was a participant observer, and he conducted intensive interviews with members of twelve families, six of them with an emotionally disturbed child and six with normal children. He also administered questionnaires to sixty families in seven other communities. Other sources of information included expert informants in various cities, discussions with Japanese and American scholars interested in the Japanese family, and a number of opinion surveys conducted in Japan by social scientists.

Vogel's primary focus is the "salary man," a prototype in Japanese culture that parallels the "organization man" of the period following World War II in the United States. The emergence of rational bureaucracy is central to Vogel's analysis, for it has created the salary man. (The term "rational bureaucracy" implies rule of law, written rules, efficiency, delegation of authority, etc.) The primary source of identification for both the salary man and the organization man is the corporation, which serves as a substitute for traditional community ties.

Despite this new emphasis, traditional Japanese values persist and constrain the individualism fostered by rational bureaucracy. Continuity of Japanese family patterns persists along with the gradual changes generated by the changing economic structure. Vogel's book provides insight into the relationship between family organization and changing economic institutions.

Japan is the only Asiatic nation that can be described as modern rather than traditional or developing. Therefore, the question that emerges is why traditional aspects still characterize the family within the new middle class. There are two variables relevant to the question. As Emil Lederer pointed out (Japan in Transition, 1938), *Japan's modernization was for the most part confined to the sphere of economics and technology, so that it could compete with the West on a presumption of equality. Ideologically, however, Japan remained traditionally feudal until the end of World War II.*

Modernization, at the opposite pole from traditionalism, involves not one but two processes: urbanization and industrialization. During the late Middle Ages, the Jews, who were forbidden to own land, became urban and engaged in middleman pursuits in order to survive. Max Weber and Werner Sombart, among others, pointed out this factor in The Protestant Ethic and the Spirit of Capitalism, 1930, *and* The Jews and Modern Capitalism, 1913, *respectively. However, although the stage was set for the emergence of industrial capitalism by the time of the Protestant Reformation, the fact remains that the Industrial Revolution did not take place until the eighteenth century in England and the nineteenth century in America. Although it is true that any date is at best an historian's convention, our problem is not to trace origins (witness all the research proving that the origins of modern political institutions, such as the state and the university, go well into the Dark Ages). Rather, our concern as sociologists is with the impact of dominant social norms upon family behavior. Regarded in this sense, modernization in the West is comparatively recent.*

Once an industrial revolution takes place anywhere in the world, the time necessary for additional modernization elsewhere becomes drastically telescoped. In the case of Japan, industrialization was hastened by the fact that the western powers that influenced Japan during the nineteenth century were themselves already urban, industrial, and modern. Japan's modernization in the last generation was accelerated even further by its defeat in World War II and the consequent downgrading of the role of the emperor. As a result, many people in Japan today regard themselves as modern not merely on technological but also on ideological levels. Japanese traditionalism may no longer be as effective a brake upon the speed of modernization as it used to be. It is in this light that we believe Vogel's concern with the new middle class in Japan can be reevaluated.

6 THE ITALIAN-AMERICAN FAMILY*

FRANCIS X. FEMMINELLA

Americans who are descended from Italian immigrants constitute the largest single ethnic group in American society. Italian-Americans have interested sociologists for many years and continue to do so. They have been compared with other immigrant groups in terms of residential patterns, status achievement, food, and alcohol use. Their family structure, their interest and success in education, their contributions to the arts, sciences, politics, and to business have all been described. Finally, and for many most importantly, the association called the Mafia has been imaginatively studied and described.

These studies indicate that there are recognizable and observable differences in the behavior of Italian-Americans scattered throughout the United States. These arise in part from the differences in the cultural patterns of the Italian communities of their forebears and in part from the differences in cultural patterns of their present communities. But if one generalization can validly be made regarding all Italian-Americans, it is that this subcultural group places a high value upon a strong and cohesive family life.[1] This family cohesion is most evident in circumstances where pat-

* This is an original paper published for the first time in this volume. It has been extensively revised by the editors, with the consent of the author, in order to make it consistent with the remainder of the anthology.

terns of segregation still prevail. In other words, consistent with the conclusions of much of the literature dealing with other immigrant groups as well, it would seem to be the case that if Italian-Americans, whether first, second, or third generation, remain in a ghetto, then traditional sanctions that create family solidarity will continue to prevail. Where acculturation has taken place, Americans of Italian origin begin to be characterized by the same kinds of individualism as is the case wherever the nuclear type is dominant.

This study seeks to analyze the intergenerational dimension of Italian-Americans and to assess the impact of acculturation upon this process. The data for this comparative and historical analysis are taken for the most part from ethnographic studies of Italians and Italian-Americans[2] as well as from a series of exploratory interviews.[3] Although it is not possible to generalize from the interviews beyond the cultural boundaries of the sample, these interviews are a fertile source for the development of provocative hypotheses as well as a means to illustrate the observations that are made here.

In the interest of semantic clarity, it should be pointed out that the term "patriarchy" is in general use and refers to a family unit where the father or the male members of the family exert legitimate authority and are the decision-makers. It is distinguished from the term "matriarchy" (on occasion the terms "matricentric" or "matrifocal" are substituted), which defines a unit ruled by a mother or another female, and from the term "egalitarian," wherein authority is more or less equally distributed and shared by both parents. The term "patriarchy" is also distinguished from "patricentric," "matricentric," and "filicentric," which mean that the power and authority of the decision-maker is attenuated by the force of interest and indulgence in the father, the mother, or the child, respectively, and from "patrilocal," "matrilocal," and "neolocal," which refer to residential patterns of families.

Italian-American family life at the turn of the century closely resembled the patterns of family structure found in Italy at that time. The Italian family was fundamentally patriarchal and patrilocal or neolocal. Under the system of primogeniture, the oldest son inherited the estate and status of his father and followed in his footsteps. The father was respected and feared. This family structure derived in part from the ancient Roman cultural heritage of the Italians. The classical Roman family was patriarchal and patrilocal. The father of the family, the *pater familias,* was a supreme authority who even had the power of life and death over family members under certain conditions.

An historical perspective is necessary in order to understand how the Italian-American family evolved. Whether the family type under discussion is Italian or Italian-American, its roots are to be found in social institutions that go back many centuries.

The Roman definition of the "family" subsumed all who shared a particular domicile, including, on occasion, slaves. The French historian Fustel De Coulanges equates the Latin word *familias* to the Greek word *oikos*, both of which exclude the concept of generation or kinship. What is referred to is field, house, money, and estate.[4] The English word "family" is derived from *familias* and according to Giambattista Vico[5] is related to the Latin root, *fama*, which refers to the fame of the "heroes." The "heroes" were refugees who worked for the landowners and were called *famuli* and, later, *vernae*. In time, the notion of *famuli* included the patriarch or father-prince, the ruler of the refugees. In the ancient Roman family, the father had sovereign power of life and death over his children, and despotic dominion over their property grew out of these roots. This is referred to in Roman law as *patria potestas*, a power so absolute that there was no distinction between sons and slaves with regard to ownership of property. This authority was passed on through the male heirs. Two major cultural patterns emerged: the system of primogeniture and the system of *clienteles*, both of which have directly or indirectly influenced the Italian-American family.

During the Middle Ages, Roman cultural patterns were preserved in part through the monastic institutions, which performed educational as well as missionary services throughout Europe. The cultural continuity between Roman and monastic social structure can be illustrated etymologically. The head of the monastery was called "abbot," or "father" (from the Greek *abbas*). Medieval civil authority was also assumed by the abbot, whose landownership was indicated by the title of Lord Abbot. In the hierarchy of the monastery the monk closest to the abbot was called *prior* or "first." The monks addressed each other as *frater,* "brother," and were called "sons" by the abbot. The Rule of St. Benedict, under which they lived, commanded that the younger monks obey the older and that the older love the younger. All vowed obedience to the abbot. The abbot did not have the power of life and death over his charges, but he did have the power to excommunicate.

With the rise of Italian cities and small states, the civil ruler assumed powers parallel to the Pope or abbot; but instead of being called "father," he was addressed as "leader." The secular community (e.g., the village) is in a sense a meeting place of family and landscape. The Italian village has historically been the focus of one's loyalty in the same sense as the village has been on the subcontinent of Asia. Much of Italian history chronicles rule by conquering invaders and absentee governments that plundered, robbed, and raped the people and the land. Family loyalty was therefore the only tie that Italians could trust. The Roman *pater familias* not only ruled but also protected the members of his family.[6] It was a kind of patron-client relationship.

To whom, then, must one be loyal? The ancestors of most Italian-Americans were peasants from southern Italy or Sicily. Even today, the people there continue to be ruled by traditional customs and laws. The traditional heritage serves an ideological function for the individuals of that society. Leonard W. Moss and Stephen C. Cappannari have described the deep-rooted tradition of high family solidarity in southern Italian villages.[7] An individual's loyalties are first and most importantly to the members of his immediate nuclear family. He feels that, ultimately, these are the only ones he can trust. From this source he derived his existence and nurturance, and these are the significant others in his life with whom he belongs and from whom he receives approval and acceptance. But in the larger society the name and social position of the neolocal nuclear family is inherited. And as the child in this family trusts his parents, so his parents trust theirs. The oldest son is given the name of his paternal grandfather, and he obeys, respects, and trusts him. Thus, one's loyalties must be extended to the larger consanguine *familie*. The degrees of reciprocal loyalty and trust, of obligation to help and expectation of receiving help, of authority and obedience are clearly marked in the minds of each person. In this sense, the consanguine family may be further extended by the system of *comparaggio*, that is, of godparenthood. Although initially the role of the godparent is a purely religious one of sponsorship and the setting of moral example, a surrogate parent-child relationship is established.

Finally, and least importantly, one's loyalties are given to one's *paisani*, that is, other members of one's *paese*, village. "Even with the advent of the radio, the peasant continues to identify himself with the village. Through bitter experience he has learned to trust, or distrust least, those who live within the sound of the local church bell [*campanilismo*]."[8] To paraphrase Edward C. Banfield, one sees one's neighbors, and one must deal with one's neighbors, and consequently, one must have one's neighbors as friends.[9] Moreover, it is better to trust a neighbor than a stranger, but it must be recognized that a neighbor is almost a stranger himself. Consequently, the greatest attachment and trust must lie within the nuclear family. This is where one deals with the core of another person in terms of the mystic indivisibility of belonging rather than in terms of specific interests.[10] The tradition of generous hospitality to guests and even to strangers in need follows from this sense of human belonging. In *gemeinschaft* relations, one gives totally and without regard to future recompense. In *gesellschaft* relations, one must occupy oneself with his *interesse*, that is, in Banfield's words, he must "maximize the material, short run advantage of the nuclear family; assume that all others will do likewise." [11] When dealing with another individual, one must be scrupulously honest and self-sacrificing. In all other social interaction, one must be wary. In this way, one protects and brings honor to his family. This is the "good" behavior that merits "admiration."

With the passage of time, changes, which reflect the changes in social and economic conditions, have taken place in the structure of family life on both sides of the ocean. Where *la miseria*, the degraded and impoverished condition of the peasant and his humiliation in the face of it, is intensified, the old traditions are strengthened. Where industrialization and a chance for upward social mobility have developed, a more modern and progressive family culture has evolved. The southern Italian peasant who migrated to the United States in the early 1900s was a proletarian villager unaccustomed to urban industrialization. His adjustment in this totally new physical, social, and cultural environment was guided by traditional customs and laws that were suited to the former time and place.

Therefore, the Italian and Italian-American families have in common a heritage of strong loyalty to one's most immediate relatives. The degrees of loyalties follow a kind of generic progression. These social relationships are akin to the etymological relationships that have been pointed out by Vico in his discussion of the first families of humanity:

Thus, marriage emerged as the first kind of friendship in the world; whence Homer, to indicate that Jove and Juno lay together, says with heroic gravity that "they celebrated their friendship." The Greek word for friendship, *philia*, is from the same root as *phileō*, to love; and from it is derived the Latin *filius*, son. *Philios* in Ionic Greek means friend, and mutation to a letter of similar sound yielded the Greek *phylē*, tribe.[12]

A young man develops a friendship with a young woman, falls in love, gets married, and begins his own family. In time his children will leave him and go on to develop their own families. Yet, they all remain related to each other by ties of kinship that are never really severed.

The heritage of *pater familias* in the Roman family, of strong patriarchy in the medieval Italian family, and of obedience to tradition in the southern Italian peasant families has led many students of Italian-American family life to see in it similar patterns of organization and orientation. Most American sociologists dealing with the subject have described the pattern of family structure among Italian-Americans as initially patriarchal. In subsequent generations, as Italian-Americans become assimilated, they begin to internalize American family norms and generate the kind of matricentric family structure characteristic of American family life. This is the usual view but not the only one possible. It offers a too simple answer to such a complex structure. Some obvious difficulties arise with such an interpretation. First, it presupposes a homogeneity of American cultural patterns not warranted by the literature. If anything, the range of class and regional differences among American family patterns seems to preclude significant statements of central tendency. Second, it does not take into account the partial pluralism of American society. On one hand, we do not yet have measures of the centrality and durability of ethnicity in the personalities of Americans. On the other hand, we do not fully know the extent of influence ethnicity has had on American family patterns.

Another view, or at least a refinement of the former one, that takes these objections into account is that among both Italian and Italian-American families there exists simultaneously a patriarchal and matriarchal family authority structure. The patriarchy is public and conscious, the matriarchy is "hidden" and unconscious.

A description of family authority patterns emerges from the interviews. With only one exception, all the respondents initially asserted that in their families and all Italian and Italian-American families in their experience, the father is the head of the household and is the major decision-maker. In probing the nature of this authority and this decision-making, the stereotype of *pater familias* and its denotation receded more and more. The authority role of the father appears to be one of verbalizing final decisions.

His role appears to be somewhat akin to the role of the President of the United States in signing a bill into law. Initially, like the President, the father may or may not have proposed the law. The legislators—the members of the family—debate the value of the law. They keep in mind the tenets of the Constitution, which they may or may not be amending, and the Supreme Court, which judges the constitutionality of the law. In addition, the family members consider the outside authorities of various kinds—the Church, the civil courts, the extended family, their neighbors—and they consider the ideals and norms that they have inherited. When legislators approve a bill, they send it to the President. When the family members approve a decision, it is presented to the father. The President may veto the bill, and the father may deny the new judgment. But the legislators can still enact a law over the veto of the President. Both Italian and Italian-American mothers have a similar veto power. Here, however, the analogy ends. The legislators make no pretense, offer no excuses for their exercise of the veto; the mother may never be so outright rebellious. Gathering the children (and particularly her sons) around her, she rationalizes her position and then attempts to undermine the authority of the father. Among Italian-Americans who follow the examples of their forebears, the home is the domain of the wife. Traditionally, and for practical reasons, the mother is most directly concerned with the raising of children and the care of the domicile. Consequently, she attempts in every way to reduce any disagreements to questions about the household. In this way, she brings the disagreement into an area in which she alone has jurisdiction. Thus, she avoids face-to-face confrontation and power conflict, which enables her to maintain publicly and consciously her conviction and belief in a patriarchal system while at the same time actually retaining power.

The matriarchy functions in other ways as well. The father knows that his decision must always be based on the law, that is, on what is "right." The law, however, is only vaguely defined. Italian and Italian-American mothers are often considered to be the unselfish self-sacrificing upholder of the law and, hence, is called upon to interpret it. The mother unconsciously uses this role for her own purposes. When she and her children have made a decision that the father does not agree with, she is able to point out to him that as the father of the family it is his obligation to command what is right, and she points out what the right thing is. The father, on the other hand, responds by testing whether or not the decision is related to his own field of jurisdiction—his work, his place of employment, his life outside the home. If the decision does relate to outside areas, he is apt to let these interests determine his position. Insofar as he becomes convinced that the decision affects the household, he accedes to the wishes of his wife.

This description of authority patterns in Italian and Italian-American families raises important questions concerning concepts of power, authority, and law. Therefore, some historical explanation for the existence of a matriarchy seems in order at this point.

The earliest forms of power and authority stem from the family, as Robert M. MacIver[13] points out: "In the historical state, power, property, and status were woven into a close knit trinity presiding over government . . . Authority is often defined as being power, the power to command obedience. Property conveys power and power confers status." [14] The history of the Italian states and Italy after the unification shows clearly that the seat of power rested within the monarchy and nobility. Italians and Italian-Americans retain, in simplistic form, this historical notion that status is obtained from wealth and power and that it is a function of birth or genealogy. Even among the peasant classes power and status are associated with property, and in America, Italians were able to seek power through property ownership. Thus, to own one's home is to merit prestige and higher status. For an Italian or an Italian-American, however, power is not thought of as an abstract concept. The Italian-American immigrant had little fear of the President or the governor of his state, for that relationship is to an abstract legitimate authority and not to a person with power. The *pater familias* had power as well as legitimate authority.

Although in the Italian-American family, the father is the legitimate authority who has a certain amount of power, the influences of industrialization and urbanization over the last 150 years have served to decrease the degree of power of the patriarch. The emancipation of women described by Ralph Linton[15] has not bypassed either the Italian or the Italian-American women. Besides the general forces of emancipation, however, another dynamic force seems to be at work. Simultaneously with the development of the institution of patriarchal families since the Middle Ages, an affinity for self-government has also developed among Italians. We have mentioned that the loyalties of the Italian are primarily to the nuclear family and then to the extended consanguine family. The loyalty to a foreign government has always been minimal among Italians. Consequently, Italians have long sought to establish institutions for freeing themselves. In the circumstance wherein the head of each family is a supreme head, any alliances made must of necessity guarantee the equality of the allies. In the early 1500s, democratic syndicates began to form among family heads in the Italian states. In the following 300 years, an ideology of freedom seems to have developed that culminated in the liberation and ultimate unification of Italy. In the process, institutions that guaranteed the freedom of individual family members arose, and family institutions for protection against the vagaries of arbitrary rulers also arose. Vico refers to an institution as *cosa.* Thus, what has recently been called the association of Cosa Nostra in America is more properly understood as a kind of family institution. Thus, *cosa nostra,* our institution, association, or club, must be seen as denoting the reasonable and customary right order of things. For Vico, the family itself is described as a *cosa umane,* a human institution.[16]

Thus, two contradictory elements seem to have developed. On one hand, a cultural norm demanding a strong and powerful patriarch exists, and on the other hand, a cultural norm emphasizing freedom appears. If we accept the anthropological law that cultures are integrated, we must seek an explanation for this paradox. These discontinuities are integrated in social behavior. In the family, the father rules according to ideals and law. However, the ideals are established by the family, and the law is what is taken by the members of the family as being the right thing to do.

The traditional affiliation of Italians with Roman Catholicism serves to strengthen the authority of the father in the family.[17] Further, the idealism of Roman Catholicism serves functionally to maintain the idealism of the family itself. The law of the Roman Catholic Church is styled after Roman law and in this respect is seen to be suitable for Italians. Thus, the Latin words for the Code of Canon Law are *Codex Canonici Iuris.* The Latin word *Iuris* is translated into Italian as *diritto,* which may be translated into English as the customary right thing. Thus, the law is neither absolute, unchanging, or eternal, but rather it is seen as being vital, evolutionary, and changeable according to the consciences of men.

Over the ages the distinction between the esteem associated with dignity and the esteem associated with prestige seems to have been lost. The dignity of the *mater familias* has been replaced by the prestige of the nourishing mother. The conception and bearing of children has traditionally been thought of as a sacred creative process that merits the mother prestige and other advantages, including the feeling of possessing a rich treasure. Maternal possessiveness and the care of the child has in the past been symbolically extended by the activities of caring for the home and of elaborate preparation of meals. Insofar as the mother possesses those whom she feeds, she has power over them.

These notions can now be integrated by way of recapitulation. Briefly, authority, legitimized by custom, is the power to command obedience. Power, inherited or acquired through ownership, brings prestige. The Madonna, the most prestigious of all women, bore and fed the Christ-child, and commanded him to perform a miracle. The form of the command was not a verbal dictum. Instead it pointed out a need and a right act and was a confident expectation of the outcome.

Italian-Americans in the third generation and beyond tend not to exhibit these traditional patterns, but neither do Italians living in the north of Italy. The influence of industrialization and urbanization on fertility, residential mobility, occupational choice, class status, child rearing, and on other family behavior is evident in both groups. But the judgment that Italian-Americans are losing their ethnic identity and are assimilating American culture is oversimplified and perhaps even overstated. That view is based upon observation of only the most superficial levels of behavior. On another level, a retention and reinforcement of ethnic bonds seems to be evident. In Italian-American family authority patterns, the Italian patriarchy–"hidden" matriarchy pattern is often mistaken for an evolving egalitarian or matricentric pattern that reflects American culture. In many cases this is undoubtedly true. But in the region where this study was conducted, two dynamics seem to be operating. On one hand, Italian-Americans have learned to extend their sense of loyalty beyond the *campanilismo*, the village. Their successes, possible only in the United States, have taught them to trust the government and to enter into a kind of clientele relationship with it. In war and in peace, they have given service to their government. At the same time, a second dynamic was in process. The rejection and prejudice experienced by the first- and second-generation Italian-Americans in the larger community and in the Church led many to reject their family allegiance and their heritage in order to be Americanized. These became a traditionless and socially disorganized group of individuals. Others responded to the attempts at amalgamation by reinforcing their traditional values and their "Italianness." Out of the conflict of this second group with the American community, a modification of the lives of both parties was engendered [18] so that today, as Nathan Glazer and Daniel Patrick Moynihan concluded, the ethnic group is no longer a remnant of the past but a new social form.[19] Italian-Americans in the third generation and beyond, secure in their Americanism, seem to want, consciously or unconsciously, to color and enliven their Americanism with a kind of romanticized but real Italianness. Where the larger community accepts this, those who had previously rejected their heritage now seek to reestablish their former identity socially, if not yet psychologically.

Strong and cohesive family life, albeit more filicentric than before, is again becoming an ideal. But now, rather than being characterized as "foreign," this pattern is being supported by American suburban and middle-class culture. Once Italian-Americans migrate into suburbia their ecological and sociocultural characteristics can be explained in terms of a new dimension other than their history. Characteristics that would be described as familism, Italian style, in a south Italian village or an Italian-American urban ghetto are now attributable to factors that are more or less true of Americans in general once suburbanization becomes dominant. To the extent that suburbia is familistic, it is because it is middle class, and residences are owned by the nuclear family rather than rented. If patterns of segregation prevail in suburbia, they do so for both Italian and non-Italian alike. The class factor as well as the ethnic factor characterizes suburban, as against urban, segregation. Italian cuisine in an urban ghetto is a symbol of Italian-American familism. Italian cuisine in suburbia has no ethnic boundaries. Italian restaurants are not for Italian-Americans exclusively, just as Chinese restaurants attract a diversified clientele.

The Italian or Italian-American matriarch wields power in a village or urban setting for traditional familistic reasons. If she wields power in suburbia, she does so for reasons that are characteristic of the matricentric middle class in general. It must be noted, however, that there are significant differences between Italian-Americans of the middle and professional classes and Italian-Americans of the working class. The latter group, to the extent that it is familistic, urban, or suburban, can trace its familism more clearly to traditional roots than can the middle classes.

In an age of increasing ethnic and racial polarization in American society, it is not clear how secure the Italian-American family can be in its Americanism. The rapidity of social change is probably the explanation of why, up to very recently, the third-generation Italian (like the third generation of any immigrant group) could be reasonably secure in his Americanism. Obviously, the third-generation Italian-American is much more acculturated to overall American values and life styles than his parents or grandparents are. Nevertheless, in a context of polarization, a return to a romanticized ethnic identity is not necessarily a reaction to security in Americanism but possibly a reaction to insecurity. The sources of insecurity might lie in the polarization of American society already alluded to, in revival of ethnic jokes and anecdotes in which an Italian or Italian-American is the butt of the humor and in which ethnic stereotypes are accepted uncritically, in which suburban neighborhoods, the characteristics of which are really middle class, are labeled Italian. The reason for the latter is that outsiders judge by such peripheral clues as surnames and religious associations. One index of familism in its generic, rather than ethnic, sense is that entertaining and visiting done by the middle classes increasingly tends to be with friends, business associates, and other guests of diverse backgrounds whereas visiting done by the lower classes is still almost exclusively on a familistic basis. More specifically, the word familism is in itself misleading because familism for the third-generation Italian-American refers to the solidarity of the nuclear family rather than of the traditional extended family.

First- and second-generation Italian-Americans in urban ghettos are in effect "villagers" in that their familism is derived from their ethnic background. Third-generation Italian-Americans (middle class, suburban, and upward mobile) are familistic only to the degree that others in their class, regardless of ethnicity, may also be familistic. Filicentrism, when it begins to characterize the third-generation Italian-American family, is an extension of family patterns that already characterize middle-class suburbia in general. Third-generation Italian-Americans increasingly tend to become more acculturated to dominant American norms and less hyphenated. Thus if one yearns romantically or otherwise for renewed hyphenation, this may be interpreted as a reaction to polarization or a retreat from what by traditional standards might be called anomic.

Notes

1. Cf. the following listed in the Bibliography: nos. 26, 5, 6, 13, 22, 15, 3, 12, 19, and 21. These patterns are so generally recognized that specific footnote references are superfluous.

2. In addition to the works cited in note 1, I have used the following works: nos. 1, 4, 9, 10, 11, 17, 18, 24, and 26.

3. These interviews were conducted by the author as a pilot pretest in conjunction with a larger study currently being undertaken. A sample of working and professional, single and married men and women from the New York metropolitan area, whose ancestors were largely from various centers in southern Italy and Sicily, with a small number being from northern Italy, were interviewed. The interviews were direct and open-ended and were conducted informally. Respondents were asked to talk about decision-making in their own families and in their extended kinship groups.

4. De Coulanges, no. 7, p. 107.

5. Vico, no. 23, pp. 38–39; pp. 152–153.

6. De Coulanges, no. 7, p. 115. Cf. Vico, no. 23, p. 153; and Friedmann, no. 9, p. 104.

7. Moss and Cappannari, nos. 17 and 18.

8. Moss and Cappannari, no. 17, p. 25.

9. Banfield, no. 1, p. 122.

10. Friedmann, no. 9, p. 118.

11. Banfield, no. 1, p. 85.

12. Vico, no. 23, p. 151.

13. MacIver, no. 16, p. 22.

14. *Ibid.*, p. 16.

15. Linton, no. 14, p. 167.

16. Vico, no. 23, pp. xxxii and li.

17. Cf. Femminella, no. 8.

18. Ware, no. 24, p. 122.

19. Glazer and Moynihan, no. 11, p. 16.

Commentary: Ethnicity and the Family

As Francis X. Femminella has implied, the "melting pot" theory, when applied to the Italians, is simply not borne out. This is also true of the Greeks. Ethnic enclaves remain a viable force and both cultures continue to exert their patterns on the families of younger generations of Italians and Greeks.

The extant sociological literature seems to indicate that while Greeks have moved upward more rapidly than Italians, they have nevertheless retained a greater degree of ethnic identification than Italians in the same age and social grades. Further, Italian group identification seems to remain primarily religious, whereas Greek group identification involves the interaction between religious and ethnic variables. In the United States, if a Greek loses his religion, he loses his ethnic identity as well. However, if an Italian loses his ethnic identity, he is still likely to retain his religious identity.

Because Femminella lays special stress upon intergenerational relationships within the Italian family, it might be instructive to note that Greeks define the matrifocal role in parallel fashion to the Italians. Other important similarities would include the subordination of the nuclear family to the extended kinship unit, the acceptance of patriarchal norms strengthened by concepts of family honor and solidarity, and a commitment to parochial education.

Studies of American society have indicated that the authority of the male has been reduced in both the Italian and Greek cases because the dogmatic and the patriarchal norms are less adaptable to the more egalitarian American scene. The independence of the Greek and Italian mother has increased as the father's decision-making role has weakened. What is most interesting is that the male's peripheral status in these instances is due to entirely different causes than that of the Negro lower class male. Functionally speaking, the connotations of the term "matrifocal" differ from minority group to minority group.

For Italians, Greeks, and all other ethnic groups that have accommodated themselves to the American scene, the process of acculturation or Americanization is present to a significant degree, especially in the third generation. Our intention is not to suggest that the differences between any two ethnic groups outweigh the similarities, because Americanization is always a matter of degree. The subculture cannot avoid being influenced by the dominant culture. However, Femminella's concern is largely with intergenerational problems and adjustments of the Italian family where first and second generations share the household and, therefore, have a partial insulation against these processes of acculturation. By the time the immigrant's family reaches adulthood in the third generation, there are fewer obstacles to the process of assimilation. However, recent studies by Seymour

Leventman and Judith Kramer, as well as the pioneer study by Louis Wirth (The Ghetto, *1928*), *indicate that segregation as a barrier to assimilation may still continue, but for voluntary reasons. Although segregation always has its voluntary cultural as well as its compulsory aspects, in the case of middle-class suburban Jews the voluntary basis for segregation tends to become dominant. One must realize, however, that (subjectively speaking) voluntary segregation may be a rationalization of a communal situation where there are elements of compulsion. In addition, we suggest that what is true of middle-class and suburban Jews may be true, to varying degrees, of Italians and Greeks.*

Bibliography

1. Banfield, Edward C. *The Moral Basis of a Backward Society.* New York: Free Press, 1958.
2. Bloch, Marc. *Feudal Society.* L. A. Manyon (tr.). Phoenix ed. 2 vols. Chicago: University of Chicago Press, 1964.
3. Campisi, Paul J. "Ethnic Family Patterns: The Italian Family in the United States," *American Journal of Sociology*, 53 (May 1948), 443–449.
4. Carlyle, Margaret. *The Awakening of Southern Italy.* London: Oxford University Press, 1962.
5. Child, Irvin L. *Italian or American? The Second Generation in Conflict.* New Haven, Conn.: Yale University Press, 1943.
6. Covello, Leonard. "The Social Background of the Italo-American School Child," unpublished Ph.D. dissertation, New York University, 1944.
7. De Coulanges, Fustel. *The Ancient City.* Anchor Book Edition. Garden City, N. Y.: Doubleday (n.d.). Originally published in 1864. English translation by William Small published in 1878.
8. Femminella, Francis X. "The Impact of Italian Migration and American Catholicism," *American Catholic Sociological Review*, 22 (Fall 1961), 233–241.
9. Friedmann, Frederick, G. *The Hoe and the Book: An Italian Experiment in Community Development.* Ithaca, N. Y.: Cornell University Press, 1960.
10. Gans, Herbert J. *The Urban Villagers Group and Class in the Life of Italian-Americans.* New York: Free Press, 1962.
11. Glazer, Nathan, and Daniel Patrick Moynihan. *Beyond the Melting Pot.* Cambridge, Mass.: The M.I.T. Press and Harvard University Press, 1963.
12. Ianni, Francis A. J. "The Italo-American Teenager," *The Annals*, 338 (November 1961), 70–78.
13. Lieberson, Stanley. *Ethnic Patterns in American Cities.* New York: Free Press, 1963.
14. Linton, Ralph. "Women in the Family," in M. B. Sussman, ed. *Sourcebook on Marriage and the Family.* 2nd ed. Boston: Houghton Mifflin, 1963, pp. 167–173.
15. Lolli, G. E. Serianni, G. M. Golder, and P. Luzzatto-Fegiz. *Alcohol in Italian Culture.* New York: Free Press; and New Haven, Conn.: Yale Center of Alcohol Studies, 1958.
16. MacIver, Robert M. *The Web of Government.* New York: Macmillan, 1947.
17. Moss, L. W. and S. C. Cappannari. "Patterns of Kinship, Comparaggio and Community in a South Italian Village," *Anthropological Quarterly*, 33 (January 1960), 24–32.

18. ———. "Estate and Class in a South Italian Hill Village," *American Anthropologist,* 64 (April 1962), 287–300.
19. Musmanno, Michael A. *The Story of the Italians in America.* Garden City, N. Y.: Doubleday, 1965.
20. Sforza, Count Carlo. *Italy and the Italians.* E. Hutton (tr.). New York: Dutton, 1949.
21. Sondern, Frederick, Jr. *Brotherhood of Evil: The Mafia.* New York: Farrar, Straus and Cudahy, 1959.
22. Strodtbeck, Fred L. "Family Interaction, Values and Achievement," in D. C. McClelland, A. L. Baldwin, U. Bronfenbrenner, and F. L. Strodtbeck, eds. *Talent and Society.* Princeton, N.J.: Van Nostrand, 1958, pp. 139–194.
23. Vico, Giambattista. *The New Science of Giambattista Vico.* T. G. Bergin and M. H. Fisch (trs.). Garden City, N.Y.: Doubleday, 1961.
24. Ware, Caroline F. "The Breakdown of Ethnic Solidarity: The Case of the Italian in Greenwich Village," in H. D. Stein and R. A. Cloward eds., *Social Perspectives on Behavior.* New York: Free Press, 1958, pp. 114–138.
25. Warner, W. Lloyd and L. Srole. *The Social Systems of American Ethnic Groups.* New Haven, Conn.: Yale University Press, 1945.
26. Whyte, William F. *Street Corner Society, The Social Structure of an Italian Slum.* Enlarged ed. Chicago: University of Chicago Press, 1955.
27. Zorbaugh, Harvey. *The Gold Coast and the Slum.* Chicago: University of Chicago Press, 1929.

7

INTERGENERATIONAL TENSIONS AND EXTENDED FAMILY STRUCTURES IN AFRICA[1]

ROBERT A. LE VINE

A Western observer of extended family organization in non-Western societies is likely to be impressed initially with its socially beneficial aspects. By contrast with how little a Western individual may rely on his family and kinship relations, the mutual dependence among kinsmen in many non-Western societies is indeed impressive. The extended family can be seen as providing care for the aged, the infirm, and the unemployed (thus obviating the need for public assistance to such persons); facilitating the redistribution of wealth from the economically privileged to their less fortunate kinsmen; and making each individual feel secure in the knowledge that he will not face the adversities of life alone. The author believes it is true not only that extended family relations have these beneficial functions in many societies of Africa and Asia, but also that their role is frequently indispensable at the level of economic and institutional development presently obtained in those areas.

A growing body of anthropological evidence and anecdotal material indicates that, whatever the gains to society from extended family organization, it is often accompanied by manifestations of

Robert A. Le Vine, "Intergenerational Tensions and Extended Family Structures in Africa," from Social Structure and the Family: Generational Relations, *Ethel Shanas & Gordon F. Streib, Editors,* © 1965. *Reprinted by permission of Prentice-Hall, Inc., Englewood Cliffs, New Jersey.*

fear and hostility within its cohesive groupings. We hear of the frequency of suicide among the desperate young married women of traditional China seeking to escape from their tyrannical mothers-in-law. From North India it is reported that young wives develop hysterical seizures when marital obligations force their return to residence with their husbands' families. Assassins are hired to help settle internal family quarrels in Egyptian villages. Fraternal tensions within domestic groups are extremely widespread from China to West Africa, and in Africa the prevalence of polygyny results in divisive quarrels between the paternally connected sons of different mothers. Accusations of witchcraft and sorcery—a common medium for the expression of hostility—tend to be concentrated among kinsmen in East African societies. Parricide is a marked phenomenon in at least one Uganda tribe. The antagonisms between father and son in societies with patrilineal inheritance and descent, and between mother's brother and sister's son in those of matrilineal inheritance and descent, have been repeatedly documented in African studies. The burden of such disparate fragments of data is that the very structures which entail kinship obligations beyond the nuclear family engender antagonisms which may ultimately be registered in homicide, suicide, litigation, and other forms of interpersonal conflict.

Concerning the societies of sub-Saharan Africa, the author proposes to discuss three questions which have relevance to this symposium on intergenerational relations: (1) What aspects of extended family structure generate intergenerational tensions? (2) What institutionalized mechanisms exist to "manage" these tensions, that is, to minimize their socially disruptive effects? (3) How have intergenerational relations been affected by or reacted to economic and educational changes stemming from Western contact?

Typical Tensions in African Extended Family Structures

To understand intergenerational tensions in Africa, one must bear in mind the organizational context within which such tensions arise in African extended family structures. By the latter we refer to domestic groups in which adults of two or more generations reside in close proximity and to groupings such as a minimal lineage which is based on a principle of descent and which may or may not coincide with a domestic residential group. In virtually every agricultural society of Africa there can be found some multigenerational primary group, based on kinship or a combination of kinship and residence, which represents the primary sphere of mutual dependence and common interest of its members. (In some societies an individual is a member of several such groups, with the important societal consequences that Fortes, Gluckman, and others have been at such pains to point out.) Regardless of whether this primary group is residentially concentrated, it is a multifunctional unit, usually involving joint property-holding, subsistence activities, judicial action, and ritual. These important functions, most frequently vested in extrafamilial institutions in industrial societies, require a high degree of formal organization within the African extended family structures.

The formal organization of the extended family unit involves clearly defined positions of leadership, which are invested with the power to make authoritative decisions concerning the functions of the group, that is, decisions concerning property, the allocation of economic resources, labor, the settlement of disputes, the application of sanctions to offenders, and religious activities. The occupant of a leadership position, often elderly, may have considerable common power within the group and a highly visible and respected position as its representative vis-à-vis other groups. Thus social prestige combined with the intrinsic rewards of the exercise of authority serve to make the assumption of a leadership position attractive to eligible members of an extended family group. If there is no rigid rule of succession such as primogeniture, considerations of ability, loyalty, or wealth then play a part in the selection of a successor to the leader, and the position may become the object of competition among group members. The competition may begin long before the position is vacant, and factions may form around each of the pretenders. If, on the other hand, there is a rigid rule of succession to leadership, overt competition may be eliminated, but tensions nevertheless can arise, primarily because the term of office is not definite. In many African societies the leader of an extended family group remains in office until his death. He may suspect his successor of wishing to hasten his death, and this may be more or less true. Thus the knowledge that the advancement of one is dependent upon the demise of the other causes the relations between the leader and his prospective successor to be strained, despite the high degree of respect paid to the aged.

We should not assume that these potentialities for tension over succession to leadership positions are made manifest in all or even the majority of African family situations. The tensions are widely recognized, however, and are likely to be found most conspicuously in those extended family units whose leadership positions carry with them political authority outside the family or considerable wealth.

A major task of extended family units is the allocation and transfer of those economic resources in which the group as a whole has at least residual rights and which may be jointly exploited or shared on some commonly accepted basis. The importance of this function to each individual member can hardly be overemphasized, for his livelihood and life chances are often derived entirely from his access to family property. In these agricultural societies men often spend their entire lives cultivating land and/or herding livestock which they received by virtue of their descent group membership and which will be transferred by that group upon their deaths.

In addition to inherited property, descent group membership often confers rights of usufruct for commonly held pastures, sources of water, and other economic resources. Furthermore, a man is often dependent on his kin group to raise the livestock, cash, or other goods necessary to pay his brideprice, and in the polygynous societies of Africa this is not simply a one-time occurrence in his lifetime. Unless there are extremely rigid rules for the inheritance of property upon death, its transfer before death (in case of brideprice), the sharing of income from the sale or exploitation of group property, and the sharing of usufruct rights—opportunities for competition and conflict within the descent group are likely to abound. The decision-makers of the group, in performing their allocative functions, are constantly confronted with the possibility that one member will claim to have been deprived of his rightful share and another member will attempt to gain more than his rightful share.

Where an elder may name his own heir or favor some heirs over others in the distribution of property, there is the expectable competition for his favor. Even where the rules of inheritance are rigid, inequalities within the group lead to resentments, and cases come up which are not adequately covered by the body of unwritten rules. These potentialities for conflict over economic resources exist within small-scale domestic groups as well as within corporate property-holding descent groups, although the exact nature of the conflicts vary according to the role of each unit in the allocative system.

In identifying points of tension in these extended family structures, we have been describing them almost as one would describe any formal organization in which there are positions of leadership and in which desired resources are shared, allocated, and transferred among the members. We have done this to emphasize the features which these kinship groupings have in common with any organization in which the transfer of power and property as the membership changes over time provides occasions for competition and conflict. However, as kinship groups, African extended family structures have other features which are not found in nonfamilial occupational and associational groups. One distinctive feature is that membership and experience in the organization begins at birth. Inevitably, at least some of one's fellow members are persons one has known from earliest childhood. This affords opportunities to base group solidarity on early affective ties, which may be very close, but it also means that the resentments and rivalries engendered in the early years may affect performance in adult relationships within the group. The emotional intensity of such long-standing hostilities may be greater than that characterizing the competition of strangers. While suppressed in everyday behavior, these grudges formed in childhood may flare into the open when a crisis occurs, pitting brother against brother, son against father, or nephew against uncle.

Another feature of these kinship groups not found in other formal organizations is the importance of sexuality and close affective bonds based on sexual unions. The struggle for power and property is complicated by matters relating to fertility, sexual possessiveness and jealousy, and incest taboos. Some of these matters are governed by rules which members may be tempted to violate; others (like fertility or sexual potency) may be matters of chance as far as group regulation goes, but which create inequalities and humiliations within the group which lead to resentments and jealousy.

We need not elaborate further on how a family group is different from a nonfamilial group. The point of this discussion is that the African extended family structures carry out economic and quasi-political functions in an atmosphere which is charged with emotions derived from childhood experience and sexual concerns. The tensions to be observed in such groups, then, result not only from conflicts over power and property, but from the fact that economic cooperation and authority relations are carried on between adults who have had intimate childhood contact and who are in some way concerned with each other's sexual behavior.

With this general organizational context in mind, we can proceed to the dyadic relationships in which intrafamilial tensions typically appear, and thus gain an impression of the sources of intergenerational tension. Since the points of tension vary with the type of kinship system and structural unit, we shall concentrate the discussion on one structural type, the patrilocal, polygynous extended family, which is probably most widespread in sub-Saharan Africa. By the "patrilocal, polygynous extended family" we refer to a domestic grouping typically comprised of at least one man of the senior generation with his several wives, his married sons and their wives and unmarried children, and other persons related by blood to one of the senior men. These others may be an aged parent of a senior man or a divorced or widowed sister. Such a family unit is basically a localized patrilineage plus the wives and unmarried daughters of the lineage members. In most areas each married woman and each adult male has a hut (or in some urban groups, a room) of her or his own. Groups of uterine brothers tend to form cohesive subgroups as they grow to maturity.

Two words of warning must be offered concerning the generality of the picture of this structural type being presented here. First of all, even in societies where it is most frequent, many persons will be found living in different family arrangements. This is not simply because of factors which make reality deviate from the ideal, but because the type as presented here actually represents only one phase in the developmental cycle of domestic groups in such societies.[2] These cycles also vary from one group to another, but frequently there is a formative phase in which the second generation has not yet been married and a later phase of dissolution in which the older generation has died off and the adult brothers have not yet set up their separate domestic groups. Secondly, patrilocal, polygynous extended families vary widely from one African society to another on so many characteristics—size, solidarity, internal ranking patterns, relation to wider kin groupings—that the type must be considered an abstraction of a few elements from a diverse set of instances.

The following dyadic relationships represent the most typical points of strain in patrilocal, polygynous extended families as found in sub-Saharan Africa.

Father-Son

Here the tension often centers about the father's fear that the son, particularly the eldest, will wish to hasten his death in order to gain independence from the old man or replace him as head of the family. In societies where the father is expected to transfer goods to his son for brideprice payment, conflict may arise over the father's delaying the transfer and/or the son's appropriating the goods in advance of formal permission from the father. The sexual rights of father and son also present problems: where the father exercises authoritarian domination over his sons, the danger exists that he will commit adultery with their wives, and this danger is recognized in many African groups. On the other hand, when the father is a senescent polygynist, wealthy enough to acquire numerous young wives but not virile enough to keep them sexually satisfied, the danger exists that the sons will commit adultery with his younger wives. In some groups—where the sons inherit these wives upon the father's death—this may be overlooked when the father is very old, but in others it is a real source of conflict. Illustrative material on father-son conflict is presented below.

Co-Wife

The polygynous situation is fraught with potentialities for conflict. If the husband bestows more attention or material benefits on one wife or the other or if he favors one's child over another, resentment may turn into open hostility. Even if the husband acts equitably, the sterility of a woman who has a fecund co-wife, or the failure in school of a child when the co-wife's child proves brilliant, can lead to conflict. The more the co-wife relationship involves uncertainty as to the present or future distribution of advantages among the wives and their children, the more likely that hostility will result. The hostility reaches a peak where the wives' own efforts play a part in determining how much their sons will inherit from the father. Factors which diminish conflict between co-wives are hierarchical status relations (either through the appointment of one chief wife who dominates or through a rank ordering of all), a large age differential, and the residential separation of the wives. The hostility among co-wives is frequently expressed as accusations of witchcraft and sorcery.[3]

Brother-Brother

In polygynous families it is most common for half-brothers to feel competitive and somewhat hostile to one another, while uterine brothers form a cohesive and mutually loyal group. This represents the continuation of co-wife hostility in the second generation of the family, but it may also reflect the contemporary situation in which the young men find themselves. If their mothers have been mutually hostile for a long time, their respective sons are likely to have taken over the feelings of hostility of their mothers, toward whom they feel protective and loyal. However, in some societies, uterine brothers are classed together as a single unit for purposes of inheritance, so that they have a mutual interest in fighting for a larger share for their subgroup. The sons in patrilocal, polygynous families are responsible for the care of their own mother in the latter's old age, and the recognition of this, together with the intense loyalty which sons in these families develop toward their mother, often makes them resentful of any ill treatment which she might receive from their father as she grows older. As an example of such ill treatment, the father may take young wives and seek to favor them over the older. Among the Gusii of Kenya, the author observed a situation in which a man with three wives had so antagonized his sons by the oldest wife by favoritism shown toward the youngest wife that when he sought to modernize his farm, involving moving the hut of the oldest wife but not depriving her of any economic benefits, these sons assaulted him.

More frequently, however, the sons display their loyalty to their mother in hostility to their half-brothers over the allocation of resources. Actually, uterine brothers may also enter into conflict with one another over property, especially where the family was monogamous, where no living heirs remain from the co-wives, or where the division of resources between uterine segments has already taken place and is no longer at issue. The generational equivalence of siblings makes brothers in a patrilineal inheritance system natural competitors for property and power, and if they are not strictly ranked, conflict may result.

Mother-in-law—Daughter-in-law

In the patrilocal family, the woman comes as a relative stranger to reside with her husband's family; in many African groups, she comes from people who are regarded as enemies by her husband's kinsmen. This situation occasions a certain measure of mutual suspicion at the outset of the marriage as well as considerable fear on the part of the bride. She usually is in closest contact with her mother-in-law, who inducts her into the women's life in the family and directs her work in the home, fields, and markets. If a woman does not get along well in her husband's family and wants to break off the marriage, she is likely to claim that her mother-in-law does not treat her well and that the old woman practices witchcraft. In some cases the accusation of witchcraft appears to be fabricated by the bride in order to arouse the sympathy of her own kinsmen so that they will support her efforts to get out of the marriage, but there can be no doubt that other young women are genuinely afraid of their mothers-in-law and suspect them of evil doings.

We should note, however, that the tension between a woman and her mother-in-law is primarily a phenomenon of the first year or so of marriage. If it is intense, the marriage will be broken off; otherwise, the wife is likely to be accustomed to and to become friendly with her husband's mother. The situation in African societies is quite different from that in areas like North India where the mother-in-law's extreme domination is a strain on her son's wives for many years. In the latter situation all the women are confined in the house and its adjacent courtyards, attending exclusively to domestic tasks under the supervision of the mother-in-law. In most African groups, a wife not only has her own hut but also becomes quickly autonomous in her economic activity, cultivating fields allotted to her or trading on her own in the market. She may serve her mother-in-law and relieve the older woman of many onerous tasks, but the wife's separate house, independent occupation, and freedom to travel on her own prevent her from being excessively dominated. Thus the resentment and desperation common among the younger wives in the extended families of India and other parts of Asia are rare in African societies. The author does not consider the mother-in-law–daughter-in-law relationship a point of great strain in African extended families.

From this review of tensions in dyadic relationships within the patrilocal, polygynous extended family, it is apparent that the major point of *intergenerational* strain is the father-son relationship. The sources of this strain are as follows: (1) Both father and son recognize that the latter will replace the former upon his

death in at least some of his roles (that is, as family head, posses-
sor of economic resources, sexual partner to the wives), and further that the adult son is capable of doing so immediately. This
raises the possibility that as the father becomes senile, his sons
will presume upon their inheritance, in contradiction to the patriarchal norms of the extended family, and contrary to the deepest
wishes of the father. (2) The authoritarian father may be
tempted to deprive his adult sons of the prerogatives they have as
husbands and fathers in their own right, especially by having sexual relations with their wives. (3) Uterine brothers in a polygynous family form a faction with their mother and may rise to her
defense against the father when they believe the latter is maltreat-
ing her. As this last point makes clear, any severe conflict within
an extended family of this type is likely to be translated into
father-son conflict because jural authority in the family is concentrated primarily in the father and secondarily in his sons and
eventual heirs.

Illustrative Cases of Intergenerational Tension

The two ethnographic cases which follow are examples of intergenerational tension which is overt and relatively unregulated. In
both cases the anthropologist reporting the facts has identified an
alleged structural source of tension to explain the manifestation of
hostility across generations in a family group.

In an analysis of homicide (99 cases) and suicide (68 cases)
among the Gisu of Uganda, La Fontaine found evidence to indicate that intergenerational homicide among men was more common than intragenerational killing, and that the age group most
heavily represented among the male killers—roughly 25–35—was
the same as that most heavily represented among the male sui-
cides.[4]

The ethnographer's analysis of the homicide situation is as
follows:

. . . [W]here the exact relationship is known, there are eleven fathers
and father's brothers killed to only five brothers. In two cases in which
the father's brother was killed, the father was dead and the victim of
the murder stood *in loco parentis* to the murderer. Three of the brothers are elder brothers and hence in a position of some authority vis-à-
vis the murderers. As in most patrilineal societies, a man is subject to
the authority of his senior male agnates [patrilineal kinsmen] who also

control property, land, and cattle, which is the means by which status is acquired in this society. Identity of interest, mutual loyalty and cooperation between agnates are continually stressed, and the fact that these very mutual interests may feed personal rivalries and jealousies for which there exists no outlet, means that the actual relationship is very different from the ideal. Conflict results in a greater strain on the junior party because legal and jural rights secure the position of the senior, whereas ideals of what is just are the only safeguards of the junior man's claims. Thus a "good" father in Gisu society provides his son with land and the cattle with which to obtain a wife, but the son cannot sue his father if he fails in his duty. He can extort what he considers his due only by resorting to means which are socially disapproved.[5]

. . . [H]omicide is primarily committed by young men . . .

The peak period appears to be between 25 and 30. The ethnographic facts show that this is a difficult period for Gisu men. By this time they have achieved adulthood, by undergoing the rites of circumcision. There being no further gradation of men into formal age sets, a young circumcised man has the same formal status, in the society as a whole, as his seniors. After circumcision, a man is entitled to the privileges of an adult male and the chief of these is the headship of his own family. In order to set up his own family, a man must have his own land and cattle, and it is his father's duty to provide him with them. However, the possession of large herds and much land mean high status in the community. An old man who is still vigorous is reluctant to relinquish to his son what he has acquired. To this rivalry is added another element which makes for conflict: although a man does achieve a change in ascribed status by passing through the *rite de passage* of circumcision, the structure of authority within the social group does not change. He is still subordinate to the authority of his seniors. But the inequality in terms of formal status that formerly supported this inequality of power no longer exists. Not only has the formal position changed but the newly-circumcised man begins to demand actual equality. Conflict between a man and his father is increased.[6]

La Fontaine adduces approximately the same factors to account for the high suicide rate of young men who are between the age of circumcision (at 16–20) and age 40. For a man in this age group, the disparity between his theoretical status as an independent adult equal to his father and his actual lack of access to the material advantages which would give him *de facto* independence is seen as frustrating and as resulting in suicide, as other legitimate outlets for aggression have been blocked. The ethnographer implies that some men are not equal to the struggle with their elders required to establish themselves socially, and that they are more likely to give up during this post-circumcision period than at any other time.

The second case involves a pair of *matrilineal* societies in the Nuba hills of the Sudan. As described in a well-known study by Nadel, the Korongo and Mesakin have many cultural similarities, including the pattern of the child of six or seven years of age moving from his father's house to that of his mother's brother, whose property (primarily cattle) he will eventually inherit.[7] The life of men from adolescence onwards revolves about a formal division into age classes, each of which is characterized by the right to engage in particular sporting contests—light wrestling, strenuous wrestling, and spearfighting—which serve as exhibitions of masculinity. The stage of strenuous wrestling marks the peak of physical vigor, while spearfighting is regarded as appropriate to the physical decline believed to be brought about by sexual relations, after which men must give up these exhibitions of masculinity altogether. When a boy who has reached puberty engages in his first sporting contest, his mother's brother ceremoniously bestows upon him an important gift—an animal from the uncle's herd—which Nadel refers to as the "anticipated inheritance," since the vernacular word for inheritance is applied to it.

Concerning divergences between the two groups, Nadel tells us that the Korongo "have no witchcraft beliefs at all" (which is probably an exaggeration), while the Mesakin are obsessed by fears of witchcraft:

Mesakin witchcraft is believed to operate only between maternal kin, especially between a mother's brother and a sister's son, the older relative assailing the younger. Mesakin witchcraft further operates only if there is a reason . . . and the latter is almost invariably a quarrel over the "anticipated inheritance" . . .[8]

Although the mother's brother in Korongo never refuses to give this special gift (though he may postpone it), his Mesakin counterpart always refuses to give it at first, and it often has to be taken by force, as it cannot legitimately be postponed. "Quarrels over it between the youth and his mother's brother are the rule; and if by any chance the former falls ill, dies, or suffers some other misfortune, the older man is invariably suspected of having employed witchcraft."[9]

To explain this difference in intergenerational conflict between the two groups, Nadel looks to divergences in their organization of social age. The Korongo have a total of six age grades, four of which involve the above mentioned physical contests, from which men withdraw gradually around the age of thirty, after having tapered off their participation and their visits to the young men's cattle camps. The sixth age grade begins around fifty with actual physical decline. In Mesakin, there are only three age grades of males: prepubertal, that of youths before parenthood (approximately 13–25), and that of men from parenthood until death. All of the athletic contests are concentrated in the 13–25 age grade, and a man must abruptly withdraw from them as well as from life in the cattle camps when he leaves this age grade. Nadel regards the uncle's gift to his sister's son as a reminder to the older man of his own withdrawal from the life of sport, in both societies. Among the Korongo, however, withdrawal comes later, social aging is in any event gradual, and the presentation of the gift can be postponed. The Korongo uncle is thereby cushioned against the implications which the anticipated inheritance has for the decline of his own masculinity. The Mesakin uncle, however, who is not prepared for his withdrawal and consignment to old man status, must go through it earlier and more abruptly, and he may not postpone the presentation of the gift to his newly active nephew. His resentment concerning his transition to the status of someone whose masculine vigor is being dissipated by sexual activity is vented upon his nephew—who replaces him in the life of the cattle camps—in the form of an illegitimate refusal to give the anticipated inheritance. The maternal uncle is openly jealous of his nephew, and his ungracious behavior makes him a likely target for accusations of witchcraft.

Both of these ethnographic cases of intergenerational tension involve an older man reluctant to give up status-conferring advantages to his legitimate heir at a time when it is socially required that he do so. In the Gisu case, traditional regulations favor the older man, and it is the younger who resorts to illegitimate aggression. In Mesakin, however, society is on the side of the younger man claiming his due, and it is the elder whose resentment at being pushed out of active life leads him to be hostile in an unacceptable manner. This fear by a man of symbolic replacement by his sister's son in a matrilineal society is so similar to the fear of fathers vis-à-vis their sons in patrilineal societies that it can be taken as evidence that intergenerational conflicts in African kinship systems tend to follow lines of inheritance and succession.

The best published example of overt recognition of intergenerational tension in a patrilineal society is the report by Fortes on the Tallensi of northern Ghana.[10] The most pertinent passages follow:

[A son] does eventually take the place of his father in the life of the community and could be suspected of wanting to hurry on the day when this will happen. His desire for independence is liable . . . to run counter to his father's plans and demands. Every advance in his social and economic development might be interpreted as an added threat to his father's dominance. He will not be his own master until he has no father. . . . Tallensi themselves make no bones about the matter. "Your oldest son is your rival," . . . the men say bluntly. . . . "Look at my oldest son," an elder once said to me. "He would not care if I should die tomorrow. Then he would inherit all my possessions. . . ."

This candor in fathers is not matched by their sons, who never admit the rivalry. . . . This is as one might expect, for it is the fathers who feel the threat to their dominance; and they feel it the more strongly as they grow older and their powers decline. . . .[11]

Tallensi explain the rivalry between father and son by means of the mystical concept of the *Yin* or personal Destiny. There is, they say, an inborn antagonism between the *Yin* of a father and the *Yin* of his eldest son. While the son is still young his *Yin* is weak, but as he grows older his *Yin* grows more powerful and wants to make him master of his own affairs. The son's *Yin* wants to destroy the father's *Yin;* but the father's *Yin* desires the father to live and be well and remain master of the house. . . . Therefore it will try to destroy the son's *Yin,* and if it is the stronger *Yin* it will cause misfortune and perhaps death to the son.[12]

The idea that a father might anticipate the rivalry of his son and want to kill him is not limited to the Tallensi in West Africa. For example, Melville and Frances Herskovits report that Dahomean folklore contains many tales of men who killed their sons to prevent being overthrown by them.[13]

The Control of Intergenerational Tension

In one of his B.B.C. lectures on conflict in Africa, Max Gluckman noted:

. . . [T]here is this constant general difference between African domestic relations and our own—in Africa there is a whole series of rules to regularize relations within the family. And it is striking that while on the one hand the members of the family are brought together by these rules, on the other hand they are forced apart and estranged from one another.[14]

The thesis of this section is that customary patterns of estrangement—ranging from formality of interaction to outright avoidance—operate in some African societies to prevent intergenerational tensions of the type described above from disrupting the functioning of extended family groups. In other words, these patterns are cultural reactions to the tensions, that is, institutionalized attempts to avert conflict by minimizing emotional intensity in those dyadic relationships which are fraught with tension and in which open hostility would prove disruptive to group functioning. This hypothesis contrasts with, though it does not necessarily contradict that of Gluckman, who asserts that patterns of intrafamilial estrangement have as their primary function the integration of the individual in the extrafamilial social order and the consequent strengthening of total-society cohesion.

Some illustrations are needed to indicate the strength and elaboration of intergenerational avoidance patterns in African societies. Probably the most striking example is a custom which is found in a variety of forms among many groups involving millions of people in the Western Sudan, which is on the southern margins of the Sahara Desert in West Africa. This is the custom of avoidance of the first child, which has been described by Fortes for the Tallensi, by Skinner for the Mossi of the Voltaic Republic (north of Ghana),[15] and by Smith for the Hausa of Northern Nigeria.[16] The avoidance takes a different form in different tribes.

The Hausa taboo on social intercourse between a first-born and his parents is so strong initially that first-born children shortly after weaning are often sent to be raised by relatives, and only as adults can they have even the most restrained contact with their parents, taking care not to look them in the face. Tallensi first-born, on the other hand, are raised by their own parents but observe special taboos from the age of seven onwards, concerning eating with their father and touching his property, and these taboos are intensified for the first-born son as he becomes older. Soon after the time of his marriage, a first-born son and his father must not meet face to face in the gateway of their common homestead. Eventually, when he has children reaching adolescence, the Tallensi first-born son separates himself from his father by cutting a private gateway for himself in the family homestead.

Skinner's discussion of Mossi father-son avoidance illustrates the relation of this pattern to intergenerational tension. Although the first son is most likely to be a father's heir and successor, he is raised by his maternal relatives.

A first son does not return to his father's compound until he is past puberty, but does visit him from time to time. These visits are quite formal and from very early time the first son is taught to be circumspect with his father. He learns to efface himself before his father and not to seek attention from him even though he sees younger siblings playing with him. When the boy does return home he is made to live with other young men of the extended family either within the compound or in special young men's quarters outside the compound. . . .[17]

Mossi fathers are so sensitive about being eventually replaced by their sons that they often resent the boys' growth and development. The first son is the target of this fear and hostility because he is the one who will benefit most from the father's death. However, if the first son happens to die, then the son who is next in line becomes the subject of his father's uneasiness. Mossi men have been known to upbraid their sons for growing beards, the significance of which is seen in the fact that men do grow beards as a sign of mourning on the death of their father. . . . As a rule, Mossi fathers tend to avoid any situation in which their eldest sons may be compared with them. For example, a man and his grown son do not walk together for fear of the embarrassment which would be created if a stranger, not recognizing the age differential between them, greeted the son before he greeted the father.[18]

After his father's death, the eldest son must go through a very elaborate series of ceremonies aimed at demonstrating to the father's spirit that he did not usurp his father's property or have sexual relations with his father's wives during the old man's lifetime; these ceremonies are prerequisite to his actual inheritance. Skinner interprets the prohibitions, avoidances, and ritual proofs of good will imposed on the eldest son as safeguarding the continuity of the patrilineal family group from the potentially disruptive tension inherent in Mossi father-son relations. Similarly, Fortes (in an earlier analysis) interprets the Tallensi first-born taboos primarily in terms of avoiding the danger that a son will usurp his father's status in regard to procreation, property, and ritual relation to the ancestor spirits.[19] Although the existence of such taboos in other relationships indicates they may have other functions as well, they tend to be most intense between father and son, and it is there that their role in the management of intergenerational tension to preserve family functioning and continuity is most evident.

On the other side of Africa, in the Kenya highlands north and east of Lake Victoria, are a number of related peoples who also have intergenerational taboos, although of a different type. Among the Gusii, these prohibitions exist between a person and every kinsman of his parents' generation, although they are most intense for men in regard to their own fathers.[20] The relevant persons of the parents' generation are referred to by a name which indicates that one experiences sexual shame in their presence, and indeed Gusii define the relationships in terms of the avoidance of sexual discussion or bodily contact of any kind. A man may not shake hands with these parental kinsmen, although he does with persons of his own generation, and he may not sleep in the same house with them, bathe with them, or be seen naked by them, or witness the mating of animals jointly with them. He must also be generally deferential to them and not contradict them. The taboo on sexual talk is so strong that a man may not inform his own father that his wife is pregnant; it must be done through intermediaries. These taboos, like those in the Western Sudan, put the burden of responsibility on the younger man, and in addition give the father a powerful weapon for humbling his son through extreme embarrassment or worse: a father's curse involves the old man exposing and manipulating his genitals before his mortified son. However, the avoidance pattern does work both ways: a father may not enter his married son's house even though it is part of the homestead of which he is the head. Gusii fathers adhere to this so strictly that they will not enter a son's house to take out some chairs when guests arrive, even when there are no other chairs and there is no one else at home to fetch them. Father's brothers are allowed to enter one room in their nephew's house but must enter through an inconvenient opening from the cattle pen rather than through the main door.

These customs, which may appear to an outsider like bizarre ritual inconveniences, are taken by the Gusii themselves to be at the core of their morality, and though the Gusii are not very articulate about their significance, clearly these customs symbolically represent a mutual restraint which not only prevents the sons from sexual usurpation but also excludes the elders from the most private lives of their subordinate kinsmen. Unlike many other African peoples, Gusii are not allowed to inherit their father's widows, so that they attempt to eliminate any possibility for the occurrence of sexual jealousy between father and son. The writer's own interpretation of this is that the strict sexual morality of the Gusii would tend to make sexual jealousy a more disruptive area of father-son conflict than it would be in less restrictive societies, and thus intergenerational avoidance is more elaborated in this area. In African groups such as the Tallensi where prerogatives of ritual access to the ancestors are more important than they are for the Gusii, intergenerational avoidance is concomitantly more elaborately focussed about participation in ritual.

Thus African extended family structures appear to generate not only characteristic intergenerational tensions but also characteristic institutions for managing these tensions and avoiding disruption of group functioning. As the author has asserted elsewhere,[21] the co-wife hostility characteristic in certain types of African polygynous families is diminished in some societies by increasing the distance between the residences of the co-wives, thus reducing their opportunities for contact. Intergenerational avoidance also reduces opportunities for contact—and hence friction—between potentially hostile persons, but it also tends to stereotype and inhibit their interaction by setting up explicit rules which if adhered to will allow their necessary cooperation while by-passing their areas of potential conflict. Even where avoidances do not reach the peak of explicitness described herein, there is much formality of intergenerational interaction in African extended families. This formality is another way of increasing social and emotional distance between persons whose hostility would be disruptive to operation of the family group in the many areas of life which are not usually familial functions in Western societies.

We should note, nonetheless, that avoidance and its approximation in formality were not the only ways of managing intergenerational tension in traditional Africa. An extremely important way—which amounts to avoidance but is not *prescribed*—is the emigration of those youths who had most difficulties in getting along with their elders in the domestic group. Until recently, much of Africa was in a frontier condition, with abundant land open to anyone who would cultivate it. Even in societies that might be described as patrilocal, many sons did move out to new land, and this movement provided a safety valve for tensions in the family. In fact, some of the worst cases of unregulated father-son tension described in the ethnographic literature—that of the Gisu as described above and the Nyakyusa of southern Tanganyika as described by Gulliver[22]—have occurred in areas where land scarcity has rapidly become a serious problem in recent years. In those areas—particularly the Nyakyusa—sons could fend for themselves and did not have to depend on their fathers. In consequence, father-son relations, particularly concerning property, did not have to be as strictly regulated as in other African societies. Land scarcity has made sons highly dependent on their fathers (and father's brothers) for allocation of land, and this has aroused conflicts for which the family structure was unprepared institutionally. Thus it appears that emigration as a mechanism for the control of intergenerational tension is highly vulnerable to contraction in land areas available for new settlement.

Adaptation to New Conditions

The impact of changes introduced by Western contact on the relations between generations in African families merits more extensive analysis than can be given here. However, one modern consequence of the pattern of intergenerational relations described above must be mentioned. The estrangement involved in formality and/or avoidance between fathers and sons conditions an individual to view intimacy and obligation as quite separate modes of behavior, inhering in different relationships. A son grows up recognizing many obligations to his father but is distinctly not intimate with him, and to a lesser extent this emphasis on obligation as opposed to intimacy holds for many relationships in African extended families. Thus when the individual leaves home, becomes educated in Western schools, and enters the modern occupational system, his remoteness from his natal family, though diminishing his opportunities for intimacy with them even further, does little to diminish his obligation. In fact, as a relatively privileged member of an extended kinship group, he finds himself saddled with obligations to many members of the groups with whom he was not previously acquainted let alone intimate. The claims they press upon him must nevertheless be honored in some degree, and the individual tends to yield to these claims because he was trained to recognize obligation independent of intimacy, a point which many Westerners fail to understand.

Thus the residential dispersion of individuals for reasons of employment, and their alienation from their cultural origins through Western education, occur more rapidly than the dissolution of extended kinship obligations. In the transitional situation characteristic of the most rapidly developing parts of equatorial Africa, this results in a redistribution of income from the well-paid educated elite to their poorer kinsmen, and thus militates against the development of a rigidly organized class system. Furthermore, the emphasis on obligation rather than intimacy mitigates intergenerational conflict over differing cultural standards. The uneducated, rural parent whose successful Westernized son recognizes his duty to give financial aid to family members and to exert influence on their behalf, makes relatively little protest over the son's radically different way of life. In this sense, the educated elite may be said to buy their way out of cultural conflict with the older generation. If they fulfill their heavy kinship obligations, the educated are able to make a more drastic cultural transition with less intergenerational friction than we are used to seeing in our rapidly changing Western societies.

Notes

1. The writing of this paper was assisted by a Research Career Development Award granted by the National Institutes of Health and was carried out while the author was a Fellow of the Foundations' Fund for Research in Psychiatry.
2. See P. H. Gulliver and R. F. Gray, eds., *The Family Estate in Africa* (London: Routledge & Kegan Paul, Ltd., 1964).
3. See Robert A. LeVine, "Witchcraft and Co-Wife Proximity in Southwestern Kenya," *Ethnology*, I (January, 1962), 39–45.
4. Jean La Fontaine, "Homicide and Suicide among the Gisu," *African Homicide and Suicide*, Paul Bohannon, ed. (Princeton: Princeton University Press, 1960), pp. 94–129. Copyright Princeton University Press.
5. *Ibid.*, pp. 107–108.
6. *Ibid.*, pp. 108–109.
7. Siegfried F. Nadel, "Witchcraft in Four African Societies: An Essay in Comparison," *American Anthropologist*, LIV (January, 1952), 18–29.
8. *Ibid.*, p. 23.
9. *Ibid.*
10. Meyer Fortes, *The Web of Kinship among the Tallensi* (London: Oxford University Press, 1949).
11. *Ibid.*, p. 225.
12. *Ibid.*, pp. 226–27.
13. Melville and Frances Herskovits, "Sibling Rivalry, the Oedipus Complex, and Myth," *Journal of American Folklore*, LXXI (January, 1958), 1–15.
14. Max Gluckman, *Custom and Conflict in Africa* (New York: Free Press of Glencoe, Inc., 1955), p. 55.
15. Elliott Skinner, "Intergenerational Conflict among the Mossi: Father and Son," *Journal of Conflict Resolution*, V (March, 1961), pp. 55–60.

16. M. G. Smith, "Introduction," *Baba of Karo*, M. F. Smith, ed. (New York: Philosophical Library, 1955).

17. Elliott Skinner, "Intergenerational Conflict among the Mossi: Father and Son," *op. cit.*, p. 56.

18. *Ibid.*, p. 57.

19. Fortes, *The Web of Kinship among the Tallensi, op. cit.*, pp. 225–27.

20. See Robert A. LeVine and Barbara B. LeVine, "Nyansongo: A Gusii Community in Kenya," *Six Cultures: Studies of Child Rearing*, Beatrice B. Whiting, ed. (New York: John Wiley & Sons, Inc., 1963, pp. 115–202.

21. Robert A. LeVine, "Witchcraft and Co-Wife Proximity in Southwestern Kenya," *op. cit.*

22. P. H. Gulliver, "Land Shortage, Social Change, and Social Conflict in East Africa," *Journal of Conflict Resolution*, V (March, 1961), 16–26.

8

RELATIONS BETWEEN GENERATIONS AND THE THREE-GENERATION HOUSEHOLD IN DENMARK[1]

JAN STEHOUWER

Until about the beginning of this century it was still common and sometimes even preferred that one of the adult children remain with his parents, even after marriage. This has changed. Urban growth, industrialization, and mechanization of agriculture have contributed to the individualization of the nuclear family and have made generations less dependent on each other in both urban and rural areas. There is considerable evidence that elderly people now want to live near their adult children, but not with them.[2]

Considering this development, one is inclined to wonder what has happened to the household of three generations as well as to relations between generations not living under the same roof. This paper deals with these questions in relation to the situation in Denmark. The paper is divided into three parts.

In the first part, the living arrangements of elderly people in Denmark, their proximity to children, and their contact with children are described briefly. It has often been assumed that the aged in modern industrial societies are isolated from their children, especially in urban areas. The first part of this paper will

Jan Stehouwer, "Relations Between Generations and the Three-Generation Household in Denmark," from Social Structure and the Family: Generational Relations, *Ethel Shanas & Gordon F. Streib, Editors,* © 1965. *Reprinted by permission of Prentice-Hall, Inc., Englewood Cliffs, New Jersey.*

deal with this question. Further, the situation of the aged in Denmark will be compared with equivalent data from sample surveys in Great Britain and the United States.

The second part of this paper will deal with factors which contribute to the establishment and maintenance of three-generation households and to the occurrence of such households in Denmark. Compared with non-Scandinavian European countries, Denmark has remarkably few people who live in three-generation households.

This observation leads to the third part of this paper, which deals with the relations between generations in Denmark. The fact that Denmark has a long-established tradition of social pension systems, health insurance, and housing policy for the aged makes the study of relations between generations an attractive object for cross-national comparisons.

The data of this paper derive from two sources. The first source is the study of the social well-being of the aged in Denmark, which is a part of a cross-national study in social gerontology, carried out in Britain, the United States, and Denmark.[3] The second source is the screening interview on household composition and health conditions, carried out by the Danish National Institute for Social Research in 1961, which was used as the sampling basis for three national sample surveys in Denmark. The data about the number and the composition of three-generation households in Denmark are a by-product of this sample survey.[4]

The Living Arrangements of Elderly People: The Proximity of Children and the Frequency of Contact

Urbanization and industrialization in Denmark started relatively late compared with other Western European countries. Denmark has a population of about 4.5 million people, one-third of whom live in the metropolitan area of Copenhagen. Another third live in the provincial towns, which range from less than 2,000 to almost 180,000 inhabitants. Approximately half of those in provincial towns live in communities with less than 30,000 inhabitants. The rest of the population live in the rural areas of the country.

Approximately 6 per cent of the people aged 65 and over live in institutions.[5] Among older people who live in private households it is more common to live apart from children than together with them. Those elderly who live with children live with unmarried children. Very few elderly people in Denmark live with married children.

Differences within Denmark

As one might expect, we find the largest proportion of married elderly people living with children in the rural parts of the country. Our results show that in Denmark in rural areas nearly one-fifth of the elderly people live together with children. This, however, does not mean that these households function as traditional farm families of more than two generations living and working together. This type of household has nearly disappeared in Denmark.

The elderly living in the provincial towns differ from the elderly in Copenhagen as well as from those in the extreme rural areas in living arrangements as well as in relations to their children.[6] In the provincial towns we find the largest proportion of elderly married people who live only with their spouse and the largest proportion who have their nearest child at a distance of more than 60 transport minutes, and the number of those who have not seen a child within the last month is about twice as high as that reported for Copenhagen or the extreme rural areas.

Among the unmarried aged we find almost the same pattern. Again the proportion of those who live alone is highest in the provincial towns. About twice as many in the provincial towns as in the Copenhagen area have their nearest child at a transport distance of more than 60 minutes. Contrary to the situation of married people, we find no significant differences in the frequency of contact with children for those who are single whether they live in Copenhagen, the provincial towns, or the rural areas.

Table 1 indicates that the probability that all children move away from the areas where their parents live is highest in the provincial towns, somewhat lower in the rural areas, and lowest in Copenhagen.

Our data reveal that one has to be careful with the hypothesis that urbanization leads to spatial separation between generations and towards isolation of the aged. The inclination for parents and children to see one another may still be greatest in the rural areas, but the possibilities of contact are greatest in Copenhagen —because the parents will more frequently find a child within the limited and densely populated area of Copenhagen than within any other area of the same size.

TABLE 1 *The Living Arrangements of People Aged 62 and Over, Their Proximity to Nearest Child, and Contact with Children in Areas of Denmark* *

Marital status and living arrangements	Copenhagen per cent	Provincial towns per cent	Rural areas per cent	Extreme rural per cent	Whole country per cent
Married					
Total	100.0	100.0	100.0	100.0	100.0
Living with:					
Spouse only	77.9	84.0	75.3	60.8	77.8
Unmarried children	17.3	12.3	17.6	19.6	16.5
Married children	0.3	0.4	2.8	8.4	1.4
Others	4.5	3.3	4.3	11.2	4.3
N =	353	559	324	396	1632
Unmarried					
Total	100.0	100.0	100.0	100.0	100.0
Living alone	61.8	73.7	43.9	47.0	60.8
Living with:					
Unmarried children	19.2	14.5	30.3	22.6	19.6
Married children	5.5	3.9	12.1	19.5	8.4
Others	13.5	7.9	13.7	10.9	11.2
N =	297	330	132	164	923
Married (not living with children)					
Nearest child more than hour away	6.4	25.0	17.4	19.0	18.1
Child not seen in last month	4.0	8.3	8.5	4.3	6.5
N =	296	492	260	300	1348
Unmarried (not living with children)					
Nearest child more than hour away	8.6	17.9	16.7	12.0	14.5
Child not seen in last month	10.3	8.4	12.8	10.1	9.8
N =	233	274	78	99	648

° Includes only persons with living children.
SOURCE: Jan Stehouwer, "Urban-Rural Differences in Contact between the Aged and their Children in Denmark," paper prepared for the International Social Science Research Seminar in Gerontology, Markaryd, Sweden, 1963.

The Living Arrangements of People with Living Children, in Denmark, Great Britain, and the United States

Nearly three out of four elderly persons aged 65 or over in Denmark, Britain, and the United States have at least one living child. The proportions without children are: Great Britain, 23.6 per cent, United States, 24.4 per cent, and Denmark, 24.5 per cent. Compared with Britain and the United States, however, we find that Denmark has the lowest proportion of elderly people—single or married—who live together with their children. As Table 2

TABLE 2 *The Living Arrangements of People Aged 65 and Over Who Have Living Children*

Marital status and living arrangements	Britain per cent	United States per cent	Denmark per cent
Married			
Total	100.0	100.0	100.0
Living with:*			
Spouse only	63.8	77.9	79.8
Married daughter	4.7	1.0	0.4
Married son	0.8	1.1	1.2
Unmarried child	25.9	14.6	14.9
Sibling	1.5	1.3	0.3
Grandchild	1.5	2.3	0.7
Other relative	0.6	0.8	0.3
Nonrelative only	1.2	1.0	2.4
N =	1022	1169	1183
Divorced, widowed, or single			
Total	100.0	100.0†	100.0
Living alone	38.7	46.5	61.1
Living with:*			
Married daughter	19.7	14.5	4.5
Married son	7.4	4.1	4.1
Unmarried child	26.8	24.1	18.4
Sibling	2.6	2.5	1.0
Grandchild	0.7	2.2	1.4
Other relative	0.9	1.4	0.8
Nonrelative only	3.2	4.6	8.7
N =	889	843	828

* Listing in priority order.
† Per cents do not add to total because of rounding.

shows, we find in Denmark only 8.7 per cent of the aged who are unmarried living together with married children compared to 18.6 per cent in the United States and 24.2 per cent in Britain. In Denmark we find no difference in the proportion of elderly people living together with the family of the married daughter or married son. In Britain, the majority of the elderly, single as well as married, who live with married children live together with the family of a married daughter.[7] In the United States typically single persons living with married children, live together with a daughter's family.

The Proximity of Children and the Frequency of
Contact Between Aged Parents and Their Children

Although relatively few people in Denmark live together with their children, most old people live within a short distance from at least one child. Table 3 shows that about one out of eight elderly people in Denmark and Britain have their nearest child at a distance of more than 60 transport minutes. In the United States the proportion is one to six. Our data support results from other surveys, which show that parents and children generally settle in the vicinity of each other.[8] In this respect, we find striking similarities among the three countries. Looking at the proportion of children living at a long distance from their parents, we must remember that the three countries vary greatly in size, which makes the relatively small number of elderly people with their nearest child within more than 60 transport minutes in the United States even more surprising compared with the corresponding proportions found in Denmark and Great Britain.

TABLE 3 *The Proximity of the Nearest Child to People Aged 65 and Over in Great Britain, the United States, and Denmark* *

	People with living children		
Proximity of the nearest child	Britain per cent	United States per cent	Denmark per cent
Total	100.0†	100.0	100.0
Same household	41.9	27.6	20.1
10 minute's journey or less	23.5	33.1	32.0
11–30 minute's journey	15.9	15.7	23.0
31 minute's–1 hour	7.6	7.2	12.4
Over 1 hour but less than one day	9.1	11.2	11.2
1-day journey or more	1.9	5.2	1.3
N =	1911	2012	2009

° Unclassifiable 0, 0, and 4 respectively.
† Per cents do not add to total because of rounding.
SOURCE: Adapted from Peter Townsend, "The Family of Three Generations," paper prepared for the International Social Science Research Seminar in Gerontology, Markaryd, Sweden, August 1963.

The majority of elderly people with living children are in daily or weekly contact with at least one of them. The proportion of people who have not seen a child within the last week is one in six in the United States and even smaller in Denmark and Britain. In

Denmark this means that although very few elderly people live together with their children, the majority of them have daily or weekly contact with at least one child. Table 4 shows that about two-thirds of the elderly in each country have seen at least one of their children today or yesterday. Among the British about 40 per cent of those with children live with a child, in Denmark only about 20 per cent. The data in Table 4 indicate that "not living together in Denmark" is highly compensated for by daily contact.

TABLE 4   When People Aged 65 and Over Last Saw One of Their Children*

	People with living children		
	Britain	United States	Denmark
Last time child seen	per cent	per cent	per cent
Total	100.0	100.0	100.0
Today or yesterday	69.3	65.0	62.3
Within previous seven days	17.3	18.7	21.8
Within previous month	7.4	6.8	9.8
Within previous year	4.2	7.0	4.8
More than a year ago	1.8	2.5	1.3
N =	1906	1996	2001

* Unclassifiable 6, 16, and 12 for Britain, the United States, and Denmark respectively.

Summarizing our major results as to the living arrangements of the aged in Denmark, the proximity of children, and the frequency of contact with children, and the comparison with Great Britain and the United States, we can conclude that in spite of the fact that Denmark has a very high proportion of aged who live apart from their children, we find no differences in the proximity of the nearest child and the frequencies of contact with children between Denmark and the two other countries involved in this cross-national survey.

These results raise two questions: first, what has happened to the household of three generations in Denmark and, secondly, what are the relations between generations when elderly people do not live together with their children. In the next two sections we will try to throw some light on these problems.

The Three-Generation Household

Why do so few elderly people in Denmark live in households consisting of three successive generations? Why in general do we find so few elderly people in Denmark who live with their children? The higher degree of institutionalization of elderly people in Denmark, compared for example with the United States, 6 per cent compared to 4 per cent, may have caused some of the difference—but evidently not the whole. The next pages shall first deal with factors which contribute to the establishment of three-generational living, secondly we shall summarize some recent evidence about the occurrence of three-generation households in Western European countries, and finally we shall describe the structure of the three-generation households which are still found in Denmark.

The Establishment of Three-Generation Households

Various reasons exist for the establishment of temporary or permanent three-generation households. In general, two main causes for such households can be distinguished: (1) dependence originating because the family functions as a joint enterprise involving two or more generations working together, and (2) need for help and care, offered either by first or second generation.

Economic dependence has traditionally been considered as one of the main reasons which have led to the establishment of three-generation households. Le Play's "La Famille Souche" in which one of the sons inherits the farm or business owned by his father, and continues to keep it for the family, is a good example of this kind of economic and functional dependence which leads to three-generational living, especially among farmers and small entrepreneurs.[9] In rural areas of Western Europe this type of farm family has been rather common and mainly patrilocal in structure.[10]

The need for help and care can be the reason for three-generational living in various circumstances. In some instances, the first or older generation offers help. Some such households are established, more or less on a temporary basis, for example, when an adult child marries, and the young couple must wait to get a dwelling for themselves. In these cases, a housing shortage may be a factor which contributes to the establishment of temporary three-generation households. A recent study of the housing conditions of newly married couples in Copenhagen, for example, has shown that 23 per cent of all couples start married life living with either his or her parents, and in a great number of cases the first child is born in this household.[11] Young and Willmot reported the same sort of households in East London.[12]

Another typical example of help offered by the first generation is seen when an unmarried daughter (or married, but temporarily separated from her husband) continues or returns to live with her own family. This has been a common pattern especially in times of war.[13]

Evacuation and acute shortage of houses caused by the destruction of war have also been common reasons for temporary and even permanent establishment of three-generation households, either in the family of the first or second generation.[14]

Finally, declining health among elderly people and the reduction of their capacity to take care of themselves are common reasons for the establishment of three-generation households in many countries. Instead of moving into an institution, the aged parents move to live with their children.

Discussing the structure of the three-generation household in Germany, Baumert makes the distinction between the new and the old type of three-generational living.[15] In the old traditional type of three-generation household, at least one of the children remains with the parents and in many cases continues to work on the farm or in the business which has been owned by the family for generations. In this type of household economic and occupational dependence together with family traditions is the main reason for three-generational living. In the new type, according to Baumert, the members of the second generation move away from the parental home, establish their own families, and later invite the parent(s) to live with them in cases of the latter's widowhood, declining health, or physical incapacity.

Having no data for retrospective comparisons, it is doubtful whether we are able to speak about old and new types of three-generation households. It is indisputable that the number of three-generation households was larger about a century ago than it is now. It is also correct that the so-called "old type" or Le Play's "La Famille Souche" has been a frequent household type in the rural areas of Western Europe. This does not allow us to assume, however, that the other type of household, in which the first generation moves into the household of the second, is particularly new. Perhaps, this latter type is more urban than rural in origin. The lack of public care for the aged, the absence of medical care, and the very unattractive institutions for the aged a hundred or even only fifty years ago must have been conditions which frequently contributed to the establishment of the three-generation household in urban areas. The three-generation household in which the children take care of their parent(s) who have moved into their household is not a new one. It may well be the remainder of an old, and perhaps traditionally urban type.

The Three-Generation Household in Western Europe

Does the three-generation household still exist in Western Europe, and where do we find it? This is the next question which should be answered before we turn to a more detailed analysis of three-generational living in Denmark. There is evidence that the three-generation household is still a common arrangement among the population of poor agricultural and economically backward regions within a number of Western European countries, such as Italy,[16] the Netherlands,[17] and even Germany.[18]

The number of three-generation households in Europe is smallest in urban areas. In rural areas their frequency seems to vary with the regional traditions and the prosperity of agriculture.

Rural sociologists in the Netherlands have ascertained that relatively many three-generation households still exist along the German frontier. The extended family system in Holland is confined to the sandy areas in the east and the middle of the country— which, up to the beginning of this century, as a result of geographical as well as social factors, have been extremely isolated. The farm family in these areas until recently has been a production as well as a consumption unit. Being small, the farms need no hired labor. Each member of the family and even sometimes members of the extended kin group are to some degree engaged in the farm work.[19]

In Baumert's study of Darmstadt in 1950 (see Table 5) 42 per cent of the full-time farm families had an extended family system of three or more generations living together. In contrast, only 5 per cent of the families in the city he studied lived in a three-generation household.

In Vienna, Rosenmayr and Köckeis found that almost 4 per cent of all households consist of three generations living together.[20] In one of six of these households the members of both adult generations were still married. In all other cases, either the grandparent or the parent (or even both) were widowed. From this, Rosen-mayr and Köckeis conclude that "joint households thus seem hardly ever to be maintained throughout adult life in urban industrial society but rather re-established when other relationships break off." [21]

TABLE 5   *Number of Generations Living Together in Urban and Rural Families in a West German City and Its Hinterland, Percentage Distribution*

Number of generations	Urban families		Rural families		
	(N = 387)	Total (N = 434)	Nonfarm	Part-time farm	Full-time farm
One	36	25	27	35	7
Two	59	62	64	49	51
Three	5	12	9	15	37
Four		1		1	5

SOURCE: Gerhard Baumert, "Changes in the Family and the Position of Older Persons in Germany," *Social and Psychological Aspects of Aging*, Clark Tibbitts and Wilma Donahue, eds. (New York: Columbia University Press, 1962), p. 420.

The Three-Generation Household in Denmark

Two of every hundred households in Denmark include three or more generations. Although the majority of the three-generation households in Denmark include aged persons, in a substantial proportion the first or grandparent generation is still at the stage where the youngest children are about to get married and leave the household. Both in absolute and relative terms we find most of these in the country and only a few in the Copenhagen metropolitan area and in the provincial towns.

When we look at the population aged 65 and over who have children, we find that 5.1 per cent live in three-generation households. In the United States the proportion is 8.1 per cent and in Great Britain 13.4 per cent.

Why is the number of three-generation households so limited in Denmark? There are two main conditions in Denmark which may have prevented three-generational living and diminished the number of households of this kind. First, for the country as a whole, the long tradition of care and the housing policy for the aged have diminished dependency among generations. This tradition may have contributed to the fact that there has been far less pressure in Denmark, than, for example, in the Netherlands and the United States to make adult children take care of their aged parents.[22] Recent trends in the housing policy for the aged show that everything possible is done to keep old people independent in their own dwellings. Institutionalization is a final solution only in cases where the elderly person is not able to take care of himself. Second, the housing conditions of Denmark serve to prevent three generations from living together. Three-generational living is dependent on large housing units, and this condition exists in Denmark only to a very limited extent, especially in urban areas. In Denmark, as well as in the other Scandinavian countries, the average dwelling has only two or three rooms.

Furthermore, in rural areas, the structure of agriculture and the high degree of mechanization of farm work have limited the need of unpaid family workers (except for the wife of the smallholder). Rural areas with a long tradition of three-generation households, such as can be found in the Netherlands, do not exist in Denmark. Finally, we must take into account that Denmark has had no major part in either the First World War or the Second. The country has not had the problem of war-widows, nor the acute housing shortage caused by war destruction which is still apparent in much of Western Europe.

The Composition of Three-Generation Households in Denmark

The most common arrangement in three-generation households in Denmark is that of widowed parents living with their married children and grandchildren.

In only one of six cases do three-generation households consist of two married couples of successive generations. Households consisting of a married couple and single children and grandchildren also occur in the same proportion.

Nearly 70 per cent of the households in which the parent(s) live in the household of one of their children are found in rural areas of the country. About 50 per cent of the households with a member of the first generation as head are also found in the rural areas of the country. Neither these households, nor the ones where the parents have moved into the household of one of the children, however, represent a typical rural tradition in three-generational living. The very small numbers of different types of three-generation households indicate in themselves that we are unable to speak of tradition in this respect.

TABLE 6 *The Composition of Three-Generation Households in Denmark*

Head of household	Per cent
Total	100.0
1st generation	
Married couple, married child(ren), possibly other child(ren), grandchild(ren) and possibly others	10.5
Married couple, unmarried child(ren), and grandchild(ren) and possibly others	14.8
Unmarried head, married child(ren), and grandchild(ren) and possibly others	8.6
Unmarried head, unmarried child(ren), and grandchild(ren) and possibly others	11.7
2nd generation	
Married parents, married child(ren), and grandchild(ren) and possibly others	6.2
Married parents, unmarried child(ren), and grandchild(ren) and possibly others	1.9
Unmarried parent, married child(ren), and grandchild(ren) and possibly others	44.4
Unmarried parent, unmarried child(ren), and grandchild(ren) and possibly others	1.9
N =	162
Total number of households in sample	8634

The observation that there are households in urban areas in which two younger generations stay in the household of the first generation can be explained by current housing conditions. The proportion of elderly people who occupy large dwellings is larger than the proportion of young families with space for three-generational living.

There is considerable evidence that the three-generation house-

TABLE 7 *Distribution of Three-Generation Households, Urban and Rural Denmark*

Area	All three-generation households per cent	Generation of head		Frequency Distribution	
		First per cent	Second per cent	in total sample per cent	of total sample per cent
Total	100.0	100.0	100.0	1.9	100.0
Copenhagen area	19.1	20.3	18.2	1.2	29.9
Provincial towns and suburbs	21.6	32.4	12.5	1.2	35.1
Rural districts	59.3	47.3	69.3	3.1	35.0
N =	162	74	88		8636

hold, as it has survived in Denmark, is a subsidiary system rather than a system kept together by occupational and economic dependence. Very few households consist of two married couples.

The majority consist of a single parent, usually widowed, living with children. Of these parents, the majority are women. Data about health and physical capacity of all family members of the household show that 55.4 per cent of all three-generation households in Denmark, compared to 15.4 per cent of all households, have at least one member with health troubles or physical handicaps.

Our results correspond very closely to observations made by Rosenmayr and Köckeis. They summarize their findings from a microcensus in Vienna and two federal states in Austria by saying "that intergenerational households are nearly always retained or reestablished only if and when one of their members (either of the older or of the younger generation) would otherwise have to live quite alone, or at least not in a family household." [23]

TABLE 8 *Illness, Health Troubles, and Physical Handicaps Among Members of Three-Generation Households in Denmark* *

Members with complaints	Number of households per cent
Total	100.0
None	44.6
Head of household only	13.6
Spouse of head only	11.7
Both head and spouse	5.6
Other member, related to head	12.3
Head and other related member	6.8
Spouse of head and other related member	1.8
Head and spouse of head and other member	1.8
No information	1.8
N =	162

* Households with member(s) who are ill, have complaints about health, or have a physical handicap. Refers to long-term, not temporary illness.

Relations Between Generations in Separate Households

Since we find that Denmark has very few three-generation households, one is inclined to ask: How about relations between generations in Denmark in general? Is the vanishing three-generation household a sign of a weakening of relations between the elderly and their children?

In the beginning of this paper, we have shown that, in spite of

certain marked differences in the living arrangements of the elderly in Denmark, compared with Great Britain and the United
States, we find remarkable similarities between the elderly population of the three countries as far as the frequency of contact
with their children and the proximity of their children is concerned.

Living together in a common household imposes a functional as
well as an emotional dependence on all household members apart
from the dependence which exists because of family and kinship
ties. To what extent is the fact that generations live apart from
each other in Denmark a symbol of functional independence
between generations, although a pattern of regular contact is
maintained? In the last part of this paper we will deal with some
aspects of relations between generations which may give some answers to this question.

Patterns of Mutual Help and Assistance in Denmark

Help given to children is one of the indicators of the extent to
which the aged parent is involved in the daily life of the adult
children. In Denmark as a whole, 27.7 per cent of the people aged
65 and over reported that they are able to help their children with
various things, such as repairs, housekeeping, and taking care of
the grandchildren. The proportion of elderly people who say that
they help their children is largest in the rural areas, nearly as large
in Copenhagen, and lowest in the provincial towns.

TABLE 9   *Are You Able to Do Anything for Your Children?*

Answers of persons aged 65 and over with living children	Copenhagen area per cent	Provincial towns per cent	Rural areas per cent	Whole country per cent
Total	100.0	100.0	100.0	100.0
Yes	28.1	22.6	31.9	27.7
No	70.7	76.7	67.3	71.5
No information	1.2	0.7	0.8	0.8
N =	516	707	739	2012

When people become ill, they become dependent on help. All
elderly people in the national sample survey were asked whether
they had been in bed because of illness during the last 12 months.
Those who had been ill were asked some further questions about

TABLE 10   Expectations of Help with Meal Preparation During Illness Compared with the Help Given*

| Persons aged 65 and over with living children | Ill during last 12 months who helped with your meals? | | | | Not ill during last 12 months who would help with your meals, if you became ill? | | | |
| | unmarried | | married | | unmarried | | married | |
Priority code	Alone per cent	With others per cent	Spouse only per cent	Spouse and others per cent	Alone per cent	With others per cent	Spouse only per cent	Spouse and others per cent
Total	100.0	100.0	100.0	100.0	100.0	100.0	100.0	100.0
No one	20.6	3.6	2.5	1.5	9.3	2.0	0.6	1.2
Spouse only	....	....	65.0	61.7	....	....	71.6	63.2
Spouse and others	....	....	12.8	10.3	....	....	9.6	18.7
Child in household	4.8	58.9	0.6	16.2	3.0	51.2	0.6	7.6
Child outside household	35.8	7.1	7.2	....	36.8	9.2	5.3	1.7
Relative in household	....	11.6	....	....	0.9	16.6	....	0.6
Relative outside household	13.3	5.4	0.9	4.5	15.6	3.4	1.3	0.6
Social services	15.2	4.5	3.8	....	29.0	14.6	8.7	5.8
Others	10.3	8.9	6.9	5.8	3.6	3.0	1.3	0.6
No information	....	....	0.3	....	1.8	....	1.0	....
N =	165	112	320	68	334	205	619	171

* Total sample interviewed except 17 persons who are bedfast and 5 who did not respond to the question whether they had been ill during the last 12 months.

who helped them with various things, such as preparing meals, housekeeping, shopping, and care. Those who had not been ill were asked questions about who would help them in case of illness. The answers given by those persons with living children tell us something about the extent to which children in fact do help the elderly and to what extent the elderly expect help from them.

About four out of five elderly married people expect their spouses to prepare their meals during illness, and about the same proportion in fact received help from their spouses in this situation. Less than one of ten married elderly people expect their children to help them with meals, but the proportion of those who actually get help from their children with the preparing of meals is slightly larger.

Three out of five single people who live with a child expect one of their children to take care of meals, and something less than this proportion get this help. Among those who are single and live alone, only two of five expect and get help from children with meals. Unmarried elderly people who live alone are in the worst situation when ill. About 10 per cent of those who had not been ill during the last 12 months answered that there would be no one to help them with meals during illness. Among those who had been ill, we found about 20 per cent who had no help with meal preparation during their illness.

Finally, it is interesting to see that relatively more elderly people expect to receive help from local social agencies, such as community home helpers, than people who actually get help from these authorities. For the elderly population as a whole, we find that about one of eight expect that they will receive help during illness from local social agencies, but about one out of eighteen gets this kind of service. Table 10 shows the difference between the number of people who expect help and those who get help from social services for all categories.

Relations Between Generations in Denmark, Compared with Great Britain and the United States

As already mentioned, we find that in Denmark about one of four elderly people report that they were able to help their children. In Great Britain as well as the United States we find that the proportion of elderly people who help their children, and thus take an active part in the life of their children and grandchildren, is much higher. In Great Britain nearly half, and in the United States more than half of the elderly population aged 65 or over, reported that they helped their children.

TABLE 11 *The Living Arrangements, the Proximity of the Nearest Child, the Contact with Children, and Patterns of Mutual Help of People Aged 65 and Over with Living Children, in Denmark, Great Britain, and the United States*

Living arrangements and relationships with children	Denmark per cent	Britain per cent	United States per cent
Proximity of Children:			
Children in the same household	20.1	41.9	27.6
Nearest child at more than one hour's transport distance	12.5	11.0	16.4
Contact with Children:			
Have seen at least one child today or yesterday	62.3	69.3	65.0
Have stayed overnight with child within last 12 months	20.0	29.5	42.9
Have had child staying overnight within last 12 months	20.1	26.2	46.0
Help to Children:			
Those able to do anything for children	27.7	46.9	52.5
Those able to do anything for grandchildren *	13.3	32.8	49.6
Help from Children:			
Received a regular money allowance within last 12 months	2.5	4.1	4.2
Received occasional money gifts within last 12 months	6.2	20.3	34.9
N =	2012	1911	2012

° Percentage computed only for those who have grandchildren. Denmark N = 1845, Britain N = 1719, and United States N = 1873.

The same pattern is observed concerning help to grandchildren. Only 13.3 per cent of the Danish respondents reported that they helped their grandchildren, while the percentages in Britain and the United States are 46.9 per cent and 52.5 per cent respectively.

To stay overnight with children or to have the children staying during holidays and other occasions is relatively uncommon in Denmark, where about one out of five parents has stayed with his child(ren) or has had a child(ren) staying with him in the previous year. In the United States little less than half of all older people with children have stayed with children or have had children staying overnight with them. These differences are even more striking when we take into account that there are relatively fewer elderly people in Denmark who live with their children than in the United States.

We must, however, take into consideration, that there may be several conditions which may make staying overnight more common in the United States than in Denmark. First of all, housing conditions in the United States permit overnight visitors to a larger extent than is true in Denmark. Secondly, we must remember that Denmark is a small country, whereas the geographical conditions in the United States make it probable that at least one of the children lives at a long distance from the parents, which makes overnight stays desirable during visits.

A regular money allowance from children is rather uncommon in all three countries. The proportion of elderly people who have received a regular allowance during the past 12 months is smallest in Denmark and highest in the United States. Receiving occasional money gifts from children is a regular phenomenon in Britain and the United States, but rare in Denmark. In Denmark, one of every seventeen old people reported that they had received money gifts from their children during the last 12 months. In Britain, one of five, and in the United States, one of three had received occasional money gifts.

In comparing economic support given by children to their elderly parents in Denmark, Britain, and the United States we have to take into account that the Danish taxation system, in contrast to that of the other two countries, does not permit the deduction of economic support to relatives in the annual income declaration. We should also mention that as far back as the first codified rules on help to the poor, the sick, and the aged (1799), the Danish Social Security Acts never have had a rule that public relief of the aged (and other groups) is given on the condition that the children are unable to support their parents.

Summarizing the few comparable observations about relations between generations in the three countries, which are available at this stage of our cross-national research, it seems that elderly people in Denmark are in regular contact with their children and live close to them. Unlike Great Britain and the United States, however, contact seems to be limited to visiting and is not the result of functional dependence. Compared with Britain and the United States, the elderly in Denmark seem to take a less active part in the lives of their children. Neither do they seem to be as dependent on help from their children as are the aged in England and the United States.

In evaluating these preliminary results from our cross-national survey one has to make certain reservations. First of all, we must be aware of the fact that some of the differences in the help patterns among generations in the three countries can be explained by structural differences in the populations concerned. The fact that we find a very large number of people in Britain saying that they are able to help their children can be a function of the extremely large proportion of elderly people in Britain living with their children. In this respect the Danish and American populations are more alike—which makes the differences in help patterns between these two countries more striking. Other structural differences between the three national samples will also have to be taken into account, such as proportions of married and unmarried elderly people, and the average number of children.[24]

We have already mentioned that Denmark has a long tradition of care for the aged—and especially a long-established pension system. Health insurance societies were formed in the middle of the nineteenth century and furnished the basis upon which the present nation-wide system in Denmark is established.

The movement towards keeping the aged out of institutions— and if possible, in their own homes or in special apartment houses with a low rent—has been supported by a system of municipal home care. In this respect, the aged in Denmark are able to be more independent of their children, as far as housekeeping, nursing, and other sorts of help are concerned.

Apart from these factors, however, there are other circumstances which should prevent a complete detachment of generations. More than 30 per cent of the married women in Denmark are in the labor force, and in the large towns the proportion is even higher. Nevertheless, it seems that the grandmother in Denmark has taken the place of the mother only to a very limited extent in regard to taking care of children. The environment of the small town and the rural areas which is typical of the country ought to be ideal for the development of intensive relations between generations. This does not seem to be the case in Denmark where we find nearly equal and low proportions of elderly people in Copenhagen and rural areas who say that they help their children. Denmark seems to be an example of a country in which generations live in close contact with each other but with a relatively low degree of functional dependence.

Obviously the differences in mutual help patterns reported here only tell us something about the degree of functional interdependence of aged parents and their children and nothing about the emotional quality of intergenerational relations in these three countries.

But, in spite of these reservations, one cannot help but ask about the causes of such pronounced differences in patterns of mutual help between Denmark on one side, and Britain and the United States on the other.

Summary and Conclusions

The lengthening of the average lifetime of man in modern Western societies has increased the possibility of having family members or relatives in two or three generations apart from one's own. In spite of this development the household consisting of members from three successive generations seems to be a disappearing structure in most parts of Western Europe as well as in the United States. The increasing proportion of elderly people in the populations of almost every country with a high degree of industrialization and urbanization makes the study of intergenerational relationships a topic of general interest for theorists as well as social practitioners.

In this paper we have dealt with three aspects of intergenerational relations in Denmark. In the first part we have described living arrangements of elderly people in Denmark, their contact with children, and the proximity of children.

Observations within the country show that:

1. Urbanization has not led to spatial separation of elderly parents and their children. As expected, we find the largest proportion of elderly people who live together with adult children in the rural areas of the country. Nevertheless, relatively more elderly people in the small provincial towns than in the metropolitan area of Copenhagen live apart from their children.

2. Urbanization has not contributed to a reduction of regular visiting between the aged and their children. The

largest proportion of elderly people who have not had contact with at least one child within the last month is found in the provincial towns. The lowest proportion is found in the Copenhagen area and not in rural areas as one might expect.

Cross-national observations in this research area reveal that:

3. The proportion of people aged 65 and over with living children who share a household with their children is largest in Britain and lowest in Denmark.
4. Elderly people in all three countries tend to live in the vicinity of their children.
5. Most elderly people in all three countries are in regular contact with at least one of their children.

The second part of this paper has dealt with the household of three generations in Denmark.

In Western Europe as well as the United States the three-generation household still exists, but it is a disappearing structure, especially in highly industrialized regions, where we find only very small proportions of the population living together in households of three or more generations. Denmark, in particular, is an example of a country with a very small proportion of three-generation households, in spite of the fact that about 25 per cent of the population lives in rural areas. This situation, which may seem to contradict some beliefs about the association between rural life and three-generation households, has to be evaluated against the background of a long tradition of social policy for the aged and a typical Scandinavian tradition of small housing, factors which limit the need and the possibilities of three-generational living.

Observations based on a national household sample show that:

6. The majority of three-generation households in Denmark are found in the rural areas of the country, whereas the remainder are equally divided between Copenhagen and the provincial towns.
7. There are nearly equal proportions of households in which the first and second generations are reported to be the head of the household.
8. One-third of all three-generation households consist of a married couple in the first generation. Only one of six households consists of two married couples of suc-

cessive generations. In two out of three households we find a single member, either among the first or the second generation.

9. In more than half of all three-generation households, at least one member has health complaints or a physical incapacity.

10. Married elderly people who share a household more often live with the family of their married son than with the family of a married daughter. These households are found only in rural areas.

11. Widows more often live with married daughters than with married sons.

The traditional extended family system, consisting of three or more generations closely related to each other in an occupational and economic interdependent unit, is a type which is nearly non-existent in Denmark. Among the disappearing three-generation households in Denmark, that which remains functions as a subsidiary system in which either first- or second-generation members are dependent on care and help from other family members. This is a type of household which has a less traditional reputation but which nevertheless must have existed for centuries, perhaps especially in urban areas.

In the last part of this paper we deal with relations between generations not living together in Denmark, Great Britain, and the United States.

Our main observation is that, in spite of similarities in regard to the proximity of the children and contact with children, there are striking differences between Denmark and the other two countries. In regard to an older parent's staying overnight with children, children's staying overnight with parents, and patterns of mutual help and assistance, we find that:

12. More than twice as great a proportion of elderly people in the United States as in Denmark stay with children overnight or have children staying with them.

13. In Denmark about one of four elderly people reports that he is able to help his children. In Britain and the United States, about one of two was able to help his children.

14. Correspondingly, we find that relatively few Danish grandparents were able to help their grandchildren with various things.

15. Regular financial support from children is a rare phenomenon in all three countries. Occasional money gifts from children occur more frequently than regular financial support. The proportion of elderly people who receive occasional financial support from their children is lowest in Denmark and highest in the United States.

Our cross-national observations show that Denmark is an example of a country in which the generations live in close contact with each other but with a very low degree of mutual functional dependence. In spite of the fact that the same proportion of elderly people in Denmark, Britain, and the United States are in regular contact with their children and live near them, we find in Denmark very low proportions of elderly people who are able to help their children or who are supported by their children.

These observations have to be evaluated against the background of two conditions. First, we must remember that Denmark, being a country with a relatively moderate degree of urbanization, many small towns, and large rural areas, must be in many respects the ideal environment for the development and maintenance of strong intergenerational relations. This is confirmed by the large proportions of elderly people who are in nearly daily contact with children, and who live in the neighbourhood of their children. Second, we must take into account that Denmark has a long tradition for social security and care for the aged. This tradition may have reduced functional dependence among generations, but it does not seem to have influenced the frequency of contact between generations. Compared with the United States and Britain, Denmark seems to be a country where expectations about help between generations are reduced to a minimum, without influencing the degree of voluntary contact.

Notes

1. This research has been financed by a grant from the United States National Institute of Health, MH 05509 and the Public Health Service, Chronic Disease Division, CH 0052-03.
2. Gordon F. Streib, "Family Patterns in Retirement," *Journal of Social Issues*, XIV, No. 2 (1958), 46–60; Leopold Rosenmayr and Eva Köckeis, "Propositions for a Sociological Theory of Ageing and the Family," *International Social Science Journal*, XV, No. 3 (1963), 410–426.

3. This study is financed by grants from the United States National Institute of Mental Health and the United States Public Health Service, Community Health Services, Bureau of State Services, in all three countries. The general aim of this study is to secure comparable data about health, physical capacity, the employment status, the family relations, and the economic status of elderly people in these countries. In each country roughly 2,500 persons aged 65 and over were interviewed during April–July, 1962. The national teams used the same sampling methods, questionnaires which included mainly comparable cross-national questions, similar definitions of variables, and similar interviewer instructions. The responsible investigators are Denmark, Henning Friis and Jan Stehouwer; Great Britain, Peter Townsend; the United States, Ethel Shanas. See Henning Friis, "Cross-National Research on Old Age," *International Social Science Journal*, XV, No. 3 (1963), 451–55.

4. A 0.7 per cent stratified area probability sample of about 10,000 households.

5. There are only estimates about the number of elderly people in nonprivate households. Census data are not yet available.

6. Extreme rural areas are areas with less than 10 per cent of the population living in the built-up area of the community.

7. Peter Townsend, "The Family of Three Generations," paper presented at the International Social Science Research Seminar in Gerontology, Markaryd, Sweden, August, 1963.

8. Leopold Rosenmayr and Eva Köckeis, "A Method to Assess Living Arrangements and Housing Problems of the Aged," paper presented at the International Social Science Research Seminar in Gerontology, Markaryd, Sweden, August, 1963.

9. Frédéric Le Play, *L'Organisation de la famille,* 3rd ed. (Tours: A. Mame et fils, 1884).

10. J. P. Kruijt, "Het gezin sedert de middeleeuwen," *Sociologisch Bulletin,* 4 e Jaargang, No. 3 (1950) p. 81.

11. K. Auken, *Familien lever* (Copenhagen: Gad, 1962), pp. 59 ff.

12. Michael Young and Peter Willmott, *Family and Kinship in East London,* Pelican, A 595 (Harmondsworth, Middlesex: Penguin Book Company, 1962), p. 31.

13. William M. Smith, Jr., Joseph H. Britton, and Jean O. Britton, *Relationships Within Three-Generation Households,* College of Home Economics Research Publication No. 155 (University Park: The Pennsylvania State University, 1958), p. 16. See also K. Ishwaran, *Family Life in the Netherlands* (The Hague: Van Keulen, 1959), Chapter on: "The Impact of the War on the Family," pp. 92 ff.

14. Enrico Quarantelli, "A Note on the Protective Function of the Family in Disasters," *Marriage and Family Living,* XXII (August,

1960), 263–64. See also Marvin B. Sussman's review of the literature on this topic in his contribution in Chapter IV of this volume.

15. Gerhard Baumert, "Changes in the Family and the Position of Older Persons in Germany," *Social and Psychological Aspects of Aging*, Clark Tibbitts and Wilma Donahue, eds. (New York: Columbia University Press, 1962), pp. 416 ff.

16. Aurelia Florea, *L'Anziano in Famiglia* (Roma: Comitato Italiano Per Gli Anziani, 1962) and some unpublished tabulations from a sample survey in rural parts of North and South Italy.

17. E. W. Hofstee and G. A. Kooy, "Traditional Households and Neighborhood Groups, Survivals of the Genealogical-Territorial Societal Pattern in Eastern Parts of the Netherlands," *Transactions of the World Sociological Congress*, Vol. IV, Part II (Amsterdam: International Sociological Association, 1954), 76 ff.

18. Baumert, "Changes in the Family and the Position of Older Persons in Germany," *op. cit.*

19. Hofstee and Kooy, "Traditional Households and Neighborhood Groups," *op. cit.* See also: K. Ishwaran, *Family Life in the Netherlands, op. cit.*, p. 40: "The extended family is confined to those areas which the Netherlanders themselves describe as 'old,' 'primitive,' 'outdated' and 'underdeveloped.' "

20. Rosenmayr and Köckeis, "A Method to Assess Living Arrangements and Housing Problems of the Aged," *op. cit.*, p. 5.

21. *Ibid.* A similar conclusion is reported by Robins in an American study. Robins found that in Columbia, Missouri, the combined household was formed on an average of ten years after the children's marriage. Arthur J. Robins, "Family Relations in Three-Generation Households," *Social and Psychological Aspects of Aging*, Clark Tibbitts and Wilma Donahue, eds. (New York: Columbia University Press, 1962), p. 470.

22. See for example Ethel Shanas, *The Health of Older People: A Social Survey* (Cambridge, Mass.: Harvard University Press, 1962), Chapter VI, "Older People and Their Families," pp. 107–41; and J. Diederich, *Levensomstandighedenvan bejaarden in kleinere en middelgrote gemeenten van Nederland* (Amsterdam: Nationale Raad voor Maatschappelijk Wek's Gravenhage, Netherlands, 1958).

23. Rosenmayr and Köckeis, "A Method to Assess Living Arrangements and Housing Problems of the Aged," *op. cit.*

24. We have to take into account that the observations in intergenerational relations in the three countries are based on sample surveys with the aged in private households only. Differences in the degree of institutionalization of the aged in the three countries, however, is not great enough to be the cause of the observed difference.

Commentary: *Intergenerational Tensions: A Comparative View*

The two articles on intergenerational tensions point to the fact that a threat to one's status is to be found in underdeveloped as well as in technologically advanced countries. It may be endemic to the human condition that the very transiency of life makes one sensitive to the loss of prestige and functionality. Nevertheless, each society consciously and unconsciously erects defenses against the deleterious effects of rivalry and competition between generations. Robert A. LeVine's article focuses on the institutional mechanisms operating in equatorial Africa, where the educated son is able to sustain intergenerational stability by deferring to the norm of obligation while withholding intimacy. In this manner, tensions are muted. In Denmark, the welfare programs introduced in the last century assure the aged of reasonable security. National health insurance provides medical care, and low-cost housing is provided by the government so that there is no abrupt change in living patterns for elder citizens. Acceptance of services in old age does not carry any puritanical stigma or loss of self-esteem. These services attenuate tensions and strains between generations.

In Africa, the conditions that make for intergenerational tensions, particularly in the developing nations, which in most instances are newly emergent, are due to an entirely different set of considerations. The nuclear family in Africa, while in existence, has an ambivalent status because the entire community is in transition from tribal to national or, in more remote terms, from traditional to modern. For this reason, the extended family type is still dominant except for the few preindustrial urban communities where recent arrivals in particular are still linked to their tribal roots. In Asia, where the extended or joint family is still dominant on the subcontinent, intergenerational tension is symptomatic of an incomplete transition, not between tribal and national, as in Africa, but between village and city.

Denmark and the United States both stress individual achievement and mobility. For both, the nuclear family is the normative ideal, and the companionate aspects of the marital relationship are stressed. However, America's stress on individual achievement has led to a disregard for senior citizens. In the United States, there are over 18 million men and women who are sixty-five years old or older. Their problem is one of survival in a society that provides no economic status for them and relegates them to a life of loneliness and isolation. Given this anomic situation, it is understandable that this age group has a higher suicide rate than any other in the United States. Jan Stehouwer's study shows that the aged in the United States tend to offer more financial help to their children than do the Danes. Obviously this assistance is unnecessary in a country that has stressed welfare programs. Assistance to children leads to intergenerational stress because it imposes obligations on the nuclear family that are difficult to meet. There are no effective institutional mechanisms in the United States by which an adult is able to resolve the tensions stemming from the demands of his family and parents. A three-generational household would almost inevitably be dysfunctional for urban nuclear family types. The nuclear family, when it becomes dominant, is composed of small independent or autonomous units, follows egalitarian norms, and tends to move toward a single standard of morality. To the degree that the nuclear family is characterized by these standards, there is not room in the same household for accommodation to an older generation that is bound to a more traditional orientation. Although this type of family structure prevails in Denmark, the tensions between generations are mitigated by the fact that Danes, as providers, are assured of security in times of personal crisis by direct government support for family needs.

Asia, Africa, Denmark, and the United States, all for their own reasons, have intergenerational tensions, but the reasons may be placed on a continuum between two termini. One end expresses the dominance of the clan or consanguineal family, with the nuclear family almost totally subordinate. The other end of the continuum reflects the dominance of the nuclear family. It should be noted parenthetically that the reason we have included Asia is not merely because one of the editors has had field experience in that area, but more significantly, because Asian preindustrial traditional society on the subcontinent is, for the most part, nontribal, and this type of comparison has not been made by LeVine.

9 THE NORMAL AMERICAN FAMILY

TALCOTT PARSONS

. . . The most important processes of development in American society during the present century, as before, have been continuing differentiation in its structure, a general process of upgrading of expectations and responsibilities, and the related development of new modes of integration of persons and substructures in the increasingly complex society. As a process of very rapid social change, complicated by such external disturbances as hot and cold wars, it is a process marked by much internal disturbance, anxiety, and conflict on many different levels.

The family and its more immediate environment have been centrally involved in the general process, and the end certainly is still far away. Perhaps the best single reference point is to the structural differentiation of the nuclear family, both from other components of the kinship system and from nonkin elements. The most striking case is the performance of occupational roles outside the family in many types of employing organizations. The most massive index of this is the decline of the proportion of the labor force engaged in agriculture, but many other family-operated productive units, like small retail shops and handicraft enter-

From Man and Civilization: The Family's Search for Survival *by Farber, Mustacchi & Wilson. Copyright © 1965 by McGraw-Hill, Inc. Used by permission of McGraw-Hill Book Company.*

prises, have also been declining in number. With this, of course, has gone dependence of the family household, as consuming unit, on money income, and drastic reduction in its relative self-sufficiency.

The composition of the household has also tended increasingly to be confined to nuclear family members. Thus households with complete nuclear families, i.e., husband, wife, and their own children, increased in proportion of total persons from 80 to 82.7 per cent between 1940 and 1960. During the same period, the proportion of household members who were relatives of the head other than spouse or own children, decreased from 7.7 to 5.5 per cent. The categories of nonfamily members, lodgers, and living-in domestic servants decreased from 4.2 to 1.5 per cent; the domestic-service figure, though small, is particularly striking in decreasing from 0.8 to 0.2 per cent, i.e., being cut to one-fourth in only twenty years. Of course the other side of the picture has been a sharp increase in nonfamilial households, i.e., those composed of single persons or those unrelated, such as two women. The increase in proportions of husbands and wives living together, from 40.5 per cent of total household members to 44.1 per cent, an increase of nearly 10 per cent in twenty years, is particularly striking in the light of the high divorce rate, which remains high though it has tended to decline slowly since the postwar peak. I think the proposition is correct that we now have the largest proportion, in the history of the United States Census, of persons of marriageable age and not widowed living with their spouses and, if the children are not yet too old, with their own children. The broad picture is that of an increasingly specialized but structurally intact family.

This impression of the importance of the family is strengthened by two further facts, namely, the decreasing average age of marriage to a point of near twenty-two for males and twenty for females, and the well-known increased birth rate, which has now been sustained since about 1940—the net reproduction rate for 1959 being a little over 1.7. There have, however, been other crucial changes. One of the most important is the extension of the span of life. Though there has been relatively little change in the last decade or so, since early in the century it has been dramatic. The *average* expectance of life at birth has reached seventy years, though as of 1959 there was a differential of 6.5 years in favor of women over men. A further particularly interesting change is the compression of the childbearing period. Combined with the trend to early marriage, this meant that by 1957 (Glick) the average American mother had her *last* child when she was twenty-six years old, in spite of the higher birth rates. This, of course, means that most married couples face a much longer period of the "empty nest," when their children are independent and neither is widowed, than has previously been the case. The combination of early marriage for girls and the greater longevity of women also means that there is a considerable excess of widows over widowers.

Another important phenomenon of differentiation in the life cycle has been the enormous growth of formal education. There is, first, the extension of full secondary education to all but a decreasing minority, though the dropouts from high school constitute the core of the juvenile-delinquency problem. Second, there is the rapid increase in the college population, running to about 40 per cent beginning some kind of college, and close to 25 per cent completing a four-year college course. Finally, postgraduate professional education, though still small in percentage, is by far the most rapidly growing sector of the educational system. This has occasioned important family problems in that a rapidly increasing proportion marry before completing their formal training.

A final notable set of demographic facts in this area concerns the gainful employment of married women. Between 1950 and 1960 the proportion of single women in the labor force actually declined, presumably because more of them were in school or college. The most striking figure, however, is the increase from 24.8 to 30 per cent between 1950 and 1960 among those living with their spouse, an increase of more than 25 per cent in a decade. The employment of women who were widowed or divorced has, on the other hand, increased much more slowly. Clearly the former increase is associated with the compression of the period of responsibility for the care of small children. It is quite clear, however, that the American woman is more frequently a married woman and probably for a larger fraction of her life than ever before. She is, at the same time, becoming increasingly highly educated and, in spite of the scarcity and expense of domestic service, she is less often "only" a housewife and a volunteer church and community worker than her predecessors. Particularly over the life cycle, her roles have become much more differentiated.

It is of course a commonplace that the American family is predominantly and, in a sense, increasingly an urban middle-class family. There has indeed been, if not a very great equalization of income (though there has been some in the present century), a very substantial homogenization of patterns of life in the population with reference to a number of things. Basic to this are the employment of one or more family members outside the home; the nuclear family household without domestic service except for cleaning and baby-sitting; and the basic constituents of the standard of living, including in particular the familiar catalogue of consumer durable goods, which constitute the basic capital equipment of the household.[1]

It can then be said that, in a sense that has probably never existed before, in a society that in most respects has undergone a process of very extensive structural differentiation, there has emerged a remarkably uniform, basic type of family. It is uniform in its kinship and household composition in the sense of confinement of its composition to members of the nuclear family, which is effective at any given stage of the family cycle, and in the outside activities of its members, e.g., jobs for adult men, some participation in the labor force for women, school for children, and various other types of community participation. Indeed it is also highly uniform in the basic components of the standard of living, e.g., the private dwelling, the mechanical aids, the impingement of communications from the outside through the mass media, etc. There is one increasingly conspicuous and distressing exception to the general pattern, namely, the situation of the lowest groups by most of the socioeconomic indices, such as income, education, occupational level, etc. This problem will have to be taken up again later.

The author has, perhaps more than anyone else, been responsible for diffusing the phrase "isolated nuclear family" to describe one aspect of this unit. This concept has recently been challenged notably by two groups of sociologists, Eugene Litwack and Melvin Seeman and their associates, in the name of the importance of the network of extended kinship relations beyond the nuclear family. To my mind the two views are not contradictory but complementary. The concept of isolation applies in the first instance to kinship structure as seen in the perspective of anthropological studies in that field. In this context our system represents an extreme type, which is well described by that term. It does not, however, follow that all relations to kin outside the nuclear family are broken. Indeed the very psychological importance for the individual of the nuclear family in which he was born and brought up would make any such conception impossible.

By and large, however, as our population elements are further removed from peasant or other similar backgrounds, these extended kinship elements do not form firmly structured units of the social system. They are not residential or economic units—in the consuming, to say nothing of the producing, sense—nor are they "corporate groups" in the sense that clans and lineages in so many societies have been. There are above all two significant features of their relations to the nuclear family. First, in the maintenance of going relations, though there seems to be clear precedence of members of the families of orientation of both spouses—parents so long as they live, and siblings, even among siblings as between the two families, and much more so beyond that—there is a marked optional quality of the expectation system. There certainly are some structured preferences on kinship bases, and others on those of geographical propinquity, but still there is a strong tendency for kinship to shade into friendship in the sense of absence from the latter of ascriptive components of membership. Hence, the amount of visiting, of common activity, of telephone and written communication, etc., is highly variable within formal categories of relationship. This suggests that extended kin constitute a resource which may be selectively taken advantage of within considerable limits.

This supposition is greatly strengthened by the second consideration. This is the extent to which extended kin, especially members of the family of orientation but not only they, serve as a "reserve" of expectations of solidarity and willingness to implement them which can be mobilized in case of need. To take one primary context, there is a clear expectation that adult siblings, children, and, increasingly, parents of adults will be economically independent and should not need to be the recipients of direct financial aid from relatives. The extended family is, in this sense, normally not a solitary-operating economic unit. In case of special need, however, the first obligation to help, if there is no organized community provision and sometimes when there is, falls on close relatives who are financially able to bear the burden. Such obligations are not likely to be unlimited, but they are none the less real—in cases of sickness, of the dependency of old age, and similar cases.

An interesting case is the one mentioned above. The tendency is for earlier marriage, which, in the most highly educated groups, very frequently occurs before completion of higher education. Not only does this situation give rise to an important part of the employment of younger married women—who thereby earn the fictional degree of P.H.T. ("put hubby through"). There is also a substantial amount of aid from parents and some from older siblings which helps fill the gap. Often this is partially concealed in the form of "gifts," e.g., of a car or a vacation trip, testifying to the importance of the need for "independence." Ritual solidarity on the occasion of weddings, but even more especially funerals, fits in with this pattern.

On this background I may now turn to a few functional and analytical considerations. More than any other influence, psychoanalytic psychology has, during the last generation, made us aware of two crucial things. The first is the fundamental importance for the individual personality of the process of growing up in the intimacies of the family. Not only is mental illness to a large, though by no means exclusive, extent generated in the relations of a child to members of his family,[2] but normal personality development is highly contingent on the proper combination of influences operating in the family situation. Of course the family stands by no means alone, and as the child grows older, influences from the neighborhood, then the school and beyond become increasingly important. The family, however, lays the essential foundations and continues always to be important.

There has been a good deal of discussion of the importance of psychological "security" in this whole context. An individual's sense of security naturally depends on his experience in his family of orientation. It remains, however, an essential problem throughout life.[3] We have become increasingly aware that for the adult, in psychologically very complex ways, his family of procreation is dynamically most intimately linked with his family of orientation. The experience of parenthood is of course a recapitulation in reverse of that of the child in relation to his parents, and in important ways reactivates the psychological structures belonging to that period. Just as much, marriage is a complex organization of components in the personality which are derived from childhood experience—the common involvement of eroticism in both is the surest clue to the relationship.

For the normal adult, then, his marriage and his role as parent constitute the primary going reinforcement of his psychological security. The family can thus be seen to have two primary functions, not one. On the one hand it is the primary agent of socialization of the child, while on the other it is the primary basis of security for the normal adult. Moreover, the linkage of these two functions is very close. The point may be put by saying that their common responsibility as parents is the most important focus of the solidarity of marriage partners, and that the desire for children is the natural outcome of a solid "romantic" attraction between two persons of opposite sex. The primary link between these two functions in terms of agency is clearly the feminine role in its dual capacity as mother and as wife.

I think it reasonable to suggest that the broad pattern of the contemporary American family, sketched above in statistical terms, fits this functional analysis. It seems to be a case of a process of differentiation through which the central functions of early socialization and giving individuals a psychological security base have become separated out from others to which they have been ascribed in less differentiated societies. The sharing of the common household as the place to "live" with all its implications is the fundamental phenomenon—it is this sharing which makes the normal nuclear family a distinctive unit which cannot be confused with *any* others, based either on kinship or on other criteria. The home, its furnishings, equipment, and the rest constitute the "logistic" base for the performance of this dual set of primary functions.

The family, however, is not only a setting into which individuals escape from the pressures of the outside society; it also has profoundly important functions in that society. The keynotes to what I have in mind may be stated with reference to two concepts mentioned above, namely that of "reserves" of solidarity and that of basic trust as discussed by Erikson. Following Durkheim, I should say that one of, to me the four, essential conditions of the adequate functioning of a social system is the solidarity among its members. This may be conceived as their motivational readiness to accept their common belongingness as members of a collective system and to *trust* each other to fulfill mutual expectations attached to membership in their respective roles.

The more differentiated and the larger the scale of the social system which depends on solidarity, however, the less can solidarity be dependent on common membership in groups where norms are highly particularistic and the relations rigidly ascribed, and where loyalties are highly diffuse and grounded in immediate affective motivational interests. Thus national community and a highly generalized system of legal norms are foci of organization highly dependent on solidarity, but clearly not meeting the above criteria. The problem is, how is it possible to develop solidarity and the attendant mutuality of trust where these conditions do not obtain—or is it possible at all?

As a first approach to an answer it may be said that the family is the "primordial" solitary unit of all human societies. Indeed, in the most primitive, kinship, which includes much more than the nuclear family, is the mode of organization of *all* solidarity. Furthermore, it is within these units that all the principal human needs are met. In a modern society this can be true only for the small child. For him "dependency" in the most diffuse sense is more highly concentrated in his relations within this small unit than in any other previous social conditions—a unit which we have seen is more sharply distinguished from others, both of kinship and of nonkinship constitution. As the child matures he develops a variety of roles outside his family. First, perhaps, come neighborhood play groups, then participation in formal education in the school with, concurrently, a new order of relation to age-peers—in the elementary school period virtually confined to the same sex, later increasingly involving the opposite sex. Then more or less well coordinated in time comes emergence into the adult responsibilities of occupational roles and of marriage. The latter usually eventuates in parenthood.

One aspect of the process is that from total and intense dependency on the family of orientation the child becomes increasingly independent from *that* nuclear family, and he continues to play a wide range of nonfamilial roles in his later life. Indeed his capacity to do so successfully is one of the two principal indices of the success of the socialization function in the family of orientation. But the other dramatic aspect is the switchover from family of orientation to the new family of procreation through marriage. The intensity of its emotional significance is attested by the pattern of romantic love on the one hand and the deep concern for having children on the other—both of which are in important part motivated by residues of childhood socialization experience.

Finally, let me emphasize again that the modern family has been deprived of a whole range of its historic functions, particularly those of economic production, but also others. It has become not only a structurally differentiated but a functionally specialized agency. What then can be said about the significance of these remaining specialized functions, not only for the personalities of the individual members but for the wider society?

I suggested above that solidarity was one of four principal conditions of the functioning of a social system. The other three may be said to be economic productivity, political effectiveness, not only for the society as a whole but also for its important collectively organized subsystems, and the integrity of institutionalization of its value commitments. Comparison with one or more of these three may yield suggestions of the significance of what is gained by individuals in their families of orientation and, as it were, "stored" in those of procreation.

The comparison may seem farfetched, but I suggest quite seriously that the grounding of the value of money in "real assets" and its most elementary form in metal coinage are the "primordial" bases of productivity in a sense parallel to that in which family solidarity is the primordial basis of social solidarity generally, "guaranteed" by the personal security of the individual. It is the groundwork on which the possibility of mutual trust in ramified systems of associative relationships—and hence openness to mutual influence—is built in a complex society. Furthermore, because of the irreducible element of ascription on the parent-child relationship, this significance of family solidarity comes to focus in that of the marriage relationship. One of the striking features of modern marriage is, of course, its increasingly voluntary character. This is the product of a long evolution from maximally prescriptive marriages in kinship terms, through marriages arranged by parents and other kin. It is the prototypical, fully unfettered personal commitment to a merging of interests, fortunes, and responsibilities. It is, however, not a simple contract for the mutual furtherance of specific interests, but a diffuse merging, with understood differentiation of function, "for better, for worse, for richer, for poorer," etc. This establishes a certain presumption, that persons capable of honestly undertaking such a commitment of mutual loyalty, including the attendant responsibilities of parenthood, may be regarded as generally trustworthy persons.

It is this generalization of the presumption of trustworthiness which seems to me to be the most crucial societal asset grounded in the solidarity of the family. To help in understanding how this can work it may be recalled that in the parallel context the value of money is grounded in the economic utility, first of real assets generally, then of its metal "base." I suggest that the solidarity of marriage is parallel to the utility of gold—perhaps a not unfamiliar figure of speech. But money as medium of exchange is not a real asset in the present sense: it has no "commodity value." It is a means of acquiring real assets and in turn can itself be acquired by selling them, but as the medium it cannot be consumed. Its

significance lies in the possibility of a kind of pooling of the resources of the exchanging system. This involves increased risk for
units who put some of their resources into monetary form—as
they must if such a system is to operate. But if the value of the
medium is secure, the units taken severally and the system as a
whole gain enormously in productive potential, especially when
not only finished goods and services but the factors of production
become marketable.

The indispensable condition of security of the value of the
monetary medium cannot, however, rest only on the intrinsic
commodity value of its metallic base. It must rest just as much on
confidence in exchangeability for real assets, including the availability of such assets in the system—hence the general level of
productivity of the system.

The analogue of money as a measure of utility and medium of
economic exchange in the field of social solidarity is what, in a
technical sense, I have called influence.[4] By this I mean generalized capacity to persuade, through giving "good reasons" why the
object of influence should believe or do something in "his own
interest." The outcome of successful use of influence in this sense
is an increased level of consensus or solidarity in the system to
which both belong—though of course the relation to third parties
remains problematical.

Persuasion may be carried out by "intrinsic means," e.g., direct
information of commitment of intentions to specific action. This is
analogous to the exchange of real assets through barter. What I
mean by influence goes beyond this to persuade and thereby mobilize commitments, power of control of resources, through a generalized symbolic medium. This consists essentially in the "reputation" of the user of influence for a combination of integrity in
commitment to the values presumptively shared with the object of
influence, ability to help mobilize the necessary resources, and
competence in implementing any action implications of the
achieved consensus. Thus to take an example which is very familiar, physicians very generally use influence to get the consent of
patients or their families to recommended regimes of treatment.
Information alone would not do because so frequently the layman
is not competent to evaluate technical information even if it is
given to him. He must *trust* both the physician's competence and
his integrity. Without the institutionalization of this truth, the presumption that a physician is *trustworthy*, the effectiveness of

health care in our complex society would be very much lower than it is. This, however, is only one of many examples which could be adduced. The necessity for influence to bridge the gap between the responsibilities taken by political leadership and the competence of their constituents to evaluate the issues by themselves is certainly one of the most striking instances. The assassination of President Kennedy brought out with special vividness the extent to which not only Americans but much of the world depended on his leadership and was in fact accessible to his influence—however severe the limits to which it was subject, e.g., to Congress. This influence is, in turn, a function on the one hand of the great office of the American Presidency and on the other of the personality of the incumbent.

If, then, influence can be considered to be a generalized medium parallel to money—and to political power—it would be reasonable to believe that on the one hand its value is grounded in the "gold" of family solidarity, while on the other hand it depends on the capacity of the relevant social system or systems to achieve, maintain, and extend its solidarity, expressed above all in its capacity to achieve consensus in matters involving actual and potential conflict of interest. Clearly, trusting others, especially those with whom one does not have a prior diffuse relation of solidarity, involves risk, just as leaving one's economic assets in banks rather than in gold involves risk. The prevalence of anxiety over the risks of trust is eloquent testimony to this. Thus there is a vocal minority who consider all medical practitioners to be no better than pious frauds who simply exploit the helplessness and gullibility of their patients. Others, or many of the same people, consider all politicians to be simple parasites, who are promoting their personal interests at the expense of the public. Finally, the seriousness of basic mistrust in international affairs, especially where ideological conflicts are involved, scarcely needs further comment.

Furthermore, there are many different levels of differentiation of influence systems, which can be analyzed as parallel to that of monetary systems extending from simple market exchange, through the marketability as noted of the factors of production, notably labor and capital, to complex systems involving elaborate forms of banking and credit. The parallel to simple markets for consumers' goods lies in the use of influence to persuade people to make decisions and commitments which are immediately within their capacities or spheres of freedom of action to make. Thus a physician may use his influence to persuade a patient to accept a recommended course of treatment though at the sacrifice of time, money, and other things, including the assumption of risks.

It is a much further step in differentiation to establish systems where the factors involved in enhancing the solidarity of a system are themselves mobilized by the use of influence. A major type of example would seem to be those elements of educational processes which are essentially optional in the system in question. Thus in order to be influential, the physician must have been properly trained. We tend, in evaluating professional training, to emphasize the factor of competence, but it would seem that reputation for integrity is no less important, and indeed access to facilities—i.e., through membership in the staff of a first-rate hospital —would not be neglected. Hence from this point of view medical education may be regarded in part as an "influence-producing industry," in that it produces a class of professional people who have a far higher capacity than would otherwise be the case to persuade people to accept good health care. The ubiquitous resistances to such acceptance should make it clear that this is by no means to be taken for granted.

The analogy to credit in influence systems raises problems of sufficient complexity so that within the limits of this brief paper, it is probably best not to enter into them. One more general point about such systems does, however, need to be made. This is that the basic organizational form of influence systems is the voluntary association. This is not, however, a matter of presence or absence, but of a component in all relational systems with a collective significance. Influence, however, is a medium of persuasion and a person is not in the relevant sense genuinely persuaded unless he is entirely free to reject the influence. Intermixture with economic inducements, with explicit or implied coercive threats, or even appeal to prior commitments is not "pure" persuasion. Generally speaking, the voluntary association is the relational nexus within which there can be said to be a presumption of the achievability of consensus. It will be limited on the one hand by boundaries of membership, which may be more or less formalized, and on the other by boundaries of relevant content—thus consensus with one's physician is relevant within the sphere of health, but not, for example, within the sphere of political opinion.

In the light of these considerations, which may seem to digress a long way from the traditional interests of family sociology, let us now come back to the contemporary family. First, this functional context may throw some light on the significance of some of the trends of development of that family. My suggestion here is that it is to be expected that the family would, as the foundation of the solidarity-influence system, itself develop progressively in the direction of the voluntary association. In the aspect of marriage this is very clear indeed—namely, the trend to make marriage as nearly as possible a purely personal and voluntary relationship. This has gone to the point where the depth of commitment is considered to a high degree to be a function of its voluntary character. More problematical, but highly significant, is the tendency to bring children into the status of members of a voluntary association much earlier and more extensively than before. Of course there is an inherent limitation to this trend in that infants cannot rationally "choose" their parents, but this is clearly a major trend in the American family. Like other such trends it has undoubtedly had its excesses, and surely its limits are not yet clearly defined, but that it is a fundamental trend can scarcely be doubted. Perhaps the most important keynote is that by the isolation of the marriage pair from "structural supports" of more or less ascribed character, children are put in a position of having to trust their parents to an extremely high degree. The corollary is that parents will be expected to reciprocate this trust to an increasing degree, hence to trust children as far as possible as responsible members of the family association.

In this connection it is particularly important to note that what I call trust is *not* to be identified with moral commitment. Common values are certainly essential to the solidarity of any social system, but as *one* factor, not as its totality. Most problems of trust in the present sense arise at a different level where, presuming common values, the questions concern action within the sphere of autonomous personal responsibility. On the part of many parents, and more generally the "view-with-alarm" school of thought on the problems of contemporary youth, the tendency is to confuse the two, and to treat as essentially a moral problem what should be one of trust in the present sense. On the part of young people trained in independence, defining problems as moral tends to activate anxiety about the basic consensus—the complaint is, "Don't you trust me?"

A second major set of considerations emerges. This is that while the family is the primary locus of most elementary instrumental learning for children, e.g., walking and talking, and is for both children and adults an essential agency for meeting their biological and other needs, e.g., food, sleep, relaxation, etc., its most crucial functions lie in the area of solidarity. In socialization it is above all the agency for establishing cathexes and identification, for integration into the series of *social* systems in which the child will function as an adult. Above all, perhaps, it is the primary agency for developing his capacity to integrate with others, to trust and be trusted, to exercise influence, and to accept legitimate influence. Here, of course, two axes are essential. One is the balance of trust over distrust, the "intensity" component. The other is the component of generalization. This is the capacity to enter into solitary relations over a *range,* both of associative partners and of subject-matter areas. In view of the increasing pluralism of our type of society, this is a particularly critical factor. It has become essential for the responsible citizen to be able to balance a variety of complex contexts of obligation and expectation, to be ready to enter into many, but not arbitrarily to sacrifice the interests of some to others. My suggestion would be that the family type which approaches the pattern of voluntary association is the best instrument for laying the foundations of this capacity—though it must be supplemented by other agencies. For the adult the combination of marriage and parenthood in such a family type provides a more or less optimal basis for maintaining the motivational foundations of this more generalized capacity. In this connection socialization and adult participation are above all related in that the capacity to become a good spouse and parent is the underlying capacity for effective participation generally in solitary relations.

Finally, a third inference may be drawn. The "intrinsic utility" of gold is connected with certain features of its sheer physical stability. Its problematical feature is not this but its scarcity. The "gold" of solidarity, however, seems to be an intrinsically unstable entity. Its value depends on its being scarce in the sense that persons who disperse their deepest interpersonal loyalties too widely, e.g., through incapacity to commit them adequately to their marriages and their own children, thereby on the whole lessen their capacity for trust in more generalized and impersonal contexts. But the balances in the personality system, and the meshing of the several commitments in the family, seem to be inherently complex and precarious. This seems to be the most fundamental reason why, once socialized, the typical individual is not finished with family problems, but positively *needs* to marry and to have children.

It would seem to follow that in so far as families are placed under strain, their tendencies to breakdown and various social pathologies should be expected to be conspicuous. Hence I have long felt that what underlay the high divorce rates of our society was not, as so commonly alleged, the decline in the importance of marriage, people's "indifference" to it, but exactly the reverse.[5] Divorce is an index of the severity of the burden placed on the marriage relationship in modern society, and back of that, of the importance of its functions. It is not correct to treat it in any simple sense as a symptom of "decline," except the decline of older patterns of social organization which in any case could not be fitted in with the other principal features of modern society. Essentially the same can be said of failures in the socialization of children, which, of course, are many. Modern child training is far more difficult and demanding on the parents but also on the children themselves than before. In this matter one should not be misled by economic affluence and the like. The hard physical work of a traditional farm boy is not nearly as difficult psychologically as the demands of secondary and higher education and adjustment to peers where the relationship patterns are freely responsible and not ascribed. Whether there is a larger proportion of serious breakdowns than in earlier times is exceedingly difficult to judge—the very anxiety generated by the present difficulties certainly predisposes to the expectation of failure. But that a substantial proportion should be expected is almost in the nature of the relation of the family to the general society of which it is such an essential part.

I was asked to write about the normal American family. In doing so, however, one is eventually led to some consideration of its strains and pathologies. In conclusion, . . . it seems appropriate to say a few words about that group in which the strains and difficulties of the modern family situation, as in other respects, are most highly concentrated, namely, those who stand lowest on the familiar scales of socioeconomic status, as by family income, education, job level, housing, and type of neighborhood.

Both with respect to the family and in other respects the trends of development of modern society have led to a concentration of certain problems in this lowest group, and by differentiation to a removal or weakening of the structural supports of the kind which, for example, have been more characteristic of the lower statuses in peasant societies—though the tendency to romanticize rural life should not lead one to overlook the reality of many noxious "rural slums." From a middle-class perspective absolute levels of deprivation stand out very prominently, but sociologically it seems more important to emphasize *relative* deprivation. By this I mean that the general trend of development in our society has included a massive upgrading of standards in many respects and the inclusion of much higher proportions of the population in the groups enjoying the higher standards. Education and the general standard of living are perhaps the most conspicuous contexts, but it is also important that the proportion of the labor force in un-skilled occupations has declined greatly.

The great source of difficulty is, of course, that in spite of many improved welfare arrangements, in a society where mobility and hence competition for preferment are so conspicuous, it has not yet proved possible to prevent a very substantial residual group from failing to meet what, however vaguely, must be defined as the minimum generally acceptable standards. To a degree and in certain respects it is legitimate to treat these cases as "failures" at the individual level, but it is surely much more a failure of the society in that though some persons brought up in the lowest con-ditions succeed in lifting themselves out of them, those set in them by and large are certainly severely handicapped in a wide variety of ways.

It is well known what a wide variety of "social problems" is concentrated in this group: poverty itself; substandard housing; educational retardation and early "dropout"; juvenile delin-quency; alcoholism; illness, both physical and mental; broken families; and others. It is clearly a vicious circle which, like the high divorce rates more generally, is in important part a conse-quence of the generally rapid process of upgrading. Thus, to take one example, the very rise in general educational standards makes the position of the relatively handicapped—whether by low IQ, lack of family support, or other factors—relatively *more* difficult. I suggest that this is a major factor in juvenile delinquency.

It is a healthy sign that there are recent indications of increased concern over this situation as a national problem, a concern ap-parently brought to focus primarily by two interconnected devel-opments, namely, the new phase of the struggle of the Negro for equality and the chronic unemployment connected with automa-tion, even in an economy which is developing at a relatively nor-mal rate.

Whatever the residue of a genuine "caste" system in the South, which is certainly rapidly breaking up, on the national level it has long been clear that basically the race problem is a *class* problem, but in a dual respect. The more obvious one is that the Negro, especially in urban society, has in fact been predominantly in lower-class status, and that in so far as there is any empirical truth in his imputed characteristics, these have been the characteristics shared with other lower-class groups. Indeed in study after study, for example, of such "pathological" behavior as delinquency, it has turned out that if class is controlled sufficiently rigorously the differences by race are negligible.

The second primary aspect, however, is that the Negro has become a, if not the, primary *symbol* of lower-class status. The new phase of the protest movement testifies that he himself is coming to be much less willing to accept this imputation, but it is this symbolic status which is at the core of the whole resistance to granting equal status. Furthermore the resistance centers in the white groups who feel insecure in their own status. The nonrational "reasoning," which must be interpreted in psychoanalytic terms, is to the effect that "if to be lower class is to be black, since I am white there is no danger of *my* falling into that status." Acceptance of the Negro in basically equal status, thus, would remove an important symbolic support to the security of the least secure white elements. The latter are presumably concentrated near the margin of lower-class status, but need not be found only there.[6]

It has recently been much publicized that the Negro has double the rate of unemployment of the white labor force, which is a dramatic confirmation of this status since it is in these lower groups generally that unemployment is concentrated.

There is no space to discuss this general situation further. I would like only to point out the relevance of my main analysis to this context. It may, that is, be reasonably supposed that a major factor in the vicious circle to which the lower class, white and Negro alike, is subject lies in the field of the relations between the family and the solidarity and influence systems with which it articulates. My essential point is that this is a two-way and not a one-way relation. By nearly every criterion "family disorganization" is particularly prevalent in the lower class. Not only is this one principal source of the other social problems in that group, but in another sense it is not an isolated phenomenon. It is in part a consequence of the low input to lower-class families of influence in the special form of "social acceptance": from the point of view of the higher groups they are "the wrong kind of people."

Though it is not possible to mobilize the relevant evidence here, I think it is adequate to support the proposition that broadly the lower class, including its Negro component, is not characterized by basically different value commitments from those of the higher groups. It is true that members of the lower class are economically disadvantaged. Perhaps their least serious handicap lies in the field of political power since both the ballot and power through trade unions is available to them, though very incompletely mobilized.

My own view, however, is that the critical problem of the status of the lower class is social acceptance. From any points of view accessible to social policy, it seems to me that in particular it is futile to expect that by exhortation lower-class families will be motivated to pull themselves together. Indeed, I am of the opinion that economic subsidies will not be effective unless they are accompanied by social support on a sufficient scale. The cure for the ills of the lower-class family is a massive input of the very social medium for which the higher-class (not upper-class) family is the primary base in our society in one major set of respects—influence in the form of social acceptance.

The essential goal of any such policies would be to break down group identifications which are interpreted directly, or indirectly as by the criterion of race, as lower class in the invidious residual sense. The neighborhood, the school, and the church are probably the crucial empirical areas for the important reason that the more limited the social participation, the more it is confined to the more immediately personal concerns of the family. Thus increased income would be likely to be important only so far as it enables families to break away from lower-class identifications, e.g., by neighborhood.

It would be expected that improvement in the solidarity of families at the lowest socioeconomic levels would be perhaps the most sensitive index to the success of such social policies. There must always be a bottom of any social scale with a hierarchical aspect, and an achievement-oriented society must be partly hierarchical. But this does not mean that the "outside" status of the present lower class is inevitable. I regard this as perhaps the most important single internal challenge to American society today.

Notes

1. Another important set of facts concerns the very large proportion of single-family dwellings in this country, and within this, the high proportion of owner occupancy.
2. The psychoanalytic tendency has been to "individualize" these relations by treating a child's relation to each of the other members one at a time—his mother, his father, his rivalry with a particular sibling, etc. More recently, however, there has emerged, particularly in the work of Theodore Lidz and his associates, a tendency to treat the family as a system in such a way that both illness and normality are conceived to be a function of the impact of the system as a whole—not of particular members in isolation—on the individual.
3. Erik Erikson has, in his *Childhood and Society,* given an especially clear formulation of this point in his discussion of the importance of what he calls "basic trust" and its relation to personality development.
4. Cf. Talcott Parsons, "On the Concept of Influence," *Public Opinion Quarterly,* Spring, 1963.
5. To take an analogy which I think is appropriate, the distressing toll of highway accidents is an index of the positive importance, and even, to a degree, of the successful ordering, of vehicular traffic. There is one way to abolish such accidents, namely, to eliminate motor vehicles. Similarly, modern divorce could be quite certainly eliminated if we went back to a primitive kinship system. But we are not, in either case, ready to pay the cost.
6. It is important to note that I do not identify lower and "working" class here. The solid upper-working-class groups, especially in the more skilled trades, seem to be pretty definitely included in the main national community in a sense in which the lower are not.

Commentary: *Is There a "Normal" American Family?*

In reviewing this very provocative essay by Talcott Parsons about the "normal" American family, the implications of some recent trends that have become visible only since the publication of this article must be stressed. We agree with Hyman Rodman (Marriage, Family and Society: A Reader, 1965) *that what is a problem for the middle class often is a solution for the lower class. Although the achievement norms of the dominant Ameri-*

can family type have in the past been emulated by lower status families, there is now a definite movement either to withdraw from the requirements of competing for status in such a social system or, even if still competing, to demand a share in the decision-making that attends the striving for upward vertical mobility.

Formerly, the Negro in the urban community was never really concerned with participation in decision-making or competition for status within the social system until he became a member of the middle class. This attainment never encompassed more than a small minority of all Negroes. The majority remained in the lower class and did not have this type of incentive. Today, however, as a result of the impact of various forms of black nationalism, there is an emphasis upon demands for decision-making power, not as a consequence of upward vertical mobility but as a search for some kind of ethnic or quasi-racial identity. As a matter of fact, middle-class aspirations are increasingly rejected as a contemporary version of "Uncle Tomism" or tokenism. In fact, what used to be accepted as objective sociological analyses (studies of Negro family instability, illegitimacy, and so on) are now rejected as racial slurs. The controversy over Daniel Patrick Moynihan's report (The Negro Family, 1965) *is a case in point.*

Even more impressive evidences of reaction to middle-class achievement norms are furnished by analyses of the hippie contraculture (discussed later in June Bingham's article). In this segment of society, the emphasis is not on participation, either integrated or segregated, but upon almost total withdrawal from involvement with these norms. As a slogan, "black power" is predicated upon a demand for power on a separatist basis, either shared or unshared. The hippie withdrawal is, in effect, a rejection of power or status as goals worthy of aspiration.

In his emphasis upon family socialization, Parsons is concerned with the delineation of differentiated roles appropriate to this socialization process in the middle-class family. The question now is: What happens in the middle-class family when there is a significant commitment to equalitarian norms, a romantic ideology, and a single standard of morality? May not role reversal or role conflict under these circumstances increasingly be a sign not of anomie or dysfunction but, rather, role "normalcy"?

Although Parsons may argue with historic plausibility that "the critical problem of the status of the lower class is social accept-

ance," *an even more critical question has come to the fore: Social acceptance by whom? In other words, the definition of this social situation and the kinds of social hierarchy that result from such definition are no longer the exclusive prerogative of the "normal American family."*

Reverting to Thorstein Veblen's terminology in The Theory of the Leisure Class *(1934), we can say that those who were included in first-generation industrial capitalism during the latter portion of the nineteenth century were in a position to accumulate wealth. However, the middle-class families had to consume more or less vicariously. In today's affluent society the middle classes literally can consume, but we suggest that lower class families may have to consume vicariously. We are speaking of class norms, not marriage norms in general. A content analysis of the mass media reflects in part such a convergence (at least symbolically) between white lower class and white middle-class norms.*

Although many marriages dominated by middle-class norms result ideologically from the interaction between pressures for economic security and romantic incentives such as free choice of mate, the lower classes, in their marital choices as well as in their consumption patterns, may weigh these pressures differently. The same causal factors that motivate lower class families to rely upon brand names in consumer goods to a much greater degree than their middle-class counterparts probably indicate a concern with the patriarchal tradition in mate selection. Both reflect reliance on authority rather than rational decision.

*Family rituals, as described by James H. S. Bossard (*Ritual in Family Living, *1950), were essential in the past to the solidarity of the American middle-class family. Today family ritual becomes increasingly dysfunctional for the middle-class family and functional for the lower class family. Robert K. Merton's concept of "ritualism" (*Social Theory and Social Research, *1968) as a kind of reaction to anomie within the social structure is, therefore, a more appropriate description of what happens in the lower classes. In effect, the anxiety and conflict induced by the romantic themes emphasized in mass media tend to be compensated for by the greater weight given to family ritualism in the lower classes.*

As a result, Parsons' concept of social acceptance always has to be qualified by a concern with "for whom" and "for what pur-

pose." Merton's use of the concepts of functional and dysfunctional may also need similar qualification. For the black nationalist, for example, social acceptance to achieve an identity means acceptance by one's black peers and not acceptance by a competitive dominant middle class.

10

CRUCIBLE OF IDENTITY:
THE NEGRO
LOWER-CLASS FAMILY

LEE RAINWATER

As long as Negroes have been in America, their marital and family patterns have been subjects of curiosity and amusement, moral indignation and self-congratulation, puzzlement and frustration, concern and guilt, on the part of white Americans.[1] As some Negroes have moved into middle-class status, or acquired standards of American common-man respectability, they too have shared these attitudes toward the private behavior of their fellows, sometimes with a moral punitiveness to rival that of whites, but at other times with a hard-headed interest in causes and remedies rather than moral evaluation. Moralism permeated the subject of Negro sexual, marital, and family behavior in the polemics of slavery apologists and abolitionists as much as in the Northern and Southern civil rights controversies of today. Yet as long as the dialectic of good or bad, guilty or innocent, overshadows a concern with who, why, and what can be, it is unlikely that realistic and effective social planning to correct the clearly desperate situation of poor Negro families can begin.

This paper is concerned with a description and analysis of slum Negro family patterns as these reflect and sustain Negroes' adaptations to the economic, social, and personal situation into which

Reprinted by permission from Daedalus, *Journal of the American Academy of Arts and Sciences, Boston, Mass., Vol. 95, No. 1 (Winter 1966).*

they are born and in which they must live. As such it deals with facts of lower-class life that are usually forgotten or ignored in polite discussion. We have chosen not to ignore these facts in the belief that to do so can lead only to assumptions which would frustrate efforts at social reconstruction, to strategies that are unrealistic in the light of the actual day-to-day reality of slum Negro life. Further, this analysis will deal with family patterns which interfere with the efforts slum Negroes make to attain a stable way of life as working- or middle-class individuals and with the effects such failure in turn has on family life. To be sure, many Negro families live *in* the slum ghetto, but are not *of* its culture (though even they, and particularly their children, can be deeply affected by what happens there). However, it is the individuals who succumb to the distinctive family life style of the slum who experience the greatest weight of deprivation and who have the greatest difficulty responding to the few self-improvement resources that make their way into the ghetto. In short, we propose to explore in depth the family's role in the "tangle of pathology" which characterizes the ghetto.

The social reality in which Negroes have had to make their lives during the 450 years of their existence in the western hemisphere has been one of victimization "in the sense that a system of social relations operates in such a way as to deprive them of a chance to share in the more desirable material and non-material products of a society which is dependent, in part, upon their labor and loyalty." In making this observation, St. Clair Drake goes on to note that Negroes are victimized also because "they do not have the same degree of access which others have to the attributes needed for rising in the general class system—money, education, 'contacts,' and 'know-how.'" [2] The victimization process started with slavery; for 350 years thereafter Negroes worked out as best they could adaptations to the slave status. After emancipation, the cultural mechanisms which Negroes had developed for living the life of victims continued to be serviceable as the victimization process was maintained first under the myths of white supremacy and black inferiority, later by the doctrines of gradualism which covered the fact of no improvement in position, and finally by the modern Northern system of ghettoization and indifference.

When lower-class Negroes use the expression, "Tell it like it is," they signal their intention to strip away pretense, to describe a situation or its participants as they really are, rather than in a polite or euphemistic way. "Telling it like it is" can be used as a harsh, aggressive device, or it can be a healthy attempt to face reality rather than retreat into fantasy. In any case, as he goes about his field work, the participant observer studying a ghetto community learns to listen carefully to any exchange preceded by such an announcement because he knows the speaker is about to express his understanding of how his world operates, of what motivates its members, of how they actually behave.

The first responsibility of the social scientist can be phrased in much the same way: "Tell it like it is." His second responsibility is to try to understand why "it" is that way, and to explore the implications of what and why for more constructive solutions to human problems. Social research on the situation of the Negro American has been informed by four main goals: (1) to describe the disadvantaged position of Negroes, (2) to disprove the racist ideology which sustains the caste system, (3) to demonstrate that responsibility for the disadvantages Negroes suffer lies squarely upon the white caste which derives economic, prestige, and psychic benefits from the operation of the system, and (4) to suggest that in reality whites would be better rather than worse off if the whole jerry-built caste structure were to be dismantled. The successful accomplishment of these *intellectual* goals has been a towering achievement, in which the social scientists of the 1920's, '30's, and '40's can take great pride; that white society has proved so recalcitrant to utilizing this intellectual accomplishment is one of the great tragedies of our time, and provides the stimulus for further social research on "the white problem."

Yet the implicit paradigm of much of the research on Negro Americans has been an overly simplistic one concentrating on two terms of an argument:

White cupidity ◄─────────────── Negro suffering.

As an intellectual shorthand, and even more as a civil rights slogan, this simple model is both justified and essential. But, as a guide to greater understanding of the Negro situation as human adaptation to human situations, the paradigm is totally inadequate because it fails to specify fully enough the *process* by which Negroes adapt to their situations as they do, and the limitations one kind of adaptation places on possibilities for subsequent adaptations. A reassessment of previous social research, combined with examination of current social research on Negro ghetto communities, suggests a more complex, but hopefully more veridical, model:

White cupidity
creates
Structural Conditions Highly Inimical to Basic Social Adaptation (low-income availability, poor education, poor services, stigmatization)
to which Negroes adapt
by
Social and Personal Responses which serve to sustain the individual in his punishing world but also generate aggressiveness toward the self and others
which results in
Suffering directly inflicted by Negroes on themselves and on others.

In short, whites, by their greater power, create situations in which Negroes do the dirty work of caste victimization for them.

The white caste maintains a cadre of whites whose special responsibility is to enforce the system in brutal or refined ways (the Klan, the rural sheriff, the metropolitan police, the businessman who specializes in a Negro clientele, the Board of Education). Increasingly, whites recruit to this cadre middle-class Negroes who can soften awareness of victimization by their protective coloration. These special cadres, white and/or Negro, serve the very important function of enforcing caste standards by whatever means seems required, while at the same time concealing from an increasingly "unprejudiced" public the unpleasant facts they would prefer to ignore. The system is quite homologous to the Gestapo and concentration camps of Nazi Germany, though less fatal to its victims.

For their part, Negroes creatively adapt to the system in ways that keep them alive and extract what gratification they can find, but in the process of adaptation they are constrained to behave in ways that inflict a great deal of suffering on those with whom they make their lives, and on themselves. The ghetto Negro is constantly confronted by the immediate necessity to suffer in order to get what he wants of those few things he can have, or to make others suffer, or both—for example, he suffers as exploited student and employee, as drug user, as loser in the competitive game of his peer-group society; he inflicts suffering as disloyal spouse, petty thief, knife- or gun-wielder, petty con man.

It is the central thesis of this paper that the caste-facilitated infliction of suffering by Negroes on other Negroes and on themselves appears most poignantly within the confines of the family, and that the victimization process as it operates in families prepares and toughens its members to function in the ghetto world, at the same time that it seriously interferes with their ability to operate in any other world. This, however, is very different from arguing that "the family is to blame" for the deprived situation ghetto Negroes suffer; rather we are looking at the logical outcome of the operation of the widely ramified and interconnecting caste system. In the end we will argue that only palliative results can be expected from attempts to treat directly the disordered family patterns to be described. Only a change in the original "inputs" of the caste system, the structural conditions inimical to basic social adaptation, can change family forms.

Almost thirty years ago, E. Franklin Frazier foresaw that the fate of the Negro family in the city would be a highly destructive one. His readers would have little reason to be surprised at observations of slum ghetto life today:

. . . As long as the bankrupt system of southern agriculture exists, Negro families will continue to seek a living in the towns and cities. . . . They will crowd the slum areas of southern cities or make their way to northern cities where their families will become disrupted and their poverty will force them to depend upon charity.[3]

The Autonomy of the Slum Ghetto

Just as the deprivations and depredations practiced by white society have had their effect on the personalities and social life of Negroes, so also has the separation from the ongoing social life of the white community had its effect. In a curious way, Negroes have had considerable freedom to fashion their own adaptations within their separate world. The larger society provides them with few resources but also with minimal interference in the Negro community on matters which did not seem to affect white interests. Because Negroes learned early that there were a great many things they could not depend upon whites to provide they developed their own solutions to recurrent human issues. These solutions can often be seen to combine, along with the predominance of elements from white culture, elements that are distinctive to the Negro group. Even more distinctive is the *configuration* which emerges from those elements Negroes share with whites and those which are different.

It is in this sense that we may speak of a Negro subculture, a distinctive *patterning* of existential perspectives, techniques for coping with the problems of social life, views about what is desirable and undesirable in particular situations. This subculture, and particularly that of the lower-class, the slum, Negro, can be seen as his own creation out of the elements available to him in response to (1) the conditions of life set by white society and (2) the selective freedom which that society allows (or must put up with given the pattern of separateness on which it insists).

Out of this kind of "freedom" slum Negroes have built a culture which has some elements of intrinsic value and many more elements that are highly destructive to the people who must live in it. The elements that whites can value they constantly borrow. Negro arts and language have proved so popular that such commentators on American culture as Norman Mailer and Leslie Fiedler have noted processes of Negro-ization of white Americans as a minor theme of the past thirty years.[4] A fairly large proportion of Negroes with national reputations are engaged in the occupation of diffusing to the larger culture these elements of intrinsic value.

On the negative side, this freedom has meant, as social scientists who have studied Negro communities have long commented, that many of the protections offered by white institutions stop at the edge of the Negro ghetto: there are poor police protection and enforcement of civil equities, inadequate schooling and medical service, and more informal indulgences which whites allow Negroes as a small price for feeling superior.

For our purposes, however, the most important thing about the freedom which whites have allowed Negroes within their own world is that it has required them to work out their own ways of making it from day to day, from birth to death. The subculture that Negroes have created may be imperfect but it has been viable for centuries; it behooves both white and Negro leaders and intellectuals to seek to understand it even as they hope to change it.[5]

Negroes have created, again particularly within the lower-class slum group, a range of institutions to structure the tasks of living a victimized life and to minimize the pain it inevitably produces. In the slum ghetto these institutions include prominently those of the social network—the extended kinship system and the "street system" of buddies and broads which tie (although tenuously and unpredictably) the "members" to each other—and the institutions of entertainment (music, dance, folk tales) by which they instruct, explain, and accept themselves. Other institutions function to provide escape from the society of the victimized: the church (Hereafter!) and the civil rights movement (Now!).

The Functional Autonomy of the Negro Family

At the center of the matrix of Negro institutional life lies the family. It is in the family that individuals are trained for participation in the culture and find personal and group identity and continuity. The "freedom" allowed by white society is greatest here, and this freedom has been used to create an institutional variant more distinctive perhaps to the Negro subculture than any other. (Much of the content of Negro art and entertainment derives exactly from the distinctive characteristics of Negro family life.) At each stage in the Negro's experience of American life—slavery, segregation, *de facto* ghettoization—whites have found it less necessary to interfere in the relations between the sexes and between parents and children than in other areas of the Negro's existence. His adaptations in this area, therefore, have been less constrained by whites than in many other areas.

Now that the larger society is becoming increasingly committed to integrating Negroes into the main stream of American life, however, we can expect increasing constraint (benevolent as it may be) to be placed on the autonomy of the Negro family system.[6] These constraints will be designed to pull Negroes into meaningful integration with the larger society, to give up ways which are inimical to successful performance in the larger society, and to adopt new ways that are functional in that society. The strategic questions of the civil rights movement and of the war on poverty are ones that have to do with how one provides functional equivalents for the existing subculture before the capacity to make a life within its confines is destroyed.

The history of the Negro family has been ably documented by historians and sociologists.[7] In slavery, conjugal and family ties were reluctantly and ambivalently recognized by the slave holders, were often violated by them, but proved necessary to the slave system. This necessity stemmed both from the profitable offspring of slave sexual unions and the necessity for their nurture, and from the fact that the slaves' efforts to sustain patterns of sexual and parental relations mollified the men and women whose labor could not simply be commanded. From nature's promptings, the thinning memories of African heritage, and the example and guilt-ridden permission of the slave holders, slaves constructed a partial family system and sets of relations that generated conjugal and familial sentiments. The slave holder's recognition in advertisements for runaway slaves of marital and family sentiments as motivations for absconding provides one indication that strong family ties were possible, though perhaps not common, in the slave quarter. The mother-centered family with its emphasis on the primacy of the mother-child relation and only tenuous ties to a man, then, is the legacy of adaptations worked out by Negroes during slavery.

After emancipation this family design often also served well to cope with the social disorganization of Negro life in the late nineteenth century. Matrifocal families, ambivalence about the desirability of marriage, ready acceptance of illegitimacy, all sustained some kind of family life in situations which often made it difficult to maintain a full nuclear family. Yet in the hundred years since emancipation, Negroes in rural areas have been able to maintain full nuclear families almost as well as similarly situated whites. As we will see, it is the move to the city that results in the very high proportion of mother-headed households. In the rural system the man continues to have important functions; it is difficult for a woman to make a crop by herself, or even with the help of other women. In the city, however, the woman can earn wages just as a man can, and she can receive welfare payments more easily than he can. In rural areas, although there may be high illegitimacy rates and high rates of marital disruption, men and women have an interest in getting together; families are headed by a husband-wife pair much more often than in the city. That pair may be much less stable than in the more prosperous segments of Negro and white communities but it is more likely to exist among rural Negroes than among urban ones.

The matrifocal character of the Negro lower-class family in the United States has much in common with Caribbean Negro family patterns; research in both areas has done a great deal to increase our understanding of the Negro situation. However, there are important differences in the family forms of the two areas.[8] The impact of white European family models has been much greater in the United States than in the Caribbean both because of the relative population proportions of white and colored peoples and because equalitarian values in the United States have had a great impact on Negroes even when they have not on whites. The typical Caribbean mating pattern is that women go through several visiting and common-law unions but eventually marry; that is, they marry legally only relatively late in their sexual lives. The

Caribbean marriage is the crowning of a sexual and procreative career; it is considered a serious and difficult step.

In the United States, in contrast, Negroes marry at only a slightly lower rate and slightly higher age than whites.[9] Most Negro women marry relatively early in their careers; marriage is not regarded as the same kind of crowning choice and achievement that it is in the Caribbean. For lower-class Negroes in the United States marriage ceremonies are rather informal affairs. In the Caribbean, marriage is regarded as quite costly because of the feasting which goes along with it; ideally it is performed in church.

In the United States, unlike the Caribbean, early marriage confers a kind of permanent respectable status upon a woman which she can use to deny any subsequent accusations of immorality or promiscuity once the marriage is broken and she becomes sexually involved in visiting or common-law relations. The relevant effective status for many Negro women is that of "having been married" rather than "being married"; having the right to be called "Mrs." rather than currently being Mrs. Someone-in-Particular.

For Negro lower-class women, then, first marriage has the same kind of importance as having a first child. Both indicate that the girl has become a woman but neither one that this is the last such activity in which she will engage. It seems very likely that only a minority of Negro women in the urban slum go through their childrearing years with only one man around the house.

Among the Negro urban poor, then, a great many women have the experience of heading a family for part of their mature lives, and a great many children spend some part of their formative years in a household without a father-mother pair. From Table 1

TABLE 1 *Proportion of Female Heads for Families with Children by Race, Income, and Urban-Rural Categories*

	Rural	Urban	Total
Negroes			
under $3000	18%	47%	36%
$3000 and over	5%	8%	7%
Total	14%	23%	21%
Whites			
under $3000	12%	38%	22%
$3000 and over	2%	4%	3%
Total	4%	7%	6%

SOURCE: U.S. Census: 1960, PC (1) D. U. S. Volume, Table 225; State Volume, Table 140.

we see that in 1960, forty-seven per cent of the Negro poor urban families with children had a female head. Unfortunately cumulative statistics are hard to come by; but, given this very high level for a cross-sectional sample (and taking into account the fact that the median age of the children in these families is about six years), it seems very likely that as many as two-thirds of Negro urban poor children will not live in families headed by a man and a woman throughout the first eighteen years of their lives.

One of the other distinctive characteristics of Negro families, both poor and not so poor, is the fact that Negro households have a much higher proportion of relatives outside the mother-father-children triangle than is the case with whites. For example, in St. Louis Negro families average 0.8 other relatives per household compared to only 0.4 for white families. In the case of the more prosperous Negro families this is likely to mean that an older relative lives in the home providing baby-sitting services while both the husband and wife work and thus further their climb toward stable working- or middle-class status. In the poor Negro families it is much more likely that the household is headed by an older relative who brings under her wings a daughter and that daughter's children. It is important to note that the three-generation household with the grandmother at the head exists only when there is no husband present. Thus, despite the high proportion of female-headed households in this group and despite the high proportion of households that contain other relatives, we find that almost all married couples in the St. Louis Negro slum community have their own household. In other words, when a couple marries it establishes its own household; when that couple breaks up the mother either maintains that household or moves back to her parents or grandparents.

Finally we should note that Negro slum families have more children than do either white slum families or stable working- and middle-class Negro families. Mobile Negro families limit their fertility sharply in the interest of bringing the advantages of mobility more fully to the few children that they do have. Since the Negro slum family is both more likely to have the father absent and more likely to have more children in the family, the mother has a more demanding task with fewer resources at her disposal. When we examine the patterns of life of the stem family we shall see that even the presence of several mothers does not necessarily lighten the work load for the principal mother in charge.

The Formation and Maintenance of Families

We will outline below the several stages and forms of Negro lower-class family life. At many points these family forms and the interpersonal relations that exist within them will be seen to have characteristics in common with the life styles of white lower-class families.[10] At other points there are differences, or the Negro pattern will be seen to be more sharply divergent from the family life of stable working- and middle-class couples.

It is important to recognize that lower-class Negroes know that their particular family forms are different from those of the rest of the society and that, though they often see these forms as representing the only ways of behaving given their circumstances, they also think of the more stable family forms of the working class as more desirable. That is, lower-class Negroes know what the "normal American family" is supposed to be like, and they consider a stable family-centered way of life superior to the conjugal and familial situations in which they often find themselves. Their conceptions of the good American life include the notion of a father-husband who functions as an adequate provider and interested member of the family, a hard working home-bound mother who is concerned about her children's welfare and her husband's needs, and children who look up to their parents and perform well in school and other outside places to reflect credit on their families. This image of what family life can be like is very real from time to time as lower-class men and women grow up and move through adulthood. Many of them make efforts to establish such families but find it impossible to do so either because of the direct impact of economic disabilities or because they are not able to sustain in their day-to-day lives the ideals which they hold.[11] While these ideals do serve as a meaningful guide to lower-class couples who are mobile out of the group, for a great many others the existence of such ideas about normal family life represents a recurrent source of stress within families as individuals become aware that they are failing to measure up to the ideals, or as others within the family and outside it use the ideals as an aggressive weapon for criticizing each other's performance. It is not at all uncommon for husbands or wives or children to try to hold others in the family to the norms of stable family life while they themselves engage in behaviors which violate these norms. The effect of such criticism in the end is to deepen commitment to the deviant sexual and parental norms of a slum subculture. Unless they are careful, social workers and other professionals exacerbate the tendency to use the norms of "American family life" as weapons by supporting these norms in situations where they are in reality unsupportable, thus aggravating the sense of failing and being failed by others which is chronic for lower-class people.

Going Together

The initial steps toward mating and family formation in the Negro slum take place in a context of highly developed boys' and girls' peer groups. Adolescents tend to become deeply involved in their peer-group societies beginning as early as the age of twelve or thirteen and continue to be involved after first pregnancies and first marriages. Boys and girls are heavily committed both to their same sex peer groups and to the activities that those groups carry out. While classical gang activity does not necessarily characterize Negro slum communities everywhere, loosely-knit peer groups do.

The world of the Negro slum is wide open to exploration by adolescent boys and girls: "Negro communities provide a flow of common experience in which young people and their elders share, and out of which delinquent behavior emerges almost imperceptibly." [12] More than is possible in white slum communities, Negro adolescents have an opportunity to interact with adults in various "high life" activities; their behavior more often represents an identification with the behavior of adults than an attempt to set up group standards and activities that differ from those of adults.

Boys and young men participating in the street system of peer-group activity are much caught up in games of furthering and enhancing their status as significant persons. These games are played out in small and large gatherings through various kinds of verbal contests that go under the names of "sounding," "signifying," and "working game." Very much a part of a boy's or man's status in this group is his ability to win women. The man who has several women "up tight," who is successful in "pimping off" women for sexual favors and material benefits, is much admired. In sharp contrast to white lower-class groups, there is little tendency for males to separate girls into "good" and "bad" categories.[13] Observations of groups of Negro youths suggest that girls and women are much more readily referred to as "that bitch" or "that whore" than they are by their names, and this seems to be a universal tendency carrying no connotation that "that bitch" is morally inferior to or different from other women. Thus, all women are essentially the same, all women are legitimate targets, and no girl or woman is expected to be virginal except for reason of lack of opportunity or immaturity. From their participation in the peer group and according to standards legitimated by the total Negro slum culture, Negro boys and young men are propelled in the direction of girls to test their "strength" as seducers. They are mercilessly rated by both their peers and the opposite sex in their ability to "talk" to girls; a young man will go to great lengths to avoid the reputation of having a "weak" line.[14]

The girls share these definitions of the nature of heterosexual relations; they take for granted that almost any male they deal with will try to seduce them and that given sufficient inducement (social not monetary) they may wish to go along with his line. Although girls have a great deal of ambivalence about participating in sexual relations, this ambivalence is minimally moral and has much more to do with a desire not to be taken advantage of or get in trouble. Girls develop defenses against the exploitative orientations of men by devaluing the significance of sexual relations ("he really didn't do anything bad to me"), and as time goes on by developing their own appreciation of the intrinsic rewards of sexual intercourse.

The informal social relations of slum Negroes begin in adolescence to be highly sexualized. Although parents have many qualms about boys and, particularly, girls entering into this system, they seldom feel there is much they can do to prevent their children's sexual involvement. They usually confine themselves to counseling somewhat hopelessly against girls becoming pregnant or boys being forced into situations where they might have to marry a girl they do not want to marry.

Girls are propelled toward boys and men in order to demonstrate their maturity and attractiveness; in the process they are constantly exposed to pressures for seduction, to boys "rapping" to them. An active girl will "go with" quite a number of boys, but she will generally try to restrict the number with whom she has intercourse to the few to whom she is attracted or (as happens not infrequently) to those whose threats of physical violence she cannot avoid. For their part, the boys move rapidly from girl to girl seeking to have intercourse with as many as they can and thus build up their "reps." The activity of seduction is itself highly cathected; there is gratification in simply "talking to" a girl as long as the boy can feel that he has acquitted himself well.

At sixteen Joan Bemias enjoys spending time with three or four very close girl friends. She tells us they follow this routine when the girls want to go out and none of the boys they have been seeing lately is available: "Every time we get ready to go someplace we look through all the telephone numbers of boys we'd have and we call them and talk so sweet to them that they'd come on around. All of them had cars you see. (I: What do you do to keep all these fellows interested?) Well nothing. We don't have to make love with all of them. Let's see, Joe, J.B., Albert, and Paul, out of all of them I've been going out with I've only had sex with four boys, that's all." She goes on to say that she and her girl friends resist boys by being unresponsive to their lines and by breaking off relations with them on the ground that they're going out with other girls. It is also clear from her comments that the girl friends support each other in resisting the boys when they are out together in groups.

Joan has had a relationship with a boy which has lasted six months, but she has managed to hold the frequency of intercourse down to four times. Initially she managed to hold this particular boy off for a month but eventually gave in.

Becoming Pregnant

It is clear that the contest elements in relationships between men and women continue even in relationships that become quite steady. Despite the girls' ambivalence about sexual relations and their manifold efforts to reduce its frequency, the operation of chance often eventuates in their becoming pregnant.[15] This was the case with Joan. With this we reach the second stage in the formation of families, that of premarital pregnancy. (We are outlining an ideal-typical sequence and not, of course, implying that all girls in the Negro slum culture become pregnant before they marry but only that a great many of them do.)

Joan was caught despite the fact that she was considerably more sophisticated about contraception than most girls or young women in the group (her mother had both instructed her in contraceptive techniques and constantly warned her to take precautions). No one was particularly surprised at her pregnancy although she, her boy friend, her mother, and others regarded it as unfortunate. For girls in the Negro slum, pregnancy before marriage is expected in much the same way that parents expect their children to catch mumps or chicken pox; if they are lucky it will not happen but if it happens people are not too surprised and everyone knows what to do about it. It was quickly decided that Joan and the baby would stay at home. It seems clear from the preparations that Joan's mother is making that she expects to have the main responsibility for caring for the infant. Joan seems quite indifferent to the baby; she shows little interest in mothering the child although she is not particularly adverse to the idea so long as the baby does not interfere too much with her continued participation in her peer group.

Establishing who the father is under these circumstances seems to be important and confers a kind of legitimacy on the birth; not to know who one's father is, on the other hand, seems the ultimate in illegitimacy. Actually Joan had a choice in the imputation of fatherhood; she chose J.B. because he is older than she, and because she may marry him if he can get a divorce from his wife. She could have chosen Paul (with whom she had also had intercourse at about the time she became pregnant), but she would have done this reluctantly since Paul is a year younger than she and somehow this does not seem fitting.

In general, when a girl becomes pregnant while still living at home it seems taken for granted that she will continue to live there and that her parents will take a major responsibility for rearing the children. Since there are usually siblings who can help out and even siblings who will be playmates for the child, the addition of a third generation to the household does not seem to place a great stress on relationships within the family. It seems common for the first pregnancy to have a liberating influence on the mother once the child is born in that she becomes socially and sexually more active than she was before. She no longer has to be concerned with preserving her status as a single girl. Since her mother is usually willing to take care of the child for a few years, the unwed mother has an opportunity to go out with girl friends and with men and thus become more deeply involved in the peer-group society of her culture. As she has more children and perhaps marries she will find it necessary to settle down and spend more time around the house fulfilling the functions of a mother herself.

It would seem that for girls pregnancy is the real measure of maturity, the dividing line between adolescence and womanhood. Perhaps because of this, as well as because of the ready resources for child care, girls in the Negro slum community show much less concern about pregnancy than do girls in the white lower-class community and are less motivated to marry the fathers of their children. When a girl becomes pregnant the question of marriage certainly arises and is considered, but the girl often decides that she would rather not marry the man either because she does not want to settle down yet or because she does not think he would make a good husband.

It is in the easy attitudes toward premarital pregnancy that the matrifocal character of the Negro lower-class family appears most clearly. In order to have and raise a family it is simply not necessary, though it may be desirable, to have a man around the house. While the AFDC program may make it easier to maintain such attitudes in the urban situation, this pattern existed long before the program was initiated and continues in families where support comes from other sources.

Finally it should be noted that fathering a child similarly confers maturity on boys and young men although perhaps it is less salient for them. If the boy has any interest in the girl he will tend to feel that the fact that he has impregnated her gives him an additional claim on her. He will be stricter in seeking to enforce his exclusive rights over her (though not exclusive loyalty to her). This exclusive right does not mean that he expects to marry her but only that there is a new and special bond between them. If the girl is not willing to accept such claims she may find it necessary to break off the relationship rather than tolerate the man's jealousy. Since others in the peer group have a vested interest in not allowing a couple to be too loyal to each other they go out of their way to question and challenge each partner about the loyalty of the other, thus contributing to the deterioration of the relationship. This same kind of questioning and challenging continues if the couple marries and represents one source of the instability of the marital relationship.

Getting Married

As noted earlier, despite the high degree of premarital sexual activity and the rather high proportion of premarital pregnancies, most lower-class Negro men and women eventually do marry and stay together for a shorter or longer period of time. Marriage is an intimidating prospect and is approached ambivalently by both parties. For the girl it means giving up a familiar and comfortable home that, unlike some other lower-class subcultures, places few real restrictions on her behavior. (While marriage can appear to be an escape from interpersonal difficulties at home, these difficulties seldom seem to revolve around effective restrictions placed on her behavior by her parents.) The girl also has good reason to be suspicious of the likelihood that men will be able to perform stably in the role of husband and provider; she is reluctant to be tied down by a man who will not prove to be worth it.

From the man's point of view the fickleness of women makes marriage problematic. It is one thing to have a girl friend step out on you, but it is quite another to have a wife do so. Whereas premarital sexual relations and fatherhood carry almost no connotation of responsibility for the welfare of the partner, marriage is supposed to mean that a man behaves more responsibly, becoming a provider for his wife and children even though he may not be expected to give up all the gratifications of participation in the street system.

For all of these reasons both boys and girls tend to have rather negative views of marriage as well as a low expectation that marriage will prove a stable and gratifying existence. When marriage does take place it tends to represent a tentative commitment on the part of both parties with a strong tendency to seek greater commitment on the part of the partner than on one's own part. Marriage is regarded as a fragile arrangement held together primarily by affectional ties rather than instrumental concerns.

In general, as in white lower-class groups, the decision to marry seems to be taken rather impulsively.[16] Since everyone knows that sooner or later he will get married, in spite of the fact that he may not be sanguine about the prospect, Negro lower-class men and women are alert for clues that the time has arrived. The time may arrive because of a pregnancy in a steady relationship that seems gratifying to both partners, or as a way of getting out of what seems to be an awkward situation, or as a self-indulgence during periods when a boy and a girl are feeling very sorry for themselves. Thus, one girl tells us that when she marries her husband will cook all of her meals for her and she will not have any housework; another girl says that when she marries it will be to a man who has plenty of money and will have to take her out often and really show her a good time.

Boys see in marriage the possibility of regular sexual intercourse without having to fight for it, or a girl safe from venereal disease, or a relationship to a nurturant figure who will fulfill the functions of a mother. For boys, marriage can also be a way of asserting their independence from the peer group if its demands become burdensome. In this case the young man seeks to have the best of both worlds.[17]

Marriage as a way out of an unpleasant situation can be seen in the case of one of our informants, Janet Cowan:

Janet has been going with two men, one of them married and the other single. The married man's wife took exception to their relationship and killed her husband. Within a week Janet and her single boy friend, Howard, were married. One way out of the turmoil the murder of her married boy friend stimulated (they lived in the same building) was to choose marriage as a way of "settling down." However, after marrying the new couple seemed to have little idea how to set themselves up as a family. Janet was reluctant to leave her parents' home because her parents cared for her two illegitimate children. Howard was unemployed and therefore unacceptable in his parents-in-law's home, nor were his own parents willing to have his wife move in with them. Howard was also reluctant to give up another girl friend in another part of town. Although both he and his wife maintained that it was all right for a couple to step out on each other so long as the other partner did not know about it, they were both jealous if they suspected anything of this kind. In the end they gave up on the idea of marriage and went their separate ways.

In general, then, the movement toward marriage is an uncertain and tentative one. Once the couple does settle down together in a household of their own, they have the problem of working out a mutually acceptable organization of rights and duties, expectations and performances, that will meet their needs.

Husband-Wife Relations

Characteristic of both the Negro and white lower class is a high degree of conjugal role segregation.[18] That is, husbands and wives tend to think of themselves as having very separate kinds of functioning in the instrumental organization of family life, and also as pursuing recreational and outside interests separately. The husband is expected to be a provider; he resists assuming functions around the home so long as he feels he is doing his proper job of bringing home a pay check. He feels he has the right to indulge himself in little ways if he is successful at this task. The wife is expected to care for the home and children and make her husband feel welcome and comfortable. Much that is distinctive to Negro family life stems from the fact that husbands often are not stable providers. Even when a particular man is, his wife's conception of men in general is such that she is pessimistic about the likelihood that he will continue to do well in this area. A great many Negro wives work to supplement the family income. When this is so the separate incomes earned by husband and wife tend to be treated not as "family" income but as the individual property of the two persons involved. If their wives work, husbands are likely to feel that they are entitled to retain a larger share of the income they provide; the wives, in turn, feel that the husbands have no right to benefit from the purchases they make out of their own money. There is, then, "my money" and "your money." In this situation the husband may come to feel that the wife should support the children out of her income and that he can retain all of his income for himself.

While white lower-class wives often are very much intimidated by their husbands, Negro lower-class wives come to feel that they have a right to give as good as they get. If the husband indulges himself, they have the right to indulge themselves. If the husband steps out on his wife, she has the right to step out on him. The commitment of husbands and wives to each other seems often a highly instrumental one after the "honeymoon" period. Many wives feel they owe the husband nothing once he fails to perform his provider role. If the husband is unemployed the wife increasingly refuses to perform her usual duties for him. For example one woman, after mentioning that her husband had cooked four eggs for himself, commented, "I cook for him when he's working but right now he's unemployed; he can cook for himself." It is important, however, to understand that the man's status in the home depends not so much on whether he is working as on whether he brings money into the home. Thus, in several of the families we have studied in which the husband receives disability payments his status is as well-recognized as in families in which the husband is working.[19]

Because of the high degree of conjugal role segregation, both white and Negro lower-class families tend to be matrifocal in comparison to middle-class families. They are matrifocal in the sense that the wife makes most of the decisions that keep the family going and has the greatest sense of responsibility to the family. In white as well as in Negro lower-class families women tend to look to their female relatives for support and counsel, and to treat their husbands as essentially uninterested in the day-to-day problems of family living.[20] In the Negro lower-class family these tendencies are all considerably exaggerated so that the matrifocality is much clearer than in white lower-class families.

The fact that both sexes in the Negro slum culture have equal right to the various satisfactions of life (earning an income, sex, drinking, and peer-group activity which conflicts with family responsibilities) means that there is less pretense to patriarchal authority in the Negro than in the white lower class. Since men find the overt debasement of their status very threatening, the Negro family is much more vulnerable to disruption when men are temporarily unable to perform their provider roles. Also, when men are unemployed the temptations for them to engage in street adventures which repercuss on the marital relationship are much greater. This fact is well-recognized by Negro lower-class wives; they often seem as concerned about what their unemployed husbands will do instead of working as they are about the fact that the husband is no longer bringing money into the home.

It is tempting to cope with the likelihood of disloyalty by denying the usual norms of fidelity, by maintaining instead that extramarital affairs are acceptable as long as they do not interfere with family functioning. Quite a few informants tell us this, but we have yet to observe a situation in which a couple maintains a stable relationship under these circumstances without a great deal of conflict. Thus one woman in her forties who has been married for many years and has four children first outlined this deviant norm and then illustrated how it did not work out:

My husband and I, we go out alone and sometimes stay all night. But when I get back my husband doesn't ask me a thing and I don't ask him anything. . . . A couple of years ago I suspected he was going out on me. One day I came home and my daughter was here. I told her to tell me when he left the house. I went into the bedroom and got into bed and then I heard him come in. He left in about ten minutes and my daughter came in and told me he was gone. I got out of bed and put on my clothes and started following him. Soon I saw him walking with a young girl and I began walking after them. They were just laughing and joking right out loud right on the sidewalk. He was carrying a large package of hers. I walked up behind them until I was about a yard from them. I had a large dirk which I opened and had decided to take one long slash across the both of them. Just when I decided to swing at them I lost my balance—I have a bad hip. Anyway, I didn't cut them because I lost my balance. Then I called his name and he turned around and stared at me. He didn't move at all. He was shaking all over. That girl just ran away from us. He still had her package so the next day she called on the telephone and said she wanted to come pick it up. My husband washed his face, brushed his teeth, took out his false tooth and started scrubbing it and put on a clean shirt and everything, just for her. We went downstairs together and gave her the package and she left.

So you see my husband does run around on me and it seems like he does it a lot. The thing about it is he's just getting too old to be pulling that kind of stuff. If a young man does it then that's not so bad—but an old man, he just looks foolish. One of these days he'll catch me but I'll just tell him, "Buddy you owe me one," and that'll be all there is to it. He hasn't caught me yet though.

In this case, as in others, the wife is not able to leave well enough alone; her jealousy forces her to a confrontation. Actually seeing her husband with another woman stimulates her to violence.

With couples who have managed to stay married for a good many years, these peccadillos are tolerable although they generate a great deal of conflict in the marital relationship. At earlier ages the partners are likely to be both prouder and less innured to the hopelessness of maintaining stable relationships; outside involvements are therefore much more likely to be disruptive of the marriage.

Marital Breakup

The precipitating causes of marital disruption seem to fall mainly into economic or sexual categories. As noted, the husband has little credit with his wife to tide him over periods of unemployment. Wives seem very willing to withdraw commitment from husbands who are not bringing money into the house. They take the point of view that he has no right to take up space around the house, to use its facilities, or to demand loyalty from her. Even where the wife is not inclined to press these claims, the husband tends to be touchy because he knows that such definitions are usual in his group, and he may, therefore, prove difficult for even a well-meaning wife to deal with. As noted above, if husbands do not work they tend to play around. Since they continue to maintain some contact with their peer groups, whenever they have time on their hands they move back into the world of the street system and are likely to get involved in activities which pose a threat to their family relationships.

Drink is a great enemy of the lower-class housewife, both white and Negro. Lower-class wives fear their husband's drinking because it costs money, because the husband may become violent and take out his frustrations on his wife, and because drinking may lead to sexual involvements with other women.[21]

The combination of economic problems and sexual difficulties can be seen in the case of the following couple in their early twenties:

When the field worker first came to know them, the Wilsons seemed to be working hard to establish a stable family life. The couple had been married about three years and had a two-year-old son. Their apartment was very sparsely furnished but also very clean. Within six weeks the couple had acquired several rooms of inexpensive furniture and obviously had gone to a great deal of effort to make a liveable home. Husband and wife worked on different shifts so that the husband could take care of the child while the wife worked. They looked forward to saving enough money to move out of the housing project into a more desirable neighborhood. Six weeks later, however, the husband had lost his job. He and his wife were in great conflict. She made him feel unwelcome at home and he strongly suspected her of going out with other men. A short time later they had separated. It is impossible to disentangle the various factors involved in this separation into a sequence of cause and effect, but we can see something of the impact of the total complex.

First Mr. Wilson loses his job: "I went to work one day and the man told me that I would have to work until 1:00. I asked him if there would be any extra pay for working overtime and he said no. I asked him why and he said, 'If you don't like it you can kiss my ass.' He said that to me. I said, 'Why do I have to do all that?' He said, 'Because I said so.' I wanted to jam (fight) him but I said to myself I don't want to be that ignorant, I don't want to be as ignorant as he is, so I just cut out and left. Later his father called me (it was a family firm) and asked why I left and I told him. He said, 'If you don't want to go along with my son then you're fired.' I said O.K. They had another Negro man come in to help me part time before they fired me. I think they were trying to have him work full time because he worked for them before. He has seven kids and he takes their shit."

The field worker observed that things were not as hard as they could be because his wife had a job, to which he replied, "Yeah, I know, that's just where the trouble is. My wife has become independent since she began working. If I don't get a job pretty soon I'll go crazy. We have a lot of little arguments about nothing since she got so independent." He went on to say that his wife had become a completely different person recently; she was hard to talk to because she felt that now that she was working and he was not there was nothing that he could tell her. On her last pay day his wife did not return home for three days; when she did she had only seven cents left from her pay check. He said that he loved his wife very much and had begged her to quit fooling around. He is pretty sure that she is having an affair with the man with whom she rides to work. To make matters worse his wife's sister counsels her that she does not have to stay home with him as long as he is out of work. Finally the wife moved most of their furniture out of the apartment so that he came home to find an empty apartment. He moved back to his parents' home (also in the housing project).

One interesting effect of this experience was the radical change in the husband's attitudes toward race relations. When he and his wife were doing well together and had hopes of moving up in the world he was quite critical of Negroes; "Our people are not ready for integration in many cases because they really don't know how to act. You figure if our people don't want to be bothered with whites then why in hell should the white man want to be bothered with them. There are some of us who are ready; there are others who aren't quite ready yet so I don't see why they're doing all of this hollering." A scarce eight months later he addressed white people as he spoke for two hours into a tape recorder, "If we're willing to be with you, why aren't you willing to be with us? Do our color make us look dirty and low down and cheap? Or do you know the real meaning of 'nigger'? Anyone can be a nigger, white, colored, orange or any other color. It's something that you labeled us with. You put us away like you put a can away on the shelf with a label on it. The can is marked 'Poison: stay away from it.' You want us to help build your country but you don't want us to live in it. . . . You give me respect; I'll give you respect. If you threaten to take my life, I'll take yours and believe me I know how to take a life. We do believe that man was put here to live together as human beings; not one that's superior and the one that's a dog, but as human beings. And if you don't want to live this way then you become the dog and we'll become the human beings. There's too much corruption, too much hate, too much one individual trying to step on another. If we don't get together in a hurry we will destroy each other." It was clear from what the respondent said that he had been much influenced by Black Muslim philosophy, yet again and again in his comments one can see the displacement into a public, race relations dialogue of the sense of rage, frustration and victimization that he had experienced in his ill-fated marriage.[22]

Finally, it should be noted that migration plays a part in marital disruption. Sometimes marriages do not break up in the dramatic way described above but rather simply become increasingly unsatisfactory to one or both partners. In such a situation the temptation to move to another city, from South to North, or North to West, is great. Several wives told us that their first marriages were broken when they moved with their children to the North and their husbands stayed behind.

"After we couldn't get along I left the farm and came here and stayed away three or four days. I didn't come here to stay. I came to visit but I liked it and so I said, 'I'm gonna leave!' He said, 'I'll be glad if you do.' Well, maybe he didn't mean it but I thought he did. . . . I miss him sometimes, you know. I think about him I guess. But just in a small way. That's what I can't understand about life sometimes; you know—how people can go on like that and still break up and meet somebody else. Why couldn't—oh, I don't know!"

The gains and losses in marriage and in the post-marital state often seem quite comparable. Once they have had the experience of marriage, many women in the Negro slum culture see little to recommend it in the future, important as the first marriage may have been in establishing their maturity and respectability.

The House of Mothers

As we have seen, perhaps a majority of mothers in the Negro slum community spend at least part of their mature life as mothers heading a family. The Negro mother may be a working mother or she may be an AFDC mother, but in either case she has the problems of maintaining a household, socializing her children, and achieving for herself some sense of membership in relations with other women and with men. As is apparent from the earlier discussion, she often receives her training in how to run such a household by observing her own mother manage without a husband. Similarly she often learns how to run a three-generation household because she herself brought a third generation into her home with her first, premarital, pregnancy.

Because men are not expected to be much help around the house, having to be head of the household is not particularly intimidating to the Negro mother if she can feel some security about income. She knows it is a hard, hopeless, and often thankless task, but she also knows that it is possible. The maternal household in the slum is generally run with a minimum of organization. The children quickly learn to fend for themselves, to go to the store, to make small purchases, to bring change home, to watch after themselves when the mother has to be out of the home, to amuse themselves, to set their own schedules of sleeping, eating, and going to school. Housekeeping practices may be poor, furniture takes a terrific beating from the children, and emergencies constantly arise. The Negro mother in this situation copes by not setting too high standards for herself, by letting things take their course. Life is most difficult when there are babies and preschool children around because then the mother is confined to the home. If she is a grandmother and the children are her daughter's, she is often confined since it is taken as a matter of course that the mother has the right to continue her outside activities and that the grandmother has the duty to be responsible for the child.

In this culture there is little of the sense of the awesome responsibility of caring for children that is characteristic of the working and middle class. There is not the deep psychological involvement with babies which has been observed with the working-class mother.[23] The baby's needs are cared for on a catch-as-catch-can basis. If there are other children around and they happen to like babies, the baby can be over-stimulated; if this is not the case, the baby is left alone a good deal of the time. As quickly as he can move around he learns to fend for himself.

The three-generation maternal household is a busy place. In contrast to working- and middle-class homes it tends to be open to the world, with many non-family members coming in and out at all times as the children are visited by friends, the teenagers by their boy friends and girl friends, the mother by her friends and perhaps an occasional boy friend, and the grandmother by fewer friends but still by an occasional boy friend.

The openness of the household is, among other things, a reflection of the mother's sense of impotence in the face of the street system. Negro lower-class mothers often indicate that they try very hard to keep their young children at home and away from the streets; they often seem to make the children virtual prisoners in the home. As the children grow and go to school they inevitably do become involved in peer-group activities. The mother gradually gives up, feeling that once the child is lost to this pernicious outside world there is little she can do to continue to control him and direct his development. She will try to limit the types of activities that go on in the home and to restrict the kinds of friends that her children can bring into the home, but even this she must give up as time goes on, as the children become older and less attentive to her direction.

The grandmothers in their late forties, fifties, and sixties tend increasingly to stay at home. The home becomes a kind of court at which other family members gather and to which they bring their friends for sociability, and as a by-product provide amusement and entertainment for the mother. A grandmother may provide a home for her daughters, their children, and sometimes their children's children, and yet receive very little in a material way from them; but one of the things she does receive is a sense of human involvement, a sense that although life may have passed her by she is not completely isolated from it.

The lack of control that mothers have over much that goes on in their households is most dramatically apparent in the fact that their older children seem to have the right to come home at any time once they have moved and to stay in the home without contributing to its maintenance. Though the mother may be resentful about being taken advantage of, she does not feel she can turn her children away. For example, sixty-five-year-old Mrs. Washington plays hostess for weeks or months at a time to her forty-year-old daughter and her small children, and to her twenty-three-year-old granddaughter and her children. When these daughters come home with their families the grandmother is expected to take care of the young children and must argue with her daughter and granddaughter to receive contributions to the daily household ration of food and liquor. Or, a twenty-year-old son comes home from the Air Force and feels he has the right to live at home without working and to run up an eighty-dollar long-distance telephone bill.

Even aged parents living alone in small apartments sometimes acknowledge such obligations to their children or grandchildren. Again, the only clear return they receive for their hospitality is the reduction of isolation that comes from having people around and interesting activity going on. When in the Washington home the daughter and granddaughter and their children move in with the grandmother, or when they come to visit for shorter periods of time, the occasion has a party atmosphere. The women sit around talking and reminiscing. Though boy friends may be present, they take little part; instead they sit passively, enjoying the stories and drinking along with the women. It would seem that in this kind of party activity the women are defined as the stars. Grandmother, daughter, and granddaughter in turn take the center of the stage telling a story from the family's past, talking about a particularly interesting night out on the town or just making some general observation about life. In the course of these events a good deal of liquor is consumed. In such a household as this little attention is paid to the children since the competition by adults for attention is stiff.

Boy Friends, not Husbands

It is with an understanding of the problems of isolation which older mothers have that we can obtain the best insight into the role and function of boy friends in the maternal household. The older mothers, surrounded by their own children and grandchildren, are not able to move freely in the outside world, to participate in the high life which they enjoyed when younger and more foot-loose. They are disillusioned with marriage as providing any more secure economic base than they can achieve on their own. They see marriage as involving just another responsibility without a concomitant reward—"It's the greatest thing in the world to come home in the afternoon and not have some curly headed twot in the house yellin' at me and askin' me where supper is, where

I've been, what I've been doin', and who I've been seein'." In this situation the woman is tempted to form relationships with men that are not so demanding as marriage but still provide companionship and an opportunity for occasional sexual gratification.

There seem to be two kinds of boy friends. Some boy friends "pimp" off mothers; they extract payment in food or money for their companionship. This leads to the custom sometimes called "Mother's Day," the tenth of the month when the AFDC checks come.[24] On this day one can observe an influx of men into the neighborhood, and much partying. But there is another kind of boy friend, perhaps more numerous than the first, who instead of being paid for his services pays for the right to be a pseudo family member. He may be the father of one of the woman's children and for this reason makes a steady contribution to the family's support, or he may simply be a man whose company the mother enjoys and who makes reasonable gifts to the family for the time he spends with them (and perhaps implicitly for the sexual favors he receives). While the boy friend does not assume fatherly authority within the family, he often is known and liked by the children. The older children appreciate the meaningfulness of their mother's relationship with him—one girl said of her mother's boy friend:

"We don't none of us (the children) want her to marry again. It's all right if she wants to live by herself and have a boy friend. It's not because we're afraid we're going to have some more sisters and brothers, which it wouldn't make us much difference, but I think she be too old."

Even when the boy friend contributes ten or twenty dollars a month to the family he is in a certain sense getting a bargain. If he is a well-accepted boy friend he spends considerable time around the house, has a chance to relax in an atmosphere less competitive than that of his peer group, is fed and cared for by the woman, yet has no responsibilities which he cannot renounce when he wishes. When women have stable relationships of this kind with boy friends they often consider marrying them but are reluctant to take such a step. Even the well-liked boy friend has some shortcomings—one woman said of her boy friend:

"Well he works; I know that. He seems to be a nice person, kind hearted. He believes in survival for me and my family. He don't much mind sharing with my youngsters. If I ask him for a helping hand he don't seem to mind that. The only part I dislike is his drinking."

The woman in this situation has worked out a reasonably stable adaptation to the problems of her life; she is fearful of upsetting this adaptation by marrying again. It seems easier to take the "sweet" part of the relationship with a man without the complexities that marriage might involve.

It is in the light of this pattern of women living in families and men living by themselves in rooming houses, odd rooms, here and there, that we can understand Daniel Patrick Moynihan's observation that during their mature years men simply disappear; that is, that census data show a very high sex ratio of women to men.[25] In St. Louis, starting at the age range twenty to twenty-four there are only seventy-two men for every one hundred women. This ratio does not climb to ninety until the age range fifty to fifty-four. Men often do not have real homes; they move about from one household where they have kinship or sexual ties to another; they live in flop houses and rooming houses; they spend time in institutions. They are not household members in the only "homes" that they have—the homes of their mothers and of their girl friends.

It is in this kind of world that boys and girls in the Negro slum community learn their sex roles. It is not just, or even mainly, that fathers are often absent but that the male role models around boys are ones which emphasize expressive, affectional techniques for making one's way in the world. The female role models available to girls emphasize an exaggerated self-sufficiency (from the point of view of the middle class) and the danger of allowing oneself to be dependent on men for anything that is crucial. By the time she is mature, the woman learns that she is most secure when she herself manages the family affairs and when she dominates her men. The man learns that he exposes himself to the least risk of failure when he does not assume a husband's and father's responsibilities but instead counts on his ability to court women and to ingratiate himself with them.

Identity Processes in the Family

Up to this point we have been examining the sequential development of family stages in the Negro slum community, paying only incidental attention to the psychological responses family members make to these social forms and not concerning ourselves with the effect the family forms have on the psychosocial development of the children who grow up in them. Now we want to examine the effect that growing up in this kind of a system has in terms of socialization and personality development.

Household groups function for cultures in carrying out the initial phases of socialization and personality formation. It is in the family that the child learns the most primitive categories of existence and experience, and that he develops his most deeply held beliefs about the world and about himself.[26] From the child's point of view, the household *is* the world; his experiences as he moves out of it into the larger world are always interpreted in terms of his particular experience within the home. The painful experiences which a child in the Negro slum culture has are, therefore, interpreted as in some sense a reflection of this family world. The impact of the system of victimization is transmitted through the family; the child cannot be expected to have the sophistication an outside observer has for seeing exactly where the villains are. From the child's point of view, if he is hungry it is his parents' fault; if he experiences frustrations in the streets or in the school it is his parents' fault; if that world seems incomprehensible to him it is his parents' fault; if people are aggressive or destructive toward each other it is his parents' fault, not that of a system of race relations. In another culture this might not be the case; if a subculture could exist which provided comfort and security within its limited world and the individual experienced frustration only when he moved out into the larger society, the family might not be thought so much to blame. The effect of the caste system, however, is to bring home through a chain of cause and effect all of the victimization processes, and to bring them home in such a way that it is often very difficult even for adults in the system to see the connection between the pain they feel at the moment and the structured patterns of the caste system.

Let us take as a central question that of identity formation within the Negro slum family. We are concerned with the question of who the individual believes himself to be and to be becoming. For Erikson, identity means a sense of continuity and social sameness which bridges what the individual "*was* as a child and what he is *about to become* and also reconciles his *conception of himself* and his community's recognition of him." Thus identity is a "self-realization coupled with a mutual recognition." [27] In the early childhood years identity is family-bound since the child's identity is his identity *vis-à-vis* other members of the family. Later he incorporates into his sense of who he is and is becoming his experiences outside the family, but always influenced by the interpretations and evaluations of those experiences that the family gives. As the child tries on identities, *announces* them, the family sits as judge of his pretensions. Family members are both the most important judges and the most critical ones, since who he is allowed to become affects them in their own identity strivings more crucially than it affects anyone else. The child seeks a sense of valid identity, a sense of being a particular person with a satisfactory degree of congruence between who he feels he is, who he announces himself to be, and where he feels his society places him.[28] He is uncomfortable when he experiences disjunction between his own needs and the kinds of needs legitimated by those around him, or when he feels a disjunction between his sense of himself and the image of himself that others play back to him.[29]

"Tell It Like It Is"

When families become involved in important quarrels the psychosocial underpinnings of family life are laid bare. One such quarrel in a family we have been studying brings together in one place many of the themes that seem to dominate identity problems in Negro slum culture. The incident illustrates in a particularly forceful and dramatic way family processes which our field work, and some other contemporary studies of slum family life, suggest unfold more subtly in a great many families at the lower-class level. The family involved, the Johnsons, is certainly not the most disorganized one we have studied; in some respects their way of life represents a realistic adaptation to the hard living of a family nineteen years on AFDC with a monthly income of $202 for nine people. The two oldest daughters, Mary Jane (eighteen years old) and Esther (sixteen) are pregnant; Mary Jane has one illegitimate child. The adolescent sons, Bob and Richard, are much involved in the social and sexual activities of their peer group. The three other children, ranging in age from twelve to fourteen, are apparently also moving into this kind of peer-group society.

When the argument started Bob and Esther were alone in the apartment with Mary Jane's baby. Esther took exception to Bob's playing with the baby because she had been left in charge; the argument quickly progressed to a fight in which Bob cuffed Esther around, and she tried to cut him with a knife. The police were called and subdued Bob with their nightsticks. At this point the rest of the family and the field worker arrived. As the argument continued, these themes relevant to the analysis which follows appeared:

1) The sisters said that Bob was not their brother (he is a half-brother to Esther, and Mary Jane's full brother). Indeed, they said their mother "didn't have no husband. These kids don't know who their daddies are." The mother defended herself by saying that she had one legal husband, and one common-law husband, no more.

2) The sisters said that their fathers had never done anything for them, nor had their mother. She retorted that she had raised them "to the age of womanhood" and now would care for their babies.

3) Esther continued to threaten to cut Bob if she got a chance (a month later they fought again, and she did cut Bob, who required twenty-one stitches).

4) The sisters accused their mother of favoring their lazy brothers and asked her to put them out of the house. She retorted that the girls were as lazy, that they made no contribution to maintaining the household, could not get their boy friends to marry them or support their children, that all the support came from her AFDC check. Mary Jane retorted that "the baby has a check of her own."

5) The girls threatened to leave the house if their mother refused to put their brothers out. They said they could force their boy friends to support them by taking them to court, and Esther threatened to cut her boy friend's throat if he did not co-operate.

6) Mrs. Johnson said the girls could leave if they wished but that she would keep their babies; "I'll not have it, not knowing who's taking care of them."

7) When her thirteen-year-old sister laughed at all of this, Esther told her not to laugh because she, too, would be pregnant within a year.

8) When Bob laughed, Esther attacked him and his brother by saying that both were not man enough to make babies, as she and her sister had been able to do.

9) As the field worker left, Mrs. Johnson sought his sympathy. "You see, Joe, how hard it is for me to bring up a family. . . . They sit around and talk to me like I'm some kind of a dog and not their mother."

10) Finally, it is important to note for the analysis which follows that the following labels—"black-assed," "black bastard," "bitch," and other profane terms—were liberally used by Esther and Mary Jane, and rather less liberally by their mother, to refer to each other, to the girls' boy friends, to Bob, and to the thirteen-year-old daughter.

Several of the themes outlined previously appear forcefully in the course of this argument. In the last year and a half the mother has become a grandmother and expects shortly to add two more grandchildren to her household. She takes it for granted that it is her responsibility to care for the grandchildren and that she has the right to decide what will be done with the children since her own daughters are not fully responsible. She makes this very clear to them when they threaten to move out, a threat which they do not really wish to make good nor could they if they wished to.

However, only as an act of will is Mrs. Johnson able to make this a family. She must constantly cope with the tendency of her adolescent children to disrupt the family group and to deny that they are in fact a family—"He ain't no brother of mine"; "The baby has a check of her own." Though we do not know exactly what processes communicate these facts to the children it is clear that in growing up they have learned to regard themselves as not fully part of a solitary collectivity. During the quarrel this message was reinforced for the twelve-, thirteen-, and fourteen-year-old daughters by the four-way argument among their older sisters, older brother, and their mother.

The argument represents vicious unmasking of the individual members' pretenses to being competent individuals.[30] The efforts of the two girls to present themselves as masters of their own fate are unmasked by the mother. The girls in turn unmask the pretensions of the mother and of their two brothers. When the thirteen-year-old daughter expresses some amusement they turn on her, telling her that it won't be long before she too becomes pregnant. Each member of the family in turn is told that he can expect to be no more than a victim of his world, but that this is somehow inevitably his own fault.

In this argument masculinity is consistently demeaned. Bob has no right to play with his niece, the boys are not really masculine because at fifteen and sixteen years they have yet to father children, their own fathers were no goods who failed to do anything for their family. These notions probably come originally from the mother, who enjoys recounting the story of having her common-law husband imprisoned for nonsupport, but this comes back to haunt her as her daughters accuse her of being no better than they in ability to force support and nurturance from a man. In contrast, the girls came off somewhat better than the boys, although they must accept the label of stupid girls because they have similarly failed and inconveniently become pregnant in the first place. At least they can and have had children and therefore have some meaningful connection with the ongoing substance of life. There is something important and dramatic in which they participate, while the boys, despite their sexual activity, "can't get no babies."

In most societies, as children grow and are formed by their

elders into suitable members of the society they gain increasingly a sense of competence and ability to master the behavioral environment their particular world presents. But in Negro slum culture growing up involves an ever-increasing appreciation of one's shortcomings, of the impossibility of finding a self-sufficient and gratifying way of living.[31] It is in the family first and most devastatingly that one learns these lessons. As the child's sense of frustration builds he too can strike out and unmask the pretensions of others. The result is a peculiar strength and a pervasive weakness. The strength involves the ability to tolerate and defend against degrading verbal and physical aggressions from others and not to give up completely. The weakness involves the inability to embark hopefully on any course of action that might make things better, particularly action which involves cooperating and trusting attitudes toward others. Family members become potential enemies to each other, as the frequency of observing the police being called in to settle family quarrels brings home all too dramatically.

The conceptions parents have of their children are such that they are constantly alert as the child matures to evidence that he is as bad as everyone else. That is, in lower-class culture human nature is conceived of as essentially bad, destructive, immoral.[32] This is the nature of things. Therefore any one child must be inherently bad unless his parents are very lucky indeed. If the mother can keep the child insulated from the outside world, she feels she may be able to prevent his inherent badness from coming out. She feels that once he is let out into the larger world the badness will come to the fore since that is his nature. This means that in the identity development of the child he is constantly exposed to identity labeling by his parents as a bad person. Since as he grows up he does not experience his world as particularly gratifying, it is very easy for him to conclude that this lack of gratification is due to the fact that something is wrong with him. This, in turn, can readily be assimilated to the definitions of being a bad person offered him by those with whom he lives.[33] In this way the Negro slum child learns his culture's conception of being-in-the-world, a conception that emphasizes inherent evil in a chaotic, hostile, destructive world.

Blackness

To a certain extent these same processes operate in white lower-class groups, but added for the Negro is the reality of blackness.

"Black-assed" is not an empty pejorative adjective. In the Negro slum culture several distinctive appellations are used to refer to oneself and others. One involves the terms, "black" or "nigger." Black is generally a negative way of naming, but nigger can be either negative or positive, depending upon the context. It is important to note that, at least in the urban North, the initial development of racial identity in these terms has very little directly to do with relations with whites. A child experiences these identity placements in the context of the family and in the neighborhood peer group; he probably very seldom hears the same terms used by whites (unlike the situation in the South). In this way, one of the effects of ghettoization is to mask the ultimate enemy so that the understanding of the fact of victimization by a caste system comes as a late acquisition laid over conceptions of self and of other Negroes derived from intimate, and to the child often traumatic, experience within the ghetto community. If, in addition, the child attends a ghetto school where his Negro teachers either overtly or by implication reinforce his community's negative conceptions of what it means to be black, then the child has little opportunity to develop a more realistic image of himself and other Negroes as being damaged by whites and not by themselves. In such a situation, an intelligent man like Mr. Wilson (quoted on pages 236–237) can say with all sincerity that he does not feel most Negroes are ready for integration—only under the experience of certain kinds of intense personal threat coupled with exposure to an ideology that places the responsibility on whites did he begin to see through the direct evidence of his daily experience.

To those living in the heart of a ghetto, black comes to mean not just "stay back," but also membership in a community of persons who think poorly of each other, who attack and manipulate each other, who give each other small comfort in a desperate world. Black comes to stand for a sense of identity as no better than these destructive others. The individual feels that he must embrace an unattractive self in order to function at all.

We can hypothesize that in those families that manage to avoid the destructive identity imputations of "black" and that manage to maintain solidarity against such assaults from the world around, it is possible for children to grow up with a sense of both Negro and personal identity that allows them to socialize themselves in an anticipatory way for participation in the larger society.[34] This broader sense of identity, however, will remain a brittle one as long as the individual is vulnerable to attack from within the Negro community as "nothing but a nigger like everybody else" or from the white community as "just a nigger." We can hypothesize further that the vicious unmasking of essential identity as black described above is least likely to occur within families where the parents have some stable sense of security, and where they therefore have less need to protect themselves by disavowing responsibility for their children's behavior and denying the children their patrimony as products of a particular family rather than of an immoral nature and an evil community.

In sum, we are suggesting that Negro slum children as they grow up in their families and in their neighborhoods are exposed to a set of experiences—and a rhetoric which conceptualizes them —that brings home to the child an understanding of his essence as a weak and debased person who can expect only partial gratification of his needs, and who must seek even this level of gratification by less than straight-forward means.

Strategies for Living

In every society complex processes of socialization inculcate in their members strategies for gratifying the needs with which they are born and those which the society itself generates. Inextricably linked to these strategies, both cause and effect of them, are the existential propositions which members of a culture entertain about the nature of their world and of effective action within the world as it is defined for them. In most of American society two grand strategies seem to attract the allegiance of its members and guide their day-to-day actions. I have called these strategies those of *the good life* and of *career success*.[35] A good life strategy involves efforts to get along with others and not to rock the boat, a comfortable familism grounded on a stable work career for husbands in which they perform adequately at the modest jobs that enable them to be good providers. The strategy of career success is the choice of ambitious men and women who see life as providing opportunities to move from a lower to a higher status, to "accomplish something," to achieve greater than ordinary material well-being, prestige, and social recognition. Both of these strategies are predicated on the assumption that the world is inherently rewarding if one behaves properly and does his part. The rewards of the world may come easily or only at the cost of great effort, but at least they are there.

In the white and particularly in the Negro slum worlds little in the experience that individuals have as they grow up sustains a belief in a rewarding world. The strategies that seem appropriate are not those of a good, family-based life or of a career, but rather *strategies for survival.*

Much of what has been said above can be summarized as encouraging three kinds of survival strategies. One is the strategy of the *expressive life style* which I have described elsewhere as an effort to make yourself interesting and attractive to others so that you are better able to manipulate their behavior along lines that will provide some immediate gratification.[36] Negro slum culture provides many examples of techniques for seduction, of persuading others to give you what you want in situations where you have very little that is tangible to offer in return. In order to get what you want you learn to "work game," a strategy which requires a high development of a certain kind of verbal facility, a sophisticated manipulation of promise and interim reward. When the expressive strategy fails or when it is unavailable there is, of course, the great temptation to adopt a *violent strategy* in which you force others to give you what you need once you fail to win it by verbal and other symbolic means.[37] Finally, and increasingly as members of the Negro slum culture grow older, there is the *depressive strategy* in which goals are increasingly constricted to the bare necessities for survival (not as a social being but simply as an organism).[38] This is the strategy of "I don't bother anybody and I hope nobody's gonna bother me; I'm simply going through the motions to keep body (but not soul) together." Most lower-class people follow mixed strategies, as Walter Miller has observed, alternating among the excitement of the expressive style, the desperation of the violent style, and the deadness of the depressed style.[39] Some members of the Negro slum world experiment from time to time with mixed strategies that also incorporate the stable working-class model of the good American life, but this latter strategy is exceedingly vulnerable to the threats of unemployment or a less than adequate pay check, on the one hand, and the seduction and violence of the slum world around them, on the other.

Remedies

Finally, it is clear that we, no less than the inhabitants of the ghetto, are not masters of their fate because we are not masters of our own total society. Despite the battles with poverty on many fronts we can find little evidence to sustain our hope of winning the war given current programs and strategies.

The question of strategy is particularly crucial when one moves from an examination of destructive cultural and interaction patterns in Negro families to the question of how these families might achieve a more stable and gratifying life. It is tempting to see the family as the main villain of the piece, and to seek to develop programs which attack directly this family pathology. Should we not have extensive programs of family therapy, family counseling, family-life education, and the like? Is this not the prerequisite to enabling slum Negro families to take advantage of other opportunities? Yet, how pale such efforts seem compared to the deep-seated problems of self-image and family process described above. Can an army of social workers undo the damage of three hundred years by talking and listening without massive changes in the social and economic situations of the families with whom they are to deal? And, if such changes take place, will the social-worker army be needed?

If we are right that present Negro family patterns have been created as adaptations to a particular socioeconomic situation, it would make more sense to change that socioeconomic situation and then depend upon the people involved to make new adaptations as time goes on. If Negro providers have steady jobs and decent incomes, if Negro children have some realistic expectation of moving toward such a goal, if slum Negroes come to feel that they have the chance to affect their own futures and to receive respect from those around them, then (and only then) the destructive patterns described are likely to change. The change, though slow and uneven from individual to individual, will in a certain sense be automatic because it will represent an adaptation to changed socioeconomic circumstances which have direct and highly valued implications for the person.

It is possible to think of three kinds of extra-family change that are required if family patterns are to change; these are outlined below as pairs of current deprivations and needed remedies:

Deprivation effect of caste victimization	Needed remedy
I. Poverty	Employment income for men; income maintenance for mothers
II. Trained incapacity to function in a bureaucratized and industrialized world	Meaningful education of the next generation
III. Powerlessness and stigmatization	Organizational participation for aggressive pursuit of Negroes' self-interest
	Strong sanctions against callous or indifferent service to slum Negroes
	Pride in group identity, Negro *and* American

Unless the major effort is to provide these kinds of remedies, there is a very real danger that programs to "better the structure of the Negro family" by direct intervention will serve the unintended functions of distracting the country from the pressing needs for socioeconomic reform and providing an alibi for the failure to embark on the basic institutional changes that are needed to do anything about abolishing both white and Negro poverty. It would be sad, indeed, if, after the Negro revolt brought to national prominence the continuing problem of poverty, our expertise about Negro slum culture served to deflect the national impulse into symptom-treatment rather than basic reform. If that happens, social scientists will have served those they study poorly indeed.

Let us consider each of the needed remedies in terms of its probable impact on the family. First, the problem of poverty: employed men are less likely to leave their families than are unemployed men, and when they do stay they are more likely to have the respect of their wives and children. A program whose sole effect would be to employ at reasonable wages slum men for work using the skills they now have would do more than any other possible program to stabilize slum family life. But the wages must be high enough to enable the man to maintain his self-respect as a provider, and stable enough to make it worthwhile to change the nature of his adaptation to his world (no one-year emergency programs will do). Once men learn that work pays off it would be possible to recruit men for part-time retraining for more highly skilled jobs, but the initial emphasis must be on the provision of full-time, permanent unskilled jobs. Obviously it will be easier to do this in the context of full employment and a tight labor market.[40]

For at least a generation, however, there will continue to be a large number of female-headed households. Given the demands of socializing a new generation for non-slum living, it is probably uneconomical to encourage mothers to work. Rather, income maintenance programs must be increased to realistic levels, and mothers must be recognized as doing socially useful work for which they are paid rather than as "feeding at the public trough." The bureaucratic morass which currently hampers flexible strategies of combining employment income and welfare payments to make ends meet must also be modified if young workers are not to be pushed prematurely out of the home.

Education has the second priority. (It is second only because without stable family income arrangements the school system must work against the tremendous resistance of competing life-style adaptations to poverty and economic insecurity.) As Kenneth Clark has argued so effectively, slum schools now function more to stultify and discourage slum children than to stimulate and train them. The capacity of educators to alibi their lack of commitment to their charges is protean. The making of a different kind of generation must be taken by educators as a stimulating and worthwhile challenge. Once the goal has been accepted they must be given the resources with which to achieve it and the flexibility necessary to experiment with different approaches to accomplish the goal. Education must be broadly conceived to include much more than classroom work, and probably more than a nine-months schedule.[41]

If slum children can come to see the schools as representing a really likely avenue of escape from their difficult situation (even before adolescence they know it is the only *possible* escape) then their commitment to school activities will feed back into their families in a positive way. The parents will feel proud rather than ashamed, and they will feel less need to damn the child as a way to avoid blaming themselves for his failure. The sense of positive family identity will be enriched as the child becomes an attractive object, an ego resource, to his parents. Because he himself feels more competent, he will see them as less depriving and weak. If children's greater commitment to school begins to reduce their involvement in destructive or aimless peer-group activities this too will repercuss positively on the family situation since parents will worry less about their children's involvement in an immoral outside world, and be less inclined to deal with them in harsh, rejecting, or indifferent ways.

Cross-cutting the deprivations of poverty and trained incapacity is the fact of powerlessness and stigmatization. Slum people know that they have little ability to protect themselves and to force recognition of their abstract rights. They know that they are looked down on and scape-goated. They are always vulnerable to the slights, insults, and indifference of the white and Negro functionaries with whom they deal—policemen, social workers, school teachers, landlords, employers, retailers, janitors. To come into contact with others carries the constant danger of moral attack and insult.[42] If processes of status degradation within families are to be interrupted, then they must be interrupted on the outside first.

One way out of the situation of impotence and dammed-up in-group aggression is the organization of meaningful protest against the larger society. Such protest can and will take many forms, not always so neat and rational as the outsider might hope. But, coupled with, and supporting, current programs of economic and educational change, involvement of slum Negroes in organizational activity can do a great deal to build a sense of pride and potency. While only a very small minority of slum Negroes can be expected to participate personally in such movements, the vicarious involvement of the majority can have important effects on their sense of self-respect and worth.

Some of the needed changes probably can be made from the top, by decision in Washington, with minimal effective organization within the slum; but others can come only in response to aggressive pressure on the part of the victims themselves. This is probably particularly true of the entrenched tendency of service personnel to enhance their own sense of self and to indulge their middle-class *ressentiment* by stigmatizing and exploiting those they serve. Only effective protest can change endemic patterns of police harassment and brutality, or teachers' indifference and insults, or butchers' heavy thumbs, or indifferent street cleaning and garbage disposal. And the goal of the protest must be to make this kind of insult to the humanity of the slum-dweller too expensive for the perpetrator to afford; it must cost him election defeats, suspensions without pay, job dismissals, license revocations, fines, and the like.

To the extent that the slum dweller avoids stigmatization in the outside world, he will feel more fully a person within the family and better able to function constructively within it since he will not be tempted to make up deficits in self-esteem in ways that are destructive of family solidarity. The "me" of personal identity and the multiple "we" of family, Negro, and American identity are all inextricably linked; a healthier experience of identity in any one sector will repercuss on all the others.

Notes

1. This paper is based in part on research supported by a grant from the National Institute of Mental Health, Grant No. MH-09189, "Social and Community Problems in Public Housing Areas." Many of the ideas presented stem from discussion with the senior members of the Pruitt-Igoe research staff—Alvin W. Gouldner, David J. Pittman, and Jules Henry—and with the research associates and assistants on the project. I have made particular use of ideas developed in discussions with Boone Hammond, Joyce Ladner, Robert Simpson, David Schulz, and William Yancey. I also wish to acknowledge helpful suggestions and criticisms by Catherine Chilman, Gerald Handel, and Marc J. Swartz. Although this paper is not a formal report of the Pruitt-Igoe research, all of the illustrations of family behavior given in the text are drawn from interviews and observations that are part of that study. The study deals with the residents of the Pruitt-Igoe housing projects in St. Louis. Some 10,000 people live in these projects which comprise forty-three eleven-story buildings near the downtown area of St. Louis. Over half of the households have female heads, and for over half of the households the principal income comes from public assistance of one kind or another. The research has been in the field for a little over two years. It is a broad community study which thus far has relied principally on methods of participant observation and open-ended interviewing. Data on families come from repeated interviews and observations with a small group of families. The field workers are identified as graduate students at Washington University who have no connection with the housing authority or other officials, but are simply interested in learning about how families in the project live. This very intensive study of families yields a wealth of information (over 10,000 pages of interview and observation reports) which obviously cannot be analyzed within the limits of one article. In this article I have limited myself to outlining a typical family stage sequence and discussing some of the psychosocial implications of growing up in families characterized by this sequence. In addition, I have tried to limit myself to findings which other literature on Negro family life suggests are not limited to the residents of the housing projects we are studying.

2. St. Clair Drake, "The Social and Economic Status of the Negro in the United States," *The Negro American* (Boston, 1966), p. 4.

3. E. Franklin Frazier, *The Negro Family in the United States* (Chicago, 1939), p. 487.

4. Norman Mailer, "The White Negro" (City Light Books, San Francisco, Calif., 1957); and Leslie Fiedler, *Waiting For The End* (New York, 1964), pp. 118–137.

5. See Alvin W. Gouldner, "Reciprocity and Autonomy in Functional Theory," in Llewellyn Gross (ed.), *Symposium of Sociological Theory* (Evanston, Ill., 1958), for a discussion of functional autonomy and dependence of structural elements in social systems. We are suggesting here that lower-class groups have a relatively high degree of functional autonomy *vis à vis* the total social system because that system does little to meet their needs. In general the fewer the rewards a society offers members of a particular group in the society, the more autonomous will that group prove to be with reference to the norms of the society. Only by constructing an elaborate repressive machinery, as in concentration camps, can the effect be otherwise.

6. For example, the lead sentence in a *St. Louis Post Dispatch* article of July 20, 1965, begins "A White House study group is laying the ground work for an attempt to better the structure of the Negro family."

7. See Kenneth Stampp, *The Peculiar Institution* (New York, 1956); John Hope Franklin, *From Slavery to Freedom* (New York, 1956); Frank Tannenbaum, *Slave and Citizen* (New York, 1946); E. Franklin Frazier, *op. cit.;* and Melville J. Herskovits, *The Myth of the Negro Past* (New York, 1941).

8. See Raymond T. Smith, *The Negro Family in British Guiana* (New York, 1956); J. Mayone Stycos and Kurt W. Back, *The Control of Human Fertility in Jamaica* (Ithaca, N. Y., 1964); F. M. Henriques, *Family and Colour in Jamaica* (London, 1953); Judith Blake, *Family Structure in Jamaica* (Glencoe, Ill., 1961); and Raymond T. Smith, "Culture and Social Structure in The Caribbean," *Comparative Studies in Society and History,* Vol. VI (The Hague, The Netherlands, October 1963), pp. 24–46. For a broader comparative discussion of the matrifocal family see Peter Kunstadter, "A Survey of the Consanguine or Matrifocal Family," *American Anthropologist,* Vol. 65, No. 1 (February 1963), pp. 56–66; and Ruth M. Boyer, "The Matrifocal Family Among the Mescalero: Additional Data," *American Anthropologist,* Vol. 66, No. 3 (June 1964), pp. 593–602.

9. Paul C. Glick, *American Families* (New York, 1957), pp. 133 ff.

10. For discussions of white lower-class families, see Lee Rainwater, Richard P. Coleman, and Gerald Handel, *Workingman's Wife*

(New York, 1959); Lee Rainwater, *Family Design* (Chicago, 1964); Herbert Gans, *The Urban Villagers* (New York, 1962); Albert K. Cohen and Harold M. Hodges, "Characteristics of the Lower-Blue-Collar-Class," *Social Problems,* Vol. 10, No. 4 (Spring 1963), pp. 303–334; S. M. Miller, "The American Lower Classes: A Typological Approach," in Arthur B. Shostak and William Gomberg, *Blue Collar World* (Englewood Cliffs, N. J., 1964); and Mirra Komarovsky, *Blue Collar Marriage* (New York, 1964). Discussions of Negro slum life can be found in St. Clair Drake and Horace R. Cayton, *Black Metropolis* (New York, 1962), and Kenneth B. Clark, *Dark Ghetto* (New York, 1965); and of Negro community life in small-town and rural settings in Allison Davis, Burleigh B. Gardner, and Mary Gardner, *Deep South* (Chicago, 1944), and Hylan Lewis, *Blackways of Kent* (Chapel Hill, N. C., 1955).

11. For general discussions of the extent to which lower-class people hold the values of the larger society, see Albert K. Cohen, *Delinquent Boys* (New York, 1955); Hyman Rodman, "The Lower Class Value Stretch," *Social Forces,* Vol. 42, No. 2 (December 1963), pp. 205 ff; and William L. Yancey, "The Culture of Poverty: Not So Much Parsimony," unpublished manuscript, Social Science Institute, Washington University.

12. James F. Short, Jr., and Fred L. Strodtbeck, *Group Process and Gang Delinquency* (Chicago, 1965), p. 114. Chapter V (pages 102–115) of this book contains a very useful discussion of differences between white and Negro lower-class communities.

13. Discussions of white lower-class attitudes toward sex may be found in Arnold W. Green, "The Cult of Personality and Sexual Relations," *Psychiatry,* Vol. 4 (1941), pp. 343–348; William F. Whyte, "A Slum Sex Code," *American Journal of Sociology,* Vol. 49, No. 1 (July 1943), pp. 24–31; and Lee Rainwater, "Marital Sexuality in Four Cultures of Poverty," *Journal of Marriage and the Family,* Vol. 26, No. 4 (November 1964), pp. 457–466.

14. See Boone Hammond, "The Contest System: A Survival Technique," Master's Honors paper, Washington University, 1965. See also Ira L. Reiss, "Premarital Sexual Permissiveness Among Negroes and Whites," *American Sociological Review,* Vol. 29, No. 5 (October 1964), pp. 688–698.

15. See the discussion of aleatory processes leading to premarital fatherhood in Short and Strodtbeck, *op. cit.,* pp. 44–45.

16. Rainwater, *And the Poor Get Children, op. cit.,* pp. 61–63. See also, Carlfred B. Broderick, "Social Heterosexual Development Among Urban Negroes and Whites," *Journal of Marriage and the Family,* Vol. 27 (May 1965), pp. 200–212. Broderick finds that although white boys and girls, and Negro girls become more in-

terested in marriage as they get older, Negro boys become *less* interested in late adolescence than they were as preadolescents.

17. Walter Miller, "The Corner Gang Boys Get Married," *Trans-action*, Vol. 1, No. 1 (November 1963), pp. 10–12.

18. Rainwater, *Family Design, op. cit.*, pp. 28–60.

19. Yancey, *op. cit.* The effects of unemployment on the family have been discussed by E. Wright Bakke, *Citizens Without Work* (New Haven, Conn., 1940); Mirra Komarovsky, *The Unemployed Man and His Family* (New York, 1960); and Earl L. Koos, *Families in Trouble* (New York, 1946). What seems distinctive to the Negro slum culture is the short time lapse between the husband's loss of a job and his wife's considering him superfluous.

20. See particularly Komarovsky's discussion of "barriers to marital communications" (Chapter 7) and "confidants outside of marriage" (Chapter 9), in *Blue Collar Marriage, op. cit.*

21. Rainwater, *Family Design, op. cit.*, pp. 305–308.

22. For a discussion of the relationship between Black Nationalist ideology and the Negro struggle to achieve a sense of valid personal identity, see Howard Brotz, *The Black Jews of Harlem* (New York, 1963), and E. U. Essien-Udom, *Black Nationalism: A Search for Identity in America* (Chicago, 1962).

23. Rainwater, Coleman, and Handel, *op. cit.*, pp. 88–102.

24. Cf. Michael Schwartz and George Henderson, "The Culture Unemployment: Some Notes on Negro Children," in Shostak and Gomberg, *op. cit.*

25. Daniel Patrick Moynihan, "Employment, Income, and the Ordeal of the Negro Family," *The Negro American* (Boston, 1966), pp. 149–50.

26. Talcott Parsons concludes his discussion of child socialization, the development of an "internalized family system" and internalized role differentiation by observing, "The internalization of the family collectivity as an object and its values should not be lost sight of. This is crucial with respect to . . . the assumption of representative roles outside the family on behalf of it. Here it is the child's family membership which is decisive, and thus his acting in a role in terms of its values for 'such as he.'" Talcott Parsons and Robert F. Bales, *Family, Socialization and Interaction Process* (Glencoe, Ill., 1955), p. 113.

27. Erik H. Erikson, "Identity and the Life Cycle," *Psychological Issues*, Vol. 1, No. 1 (1959).

28. For discussion of the dynamics of the individual's *announcements* and the society's *placements* in the formation of identity, see Gregory Stone, "Appearance and the Self," in Arnold Rose, *Human Behavior in Social Process* (Boston, 1962), pp. 86–118.

29. The importance of identity for social behavior is discussed in detail

in Ward Goodenough, *Cooperation and Change* (New York, 1963), pp. 176–251, and in Lee Rainwater, "Work and Identity in the Lower Class," in Sam H. Warner, Jr., *Planning for the Quality of Urban Life* (Cambridge, Mass., forthcoming). The images of self and of other family members is a crucial variable in Hess and Handel's psychosocial analysis of family life; see Robert D. Hess and Gerald Handel, *Family Worlds* (Chicago, 1959), especially pp. 6–11.

30. See the discussion of "masking" and "unmasking" in relation to disorganization and re-equilibration in families by John P. Spiegel, "The Resolution of Role Conflict within the Family," in Norman W. Bell and Ezra F. Vogel, *A Modern Introduction to the Family* (Glencoe, Ill., 1960), pp. 375–377.

31. See the discussion of self-identity and self-esteem in Thomas F. Pettigrew, *A Profile of the Negro American* (Princeton, N. J., 1964), pp. 6–11.

32. Rainwater, Coleman, and Handel, *op. cit.,* pp. 44–51. See also the discussion of the greater level of "anomie" and mistrust among lower-class people in Ephriam Mizruchi, *Success and Opportunity* (New York, 1954). Unpublished research by the author indicates that for one urban lower-class sample (Chicago) Negroes scored about 50 per cent higher on Srole's anomie scale than did comparable whites.

3. For a discussion of the child's propensity from a very early age for speculation and developing explanations, see William V. Silverberg, *Childhood Experience and Personal Destiny* (New York, 1953), pp. 81 ff.

34. See Ralph Ellison's autobiographical descriptions of growing up in Oklahoma City in his *Shadow and Act* (New York, 1964). . . .

35. Rainwater, "Work and Identity in the Lower Class," *op. cit.*

36. *Ibid.*

37. Short and Strodtbeck see violent behavior in juvenile gangs as a kind of last resort strategy in situations where the actor feels he has no other choice. See Short and Strodtbeck, *op. cit.,* pp. 248–264.

38. Wiltse speaks of a "pseudo depression syndrome" as characteristic of many AFDC mothers. Kermit T. Wiltse, "Orthopsychiatric Programs for Socially Deprived Groups," *American Journal of Orthopsychiatry*, Vol. 33, No. 5 (October 1963), pp. 806–813.

39. Walter B. Miller, "Lower Class Culture as a Generating Milieu of Gang Delinquency," *Journal of Social Issues*, Vol. 14, No. 3 (1958), pp. 5–19.

40. This line of argument concerning the employment problems of Negroes, and poverty war strategy more generally, is developed with great cogency by James Tobin, "On Improving the Economic

Status of the Negro," *Dædalus* (Fall 1965), and previously by Gunnar Myrdal, in his *Challenge to Affluence* (New York, 1963), and Orville R. Gursslin and Jack L. Roach, in their "Some Issues in Training the Employed," *Social Problems,* Vol. 12, No. 1 (Summer 1964), pp. 68–77.

41. See Chapter 6 (pages 111–153) of Kenneth Clark, *op. cit.,* for a discussion of the destructive effects of ghetto schools on their students.

42. See the discussion of "moral danger" in Lee Rainwater, "Fear and the House-as-Haven in the Lower Class," *Journal of the American Institute of Planners,* February 1966.

Commentary: *The Search for Identity*

Lee Rainwater is concerned with the problem of finding an identity. He finds a sense of individual and group identity emerging from the "crucible" in which the Negro of the lower class family finds himself. This identity may be negative, that is, it may involve such symptoms as self-hatred and exploitation of on member of the minority by another. Or the identity may be pos tive to the degree that segregation, according to some, may be a stepping stone toward a sense of pride or an incentive for self improvement. Historically, the lower class Negro family has been structured by the kinds of situations that result in what Rainwater calls "caste victimization." This observation in itself would not be an original insight, but Rainwater is most provocative in his assertion that victimization has been functional and not dysfunctional, as so many writers on the Negro family believe. After all, victimization of the Negro family in the urban ghetto has provided it with functional autonomy wherein the members of the family are provided, in the course of the socialization process, with an arena in which they may be more realistically prepared for conflict with and survival in the world outside.

*A second point is that the "matrifocal" * family gains its cohesion*

---

* *Although "matriarchal" is the dictionary opposite of patriarchal, the sociological opposite of patriarchal is egalitarian. Cultural anthropologists, for the most part, doubt that there is anything anywhere, in terms of sexual division of labor or allocation of power within the social system, that is genuinely matriarchal. The term "matricentric," although better, may include judg-*

from identifying with a set of norms radically different from those of the dominant middle class, white or black. For example, illegitimacy and premarital pregnancy are problems to the middle class, but they are solutions and essentially a source of pride and solidarity to the matrifocal lower class. In addition, even the existence of three-generation matrifocal households does not alter the fact that the larger social system is still structured in terms of patriarchal rules and regulations. The lesson this teaches the analyst of family behavior is that an individual family may be patriarchal, equalitarian, matrifocal, or somewhere in between and still not provide a crucial test for overall societal change in family norms.

Rainwater was singularly prophetic and perceptive about the direction of ideological change. In the years that have followed since he published the essay in 1966, the feeling has arisen in the new Negro leadership that aspiring toward middle-class status, instead of solving problems through social action on community levels, made the Negro more vulnerable to victimization. This earlier goal placed him in conflict with the vast majority of lower class Negroes. To the black nationalists, blackness as a basis for racial solidarity connotes pride rather than self-hatred or escape. In 1966 identification with middle-class goals as structured by the dominant group was still a legitimate objective.

Murray A. Straus, in "Communication, Creativity, and Problem-Solving Ability of Middle- and Working-Class Families in Three Societies," in the American Journal of Sociology *(January 1968), has added a crucial dimension to the variable of social class and its impact upon the family that seems to support Rainwater's thesis. Straus finds that there are significant differences in communication, creativity, and problem-solving ability between middle- and working-class families. This observation in itself would not be a new finding. However, his cross-cultural research design is quite striking because he finds a class difference in three samples far removed from each other both geographically and culturally; namely, Minneapolis, San Juan, and Bombay. His conclusion reinforces what we have been trying to argue throughout this anthology: urbanization coupled with industrialization (as in the case of Minneapolis) tends to reduce the gap between*

---

ments as to female dominance that are ambiguous. This is why we prefer the term "matrifocal" as most neutral in its connotations.

middle-class and lower class families. This applies not only to Rainwater's theme but also to Talcott Parson's analysis. Interestingly enough, the lower class white has a higher index of aspiration to middle-class values than the lower class Negro. This lack of aspiration is especially true when the Negro is influenced by black nationalist appeals.

In Puerto Rico and India, the family samples studied by Straus were urban but preindustrial, so that the differences between lower class and middle-class families were much sharper. Because they are irrevocably part of a modern urban and industrial social order, lower class Negro families in the United States are paradoxically influenced by middle-class norms—even when they rebel against them most in separatist fashion.

11

EQUALITY BETWEEN THE SEXES: AN IMMODEST PROPOSAL

ALICE S. ROSSI

Introduction

When John Stuart Mill wrote his essay on "The Subjection of Women" in 1869, the two major things he argued for with elegance and persuasion were to extend the franchise to women, and to end the legal subordination of married women to their husbands. The movement for sex equality had already gathered considerable momentum in England and the United States by 1869, reaching its peak fifty years later, when the franchise was won by American women in 1920. In the decades since 1920, this momentum has gradually slackened, until by the 1960's American society has been losing rather than gaining ground in the growth toward sex equality. American women are not trying to extend their claim to equality from the political to the occupational and social arenas and often do not even seem interested in exercising the rights so bitterly won in the early decades of the twentieth century in politics and higher education. The constitutional amendment on equal rights for men and women has failed to pass Congress for seventeen consecutive years, and today a smaller proportion of college graduates are women than was true thirty years ago.

There is no overt antifeminism in our society in 1964, not because sex equality has been achieved, but because there is practi-

Reprinted by permission from Daedalus, *Journal of the American Academy of Arts and Sciences, Boston, Mass., Vol. 93, No. 2 (Spring 1964).*

cally no feminist spark left among American women. When I ask the brightest of my women college students about their future study and work plans, they either have none because they are getting married in a few months, or they show clearly that they have lowered their aspirations from professional and research fields that excited them as freshmen, to concentrate as juniors on more practical fields far below their abilities. Young women seem increasingly uncommitted to anything beyond early marriage, motherhood and a suburban house. There are few Noras in contemporary American society because women have deluded themselves that the doll's house is large enough to find complete personal fulfillment within it.

It will be the major thesis of this essay that we need to reassert the claim to sex equality and to search for the means by which it can be achieved. By sex equality I mean a socially androgynous conception of the roles of men and women, in which they are equal and similar in such spheres as intellectual, artistic, political and occupational interests and participation, complementary only in those spheres dictated by physiological differences between the sexes. This assumes the traditional conceptions of masculine and feminine are inappropriate to the kind of world we can live in in the second half of the twentieth century. An androgynous conception of sex role means that each sex will cultivate some of the characteristics usually associated with the other in traditional sex role definitions. This means that tenderness and expressiveness should be cultivated in boys and socially approved in men, so that a male of any age in our society would be psychologically and socially free to express these qualities in his social relationships. It means that achievement need, workmanship and constructive aggression should be cultivated in girls and approved in women so that a female of any age would be similarly free to express these qualities in her social relationships. This is one of the points of contrast with the feminist goal of an earlier day: rather than a one-sided plea for women to adapt a masculine stance in the world, this definition of sex equality stresses the enlargement of the common ground on which men and women base their lives together by changing the social definitions of approved characteristics and behavior for both sexes.

It will be an assumption of this essay that by far the majority of the differences between the sexes which have been noted in social research are socially rather than physiologically determined. What proportion of these sex differences are physiologically based and what proportion are socially based is a question the social and physiological sciences cannot really answer at the present time. It is sufficient for my present purposes to note that the opportunities for social change toward a closer approximation of equality between the sexes are large enough within the area of sex differences now considered to be socially determined to constitute a challenging arena for thought and social action. This is my starting point. I shall leave to speculative discourse and future physiological research the question of what constitutes irreducible differences between the sexes.

There are three main questions I shall raise in this essay. Why was the momentum of the earlier feminist movement lost? Why should American society attempt to reach a state of sex equality as I have defined it above? What are the means by which equality between the sexes can be achieved?

Why Feminism Declined

I shall discuss three factors which have been major contributors to the waning of feminism. The chief goals of the early leaders of the feminist movement were to secure the vote for women and to change the laws affecting marriage so that women would have equal rights to property and to their own children. As in any social reform movement or social revolution, the focus in the first stage is on change in the legal code, whether this is to declare independence from a mother country, establish a constitution for a new nation, free the slaves, or secure the right of women to be equal citizens with men. But the social changes required to translate such law into the social fabric of a society are of a quite different order. Law by itself cannot achieve this goal. It is one thing to declare slaves free or to espouse a belief in racial equality; quite another matter to accept racial integration in all spheres of life, as many northern communities have learned in recent years. In a similar way, many people accept the legal changes which have reduced the inequality between men and women and espouse belief in sex equality, but resist its manifestation in their personal life. If a social movement rests content with legal changes without making as strong an effort to change the social institutions through which they are expressed, it will remain a hollow victory.

This is one of the things which occurred in the case of the feminist movement. Important as the franchise is, or the recent change in Civil Service regulations which prevents the personnel specification of "male only," the new law or regulation can be successful only to the extent that women exercise the franchise, or are trained to be qualified for and to aspire for the jobs they are now permitted to hold. There is no sex equality until women participate on an equal basis with men in politics, occupations and the family. Law and administrative regulations must permit such participation, but women must want to participate and be able to participate. In politics and the occupational world, to be able to participate depends primarily on whether home responsibilities can be managed simultaneously with work or political commitments. Since women have had, and probably will continue to have, primary responsibility for child-rearing, their participation in politics, professions or the arts cannot be equal to that of men unless ways are devised to ease the combination of home and work responsibilities. This is precisely what has not occurred; at the same time, since fewer women today choose a career over marriage, the result has been a reduction in women's representation in the more challenging and demanding occupations.

By itself, the stress on legal change to the neglect of institutional change in the accommodations between family and work does not go very far in explaining why the feminist movement has lost momentum. There is an important second factor which must be viewed in conjunction with this first one. The feminist movement has always been strongest when it was allied with other social reform movements. In the nineteenth century its linkage was with the antislavery movement, and in the early twentieth century it was allied to the social welfare movement. There is an interesting and a simple explanation of this: unlike any other type of social inequality, whether of race, class, religion or nationality, sex is the only instance in which representatives of the unequal groups live in more intimate association with each other than with members of their own group. A woman is more intimately associated with a man than she is with any woman.* This was not the case for lord-serf, master-slave, Protestant-Roman Catholic, white-Negro relationships unless or until the social groups involved reach a full equality. By linking the feminist cause to the antislavery or social welfare movement, women were able to work to-

---

* This is one among many points of crucial and still relevant significance to be found in John Stuart Mill's essay "The Subjection of Women" (London, 1869).

gether with men of similar sympathies and in the process they enlisted the support of these men for the feminist cause. To a greater extent than any other underprivileged group, women need not only vigorous spokesmen and pacesetters of their own sex, but the support of men, to effect any major change in the status of women, whether in the personal sphere of individual relationships or on the level of social organization.* The decline of political radicalism and the general state of affluence and social conservatism in American society since World War II have contributed in subtle ways to the decline of feminism, for women are not joined with men in any movement affecting an underprivileged group in American society. At the present time, marriage remains the only major path of social mobility for women in our society.

The general conservatism of the total society has also penetrated the academic disciplines, with side effects on the motivation and ability of women to exercise the rights already theirs or to press for an extension of them. Feminism has been undermined by the conservatism of psychology and sociology in the postwar period. Sociologists studying the family have borrowed heavily from selective findings in social anthropology and from psychoanalytic theory and have pronounced sex to be a universally necessary basis for role differentiation in the family. By extension, in the larger society women are seen as predominantly fulfilling nurturant, expressive functions and men the instrumental, active functions. When this viewpoint is applied to American society, intellectually aggressive women or tender expressive men are seen as deviants showing signs of "role conflict," "role confusion," or neurotic disturbance. They are not seen as a promising indication of a desirable departure from traditional sex role definitions.† In a

---

* In recent years of acute manpower shortages in scientific, professional and technical fields, there has been a growing awareness of the fact that women constitute the only sizable remaining reservoir of such talent. Many men whose administrative or policy responsibilities alert them to this fact have been eagerly exploring the ways by which female brainpower could be added to the national pool of skilled manpower. The contemporary period is therefore ripe with opportunities for talented women, and women can anticipate a welcome from male colleagues and employers. I shall not discuss any further the current societal need for women in the labor force, because I would argue for an extension of female participation in the higher levels of occupations even in an era with *no* pressing manpower shortages, on the grounds of the more general principles to be developed in this essay.

† Often the conclusion that sex differentiation is a basic and universal phenomenon is buttressed by pointing to a large number of societies, all of which manifest such sex differentiation. Since Americans are easily impressed by large numbers, this does indeed sound like conclusive evidence against the likelihood of any society's achieving full sex equality. Closer examination

similar way, the female sphere, the family, is viewed by social theorists as a passive, pawnlike institution, adapting to the requirements of the occupational, political or cultural segments of the social structure, seldom playing an active role either in affecting the nature of other social institutions or determining the nature of social change.* The implicit assumption in problem after problem in sociology is that radical social innovations are risky and may have so many unintended consequences as to make it unwise to propose or support them. Although the sociologist describes and analyzes social change, it is change already accomplished, seldom anticipated purposive social change.† When the changes are in process, they are defined as social problems, seldom as social opportunities.

Closely linked to this trend in sociology and social anthropology, and in fact partly attributable to it, is the pervasive permeation of psychoanalytic thinking throughout American society. Individual psychoanalysts vary widely among themselves, but when their theories are popularized by social scientists, marriage and family counselors, writers, social critics, pediatricians and mental health specialists, there emerges a common and conservative image of the woman's role. It is the traditional image of woman which is popularized: the woman who finds complete self-fulfillment in her exclusive devotion to marriage and parenthood.

---

of such samples, however, reveals two things: very little representation of numerous African societies in which the instrumental-expressive distinction is simply *not* linked to sex in the predicted direction, and second, they are largely primitive societies, a half dozen of which might equal the size of a very small American city. Such cultural comparisons assume every possible kind of societal arrangement is represented, but this is not the case: Sweden, China, Yugoslavia, the Soviet Union, Israel are not represented on such a continuum. I believe we may learn more that is of relevance to a future America by studying family patterns in these societies than from a study of all the primitive societies in the world. Unfortunately, most of contemporary sociology and social anthropology is far less concerned with the future than the present as molded by the past.

* A rare exception is the recent work by William J. Goode, who has focussed precisely on the active role of the family in determining the course of social change in the non-family segments of social structure. See his *World Revolution and Family Patterns* (Glencoe: The Free Press, 1963).

† When the sociologist finds, for example, that the incidence of divorce is higher for those who marry outside their religion than for those who do not, he concludes that intermarriage is "bad" or "risky"; he does not say such marital failures may reflect the relative newness of the social pattern of intermarriage, much less suggest that such failures may decline once this pattern is more prevalent. In fact, the only aspect of intermarriage which is studied is the incidence of its failure. Sociologists have not studied *successful* intermarriages.

Women who thirty years ago might have chosen a career over a marriage, or restricted their family size to facilitate the combination of family and work roles, have been persuaded to believe that such choices reflect their inadequacy as women. It is this sense of failure as a woman that lies behind the defensive and apologetic note of many older unmarried professional women, the guilt which troubles the working mother (which I suspect goes up in direct proportion to the degree to which she is familiar with psychoanalytic ideas), the restriction of the level of aspiration of college women, the early plunge into marriage, the closed door of the doll's house.

Our society has been so inundated with psychoanalytic thinking that any dissatisfaction or conflict in personal and family life is considered to require solution on an individual basis. This goes well with the general American value stress on individualism, and American women have increasingly resorted to psychotherapy, the most highly individualized solution of all, for the answers to the problems they have as women. In the process the idea has been lost that many problems, even in the personal family sphere, cannot be solved on an individual basis, but require solution on a societal level by changing the institutional contexts within which we live.

The consequences of this acceptance of psychoanalytic ideas and conservatism in the social sciences have been twofold: first, the social sciences in the United States have contributed very little since the 1930's to any lively intellectual dialogue on sex equality as a goal or the ways of implementing that goal. Second, they have provided a quasi-scientific underpinning to educators, marriage counselors, mass media and advertising researchers, who together have partly created, and certainly reinforced, the withdrawal of millions of young American women from the mainstream of thought and work in our society.[*]

[*] A full picture of this post-World War II development is traced in Betty Friedan's *The Feminine Mystique* (New York: W. W. Norton, 1963). See particularly Chapters 6 and 7 on the "Functional Freeze" and the "Sex-Directed Educators."

Why Seek Equality Between the Sexes

This brings us to the second question: why should American society attempt to reach a state of sex equality? If women seem satisfied with a more narrowly restricted life pattern than men would be, why should we seek to disturb this pattern? To begin with, I do not think this question is really relevant to the issue. There have been underprivileged groups throughout history which contained sizable proportions of contented, uncomplaining members, whether slaves, serfs or a low status caste. But the most enlightened members of both the privileged and underprivileged groups in such societies came to see that inequality not only depressed the human potential of the subject groups but corrupted those in the superordinate groups. The lives of southern whites are as crippled by racial inequality as the lives of southern Negroes are impoverished. In the same way, many men spend their daytime hours away from home as vital cognitive animals and their nights and weekends in mental passivity and vegetation. Social and personal life is impoverished for some part of many men's lives because so many of their wives live in a perpetual state of intellectual and social impoverishment.

A second reason why American society should attempt to reach a state of full sex equality is that at the level our industrial society has now reached, it is no longer necessary for women to confine their life expectations to marriage and parenthood. Certain of the reasons for this have been increasingly stressed in recent years: with increased longevity, and smaller sized families, the traditional mother role simply does not occupy a sufficient portion of a woman's life span to constitute any longer the exclusive adult role for which a young woman should be prepared.* American girls spend more time as apprentice mothers with their dolls than they will as adult women with their own babies, and there is half a lifetime still ahead by the time the youngest child enters high school. Although studies have shown that women today are working in the home roughly the same number of hours a week as their mothers did,[1] this is not because they have to do so: technological

* Demographic changes in the family life cycle between 1890 and 1950 are shown in great detail in Paul Glick's *American Families* (New York: John Wiley, 1957). It should also be noted that even in contemporary families with four or five children, child-bearing occupies a far shorter portion of a woman's life span than it did to achieve this size family fifty years ago, because infant mortality has been so drastically reduced.

innovations in the production and distribution of food, clothing and other household equipment have been such that homemaking no longer requires the specialized skills and time-consuming tasks it did until early in our century. Contemporary women often turn what should be labor-saving devices into labor-making devices. In the light of the many time-consuming tasks the American mother fifty years ago had to perform, and the much longer work day for those in the labor force then, the woman in 1964 who holds down a full-time job will probably have as much or more time with her children as her grandmother had. Furthermore, most of the skills needed for adulthood are no longer taught within the family: child socialization is increasingly a shared enterprise between the parent and teachers, doctors, nurses, club leaders and instructors in an assortment of special skills.

These are perhaps all familiar points. What has not been seen is the more general point that *for the first time in the history of any known society, motherhood has become a full-time occupation for adult women.* In the past, whether a woman lived on a farm, a Dutch city in the seventeenth century, or a colonial town in the eighteenth century, women in all strata of society except the very top were never able to be full-time mothers as the twentieth-century middle class American woman has become. These women were productive members of farm and craft teams along with their farmer, baker or printer husbands and other adult kin. Children either shared in the work of the household or were left to amuse themselves; their mothers did not have the time to organize their play, worry about their development, discuss their problems. These women were not lonely because the world came into their homes in the form of customers, clients or patients in villages and towns, or farmhands and relatives on the farm; such women had no reason to complain of the boredom and solitude of spending ten-hour days alone with babies and young children because their days were peopled with adults. There were no child specialists to tell the colonial merchant's wife or pioneer farmer's wife that her absorption in spinning, planting, churning and preserving left her children on their own too much, that how she fed her baby would shape his adult personality, or that leaving children with a variety of other adults while she worked would make them insecure.

There are two important questions this analysis raises: why has full-time motherhood been accepted by the overwhelming majority of American women, and how successful has been the new pattern of full-time motherhood of the past forty years or so? I believe the major answer to the first question is that the American woman has been encouraged by the experts to whom she has turned for guidance in child-rearing to believe that her children need her continuous presence, supervision and care and that she should find complete fulfillment in this role. If, for example, a woman reads an article by Dr. Spock on working mothers, she is informed that any woman who finds full-time motherhood produces nervousness is showing a "residue of difficult relationships in her own childhood"; if irritability and nervousness are not assuaged by a brief trip or two, she is probably in an emotional state which can be "relieved through regular counseling in a family social agency, or, if severe, through psychiatric treatment"; and finally, "any mother of a preschool child who is considering a job should discuss the issues with a social worker before making her decision." [2] Since the social worker shares the same analytic framework that Dr. Spock does, there is little doubt what the advice will be; the woman is left with a judgment that wanting more than motherhood is not natural but a reflection of her individual emotional disturbance.

The fundamental tenet of the theory underlying such advice is that the physically and emotionally healthy development of the infant requires the loving involvement of the mother with the child. If an infant does not receive stable continuous mothering there is almost invariably severe physical and emotional disturbance. There is apparently ample clinical evidence to support these points. Studies have suggested that prolonged separation from parents, and particularly from the mother, has serious effects upon infants and young children.[3] However, practitioners make unwarranted extrapolations from these findings when they advise that *any* separation of mother and child is risky and hazardous for the healthy development of the child.[*] Despite the fact that the empirical evidence stems from instances of prolonged, traumatic separation caused by such things as the death or serious illness of the mother, or the institutionalization of the child, this viewpoint is applied to the situation of an employed mother absent from the

---

[*] A few authors have seen this claim that all separation of the child from the biological mother or mother surrogate, even for a few days, is inevitably damaging to the child, as a new and subtle form of anti-feminism, by which men, under the guise of exacting the importance of maternity, are tying women more tightly to their children than any real clinical or cultural evidence indicates is necessary. See Hilde Bruch, *Don't Be Afraid of Your Child* (New York: Farrar, Straus & Young, 1952); and Margaret Mead, "Some Theoretical Considerations on the Problem of Mother-Child Separation," *American Journal of Orthopsychiatry* (1954), 24: 471–483.

home on a regular basis. No one predicts that any dire consequences will flow from a woman's absence from home several
afternoons a week to engage in a shopping spree, keep medical
appointments or play bridge; nor is a father considered to produce severe disturbance in his young children even if his work
schedule reduces contact with them to the daylight hours of a
weekend. But women who have consulted pediatricians and family counselors about their resuming work are firmly told that they
should remain at home, for the sake of their children's emotional
health.*

What effect *does* maternal employment have upon children?
Many sociologists of the family have raised this question during
the past fifteen years, expecting to find negative effects as psychoanalytic theory predicted. In fact, the focus of most maternal employment studies has been on the effect of mothers' working upon
the personalities of their children, somewhat less often on the tensions and strains between the mother role and the occupational
role,† seldom on the question of how maternal employment
affects the woman's satisfactions with herself, her home and marriage. To date, *there is no evidence of any negative effects trace-
able to maternal employment;* children of working mothers are no
more likely than children of non-working mothers to become delinquent, to show neurotic symptoms, to feel deprived of maternal
affection, to perform poorly in school, to lead narrower social
lives, etc.[4] Many of the researchers in the 1950's frankly admitted
surprise at their negative findings. In a study reported in 1962,[5]

* It is interesting in this connection that studies concerning the separation
of the mother and child are frequently cited as cases of *maternal deprivation,*
but those concerning the separation of the father and child are cited more
neutrally as cases of *father absence,* never as *paternal deprivation.*

† Social scientists raise the question of whether there are not such diamet-
rically opposed requirements of an occupational role from the mother role as
to involve great strain between the two. It is argued that because of this
contrast between the two spheres, one or the other role must "suffer," there
will be "role conflict." The researchers were not prepared to find either that
women could slip back and forth between these two spheres just as men
have done for decades without any of the same difficulty predicted for
women, or that the mother role may be subtly changed in the direction of
more rationality, greater stress on independence and autonomy in children
than is found in the child-rearing values of non-working mothers (See Faye
VonMering, "Professional and Non-Professional Women as Mothers," *Journal of Social Psychology* [August, 1955], 42: 21–34). Rather, the researcher
expected to find maternal neglect, negative effect on children's personality,
or inadequacy in occupational roles, such as absenteeism, overly personal
view of work relationships, etc. As in many areas in which role conflict has
been predicted, human beings have a greater tolerance for sharp contrasts in
role demands than social scientists credit them with.

the only significant difference found between working and non-working mothers was the mother's confidence about her role as mother: 42 per cent of the working mothers but only 24 per cent of the non-working mothers expressed concern about their maternal role, "often by explicit questioning and worry as to whether working is interfering with their relationships and the rearing of their children." Yet these working women did not actually differ from the at-home mothers in the very things that concerned them: there were no differences between these women in the emotional relationships with their children, household allocation of responsibilities, principles of child-rearing, etc. The working mothers appeared to share the prevailing view that their children would suffer as a result of their employment, though in fact their children fare as well as those of non-working mothers.[6]

It would appear, therefore, that the employment of women when their children are eight years of age or older has no negative effect on the children. What about the earlier years, from infancy until school age? In the American literature, there is little to refer to as yet which bears directly upon the effect of maternal employment on the infant or toddler, partly because employment of mothers with preschool children is so negligible in the United States, partly because the measurement of "effects" on young children is difficult and cannot be done with the research tools which have been used in most studies of maternal employment effects—questionnaires administered to mothers and to their school-age children.*

There is, however, one significant body of data which is of considerable relevance to the question of the effect of maternal employment upon infants and very young children. Maternal employment is a regular pattern of separation of mother and child: the Israeli kibbutzim are collective settlements with several decades of experience in precisely this pattern. On the kibbutz, infants live in children's houses where their physical care and training are largely handled. During the infancy months the mother visits the

---

* The Burchinal-Rossman research cited previously did give special attention to employment of mothers during the child's early years. Their 7th- and 11th-grade students were divided according to when the maternal employment occurred—i.e., whether during the first three years of the child's life, second three, between the ages of 1 and 6, only within the previous 30 months or for the child's entire life. How long the mother has been working, or when in the growth of the child she began work, showed no significant effect upon the children's development: those whose mothers were working when they were under three years of age did not differ from those whose mothers began working when they were adolescents.

house to feed the infant; as toddlers, children begin a pattern of visiting with their parents for a few hours each day, living in the children's houses for the remaining portions of their days and nights. A number of studies have been conducted to investigate the effect of this intermittent multiple mothering on the young child.[7] They all point to essentially the same conclusion; the kibbutz child-rearing practices have no deleterious effects upon the subsequent personality development of the children involved. In fact, there are a number of respects in which the kibbutz-reared Israeli children exceed those reared in the traditional farm family: the kibbutz children showed a more accurate perception of reality, more breadth of interest and cultural background, better emotional control and greater overall maturity.

Continuous mothering, even in the first few years of life, does not seem to be necessary for the healthy emotional growth of a child.* The crux of the matter appears to be in the nature of the care which is given to the child.† If a child is reared by a full-time mother who is rejecting and cold in her treatment of him, or if a child is reared in an institutional setting lacking in warmth and stimulation and with an inadequate staff, both children will show personality disturbances in later years. If the loving care of the biological mother is shared by other adults who provide the child with a stable loving environment, the child will prosper at least as well as and potentially better than one with a good full-time mother.‡ In the section below on child care and careers, I

---

* There are of course other instances of infant and toddler care by persons supplementing the biological mother, notable among them being the creche and nursery school systems in the Soviet Union. What effect these early experiences of creche care have upon the subsequent personality development of Soviet young people is not known. Western observers who have visited them during the past several years have been impressed with the facilities, quality of staff personnel, and general happy mood of the children seen in them, but there is no rigorous evidence to substantiate these impressions, or assess the effect of such early separation from the mother upon personality.

† In this analysis, I am placing primary emphasis on the quality of the care given to the children. Another specification of maternal employment involves introducing the motivations and satisfactions of working and non-working mothers: many women work who do not wish to work, and many women are at home who do not wish to be at home. One recent study which took these factors into consideration found that the non-working mothers who are dissatisfied with not working (who want to work but, out of a sense of "duty," do not work) show the greatest problems in child rearing— more difficulty controlling their children, less emotional satisfaction in relationships to their children, less confidence in their functioning as mothers. Cf. Marian Radke Yarrow *et al., op. cit.*

‡ This shifts the ground of the problem of maternal employment to a very

shall suggest institutional innovations which would ensure good quality care for children and ease the combination of work and child-rearing for women.

Turning now to the second question raised above: how successful has the new pattern of full-time motherhood been? Are women more satisfied with their lives in the mid-twentieth century than in the past? Does motherhood fulfill them, provide them with a sufficient canvas to occupy a lifetime? Are contemporary children living richer lives, developing greater ego strength to carry them through a complex adulthood? Are children better off for having full-time mothers?

I think the answer to all the questions posed above is a firm *no*. Educators, child psychologists and social analysts report an increasing tendency for American middle-class children to be lacking in initiative, excessively dependent on others for direction and decision, physically soft.[8] Our children have more toys and play equipment than children in any other society, yet they still become bored and ask their mothers for "something to do." No society has as widespread a problem of juvenile delinquency and adolescent rebellion as the United States. Alcoholism, compulsive sex-seeking and adolescent delinquency are no longer social problems confined to the working class, socially disorganized sections of our cities, but have been on the increase in the middle-class suburb in the past twenty years, and involve more women and girls than in the past. There is a strong strand of male protest against the mother or "matriarch" in both our beatnik culture and our

---

different level from the one on which it is usually discussed. As a research problem, the crucial question is not whether the mother is employed or not, but what is the quality of the care given to the children—whether by the mother alone or a combination of other adults. Since full-time mothers vary from loving care to rejecting neglect, and mother substitutes may be presumed to vary in the same way, it is scarcely surprising that maternal employment *per se* shows very little effect upon the personality of children. Social scientists have uncritically borrowed the assumption of the psychoanalysts that the mental health of the child is possible only with continuous care by the biological mother. What is clearly called for is a shift in research definition from maternal employment versus full-time motherhood, to the quality of the care the child receives under conditions of full- and part-time working or non-working mothers. There is also a need for research which is based on a clear conceptualization of the variables of both "maternal care" and "maternal deprivation." For a careful review of crucial dimensions of maternal care and their effect upon infants, see Leon J. Yarrow, "Research in Dimensions of Early Maternal Care," *Merrill-Palmer Quarterly*, 9 (April, 1963), 101–114. The same author has written a careful re-evaluation of the concept of maternal deprivation: "Maternal deprivation: toward an empirical and conceptual reevaluation," *Psychological Bulletin*, 58 (1961), 459–490.

avant-garde literature: social and artistic extremes are seldom fully deviant from the middle range in a society, but show in an exaggerated heightened way the same though less visible tendencies in the social majority.

In a large proportion of cases, the etiology of mental illness is linked to inadequacy in the mother-child relationship. A high proportion of the psychoneurotic discharges from the army during World War II was traced to these young soldiers' overly dependent relationships to their mothers.[9] This has been the subject of much earnest discussion in the years since the war, but the focus has remained on the mother-*son* relationship, I suspect only because as a fighter, a professional man or a worker, male performance is seen to be more crucial for society than female performance. But dependence, immaturity and ego diffusion have been characteristic of daughters as well as sons. The only difference is that, in the case of daughters, this less often reaches the overt level of a social problem because young women move quickly from under their mothers' tutelage into marriage and parenthood of their own: female failures are therefore not as socially visible, for they are kept within the privacy of family life and psychoanalytic case records. It is a short-sighted view indeed to consider the immature wife, dominating mother or interfering mother-in-law as a less serious problem to the larger society than the male homosexual, psychoneurotic soldier or ineffectual worker, for it is the failure of the mother which perpetuates the cycle from one generation to the next, affecting sons and daughters alike.

Disturbing trends of this sort cannot all be traced to the American woman's excessive and exclusive involvement with home and family. We live in turbulent times, and some part of these trends reflects the impact of world tension and conflict. But there is no reason to assume that world tension is relevant to many of them. Emotional and physical difficulties after childbirth or during the menopause years, the higher incidence of college girl than college boy breakdowns, the shrunken initiative and independence of children, are clearly not explained by world conflict. Besides, vast sections of American society remain totally unmoved and unaffected by international political and military events until they directly impinge on their own daily lives. Since history is both written and produced more by men than by women, the fact that our writers are preoccupied with the relationship to the mother points to difficulties in our family system more than the course of world events.

It is a paradox of our social history that motherhood has become a full-time occupation in precisely the era when objectively it could, and perhaps should, be a part-time occupation for a short phase of a woman's life span. I suspect that the things women do for and with their children have been needlessly elaborated to make motherhood a full-time job. Unfortunately, in this very process the child's struggle for autonomy and independence, for privacy and the right to worry things through for himself are subtly and pervasively reduced by the omnipresent mother. As a young child he is given great permissive freedom, but he must exercise it under supervision. As an adolescent he is given a great deal of freedom, but his parents worry excessively about what he does with it. Edgar Friedenberg has argued that there is entirely too much parental concentration on adolescent children, with the result that it has become increasingly difficult to *be* an adolescent in American society.[10] He suggests that parents are interested in youth to the extent that they find their own stage of life uninteresting. Middle-class children are observed and analyzed by their mothers as though they were hothouse plants psychologically, on whose personalities any pressure might leave an indelible bruise. If a woman's adult efforts are concentrated exclusively on her children, she is likely more to stifle than broaden her children's perspective and preparation for adult life. Any stress or failure in a child becomes a failure of herself, and she is therefore least likely to truly help her child precisely when the child most needs support.[11] In myriad ways the mother binds the child to her, dampening his initiative, resenting his growing independence in adolescence; creating a subtle dependence which makes it difficult for the child to achieve full adult stature without a rebellion which leaves him with a mixture of resentment and guilt that torments him in his mother's declining years.

It seems to me no one has linked these things together adequately. Psychiatric counselors of college students frequently have as their chief task that of helping their young patients to free themselves from the entangling web of dependence upon their parents, primarily their mothers, and encouraging them to form stable, independent lives of their own. In other words, if the patient is eighteen years old the analyst tries to help her free herself from her mother, but if the next patient is twenty-five years old with young children at home, the analyst tells her the children would suffer emotional damage if she left them on a regular basis to hold down a job. The very things which would reduce the excessive dependency of children before it becomes a critical problem are discouraged by the counselor or analyst during the years when the dependency is being formed. If it is true that the adult is what the child was, and if we wish adults to be assertive, independent, responsible people, then they should be reared in a way which prevents excessive dependence on a parent. They should be cared for by a number of adults in their childhood, and their parents should truly encourage their independence and responsibility during their youthful years, not merely give lip service to these parental goals. The best way to encourage such independence and responsibility in the child is for the mother to be a living model of these qualities herself. If she had an independent life of her own, she would find her stage of life interesting, and therefore be less likely to live for and through her children. By maintaining such an independent life, the American mother might finally provide her children with something she can seldom give when she is at home —a healthy dose of inattention, and a chance for adolescence to be a period of fruitful immaturity and growth.* If enough American women developed vital and enduring interests outside the family and remained actively in them throughout the child-bearing years, we might then find a reduction in extreme adolescent rebellion, immature early marriages, maternal domination of children, and interference by mothers and mothers-in-law in the lives of married children.

There remains one further general characteristic of our industrial society which has relevance to the question of why American society should achieve full sex equality. Our family unit is small, for the most part geographically if not socially isolated from its kin. This small family unit is possible because of the increased longevity in highly industrialized societies. In agricultural societies, with their high rate of mortality, many parents die before they have completed the rearing of their young. The extended family provided substitutes for such parents without disturbing the basic lines of kin affiliation and property rights of these children. In our modern family system it is an unusual event for women or men to be widowed while they have young dependent children. This also means, however, that American families must fend for themselves in the many emergencies less critical than the death of a spouse:

* This has been argued by Eric Larrabee, though he does not suggest the employment of the mother as the way to make the older woman's life more interesting. See Eric Larrabee, "Childhood in Twentieth Century America," Eli Ginzberg (ed.), *The Nation's Children*, Vol. 3, *Problems and Prospects* (New York: Columbia University Press, 1960), pp. 199–216.

army service, long business or professional trips, prolonged physical or emotional illness, separation or divorce often require that one spouse carry the primary responsibility for the family, even if this is cushioned or supplemented by insurance, government aid, paid helpers or relatives. The insurance advertisements which show fathers bending over a cradle and begin "what would happen if?" evoke a twinge of fear in their readers precisely because parents recognize the lonely responsible positions they would be in if serious illness or death were to strike their home. In our family system, then, it is a decided asset if men and women can quickly and easily substitute for or supplement each other as parents and as breadwinners. I believe these are important elements in the structure of our economy and family system which exert pressure toward an equality between men and women. It is not merely that a companionate or equalitarian marriage is a desirable relationship between wife and husband, but that the functioning of an urban industrial society is facilitated by equality between men and women in work, marriage and parenthood.

The conclusions I have drawn from this analysis are as follows: full-time motherhood is neither sufficiently absorbing to the woman nor beneficial to the child to justify a contemporary woman's devoting fifteen or more years to it as her exclusive occupation. Sooner or later—and I think it should be sooner—women have to face the question of who they are besides their children's mother.

A major solution to this quest would be found in the full and equal involvement of women in the occupational world, the culmination of the feminist movement of the last one hundred and fifty years. This is not to overlook the fact that involvement as a volunteer in politics or community organizations or a serious dedication to a creative art can be a solution for many women. These areas of participation and involvement provide innumerable women with a keen sense of life purpose, and women are making significant and often innovative contributions in these pursuits. A job *per se* does not provide a woman, or a man either, with any magical path to self-fulfillment; nor does just any community volunteer work, or half-hearted dabbling in a creative art.

Women are already quite well represented in volunteer organizations in American communities. However, broadening the range of alternatives open to women and chosen by women for their life patterns is still to be achieved in the occupational world. It is also true that at the most challenging reaches of both political and community volunteer work, the activities have become increasingly professionalized. Thus while many women have and will continue to make innovative contributions to these fields as volunteers, such opportunities have become limited. Furthermore, many such women often find themselves carrying what amounts to a full-time job as a "volunteer executive," yet neither the recognition nor the rewards are equivalent to what they would receive in comparable positions in the occupational system.[12] Hence, the major focus in this essay will be on the means by which the full and equal involvement of well-educated women in the occupational world may be achieved. For reasons which will become clear later, I believe that the occupational involvement of women would also be the major means for reducing American women's dominance in marriage and parenthood, and thus for allowing for the participation of men as equal partners in family life.

Of course there have already been changes in the extent and the nature of women's participation in the American labor force. Indeed, this is sometimes cited as proof that sex equality has been achieved in the United States. There are roughly twenty-three million American women in the labor force, and it is predicted that this will swell to thirty million by 1970. About three-fifths of these women are married, an increase of well over 20 per cent since 1940. It should be noted that this increase came predominantly from women between the ages of 35 and 54 years, after the child-rearing years and before the usual retirement age for workers. This is a major social change, to be sure, and people who still raise the question of whether married women should work are arguing after the fact, for such women are doing so at increasing rates. The point is, however, that most American women—65 per cent—do *not* work outside the home, and those who do are found largely in blue collar or low-skill white collar occupations. Men fill roughly 85 per cent of the very top professional and technical jobs in the United States. Furthermore, only a very small proportion of American wives work if their husbands are in the middle and top income brackets, or if they have young children. Finally, the distribution of the female labor force by age shows two major peaks of female participation, before and for a short time after marriage, and then for the fifteen years from their early forties through middle fifties. Withdrawal and re-entry many years later is now a common female work pattern in the United States. As long as this pattern continues, women will not increase their representation in the top professional and technical occupations.*

Over the past twenty years, women in many European countries have doubled or more their representation in the professional occupations. By comparison, American women constitute a smaller proportion of the professional world today than they did twenty years ago. That this reflects a lowering of ambition among American women is suggested by the fact that of all the women capable of doing college work, only one out of four do so, compared to one out of two men. This is the point at which we begin to tap a deeper root of women's motivations in the United States. Whether a woman works steadily throughout her marriage or returns to work after the child-rearing period, no significant increase of women in the professional and high-skill job categories will occur unless American women's attitude toward education and work is changed.[13] To study and to prepare for a future job "in case I have to work" is just as poor a preparation for occupational participation as the postponement of learning domestic skills "until I have to" is a poor preparation for the homemaker role. Both views reflect a digging in of the heels into the adolescent moment of a lifetime. In many ways the middle-class girl considers only the present, the here-and-now, as do most members of the working class, and not the future, as do her father, brothers and male friends. There is evidence to suggest that such an emphasis on the present is characteristic not only of the American woman at college age, but also more generally throughout her life span. Thus, Gallup's portrait of the American woman shows the same characteristic at all points during the younger half of the life cycle: young unmarried women as well as mature women with their children now entering high school give little thought to and no preparation for their life over forty years of age.[14]

The middle-class wife of a successful business executive or professional man has a special problem. To earn a salary in the occupational world, she will be judged by her own achieved merits without regard to her social position or her husband's influence. Unless she has had the education and experience necessary to hold a position of some prestige, she will experience social and personal barriers to entering the labor force. In the absence of

---

* Viola Klein's study of English working women shows the same pattern: withdrawal and return to work at a later age is paid for by a loss of occupational status. See Viola Klein, *Working Wives*, Occasional Papers No. 15 (London: Institute of Personnel Management, 1960), pp. 21–24.

such education and experience, she is qualified to be only the occupational subordinate of men who are her equals socially, a status incongruity few women are likely to tolerate. By contrast, no matter how menial, her service as a volunteer will be socially approved. Unless such women secure specialized training before marriage, or acquire it after marriage, there will be little increase in the proportion of working wives and mothers in the upper half of the middle class. Many such women with a flair for organization have found full scope for their independent fulfillment in volunteer work in politics, education, social welfare and the arts. Unfortunately, there are innumerable other women for whom such outlets have little attraction who realize they have missed their chance for independent self-fulfillment, and who have little opportunity for a second chance by their late forties.

It has been argued by some sociologists that the American marriage is already too fragile to sustain competition at comparable skill levels between spouses.[15] If this were true, and women are also reluctant to work at lower prestige jobs than their husbands, this would effectively freeze most middle-class women out of the occupational world. I would raise three points concerning this assumption. First, husbands and working wives are usually found in different segments of the occupational system, which makes comparison of success a difficult matter. For example, is an architect working for a large firm and earning $20,000 a year more or less successful than his wife who directs a large family welfare agency and earns $15,000 a year? Second, even were such achievements in nonfamily roles to provoke some competitive feeling between husband and wife, I think the consequences of this competition are far less potentially harmful to the marriage or to the children than the situation of the well-educated able woman who is not working and engages instead in a competition with her husband for the affections and primary loyalties of the children. If a woman is markedly more successful than her husband, it would probably create difficulty in the marriage, particularly if there are residues of traditional expectations of male breadwinner dominance on the part of either partner to the marriage. But competition does not necessarily mean conflict. It can be a social spice and a source of pride and stimulation in a marriage of equals. Last, one must face up to the fact that a new social goal exacts a price. A change toward sex equality may cause some temporary marital dislocations, but this is not sufficient reason to expect all women to remain enclosed in the past.

Institutional Levers for Achieving
Sex Equality

In turning to the problem of how equality between the sexes may be implemented as a societal goal, I shall concentrate on the three major areas of child care, residence and education. Institutional change in these areas in no sense exhausts the possible spheres in which institutional change could be effected to facilitate the goal of sex equality. Clearly government and industry, for example, could effect highly significant changes in the relations between the sexes. But one must begin somewhere, and I have chosen these three topics, for they all involve questions of critical significance to the goal of equality between men and women.

1. It is widely assumed that rearing children and maintaining a career is so difficult a combination that except for those few women with an extraordinary amount of physical strength, emotional endurance and a dedicated sense of calling to their work, it is unwise for women to attempt the combination. Women who have successfully combined child-rearing and careers are considered out of the ordinary, although many men with far heavier work responsibilities who yet spend willing loving hours as fathers, and who also contribute to home maintenance, are cause for little comment. We should be wary of the assumption that home and work combinations are necessarily difficult. The simplified contemporary home and smaller sized family of a working mother today probably represent a lesser burden of responsibility than that shouldered by her grandmother.

This does not mean that we should overlook the real difficulties that are involved for women who attempt this combination. Working mothers do have primary responsibility for the hundreds of details involved in home maintenance, as planners and managers, even if they have household help to do the actual work. No one could suggest that child-rearing and a career are easy to combine, or even that this is some royal road to greater happiness, but only that the combination would give innumerable intelligent and creative women a degree of satisfaction and fulfillment that they cannot obtain in any other way. Certainly many things have to "give" if a woman works when she also has young children at home. Volunteer and social activities, gardening and entertaining may all have to be curtailed. The important point to recognize is that as children get older, it is far easier to resume these social activities than it is to resume an interrupted career. The major difficulty, and the one most in need of social innovation, is the problem of providing adequate care for the children of working mothers.

If a significant number of American middle-class women wish to work while their children are still young and in need of care and supervision, who are these mother-substitutes to be? In the American experience to date, they have been either relatives or paid domestic helpers. A study conducted by the Children's Bureau in 1958 outlines the types of child-care arrangements made by women working full time who had children under twelve years of age.[16] The study showed that the majority of these children (57 per cent) were cared for by relatives: fathers, older siblings, grandparents and others. About 21 per cent were cared for by nonrelatives, including neighbors as well as domestic helpers. Only 2 per cent of the children were receiving group care—in day nurseries, day-care centers, settlement houses, nursery schools and the like. Of the remainder, 8 per cent were expected to take care of themselves, the majority being the "latchkey" youngsters of ten and twelve years of age about whom we have heard a good deal in the press in recent years.

These figures refer to a national sample of employed mothers and concern women in blue collar jobs and predominantly low-skill white collar jobs. Presumably the proportion of middle-class working mothers who can rely on either relatives or their husbands would be drastically lower than this national average, and will probably decline even further in future years. Many of today's, and more of tomorrow's American grandmothers are going to be wage earners themselves and not baby-sitters for their grandchildren. In addition, as middle-class women enter the occupational world, they will experience less of a tug to remain close to the kinswomen of their childhood, and hence may contribute further to the pattern of geographic and social separation between young couples and both sets of their parents. Nor can many middle-class husbands care for their children, for their work hours are typically the same as those of their working wives: there can be little dovetailing of the work schedules of wives and husbands in the middle class as there can be in the working class.

At present, the major child-care arrangement for the middle-class woman who plans a return to work has to be hired household help. In the 1920's the professional and business wife-mother had little difficulty securing such domestic help, for there were thousands of first generation immigrant girls and women in our large cities whose first jobs in America were as domestic servants.* In the 1960's, the situation is quite different: the major source of domestic help in our large cities is Negro and Puerto Rican women. Assuming the continuation of economic affluence and further success in the American Negro's struggle for equal opportunity in education, jobs and housing, this reservoir will be further diminished in coming decades. The daughters of many present-day Negro domestic servants will be able to secure far better paying and more prestigeful jobs than their mothers can obtain in 1964. There will be increasing difficulty of finding adequate child-care help in future years as a result.

The problem is not merely that there may be decreasing numbers of domestic helpers available at the same time more women require their aid. There is an even more important question involved: are domestic helpers the best qualified persons to leave in charge of young children? Most middle-class families have exacting standards for the kind of teachers and the kind of schools they would like their children to have. But a working mother who searches for a competent woman to leave in charge of her home has to adjust to considerably lower standards than she would tolerate in any nursery school program in which she placed her young son or daughter, either because such competent help is scarce, or because the margin of salary left after paying for good child care and the other expenses associated with employment is very slight.

One solution to the problem of adequate child care would be an attempt to upgrade the status of child-care jobs. I think one productive way would be to develop a course of study which would yield a certificate for practical mothering, along the lines that such courses and certificates have been developed for practical nursing. There would be several important advantages to such a program. There are many older women in American communities whose lives seem empty because their children are grown and their grandchildren far away, yet who have no interest in factory or

* In one study conducted for the Bureau of Vocational Information in 1925, Collier found that 42% of the one hundred professional and business mothers she interviewed had two or more full-time domestic servants to maintain their homes and care for their children during the day; only 9 of these 100 women had no full-time servants, five of whom had their mothers living with them. Virginia MacMakin Collier, *Marriage and Careers: A Study of One Hundred Women who are Wives, Mothers, Homemakers and Professional Women* (New York: The Channel Bookshop, 1926), pp. 59 and 74.

sales work, for they are deeply committed to life and work within the context of a home. Indeed, there are many older women who now work in factories or as cashiers or salesclerks who would be much more satisfied with child-care jobs, if the status and pay for such jobs were upgraded. These are the women, sometimes painfully lonely for contact with children, who stop young mothers to comment on the baby in the carriage, to talk with the three-year-old and to discuss their own distant grandchildren. I think many of these women would be attracted by a program of "refresher" courses in first aid, child development, books and crafts appropriate for children of various ages, and the special problems of the mother substitute-child relationship. Such a program would build upon their own experiences as mothers but would update and broaden their knowledge, bringing it closer to the values and practices of the middle-class woman who is seeking a practical mother for her family. Substitute motherhood for which she earns a wage, following active motherhood of her own, could provide continuity, meaning and variety to the life-span of those American women who are committed to the traditional conception of woman's role. Such a course of study might be developed in a number of school contexts—a branch of a college department of education, an adult education extension program or a school of nursing.

A longer-range solution to the problem of child care will involve the establishment of a network of child-care centers.* Most of the detailed plans for such centers must be left for future discussion, but there are several important advantages to professionally run child-care centers which should be noted. Most important, better care could be provided by such centers than any individual mother can provide by hiring a mother's helper, housekeeper or even the practical mother I have just proposed. In a

---

* Child-care centers would not be an entirely new phenomenon in the United States, for there were a number of municipal day-care centers established during World War II when the need for womanpower in factories engaged in war production made them necessary to free women to accept employment. There have also been continuing debates about the provision of child-care centers for other mothers, such as the ADC mother, the problem revolving about whether such women should be given sufficient money from municipal funds to stay at home and care for her children, or to establish child-care centers and thus enable such women to hold down jobs and at least partially support their children. In either case, the focus has been upon working-class women. Child-care centers as an institutional device to facilitate the combination of job and family by women in professional and technical occupations in the middle class are very rare, and are largely confined to small private ventures in the large metropoli.

child-care center, there can be greater specialization of skills, better facilities and equipment, and play groups for the children. Second, a child-care center would mean less expense for the individual working mother, and both higher wages and shorter hours for the staff of the center. Third, these centers could operate on a full-time, year-round schedule, something of particular importance for women trained in professional or technical fields, the majority of which can be handled only on a full-time basis. Except for the teaching fields, such women must provide for the afternoon care of their nursery school and kindergarten-age children, after-school hours for older children and three summer months for all their children. Fourth, a child-care center could develop a roster of home-duty practical mothers or practical nurses to care for the ill or convalescent child at home, in much the way school systems now call upon substitute teachers to cover the classes of absent regular teachers.

A major practical problem is where to locate such child-care centers. During the years of experimentation which would follow acceptance of this idea, they might be in a variety of places, under a variety of organizational auspices, as a service facility offered by an industrial firm, a large insurance company, a university, the federal or a state government. Community groups of women interested in such service might organize small centers of their own much as they have informal pooled baby-sitting services and cooperatively run nursery schools at the present time.

I believe that one of the most likely contexts for early experimentation with such child-care centers is the large urban university. As these universities continue to expand in future years, in terms of the size of the student body, the varied research institutes associated with the university and the expansion of administrative, technical and counseling personnel, there will be increasing opportunity and increasing need for the employment of women. A child-care center established under the auspices of a major university would facilitate the return for training of older women to complete or refresh advanced training, forestall the dropping out of younger graduate married women with infants and young children to care for, and attract competent professional women to administrative, teaching or research positions, who would otherwise withdraw from their fields for the child-rearing years. It would also be an excellent context within which to innovate a program of child care, for the university has the specialists in psychology, education and human development on whom to call for the planning, research and evaluation that the establishment of child-care centers would require. If a university-sponsored child-care program were successful and widely publicized, it would then constitute an encouragement and a challenge to extend child-care centers from the auspices of specific organizations to a more inclusive community basis. A logical location for community child-care centers may be as wings of the elementary schools, which have precisely the geographic distribution throughout a city to make for easy access between the homes of very young children and the centers for their daytime care. Since school and center would share a location, it would also facilitate easy supervision of older children during the after-school hours. The costs of such care would also be considerably reduced if the facilities of the school were available for the older children during after-school hours, under the supervision of the staff of the child-care center. There are, of course, numerous problems to be solved in working out the details of any such program under a local educational system, but assuming widespread support for the desirability of community facilities for child care, these are technical and administrative problems well within the competence of school and political officials in our communities.

I have begun this discussion of the institutional changes needed to effect equality between the sexes with the question of child-care provision because it is of central importance in permitting women to enter and remain in the professional, technical and administrative occupations in which they are presently so underrepresented. Unless provision for child care is made, women will continue to find it necessary to withdraw from active occupational involvement during the child-rearing years. However, the professional and scientific fields are all growing in knowledge and skill, and even a practitioner who remains in the field often has difficulty keeping abreast of new developments. A woman who withdraws for a number of years from a professional field has an exceedingly difficult time catching up. The more exacting the occupation, then, the shorter the period of withdrawal should probably be from active participation in the labor force. If a reserve of trained practical mothers were available, a professional woman could return to her field a few months after the birth of a child, leaving the infant under the care of a practical mother until he or she reached the age of two years, at about which age the child could enter a child-care center for daytime care. Assuming a two-child family, this could mean not more than one year of withdrawal from her professional field for the working mother.

2. The preferred residential pattern of the American middle class in the postwar decades has been suburban. In many sections of the country it is difficult to tell where one municipality ends and another begins, for the farm, forest and waste land between towns and cities have been built up with one housing development after another. The American family portrayed in the mass media typically occupies a house in this sprawling suburbia, and here too, are the American women, and sometimes men, whose problems are aired and analyzed with such frequency. We know a good deal about the characteristics and quality of social life in the American suburb[17] and the problems of the men and women who live in them. We hear about the changing political complexion of the American suburbs, the struggle of residents to provide sufficient community facilities to meet their growing needs. But the social and personal difficulties of suburban women are more likely to be attributed to their early family relationships or to the contradictory nature of the socialization of girls in our society than to any characteristic of the environment in which they now live. My focus will be somewhat different: I shall examine the suburban residence pattern for the limitations it imposes on the utilization of women's creative work abilities and the participation of men in family life. Both limitations have important implications for the lives of boys and girls growing up in the suburban home.

The geographic distance between home and work has a number of implications for the role of the father-husband in the family. It reduces the hours of possible contact between children and their fathers. The hour or more men spend in cars, buses or trains may serve a useful decompression function by providing time in which to sort out and assess the experiences at home and the events of the work day, but it is questionable whether this outweighs the disadvantage of severely curtailing the early morning and late afternoon hours during which men could be with their children.

The geographic distance also imposes a rigid exclusion of the father from the events which highlight the children's lives. Commuting fathers can rarely participate in any special daytime activities at home or at school, whether a party, a play the child performs in or a conference with a teacher. It is far less rewarding to a child to report to his father at night about such a party or part in a play than to have his father present at these events. If the husband-father must work late or attend an evening function in the city, he cannot sandwich in a few family hours but must remain in the city. This is the pattern which prompted Margaret Mead to characterize the American middle-class father as the "children's mother's husband," and partly why mother looms so oversized in the lives of suburban children.

Any social mixing of family-neighborhood and job associates is reduced or made quite formal: a work colleague cannot drop in for an after-work drink or a Saturday brunch when an hour or more separates the two men and their families. The father-husband's office and work associates have a quality of unreality to both wife and children. All these things sharpen the differences between the lives of men and women—fewer mutual acquaintances, less sharing of the day's events, and perhaps most importantly, less simultaneous filling of their complementary parent roles. The image of parenthood to the child is mostly motherhood, a bit of fatherhood and practically no parenthood as a joint enterprise shared at the same time by father and mother. Many suburban parents, I suspect, spend more time together as verbal parents —discussing their children in the children's absence—than they do actively interacting with their children, the togetherness cult notwithstanding. For couples whose relationship in courtship and early marriage was equalitarian, the pressures are strong in the suburban setting for parenthood to be highly differentiated and skewed to an ascendant position of the mother. Women dominate the family, men the job world.

The geographic distance between home and the center of the city restricts the world of the wife-mother in a complementary fashion. Not only does she have to do and be more things to her children, but she is confined to the limitations of the suburban community for a great many of her extrafamilial experiences. That suburban children are restricted in their social exposure to other young children and relatively young adults, mostly women and all of the same social class, has often been noted. I think the social restriction of the young wife to women of her own age and class is of equal importance: with very few older persons in her immediate environment, she has little first-hand exposure to the problems attending the empty-nest stage of life which lies ahead for herself. It is easy for her to continue to be satisfied to live each day as it comes, with little thought of preparing for the thirty-odd years when her children are no longer dependent upon her. If the suburban wife-mother had more opportunity to become acquainted with older widows and grandmothers, this would be pressed home to her in a way that might encourage a change in her unrealistic expectations of the future, with some preparation for that stage of life while she is young.*

If and when the suburban woman awakens from this short-range perspective and wants either to work or to prepare for a return to work when her children are older, how is she to do this, given the suburban pattern of residence? It is all very well to urge that school systems should extend adult education, that colleges and universities must make it possible for older women to complete education interrupted ten or more years previously or to be retrained for new fields; but this is a difficult program for the suburban wife to participate in. She lives far from the center of most large cities, where the educational facilities tend to be concentrated, in a predominantly middle-class community, where do-

* George Gallup and Evan Hill, "The American Woman," *The Saturday Evening Post*, December 22, 1962. One must read this survey very carefully to get behind the gloss of the authors' rosy perspective. Gallup reports that almost half of the married women in the sample claimed that childbirth was the "most thrilling event" in their lives. He gives two quotes to illustrate why these women were so fascinated by childbirth: one stresses the point that it was "the one time in my life when everything was right"; the other points out "you've done something that's recognized as a good thing to do, and you're the center of attention." If these are truly typical, it tells us a good deal about the underlying attitude toward the thousands of days on which no child is born: things are *not* all right, and there must be some sense of being on the sidelines, of having a low level of self-esteem, if childbirth is important because "society views it as good" and it is the only time in her life that she is the important center of attention. In other parts of the article, which generally stresses the central importance of children to women, and their high satisfaction with marriage, we learn that a large proportion of American women wish the schools would do more of the socializing of these children—teach them good citizenship, how to drive, sex education; and if these women were so satisfied with their lives, why does only 10% of the sample want their daughters to live the same lives they have? Instead, these women say they want their daughters to get more education and to marry later than they did. If marriage is the perfect female state, then why wish to postpone it, unless there are unexpressed sides of the self which have not been fulfilled?

The only strong critical point made is the following: "with early weddings and extended longevity, marriage is now a part-time career for women, and unless they prepare now for the freer years, this period will be a loss. American society will hardly accept millions of ladies of leisure, or female drones, in their 40's" (p. 32). But only 31% of the sample reported they are "taking courses or following a plan to improve themselves," a third of these involving improvement of their physical shape or appearance. The photographs accompanying this article reveal the authors' own focus on the years of youth rather than of maturity: of 29 women appearing in these pictures, only 2 are clearly of women over 45 years of age.

mestic help is often difficult to arrange and transportation often erratic during the hours she would be using it.

It is for these reasons that I believe any attempt to draw a significant portion of married women into the mainstream of occupational life must involve a reconsideration of the suburban pattern of living. Decentralization of business and industry has only partly alleviated the problem: a growing proportion of the husbands living in the suburbs also work in the suburbs. There are numerous shops and service businesses providing job opportunities for the suburban wife. Most such jobs, however, are at skill levels far below the ability potential and social status of the suburban middle-class wife. Opportunities for the more exacting professional, welfare and business jobs are still predominantly in the central sections of the city. In addition, since so many young wives and mothers in this generation married very young, before their formal education was completed, they will need more schooling before they can hope to enter the fields in which their talents can be most fruitfully exercised, in jobs which will not be either dull or a status embarrassment to themselves and their husbands. Numerous retail stores have opened suburban branches; colleges and universities have yet to do so. A woman can spend in the suburb, but she can neither learn nor earn.

That some outward expansion of American cities has been necessary is clear, given the population increase in our middle- to large-sized cities. But there are many tracts in American cities between the business center and the outlying suburbs which imaginative planning and architectural design could transform and which would attract the men and women who realize the drawbacks of a suburban residence. Unless there is a shift in this direction in American housing, I do not think there can be any marked increase in the proportion of married middle-class women who will enter the labor force. That Swedish women find work and home easier to combine than American women is closely related to the fact that Sweden avoided the sprawling suburban development in its postwar housing expansion. The emphasis in Swedish housing has been on inner-city housing improvement. With home close to diversified services for schooling, child care, household help and places of work, it has been much easier in Sweden than in the United States to draw married women into the labor force and keep them there.

In contrast, the policy guiding the American federal agencies which affect the housing field, such as the FHA, have stressed the individual home, with the result that mortgage money was readily available to encourage builders to develop the sprawling peripheries of American cities. Luxury high-rise dwellings at the hub of the city and individual homes at the periphery have therefore been the pattern of middle-class housing development in the past twenty years. A shift in policy on the part of the federal government which would embrace buildings with three and four dwelling units and middle-income high-rise apartment buildings in the in-between zones of the city could go a long way to counteract this trend toward greater and greater distance between home and job. Not everyone can or will want to live close to the hub of the city. From spring through early fall, it is undoubtedly easier to rear very young children in a suburban setting with back yards for the exercise of healthy lungs and bodies. But this is at the expense of increased dependence of children on their mothers, of minimization of fathers' time with their youngsters, of restriction of the social environment of women, of drastic separation of family and job worlds and of less opportunity for even part-time schooling or work for married women.

3. Men and women must not only be able to participate equally; they must want to do so. It is necessary, therefore, to look more closely into their motivations, and the early experiences which mold their self-images and life expectations. A prime example of this point can be seen in the question of occupational choice. The goal of sex equality calls for not only an increase in the extent of women's participation in the occupational system, but a more equitable distribution of men and women in all the occupations which comprise that system. This means more women doctors, lawyers and scientists, more men social workers and school teachers. To change the sex ratio within occupations can only be achieved by altering the sex-typing of such occupations long before young people make a career decision.* Many men

* The extent of this sex-typing of occupations is shown dramatically in a study of the June, 1961 college graduates conducted by the National Opinion Research Center at the University of Chicago. Although the women in this sample of college graduates showed a superior academic performance during the college years—only 36% of the women in contrast to 50% of the men were in the "bottom half" of their class—their career aspirations differed markedly from those of men. Of those who were going on to graduate and professional schools in the fall of 1961, only 6% of those aspiring to careers in medicine were women; 7% in physics, 7% in pharmacology, 10% in business and administration, 28% in the social sciences. In contrast, women predominated in the following fields: 51% in humanities, 59% in elementary

and women change their career plans during college, but this is usually within a narrow range of relatively homogeneous fields: a student may shift from medicine to a basic science, from journalism to teaching English. Radical shifts such as from nursing to medicine, from kindergarten teaching to the law, are rare indeed. Thus while the problem could be attacked at the college level, any significant change in the career choices men and women make must be attempted when they are young boys and girls. It is during the early years of elementary school education that young people develop their basic views of appropriate characteristics, activities and goals for their sex. It is for this reason that I shall give primary attention to the sources of sex-role stereotypes and what the elementary school system could do to eradicate these stereotypes and to help instead in the development of a more androgynous conception of sex role.*

The all-female social atmosphere of the American child has been frequently noted by social scientists, but it has been seen as a problem only in its effect upon boys. It has been claimed, for example, that the American boy must fight against a feminine identification this atmosphere encourages, with the result that he becomes overly aggressive, loudly asserting his maleness. In con-

---

and secondary education, 68% in social work, 78% in health fields such as nursing, medical technology, physical and occupational therapy. In a sample of 33,782 college graduates, there were 11,000 women who expected to follow careers in elementary and secondary education, but only 285 women who hoped to enter the combined fields of medicine, law and engineering. See James A. Davis and Norman Bradburn, "Great Aspirations: Career Plans of America's June 1961 College Graduates," National Opinion Research Center Report No. 82, September, 1961 (mimeographed). Davis and Bradburn report that some 40% of the graduates had changed their career plans during their college years (p. 40).

* My attention in this section will be largely on the early years of schooling. There is a great need, however, for a return of the spirit that characterized high school and college educators of women in the 1930's. It has seemed to me that there is an insidious trend at this level of education toward discouraging women from aspiring to the most demanding and rewarding fields of work and thought. Dr. Mary Bunting, noteworthy for the imaginative Radcliffe Institute for Independent Study, now urges women to work on the "fringes" of the occupational system, away from the most competitive intellectual market places. In her first public address upon assuming the presidency of Barnard College, Dr. Rosemary Park stated that in her view college education of women in the United States should have as its goal the creation of "enlightened laymen." High school and college counselors give hearty approval if women students show talent and interest in elementary school teaching, nursing, social work; their approval is all too often very lukewarm if not discouraging, if women students show interest in physics, medicine or law.

trast, it is claimed that the American girl has an easy socialization, for she has an extensive number of feminine models in her environment to facilitate her identification as a female.

There are several important factors which this analysis overlooks. To begin with the boy: while it is certainly true that much of his primary group world is controlled by women, this does not mean that he has no image of the male social and job world as well. The content of the boy's image of man's work has a very special quality to it, however. Although an increasingly smaller proportion of occupations in a complex industrial society relies on sheer physical strength, the young boy's exposure to the work of men remains largely the occupations which do require physical strength. The jobs he can see are those which are socially visible, and these are jobs in which men are reshaping and repairing the physical environment. The young boy sees working class men operating trucks, bulldozers, cranes; paving roads; building houses; planting trees; delivering groceries. This image is further reinforced by his television viewing: the gun-toting cowboy, the bat-swinging ballplayer, the arrow-slinging Indian. Space operas suggest not scientific exploration but military combat, the collision and collusion of other worlds. In short, even if the boy sees little of his father and knows next to nothing of what his father does away from home, there is some content to his image of men's work in the larger society. At least some part of his aggressive active play may be as much acting out similar male roles in response to the cultural cues provided by his environment as it is an over-reaction to his feminine environment or an identification with an aggressor-father.

And what of the girl? What image of the female role is she acquiring during her early years? In her primary group environment, she sees women largely in roles defined in terms that relate to her as a child—as mother, aunt, grandmother, baby-sitter—or in roles relating to the house—the cleaning, cooking, mending activities of mother and domestic helpers. Many mothers work outside the home, but the daughter often knows as little of that work as she does of her father's. Even if her own mother works, the reasons for such working that are given to the child are most often couched in terms of the mother or housewife role. Thus, a girl is seldom told that her mother works because she enjoys it or finds it very important to her own satisfaction in life, but because the money she earns will help pay for the house, a car, the daughter's

clothes, dancing lessons or school tuition.* In other words, working is something mothers sometimes have to do as mothers, not
something mothers do as adult women. This is as misleading and
distorted an image of the meaning of work as the father who tells
his child he works "to take care of mummy and you" and neglects
to mention that he also works because he finds personal satisfaction in doing so, or that he is contributing to knowledge, peace or
the comfort of others in the society.

The young girl also learns that it is only in the family that
women seem to have an important superordinate position. However high her father's occupational status outside the home, when
he returns at night, he is likely to remove his white shirt and become a blue collar Mr. Fixit or mother's helper. The traditional
woman's self-esteem would be seriously threatened if her husband
were to play a role equal to her own in the lives and affections of
her children or in the creative or managerial aspect of home management, precisely because her major sphere in which to acquire
the sense of personal worth is her home and children.† The lesson is surely not lost on her daughter, who learns that at home
father does not know best, though outside the home men are the
bosses over women, as she can see only too well in the nurse-doc-
tor, secretary-boss, salesclerk-store manager, space Jane-space
John relationships that she has an opportunity to observe.

The view that the socialization of the girl is an easy one compared with the boy depends on the kind of woman one has in

---

* Although her sample was upper-middle-class mothers of girls in progressive schools in New York City, Ruth Hartley reports that the working
mothers in her sample told their children they were working out of the home
because of financial need: "They express guilt about their working and
appear to hold quite traditional concepts of appropriate 'feminine' behavior
which they feel they are violating." An example is provided by a well-to-do
working mother who obviously loves her work but told her daughter that she
works because of financial necessity. When asked why she doesn't let her
daughter know she enjoys her work, she answered, "well, then what excuse
would I have for working?" Ruth Hartley and A. Klein, "Sex Role Concepts
among Elementary School-Age Girls," *Marriage and Family Living*, 21
(February, 1959), 59–64.

† Women enhance their own self-esteem when they urge their children to
"be good when father gets home" because he is tired and needs to rest.
They are not only portraying an image of the father as a fragile person, a
"Dresden cup" as Irene Joselyn expresses it, but by expanding their maternal-
ism to include the father, they are symbolically relegating him to the subordinate position of the child in the family structure. See Irene Joselyn,
"Cultural Forces, Motherliness and Fatherliness," *American Journal of Orthopsychiatry*, 26 (1956), 264–271.

mind as an end-product of socialization. Only if the woman is to be the traditional wife-mother is present-day socialization of young girls adequate, for from this point of view the confinement to the kinds of feminine models noted above and the superordinate position of the mother in the family facilitate an easy identification. If a girl sees that women reign only at home or in a history book, whereas outside the home they are Girl Fridays to men, then clearly for many young girls the wife-mother role may appear the best possible goal to have. It should be noted, however, that identification has been viewed primarily as an either-or process—the child identifies either with the mother or the father—and not as a process in which there is a fusion of the two parent models such that identification involves a modeling of the self after mother in some respects, father in others. It is possible that those women who have led exciting, intellectually assertive and creative lives did not identify exclusively with their traditional mothers, but crossed the sex line and looked to their fathers as model sources for ideas and life commitments of their own. This is to suggest that an exclusively same-sex identification between parent and child is no necessary condition for either mentally healthy or creative adults.

If I am correct about the significance of the father in the childhoods of those women who later led creative adult lives, then an increased accessibility of the middle-class father to his daughters and greater sharing of his ideas and interests could help to counteract the narrow confines of the feminine models daughters have. Beyond this, young girls need exposure to female models in professional and scientific occupations and to women with drive and dedication who are playing innovative volunteer roles in community organizations; they need an encouragement to emulate them and a preparation for an equalitarian rather than a dominant role in parenthood. Only if a woman's self-esteem is rooted in an independent life outside her family as well as her roles within the home can she freely welcome her husband to share on an equal basis the most rewarding tasks involved in child-rearing and home maintenance.

What happens when youngsters enter school? Instead of broadening the base on which they are forming their image of male and female roles, the school perpetuates the image children bring from home and their observations in the community. It has been mother who guided their preschool training; now in school it is almost exclusively women teachers who guide their first serious learning experiences. In the boy's first readers, men work at the same jobs with the same tools he has observed in his neighborhood—"T" for truck, "B" for bus, "W" for wagon. His teachers expect him to be rugged, physically strong and aggressive. After a few years he moves into separate classes for gym, woodworking and machine shop. For the girl, women are again the ones in charge of children. Her first readers portray women in aprons, brooms in their hands or babies in their arms. Teachers expect her to be quiet, dependent, with feminine interests in doll and house play and dressing up. In a few years she moves into separate classes for child care, cooking and practical nursing. In excursions into the community, elementary school boys and girls visit airports, bus terminals, construction sites, factories and farms.

What can the schools do to counteract these tendencies to either outmoded or traditional images of the roles of men and women? For one, class excursions into the community are no longer needed to introduce American children to building construction, airports or zoos. Except for those in the most underprivileged areas of our cities, American children have ample exposure to such things with their car- and plane-riding families. There are, after all, only a limited number of such excursions possible in the course of a school year. I think visits to a publishing house, research laboratory, computer firm or art studio would be more enriching than airports and zoos.

Going out into the community in this way, youngsters would observe men and women in their present occupational distribution. By a program of bringing representatives of occupations into the classroom and auditorium, however, the school could broaden the spectrum of occupations young children may link to their own abilities and interests regardless of the present sex-typing of occupations, by making a point of having children see and hear a woman scientist or doctor; a man dancer or artist; both women and men who are business executives, writers and architects.*

* In a large metropolis, resource persons could be invited through the city business and professional organizations, the Chamber of Commerce, art, music and dancing schools, etc. This could constitute a challenging program for PTA groups to handle; or a Community Resources Pool could be formed similar to that the New World Foundation has supported in New York City whereby people from business, the arts and sciences and the professions work with the public schools. Many educators and teachers might hesitate to try such a project in anticipation of parent-resistance. But parent-resistance could be a good opportunity for parent-education, if teachers and school officials were firm and informed about what they are trying to do.

Another way in which the elementary schools could help is making a concerted effort to attract male teachers to work in the lower grades. This would add a rare and important man to the primary group environment of both boys and girls. This might seem a forlorn hope to some, since elementary school teaching has been such a predominantly feminine field, and it may be harder to attract men to it than to attract women to fields presently considered masculine. It may well be that in the next decade or so the schools could not attract and keep such men as teachers. But it should be possible for graduate schools of education and also school systems to devise ways of incorporating more men teachers in the lower grades, either as part of their teacher training requirements or in the capacity of specialized teachers: the science, art or music teacher who works with children at many grade levels rather than just one or two contiguous grade levels.* His presence in the lives of very young children could help dispel their expectation that only women are in charge of children, that nurturance is a female attribute or that strength and an aggressive assault on the physical environment is the predominant attribute of man's work.

The suggestions made thus far relate to a change in the sex-linking of occupations. There is one crucial way in which the schools could effect a change in the traditional division of labor by sex within the family sphere. The claim that boys and girls are reared in their early years without any differentiation by sex is only partially true. There are classes in all elementary schools which boys and girls take separately or which are offered only to one sex. These are precisely the courses most directly relevant to adult family roles: courses in sex and family living (where communities are brave enough to hold them) are typically offered in separate classes for boys and for girls, or for girls only. Courses in shop and craft work are scheduled for boys only; courses in child care, nursing and cooking are for girls only. In departing from completely coeducational programs, the schools are reinforcing the traditional division of labor by sex which most children observe in their homes. Fifteen years later, these girls find that they

* Though predominantly a feminine field, there is one man to approximately every two women planning careers in teaching. In the "Great Aspirations" study there were 11,388 women students planning to teach in elementary and secondary schools, but also 5038 men. The problem may therefore not be as great as it seems at first: schools of education could surely do more to encourage some of these men to work in the lower grades, in part or for part of their teaching careers.

cannot fix a broken plug, set a furnace pilot light or repair a broken high chair or favorite toy. These things await the return of the child's father and family handyman in the evening. When a child is sick in the middle of the night, his mother takes over; father is only her assistant or helper.

These may seem like minor matters, but I do not think they are. They unwittingly communicate to and reinforce in the child a rigid differentiation of role between men and women in family life. If first aid, the rudiments of child care and of cooking have no place in their early years as sons, brothers and schoolboys, then it is little wonder that as husbands and fathers American men learn these things under their wives' tutelage. Even assuming these wives were actively involved in occupations of their own and hence free of the psychological pressure to assert their ascendancy in the family, it would be far better for all concerned—the married pair and the children as well—if men brought such skills with them to marriage.

This is the point where the schools could effect a change: if boys and girls took child care, nursing, cooking, shop and craft classes together, they would have an opportunity to acquire comparable skills and pave the way for true parental substitutability as adults. They would also be learning something about how to complement each other, not just how to compete with each other.* Teamwork should be taught in school in the subjects relevant to adult family roles, not just within each sex on the playground or in the gymnasium. In addition to encouraging more equality in the parental role, such preparation as school children could ease their adjustment to the crises of adult life; illness, separation due to the demands of a job or military service, divorce or death would have far less trauma and panic for the one-parent family—whether mother or father—if such equivalence and substitutability were a part of the general definition of the parental role.

A school curriculum which brought boys and girls into the same classes and trained them in social poise, the healing skills, care of children, handling of interpersonal difficulties and related subjects

---

* Bruno Bettelheim makes the point that American boys and girls learn to compete with each other, but not how to complement each other. He sees this lack of experience in complementarity as part of the difficulty in achieving a satisfactory sexual adjustment in marriage: the girl is used to "performing with males on equal grounds, but she has little sense of how to complement them. She cannot suddenly learn this in bed." See Bruno Bettelheim, "Growing Up Female," *Harper's*, November, 1962, p. 125.

would also encourage the development of skills which are increasingly needed in our complex economy. Whether the adult job is to be that of a worker in an automated industry, a professional man in law, medicine or scholarship, or an executive in a large bureaucratic organization, the skills which are needed are not physical strength and ruggedness in interpersonal combat but understanding in human dealings, social poise and persuasive skill in interpersonal relations.* All too often, neither the family nor the school encourages the development of these skills in boys. Hundreds of large business firms look for these qualities in young male applicants but often end up trying to develop them in their young executives through on-the-job training programs.

I have suggested a number of ways in which the educational system could serve as an important catalyst for change toward sex equality. The schools could reduce sex-role stereotypes of appropriate male and female attributes and activities by broadening the spectrum of occupations youngsters may consider for themselves irrespective of present sex-linked notions of man's work and woman's work, and by providing boys as well as girls with training in the tasks they will have as parents and spouses. The specific suggestions for achieving these ends which I have made should be viewed more as illustrative than as definitive, for educators themselves may have far better suggestions for how to implement the goal in the nation's classrooms than I have offered in these pages. Equality between the sexes cannot be achieved by proclamation or decree but only through a multitude of concrete steps, each of which may seem insignificant by itself, but all of which add up to the social blueprint for attaining the general goal.

Summary Profile

In the course of this essay I have suggested a number of institutional innovations in education, residence and child care which would facilitate equality between the sexes. Instead of a more conventional kind of summary, I shall describe a hypothetical case of a woman who is reared and lives out her life under the changed social conditions proposed in this essay.

She will be reared, as her brother will be reared, with a combi-

---

* These are the same skills which, when found in women, go by the names of charm, tact, intuition. See Helen Mayer Hacker, "The New Burdens of Masculinity," *Marriage and Family Living*, 19 (August, 1957), 227–233.

nation of loving warmth, firm discipline, household responsibility and encouragement of independence and self-reliance. She will not be pampered and indulged, subtly taught to achieve her ends through coquetry and tears, as so many girls are taught today. She will view domestic skills as useful tools to acquire, some of which, like fine cooking or needlework, having their own intrinsic pleasures but most of which are necessary repetitive work best gotten done as quickly and efficiently as possible. She will be able to handle minor mechanical breakdowns in the home as well as her brother can, and he will be able to tend a child, press, sew, and cook with the same easy skills and comfortable feeling his sister has.

During their school years, both sister and brother will increasingly assume responsibility for their own decisions, freely experiment with numerous possible fields of study, gradually narrowing to a choice that best suits their interests and abilities rather than what is considered appropriate or prestigeful work for men and women. They will be encouraged by parents and teachers alike to think ahead to a whole life span, viewing marriage and parenthood as one strand among many which will constitute their lives. The girl will not feel the pressure to belittle her accomplishments, lower her aspirations, learn to be a receptive listener in her relations with boys, but will be as true to her growing sense of self as her brother and male friends are. She will not marry before her adolescence and schooling are completed, but will be willing and able to view the college years as a "moratorium" from deeply intense cross-sex commitments, a period of life during which her identity can be "at large and open and various." [18] Her intellectual aggressiveness as well as her brother's tender sentiments will be welcomed and accepted as *human* characteristics, without the self-questioning doubt of latent homosexuality that troubles many college-age men and women in our era when these qualities are sex-linked.* She will not cling to her parents, nor they to her, but will establish an increasingly larger sphere of her own independent world in which she moves and works, loves and thinks, as a maturing young person. She will learn to take pleasure in her own body and a man's body and to view sex as a good and wonderful

* David Riesman has observed that this latent fear of homosexuality haunts the Ivy League campuses, putting pressure on many young men to be guarded in their relations with each other and with their male teachers, reflecting in part the lag in the cultural image of appropriate sex characteristics. See David Riesman, "Permissiveness and Sex Roles," *Marriage and Family Living*, 21 (August, 1959), 211–217.

experience, but not as an exclusive basis for an ultimate commitment to another person, and not as a test of her competence as a female or her partner's competence as a male. Because she will have a many-faceted conception of her self and its worth, she will be free to merge and lose herself in the sex act with a lover or a husband.*

Marriage for our hypothetical woman will not mark a withdrawal from the life and work pattern that she has established, just as there will be no sharp discontinuity between her early childhood and youthful adult years. Marriage will be an enlargement of her life experiences, the addition of a new dimension to an already established pattern, rather than an abrupt withdrawal

---

* It goes beyond the intended scope of this essay to discuss the effects of a social pattern of equality between men and women upon their sexual relationship. A few words are, however, necessary, since the defenders of traditional sex roles often claim that full equality would so feminize men and masculinize women that satisfactory sexual adjustments would be impossible and homosexuality would probably increase. If the view of the sex act presupposes a dominant male actor and a passive female subject, then it is indeed the case that full sex equality would probably be the death knell of this traditional sexual relationship. Men and women who participate as equals in their parental and occupational and social roles will complement each other sexually in the same way, as essentially equal partners, and not as an ascendant male and a submissive female. This does not mean, however, that equality in non-sexual roles necessarily de-eroticizes the sexual one. The enlarged base of shared experience can, if anything, heighten the salience of sex *qua* sex. In Sweden, where men and women approach equality more than perhaps any other western society, visitors are struck by the erotic atmosphere of that society. Sexually men and women do after all each lack what the other has and wishes for completion of the self; the salience of sex may be enhanced precisely in the situation of the diminished significance of sex as a differentiating factor in all other areas of life. It has always seemed paradoxical to me that so many psychoanalysts defend the traditional sex roles and warn that drastic warping of the sexual impulses may flow from full sex equality; surely they are underestimating the power and force of the very drive which is in so central a position in their theoretical framework. Maslow is one of the few psychologists who has explored the connections between sex experience and the conception of self among women. With a sample of one hundred and thirty college-educated women in their twenties, he found, contrary to traditional notions of femininity and psychoanalytic theories, that the more "dominant" the woman, the greater her enjoyment of sexuality, the greater her ability to give herself freely in love. Women with dominance feelings were free to be completely themselves, and this was crucial for their full expression in sex. They were not feminine in the traditional sense, but enjoyed sexual fulfillment to a much greater degree than the conventionally feminine women he studied. See A. H. Maslow, "Dominance, Personality and Social Behavior in Women," *Journal of Social Psychology,* 10 (1939), 3–39; and "Self-Esteem (Dominance Feeling) and Sexuality in Women," *Journal of Social Psychology,* 16 (1942), 259–294; or a review of Maslow's studies in Betty Friedan, *The Feminine Mystique,* pp. 316–326.

to the home and a turning in upon the marital relationship. Marriage will be a "looking outward in the same direction" for both the woman and her husband. She will marry and bear children only if she deeply desires a mate and children, and will not be judged a failure as a person if she decides against either. She will have few children if she does have them, and will view her pregnancies, childbirth and early months of motherhood as one among many equally important highlights in her life, experienced intensely and with joy but not as the exclusive basis for a sense of self-fulfillment and purpose in life. With planning and foresight, her early years of child bearing and rearing can fit a long-range view of all sides of herself. If her children are not to suffer from "paternal deprivation," her husband will also anticipate that the assumption of parenthood will involve a weeding out of nonessential activities either in work, civic or social participation. Both the woman and the man will feel that unless a man can make room in his life for parenthood, he should not become a father. The woman will make sure, even if she remains at home during her child's infancy, that he has ample experience of being with and cared for by other adults besides herself, so that her return to a full-time position in her field will not constitute a drastic change in the life of the child, but a gradual pattern of increasing supplementation by others of the mother. The children will have a less intense involvement with their mother, and she with them, and they will all be the better for it. When they are grown and establish adult lives of their own, our woman will face no retirement twenty years before her husband, for her own independent activities will continue and expand. She will be neither an embittered wife, an interfering mother-in-law nor an idle parasite, but together with her husband she will be able to live an independent, purposeful and satisfying third act in life.

Notes

1. Cowles and Dietz, Myrdal and Klein, and Jean Warren have shown that there has been very little change in the past quarter century in the total working time per week devoted to homemaking activities. May L. Cowles and Ruth P. Dietz, "Time Spent in Homemaking Activities by a Selected Group of Wisconsin Farm Homemakers," *Journal of Home Economics,* 48 (January, 1956), 29–35; Jean Warren, "Time: Resource or Utility," *Journal of Home*

Economics, 49 (January, 1957), 21 ff; Alva Myrdal and Viola Klein, *Women's Two Roles: Home and Work* (London: Routledge and Kegan Paul, 1956).

2. Benjamin Spock, "Should Mothers Work?" *Ladies' Home Journal,* February, 1963.

3. See Anna Freud and Dorothy T. Burlingham, *Infants Without Families* (New York: International University Press, 1944); William Goldfarb, "Psychological Deprivation in Infancy and Subsequent Adjustment," *American Journal of Orthopsychiatry,* 15 (April, 1945), 247–255; John Bowlby, *Maternal Care and Mental Health* (Geneva: World Health Organization, 1952); John Bowlby, *Child-Care and the Growth of Love* (London: Pelican Books, 1953); and James Bossard, *The Sociology of Child Development* (New York: Harper, 1954).

4. Burchinal and Rossman found no significant relationships between any kind of employment and personality characteristics or social interaction of children in the 7th and 11th grades in school—Lee G. Burchinal and Jack E. Rossman, "Relations among Maternal Employment Indices and Developmental Characteristics of Children," *Marriage and Family Living,* 23 (November, 1961), 334–340. Nye administered questionnaires to over two thousand high school students and found no significant relationships between maternal employment and educational achievement or neurotic symptoms—F. Ivan Nye, "Employment Status of Mothers and Adjustment of Adolescent Children," *Marriage and Family Living,* 21 (August, 1959), 240–244. Using scales to tap nervous symptoms, antisocial and withdrawing tendencies, Perry found no significant differences between children with working and nonworking mothers—Joseph B. Perry, "The Mother Substitutes of Employed Mothers: An Exploratory Inquiry," *Marriage and Family Living,* 23 (November, 1961), 362–367. Kligler found that employed mothers reported their maternal role suffered least from their occupations—Deborah S. Kligler, "The Effects of the Employment of Married Women on Husband and Wife Roles." Unpublished. Ph.D. dissertation, Department of Sociology, Yale University, 1954. Roy found no consistent effects of maternal employment on the social life and participation of children or their academic performance, or the affection, fairness of discipline and cooperation in the family—Prodipto Roy, "Maternal Employment and Adolescent Roles: Rural-Urban Differentials," *Marriage and Family Living,* 23 (November, 1961), 340–349. Peterson found no significant differences on employment of mothers and maternal interest in and supervision of their adolescent daughters—Evan T. Peterson, "The Impact of Maternal Employment on the Mother-Daughter Relationship," *Marriage and Family Living,* 23

(November, 1961), 355–361. In Eleanor Maccoby's reanalysis of data from the Gluecks' study of working mothers and delinquency, she shows that working or not working has little effect once the quality of child care is taken into account—Eleanor Maccoby, "Effects Upon Children of their Mothers' Outside Employment," in National Manpower Council, *Work in the Lives of Married Women* (New York: Columbia University Press, 1958), pp. 150–172. General reviews of the literature are found in: Lois M. Stolz, "Effects of Maternal Employment on Children: Evidence from Research," *Child Development*, 31 (December, 1960), 749–782; Eli Ginzberg (ed.), *The Nation's Children*, Vol. 3, *Problems and Prospects* (New York: Columbia University Press, 1960) in the chapter by Henry David on "Work, Women and Children," pp. 180–198; and Elizabeth Herzog, *Children of Working Mothers* (Washington, D. C.: U. S. Department of Health, Education and Welfare, Children's Bureau Publication #382, 1960); and most recently, a volume of research papers on the employed mother by F. Ivan Nye and Lois W. Hoffman, *The Employed Mother in America* (Chicago: Rand McNally, 1963).

5. Marian Radke Yarrow, Phyllis Scott, Louise de Leeuw, and Christine Heinig, "Child-rearing in Families of Working and Nonworking Mothers," *Sociometry*, 25 (June, 1962), 122–140.

6. Only in recent years has there been a shift in the discussion and research on maternal employment: investigators have begun to explore the *positive* effects of maternal employment. For example, Urie Bronfenbrenner has suggested that employed mothers may have a positive effect upon adolescent children by giving them a chance to develop responsibility for their own behavior—Urie Bronfenbrenner, "Family Structure and Personality Development: Report of Progress" (Ithaca, New York: Cornell University, Department of Child Development and Family Relationships, 1958 (mimeographed)). Ruth Hartley has suggested that the working mother may have "stretching effects" upon a child's perceptions and social concepts—Ruth E. Hartley, "What Aspects of Child Behavior Should be Studied in Relation to Maternal Employment," *Research Issues Related to the Effects of Maternal Employment on Children* (New York: Social Science Research Center, The Pennsylvania State University, 1961), p. 48.

7. A. I. Rabin, "Infants and Children under Conditions of 'Intermittent' Mothering in the Kibbutz," *American Journal of Orthopsychiatry*, 28 (1958), 577–584; Rabin, "Personality Maturity of Kibbutz and Non-Kibbutz Children as Reflected in Rorschach Findings," *Journal of Projective Techniques*, 21 (1957), 148–153; Rabin, "Attitudes of Kibbutz Children to Family and Parents," *American Journal of Orthopsychiatry*, 29 (1959), 172–179; Rabin,

"Some Psychosexual Differences between Kibbutz and Non-Kibbutz Israeli Boys," *Journal of Projective Techniques*, 22 (1958), 328–332; H. Faigin, "Social Behavior of Young Children in the Kibbutz," *Journal of Abnormal and Social Psychology*, 56 (1958), 117–129. A good overview of these studies can be found in David Rapaport, "The Study of Kibbutz Education and its Bearing on the Theory of Development," *American Journal of Orthopsychiatry*, 28 (1958), 587–599.

8. This passivity and softness in American young people has been noted in the following works: David Riesman, Introduction to Edgar Friedenberg, *The Vanishing Adolescent* (Boston: Beacon Press, 1959); Paul Goodman, *Growing Up Absurd* (New York: Random House, 1960); Marjorie K. McCorquodale, "What They Will Die for in Houston," *Harper's*, October, 1961; the *Dædalus* issue on *Youth: Change and Challenge*, Winter 1962. The White House attempt in recent years to revitalize physical education has been in part a response to the distressing signs of muscular deterioration and physical passivity of American youth.

9. Edward A. Strecker, *Their Mothers' Sons* (Philadelphia: Lippincott, 1946).

10. Friedenberg, *The Vanishing Adolescent*.

11. Numerous authors have analyzed the effect of women's focus on their children as their chief achievement: John Spiegel, "New Perspectives in the Study of the Family," *Marriage and Family Living*, 16 (February, 1954), 4–12; Bruno Bettelheim, "Growing Up Female," *Harper's*, October, 1962. The effects of such exclusive maternal focus on children upon relations with married children are shown in: Marvin Sussman, "Family Continuity: Selective Factors which Affect Relationships between Families at Generational Levels," *Marriage and Family Living*, 16 (May, 1954), 112–130; Paul Wallin, "Sex Differences in Attitudes toward In-Laws," *American Journal of Sociology*, 59 (1954), 466–469; Harvey Locke, *Predicting Adjustment in Marriage* (New York: Holt, 1951); Evelyn M. Duvall, *In-Laws: Pro and Con* (New York: Associated Press, 1954); and Frances Jerome Woods, *The American Family System* (New York: Harper and Brothers, 1959), pp. 265–266. These authors discuss the strains with mothers-in-law stemming from too exclusive a focus of women on their children and their subsequent difficulty in "releasing" their children when they are grown.

12. See Margaret Cussler's profile of the "volunteer executive" in her study *The Woman Executive* (New York: Harcourt, Brace, 1958), pp. 111–118.

13. Myrdal and Klein, *Women's Two Roles: Home and Work*, pp. 33–64; National Manpower Council, *Womanpower* (New York:

Columbia University Press, 1957); Florence Kluckhohn, *The American Family: Past and Present and America's Women* (Chicago: The Delphian Society, 1952), p. 116; and Rose Goldsen et al., *What College Students Think* (Princeton: D. Van Nostrand, 1960), pp. 46–59, 81–96.

14. Florence Kluckhohn, "Variations in Basic Values of Family Systems," in Norman W. Bell and Ezra F. Vogel, *A Modern Introduction to the Family* (Glencoe, Illinois: The Free Press, 1960), pp. 304–316; and George Gallup and Evan Hill, "The American Woman," *The Saturday Evening Post*, December 22, 1962, pp· 15–32.

15. Talcott Parsons, *Essays in Sociological Theory Pure and Applied* (Glencoe, Illinois: The Free Press, 1949), pp. 222–224 and 243–246.

16. Henry C. Lajewski, *Child Care Arrangements of Full-Time Working Mothers* (Washington, D. C.: U. S. Department of Health, Education and Welfare, Children's Bureau Publication No. 378, 1959); and Herzog, *Children of Working Mothers*.

17. William Whyte, *Organization Man* (New York: Simon and Schuster, 1956); Robert Wood, *Suburbia, Its People and Their Politics* (Boston: Houghton Mifflin, 1959); John Keats, *The Crack in the Picture Window* (Boston: Houghton Mifflin, 1956); A. C. Spectorsky, *The Exurbanites* (Philadelphia: J. B. Lippincott, 1955); and Nanette E. Scofield, "Some Changing Roles of Women in Suburbia: A Social Anthropological Case Study," *Transactions of the New York Academy of Sciences*, 22 (April, 1960), 6.

18. Erik Erikson, *Childhood and Society* (New York: W. W. Norton, 1950).

12

REVOLUTION
WITHOUT IDEOLOGY:
THE CHANGING PLACE
OF WOMEN IN AMERICA

CARL N. DEGLER

If feminism is defined as the belief that women are human beings and entitled to the same opportunities for self-expression as men, then America has harbored a feminist bias from the beginning. In both the eighteenth and nineteenth centuries foreign travelers remarked on the freedom for women in America. "A paradise for women," one eighteenth-century German called America, and toward the close of the nineteenth century Lord Bryce wrote that in the United States "it is easier for women to find a career, to obtain work of an intellectual as of a commercial kind, than in any part of Europe."

Certainly the long history of a frontier in America helps to account for this feminist bias. In a society being carved out of a wilderness, women were active and important contributors to the process of settlement and civilization. Moreover, because women have been scarce in America they have been highly valued. During almost the whole of the colonial period men outnumbered women, and even in the nineteenth century women remained scarce in the West. As late as 1865, for example, there were three men for each woman in California; in Colorado the ratio was as high as 20 to 1. Such disparities in the sex ratio undoubtedly ac-

Reprinted by permission from Daedalus, *Journal of the American Academy of Arts and Sciences, Boston, Mass., Vol. 93, No. 2 (Spring 1964).*

count for the West's favorable attitude toward women as in an Oregon law of 1850 that granted land to single women and, even more significant for the time, to married women; or in the willingness of western territories like Wyoming (1869) and Utah (1870) to grant the suffrage to women long before other regions where the sex ratio was more nearly equal.

Another measure of women's high esteem in American society was the rapidity with which the doors of higher education opened to women. Even without counting forerunners like Oberlin College, which admitted women in 1837, the bars against women came down faster and earlier in America than anywhere. The breakthrough came during the Civil War era, when women's colleges like Elmira, Vassar and Smith were founded, and universities like Michigan and Cornell became coeducational. The process was later and slower in Europe. Girton College, Cambridge, for example, which opened in 1869, was the sole English institution of higher education available to women until London University accorded women full privileges in 1879. Heidelberg, which was the first German university to accept women, did not do so until 1900. More striking was the fact that at its opening Girton provided six places for young women; Vassar alone, when it opened in 1865, counted some 350 students in residence. Another indication of the American feminist bias was that at the end of the century girls outnumbered boys among high school graduates.

But if the frontier experience of America helped to create a vague feminist bias that accorded women more privileges than in settled Europe, the really potent force changing women's place had little to do with the frontier or the newness of the country. It was the industrial revolution that provided the impetus to women's aspirations for equality of opportunity; it was the industrial revolution that carried through the first stage in the changing position of women—the removal of legal and customary barriers to women's full participation in the activities of the world.

Today it is axiomatic that men work outside the home. But before the industrial revolution of the nineteenth century, the great majority of men and women were co-workers on the land and in the home. Women worked in the fields when the chores of the home and childrearing permitted, so that there was not only close association between work and home for both sexes, but even a certain amount of overlap in the sexual division of labor. The coming of machine production changed all that. For a time, it is true, many unmarried women and children—the surplus labor of the day—were the mainstay of the new factory system, but that was only temporary. By the middle of the nineteenth century the bulk of industrial labor was male. The coming of the factory and the city thus wholly changed the nature of men's work. For the first time in history, work for most men was something done outside the family, psychologically as well as physically separated from the home.

The same industrial process that separated work and home also provided the opportunities for women to follow men out of the home. For that reason the feminist movement, both socially and intellectually, was a direct consequence of the industrial changes of the nineteenth century. Furthermore, just as the new industrial system was reshaping the rural men who came under its influence, so it reshaped the nature of women.

The process began with the home, which, in the early years of industrialization, was still the site of most women's work. Because of high land values, the city home was smaller than the farm house, and with less work for children, the size of the urban family was smaller than the rural. Moreover, in the city work in the home changed. Machines in factories now performed many of the tasks that had long been women's. In truth, the feminist movement began not when women felt a desire for men's jobs, but when men in factories began to take away women's traditional work. Factory-produced clothing, commercial laundries, prepared foods (e.g. prepared cereals, canned vegetables, condensed milk, bakery bread) were already available in the years after the Civil War. Toward the end of the century an advanced feminist like Charlotte Perkins Gilman, impressed by the accelerating exodus of women's chores from the middle-class home, predicted that the whole kitchen would soon be gone. She was wrong there, but even today the flight continues with precooked and frozen foods, TV dinners, cake mixes, special packaging for easy disposal, diaper services and the like.

Middle-class women were the main beneficiaries of the lightening of the chores of the home; few working-class or immigrant women could as yet take advantage of the new services and products. These middle-class women became the bone and sinew of the feminist movement, which was almost entirely an urban affair. They joined the women's clubs, organized the temperance crusades and marched in the suffrage parades. With an increasing amount of time available to them in the city, and imbued with the historic American value of work, they sought to do good. And there was much to be done in the raw, sometimes savage, urban environment of the late nineteenth century. For example, public playgrounds in the United States began in Boston only in the 1880's, when two public-spirited middle-class women caused a cartload of sand to be piled on an empty lot and set the neighborhood children loose upon it. Many a city and small town at the turn of the century owed its public library or its park to the dedicated work of women's clubs. The venerable giant redwood trees of northern California survive today because clubwomen of San Francisco and nearby towns successfully campaigned in 1900 to save them from being cut down for lumber. The saloon and prostitution were two other prevalent urban blights that prompted study and action by women's organizations.

More important than women's opposition to social evils was the widening of women's knowledge and concerns that inevitably accompanied it. What began as a simple effort to rid the community of a threat to its purity often turned into a discovery of the economic exploitation that drove young working girls into brothels and harried working men into saloons. Frances Willard for example, while head of the Women's Christian Temperance Union, broadened the WCTU's reform interests far beyond the liquor question, causing it to advocate protective legislation for working women, kindergartens and training programs for young working girls. Jane Addams, at Hull-House in Chicago's slums, quickly learned what historians have only recently discovered, that it was the urban boss's undeniable services to the immigrants that were the true sources of his great political power and the real secret of his successful survival of municipal reform campaigns.

The most direct way in which industrialization altered the social function of women was by providing work for women outside the home. Production by machine, of course, widened enormously the uses to which women's labor could be put once physical strength was no longer a consideration. And toward the end of the century, as business enterprises grew and record-keeping, communications and public relations expanded, new opportunities for women opened up in business offices. The telephone operator, the typist, the clerical worker and the stenographer now took places beside the seamstress, the cotton mill operator and the teacher.

As workers outside the home, women buried the Victorian stereotype of the lady under a mountain of reality. After all, it was difficult to argue that women as a sex were weak, timid, incompetent, fragile vessels of spirituality when thousands of them could be seen trudging to work in the early hours of the day in any city of the nation. Nor could a girl who worked in a factory or office help but become more worldly. A young woman new to a shop might have been embarrassed to ask a male foreman for the ladies' room, as some working girls' autobiographies report, but such maidenly reticence could hardly survive very long. Even gentle, naïve farm girls soon found out how to handle the inevitable, improper advances of foremen. They also learned the discipline of the clock, the managing of their own money, the excitement of life outside the home, the exhilaration of financial independence along with the drudgery of machine labor. Having learned something of the ways of the world, women could not be treated then, nor later in marriage, as the hopeless dependents Victorian ideals prescribed.

In time work transformed the outer woman, too. First to go were the hobbling, trailing skirts, which in a factory were a hazard and a nuisance. Even before the Civil War, Amelia Bloomer and other feminists had pointed out that women, if they were to work in the world as human beings, needed looser and lighter garments than those then in fashion. Until working women were numbered in the millions, no change took place. After 1890 women's skirts gradually crept up from the floor, and the neat and simple shirtwaist became the uniform of the working girl. A costume very like the original bloomer was widely worn by women factory workers during the First World War. Later the overall and the coverall continued the adaptation of women's clothes to the machine.

The most dramatic alteration in the image of woman came after the First World War, when there was a new upsurge in women's employment. The twenties witnessed the emergence of the white-collar class, and women were a large part of it. Over twice as many women entered the labor force that decade as in the previous one; the number of typists alone in 1930 was three-quarters of a million, a tenfold increase since 1900. And woman's appearance reflected the requirements of work. Except for some of the extreme flapper fashions, which were transient, the contemporary woman still dresses much as the woman of the 1920's did. In the 1920's women threw out the corset and the numerous petticoats in favor of light undergarments, a single slip, silk or rayon stockings, short skirts and bobbed hair. So rapid and widespread was the change that an investigation in the 1920's revealed that even most working-class girls no longer wore corsets, and the new interest in bobbed hair resulted between 1920 and 1930 in an increase of 400 per cent in the number of women hair dressers.

The physical freedom of dress that women acquired during the 1920's was but the superficial mark of a new social equality. The social forces behind this new equality are several. Some of these forces, like the growing number of college-trained women and the increasing number of women in the working force, go back far into the past; others, like the impact of the war and the arduous campaign for women's suffrage, were more recent. But whatever the causes, the consequences were obvious. Indeed, what is generally spoken of as the revolution in morals of the 1920's is more accurately a revolution in the position of women. Within a few short years a spectrum of taboos was shed. For the first time women began to smoke and drink in public; cigarette manufacturers discovered and exploited in advertising a virtually untouched market. As recently as 1918 it was considered daring for a New York hotel to permit women to sit at a bar. In the twenties, despite prohibition, both sexes drank in public.

Perhaps most significant, as well as symbolic, of the new stage in the position of women was their new sexual freedom. The twenties have long been associated with the discovery of Freud and a fresh, publicly acknowledged interest in sex. But insofar as these attitudes were new they represented changes in women, particularly those of the middle and upper classes. Premarital and extramarital sexuality by men had never been severely criticized, and discussion of sexual matters was commonplace wherever men gathered. Now, though, middle-class women also enjoyed that freedom. For the first time, it has been said, middle-class men carried on their extramarital affairs with women of their own social class instead of with cooks, maids and prostitutes.

An easier sexuality outside of marriage was only the most sensational side of the revolution in morals; more important, if only because more broadly based, was a new, informal, equal relationship between the sexes, culminating in a new conception of marriage. The day was long since past when Jennie June Croly could be barred, as she was in 1868, from a dinner in honor of Charles Dickens at a men's club even though her husband was a member and she was a professional writer. (Indeed, so thoroughly has such separation of the sexes been abandoned that the new Princeton Club in New York City has closed all but one of its public rooms to any man who is not accompanied by a woman!) And at least in the gatherings of the educated middle class, talk between the sexes was often free, frank and wide-ranging. The same mutual acceptance of the sexes was visible in the prevalent talk about the "new marriage," in which the woman was a partner and a companion, not simply a mother, a social convenience and a housekeeper.

The reality of the new conception of marriage was reflected in the sharp increase in the divorce rate. Because marriage, legally as well as socially, in the nineteenth century was more confining for women than for men, the early feminists had often advocated more liberal divorce laws. And even though divorce in the nineteenth century was more common in the United States than in any European country, the divorce rate in the 1920's shot up 50 per cent over what it had been only ten years before. One sign that women in the 1920's were seeking freedom from marriage if they could not secure equality in marriage was that two thirds of the divorces in that decade were instituted by women.

By the close of the twenties the ordinary woman in America was closer to a man in the social behavior expected of her, in the economic opportunities open to her and in the intellectual freedom enjoyed by her than at any time in history. To be sure there still was a double standard, but now its existence was neither taken for granted nor confidently asserted by men.

In truth, the years since the twenties have witnessed few alterations in the position of women that were not first evident in that crucial decade. The changes have penetrated more deeply and spread more widely through the social structure, but their central tendency was then already spelled out. Even the upsurge in women's employment, which was so striking in the twenties, continued in subsequent years. Each decade thereafter has counted a larger number of working women than the previous one. During the depression decade of the 1930's, even, half a million more women entered the labor force than in the prosperous twenties. By 1960 some 38 per cent of all women of working age—almost two out of five women—were employed outside the home.

The movement of women out of the home into remunerative work, however, has been neither steady nor unopposed. Undoubtedly one of the underlying conditions is an expanding economy's need for labor. But something more than that is needed to break society's traditional habits of mind about the proper work for women. Certainly here the feminist demands for equality for women played a part. But a social factor of equal importance was war. By their very disruption of the steady pulse of everyday living, wars break the cake of custom, shake up society and compel people to look afresh at old habits and attitudes. It is not accidental, for instance, that women's suffrage in England, Russia and Germany, as well as the United States, was achieved immediately after the First World War and in France and Italy after the Second.

At the very least, by making large and new demands upon the established work force, war draws hitherto unused labor into the economic process. During the Civil War, for example, young women assumed new roles in the economy as workers in metal and munitions factories, as clerks in the expanded bureaucracy in Washington and as nurses in war hospitals. Moreover, when the war was over women had permanently replaced men as the dominant sex in the teaching profession. Furthermore, since many women found a new usefulness in the Sanitary Fairs and other volunteer work, the end of hostilities left many women unwilling to slip back into the seclusion of the Victorian home. It is not simply coincidental that the women's club movement began very soon after the war.

When the First World War came to the United States, feminist leaders, perhaps recalling the gains of the Civil War, anticipated new and broad advances for their sex. And the demand for labor, especially after the United States entered the war, did open many jobs to women, just as it was doing in contemporary Great Britain and Germany. All over the United States during the war customary and legal restrictions on the employment of women fell away. Women could be seen doing everything from laying railroad ties to working in airplane factories. The war also brought to a successful climax the struggle for the suffrage. Pointedly women had argued that a war for democracy abroad should at least remedy the deficiencies of democracy at home.

If politically the war was a boon to women, economically it failed to live up to feminist anticipations. The First World War, unlike the Civil War, did not result in a large permanent increase in the number of working women. Indeed, by 1920 there were only 800,000 more women working than in 1910. But as a result of wartime demands, women did get permanent places in new job categories, like elevator operators and theater ushers. (But women street car conductors disappeared soon after the armistice.) Certain traditional professions for women, like music teaching, lost members between 1910 and 1920, while professions that required more training and provided steadier income, like library and social work and college teaching, doubled or tripled their numbers in the same period.

The Second World War, with its even more massive demands for labor and skills, brought almost four million new women workers into the nation's factories and offices. Once again jobs usually not filled by women were opened to them. For example, the number of women bank officers rose 40 per cent during the four years of the war and the number of women employees in finance has continued to rise ever since. Furthermore, unlike the situation after the First World War, the female work force after 1945 not only stayed up but then went higher.

Measured in the number of women working, the changes in the economic position of women add up to a feminist success. Twenty-four million working women cannot be ignored. But weighed in the scales of quality instead of quantity, the change in women's economic status is not so striking. It is true that women now work in virtually every job listed by the Bureau of the Census. Moreover, the popular press repeatedly tells of the inroads women are making into what used to be thought of as men's jobs. Three years ago, for example, a woman won a prize as the mutual fund salesman of the year. Women are widely represented in advertising and in real estate, and even women taxicab drivers are no longer rare. Yet the fact remains that the occupations in which the vast majority of women actually engage are remarkably similar to those historically held by women. In 1950 almost three quarters of all employed women fell into twenty occupational categories, of which the largest was stenographers, typists and secretaries—a category that first became prominent as a woman's occupation over a half century ago. Other occupations which have traditionally been women's, like domestic service, teaching, clerical work, nursing and telephone service, are also conspicuous among the twenty categories. Further than that, the great majority of women are employed in occupations in which they predominate. This sexual division of labor is clearly evident in the professions, even though women are only a small proportion of total professional workers. Two thirds of all professional women are either nurses or teachers; and even in teaching there is a division between the sexes. Most women teach in the primary grades; most men teach in high school. Women are notoriously underrepresented in the top professions like law, medicine, engineering and scientific research. No more than 7 per cent of all professional women in 1950 were in the four of these categories together. Only 6 per cent of medical doctors and 4 per cent of lawyers and judges were women. In contrast, almost three quarters of medical doctors are women in the Soviet Union; in England the figure is 16 per cent. In both France and Sweden women make up a high proportion of pharmacists and dentists; neither of those professions attracts many women in the United States.

One consequence as well as manifestation of the sexual division of labor in the United States has been the differences in pay for men and women. That difference has been a historical complaint of feminist leaders. In 1900 one study found women's wages to be, on the average, only 53 per cent of men's. The reason was, of course, that women were concentrated in the poorer paying jobs and industries of the economy. The disparity in pay between the sexes has been somewhat reduced today, but not very much. In 1955 among full-time women workers of all types the median wage was about two thirds of that for men. In short, women are still supplying the low-paid labor in the economy just as they were in the last century. (In substance, women workers and Negroes of both sexes perform a similar function in the economy.) The willingness of women to supply cheap labor may well account for their getting the large number of jobs they do; men often will not work for the wages that women will accept.

Today, there does not seem to be very much disparity between men's and women's wages for the same work, though the sexual division of labor is so nearly complete that it is difficult to find comparable jobs of the two sexes to make a definitive study.

There has been no improvement in women's position in higher education; indeed, it can be argued that women have failed to maintain the place reached much earlier. As we have seen, the United States led the world in opening higher education to women. This country also led in broadening the social base of education for women. No other country educated such a large proportion of women in its universities and colleges as did the United States. At the close of the nineteenth century, one third of American college students were women; by 1937 women made up almost 40 per cent of the students in American institutions of higher learning. In Germany, just before Hitler took power, no more than one out of ten university students was a woman; in Swedish universities in 1937 only 17 per cent of the students were women; in British universities the ratio was 22 per cent.

But since the Second World War the gap between American and European proportions of women in higher education has narrowed considerably. In 1952–1953 women constituted only 35 per cent of the American college population, while France counted women as 36 per cent of its university students and Sweden 26 per cent. The *number* of women in American colleges, of course, is considerably greater than it was in the 1920's and 1930's, but in proportion to men, women have lost ground in America while gaining it in Europe.

A further sign of the regression in the educational position of women in the United States is that in the early 1950's women earned about 10 per cent of the doctoral degrees in this country as compared with almost 15 per cent in the 1920's.

How is one to explain this uneven, almost contradictory record of women in America? How does it happen that a country with a kind of built-in feminism from the frontier falls behind more traditional countries in its training of college women; that a country with one of the highest proportions of working women in the world ends up with such a small proportion of its women in medicine, in law and in the sciences? Perhaps the correct answer is that the question should not be asked—at least not by Americans. For like so much else in American society, such contradictions are a manifestation of the national avoidance of any ideological principle, whether it be in feminist reform or in anything else. To be sure there has been no lack of feminist argument or rationale for women's work outside the home, for women's education and for other activities by women. But American women, like American society in general, have been more concerned with individual practice than with a consistent feminist ideology. If women have entered the labor force or taken jobs during a war they have done so for reasons related to the immediate individual or social circumstances and not for reasons of feminist ideology. The women who have been concerned about showing that women's capabilities can match men's have been the exception. As the limited, and low-paying, kinds of jobs women occupy demonstrate, there is not now and never has been any strong feminist push behind the massive and continuing movement of women into jobs. Most American women have been interested in jobs, not careers. To say, as many feminists have, that men have opposed and resisted the opening of opportunities to women is to utter only a half truth. The whole truth is that American society in general, which includes women, shuns like a disease any feminist ideology.

Another way of showing that the historical changes in the status of women in America bear little relation to a feminist ideology is to examine one of those rare instances when women did effect a social improvement through an appeal to ideology, for instance, the struggle for the suffrage. By the early twentieth century the feminist demand for the vote overrode every other feminist goal. Once women achieved the vote, it was argued, the evils of society would be routed, for women, because of their peculiar attributes, would bring a fresh, needed and wholesome element into political life. In form, and in the minds of many women leaders, the arguments for the suffrage came close to being a full-blown ideology of feminism.

In point of fact, of course, the Nineteenth Amendment ushered in no millennium. But that fact is of less importance than the reason why it did not. When American women obtained the vote they simply did not use it ideologically; they voted not as women but as individuals. Evidence of this was the failure of many women to vote at all. At the end of the first decade of national suffrage women still did not exercise the franchise to the extent that men did. Nor did many women run for or hold political offices. The first woman to serve in Congress was elected in 1916; in 1920, the first year of national women's suffrage, four women were elected to Congress, but until 1940 no more than nine women served at one time in the House of Representatives and the Senate together. That we are here observing an American and not simply a sexual phenomenon is shown by a comparison with European countries. In nonfeminist Germany, where the ballot came to women at about the same time as in the United States, the first Reichstag after suffrage counted forty-one women as members. In 1951 seventeen women sat in the British House of Commons as compared with ten in the United States House of Representatives. Twice the number of women have served as cabinet ministers in Britain between 1928 and 1951 as have served in the United States down to the present.

Another instance in which social change was effected by feminist ideology was prohibition. The achievement of national prohibition ran second only to the suffrage movement as a prime goal of the organized women's movement; the Eighteenth Amendment was as much a product of feminist ideology as the Nineteenth. Yet like the suffrage movement, prohibition, despite its feminist backing, failed to receive the support of women. It was *after* prohibition was enacted, after all, that women drank in public.

In the cases of both suffrage and prohibition, women acted as individuals, not as members of a sex. And so they have continued to act. It is not without relevance that the women's political organization that is most respected—the League of Women Voters —is not only nonpartisan but studiously avoids questions pertaining only to women. To do otherwise would be feminist and therefore ideological.

One further conclusion might be drawn from this examination of the non-ideological character of American women. That the changes that have come to the position of women have been devoid of ideological intent may well explain why there has been so little opposition to them. The most successful of American reforms have always been those of an impromptu and practical nature. The great revolution of the New Deal is a classic example. The American people, like F. D. R. himself, simply tried one thing after another, looking for something—anything—that would get the nation out of the depression. If lasting reforms took place too, so much the better. On the other hand, reforms that have been justified by an elaborate rationale or ideology, like abolition, have aroused strong and long-drawn-out opposition. By the same token, when women became ideological in support of suffrage and prohibition, they faced their greatest opposition and scored their most disappointing triumphs.

The achievement of the suffrage in 1920 is a convenient date for marking the end of the first phase in the changing position of women, for by then women were accorded virtually the same rights as men even if they did not always exercise them. The second phase began at about the same time. It was the participation of married women in the work force. During the nineteenth century few married women worked; when they did it was because they were childless or because their husbands were inadequate providers. Even among the poor, married women normally did not work. A survey of the slum districts in five large cities in 1893 revealed that no more than 5 per cent of the wives were employed. Only Negro wives in the South and immigrant wives in big northern cities provided any significant exceptions to this generalization.

Before the First World War, the movement of wives into the working force was barely noticeable. During the 1920's there was an acceleration, but as late as 1940 less than 17 per cent of all married women were working. Among working women in 1940, 48 per cent were single and only 31 per cent were married. The Second World War dramatically reversed these proportions—another instance of the influence of war on the position of women. By 1950 the proportion of married women living with their husbands had risen to 48 per cent of all working women while that of single women had fallen to 32 per cent. In 1960 the Census reported that almost 32 per cent of all married women were employed outside the home and that they comprised 54 per cent of all working women. No industrial country of Europe, with the exception of the Soviet Union, counted such a high proportion. Today, married women are the greatest source of new labor in the American economy. Between 1949 and 1959, for example, over four million married women entered the labor force, some 60 per cent of *all* additions, male and female.

Such a massive movement of married women out of the home was a development few of the early feminists could have anticipated. That it has taken place is at once a sign and a yardstick of the enormous change in women's position in society and in the family. In the nineteenth century work outside the home was unthinkable for the married woman. Not only were there children to care for, but there were objections from husbands and society to consider. That is why the convinced feminist of the nineteenth century often spurned marriage. Indeed, it is often forgotten that the feminist movement was a form of revolt against marriage. For it was through marriage, with the legal and social dominance of the husband, that women were most obviously denied opportunities for self-expression. Even after the legal superiority of the husband had been largely eliminated from the law, middle-class social conventions could still scarcely accommodate the working wife. To the woman interested in realizing her human capabilities, marriage in the nineteenth century was not an opportunity but a dead end. And it was indeed a minor scandal of the time that many of the "new women" did in fact reject marriage. The tendency was most pronounced, as was to be expected, among highly educated women, many of whom felt strongly their obligation to serve society through careers. Around 1900 more than one fourth of women who graduated from college never married; more than half of the women medical doctors in 1890 were single.

Like other changes in the position of women, the movement of married women into the work force—the reconciliation of marriage and work—must be related to the social changes of the last three decades. One of these social changes was the increase in contraceptive knowledge, for until married women could limit their families they could not become steady and reliable industrial workers. Information about contraceptive techniques which had been known for a generation or more to educated middle-class women did not seep down to the working class until the years of the Great Depression. In 1931, for instance, there were only 81 clinics disseminating birth control information in the United States; in 1943 there were 549, of which 166 were under public auspices. As the number of public clinics suggest, by the end of the 1930's birth control was both socially and religiously accept-able, at least among Protestants. And a method was also available then to Roman Catholics, since it was in the same decade that the rhythm method, the only one acceptable to the Roman Catholic Church, was first brought to popular attention with the approval of ecclesiastical authorities.

Another social force underlying the movement of wives and mothers in the work force was the growing affluence of an indus-trial society, especially after 1940. Higher health standards, en-larged incomes of husbands and a better standard of living in general permitted a marked alteration in the temporal cycle of women's lives. Women now lived longer, stayed in school later and married earlier. In 1890 half the girls left school at 14 or before— that is, when they finished grammar school; in 1957 the median age was 18—after graduation from high school. The girl of 1890, typically, did not marry until she was 22; the age of her counter-part in 1957 was 20, leaving no more than two years for work between the end of school and marriage. Among other things this fact explains the fall in the proportion of single women in the work force in the United States as compared with other industrial societies. Few other countries have such an early median age of marriage for girls.

Early marriages for women produce another effect. With knowledge of contraceptive techniques providing a measure of control over child-bearing, women are now having their children early and rapidly. When this tendency is combined with a younger age of marriage, the result is an early end to child-bear-ing. In 1890 the median age of a mother when her last child was born was 32; in 1957 it was 26. A modern mother thus has her children off to school by the time she is in her middle thirties, leaving her as much as thirty-five years free for work outside the home. And the fact is that almost half of working women today are over forty years of age. Put another way, 34 per cent of mar-ried women between the ages of thirty-five and forty-four years are gainfully employed.

Unquestionably, as the practical character of the woman's movement would lead us to expect, an important force behind the influx of married women into the work force is economic need. But simple poverty is not the only force. Several studies, for example, have documented the conclusion that many women who work are married to men who earn salaries in the upper income brackets, suggesting that poverty is not the controlling factor in the wife's decision to work. A similar conclusion is to be drawn from the positive correlation between education and work for married women. The more education a wife has (and therefore the better salary her husband is likely to earn) the more likely she is to be working herself. Many of these women work undoubtedly in order to raise an adequate standard of living to a comfortable one. Many others work probably because they want to realize their potentialities in the world. But that women are so poorly represented in the professions and other careers suggests that most married women who work are realizing their full capabilities neither for themselves nor for society.

Over sixty years ago, in *Women and Economics,* the feminist Charlotte Perkins Gilman cogently traced the connection between work and the fulfillment of women as human beings. In subsequent writings she grappled with the problem of how this aim might be realized for married women. As a mother herself, raising a child under the trying circumstances of divorce, Gilman knew first hand that work outside the home and child-rearing constituted *two* full-time jobs. No man, she knew, was expected or required to shoulder such a double burden. Gilman's remedies of professional domestic service and kitchenless apartments never received much of a hearing, and considering the utopian if not bizarre character of her solutions, that is not surprising. Yet the problem she raised remained without any solution other than the eminently individualistic and inadequate one of permitting a woman to assume the double burden if she was so minded. Meanwhile, as the economy has grown, the problem has entered the lives of an ever increasing number of women. Unlike most of her feminist contemporaries, who were mainly concerned with the suffrage and the final elimination of legal and customary barriers to women's opportunities, Gilman recognized that the logic of feminism led unavoidably to the working mother as the typical woman. For if women were to be free to express themselves, then they should be able to marry as well as to work. Women should not have to make a choice any more than men. To make that possible, though, would require that some way be found to mitigate the double burden which biology and society had combined to place only on women.

As women moved into the second stage of their development—the reconciliation of work and marriage—the problem which Gilman saw so early was increasingly recognized as the central issue. Virginia Collier, for example, in a book *Marriage and Careers*, published in 1926, wrote that since so many married women were working, "The question therefore is no longer should women combine marriage with careers, but how do they manage it and how does it work." Interestingly enough, her study shows that what today Betty Friedan, in *The Feminine Mystique*, has called the "problem that has no name," was already apparent in the 1920's. One working wife explained her reasons for taking a job in these words, "I am burning up with energy and it is rather hard on the family to use it up in angry frustration." Another said, "I had done everything for Polly for six years. Suddenly she was in school all day and I had nothing to do. My engine was running just as hard as ever, but my car was standing still." A year after Collier's book appeared, President William A. Neilson of Smith College observed "that the outstanding problem confronting women is how to reconcile a normal life of marriage and motherhood with intellectual activity such as her college education has fitted her for." That the issue was taken seriously is attested by an action of the Board of Trustees of Barnard College in 1932. The board voted to grant six months' maternity leave with pay to members of the staff and faculty. In announcing the decision, Dean Virginia Gildersleeve clearly voiced its import. "Neither the men nor the women of our staff," she said, "should be forced into celibacy, and cut off from that great source of experience, of joy, sorrow and wisdom which marriage and parenthood offer."

With one out of three married women working today, the problem of reconciling marriage and work for women is of a social dimension considerably larger than in the days of Charlotte Gilman or even in the 1930's. But the fundamental issue is still the same; how to make it possible, as Dean Gildersleeve said, to pursue a career or hold a job while enjoying the "experience . . . joy, sorrow and wisdom" of marriage and parenthood. The practical solutions to this central problem of the second stage in the changing position of women seem mainly collective or governmental, not individual. Child-care centers, efficient and readily available house-keeping services, and emergency child-care service such as the Swedes have instituted are obviously a minimal requirement if women are to have the double burdens of home-making and employment lightened. The individual working woman cannot be expected to compensate for the temporary disabilities consequent upon her role as mother any more than the individual farmer or industrial worker can be expected single-handedly to overcome the imbalance between himself and the market. Today both farmers and workers have government and their own organizations to assist them in righting the balance.

But as the history of farmers and industrial labor makes evident, to enact legislation or to change mores requires persuasion of those who do not appreciate the necessity for change. Those who would do so must organize the like-minded and mobilize power, which is to say they need a rationale, an ideology. And here is the rub; in pragmatic America, as we have seen, any ideology must leap high hurdles. And one in support of working wives is additionally handicapped because women themselves, despite the profound changes in their status in the last century, do not acknowledge such an ideology. Most American women simply do not want work outside the home to be justified as a normal activity for married women. Despite the counter-argument of overwhelming numbers of working wives, they like to think of it as special and exceptional. And so long as they do not advance such an ideology, American society surely will not do so, though other societies, like Israel's and the Soviet Union's, which are more ideological than ours, obviously have.

Commentary: *On Equality*

The two selections that precede this commentary address themselves to the nature of inequality between the sexes. Both provide an historical perspective outlining the social forces that have vitiated woman's drive toward equality. Alice S. Rossi focuses on the structural inadequacy of the social system to meet demands of equality and argues for a reordering of institutions in both public and private sectors. These are necessary, she argues, to permit true equality of the sexes in all patterns of living. Carl N. Degler notes that a diminished drive toward equality has taken place since World War II and argues that women should think in more ideological terms about their lives.

Both writers would agree that in the post-World War II era women responded eagerly to the clarion call of hearth and home. The Depression years, followed by those of the war, significantly vitiated the goals of feminism, that is, equality between the sexes. Despite a seeming acquiescence to home life on the part of women, we have heard much about the "suburban syndrome" and the "problem that has no name" in the last two decades. These phrases describe a pattern of life that has become meaningless and boring to women who are part of a society that has led them to different expectations. The educated American woman, after all, lives in a world where she can be satisfied with nothing except, perhaps, her marriage. This situation will continue unless or until fundamental structural change takes place in the larger society. The exclusion of other values and other roles must, of necessity, produce anxiety. Anxiety is subtle and has a disastrous way of breeding more anxiety. It is difficult to cope with a gnawing feeling that something is always wrong somewhere.

Alice Rossi would argue that the "somewhere" is located within the institutional structure, whereas Degler sees the problem as an absence of ideology—ideas, values, and tactical principles of a group. This latter view has been documented in recent literature which has traced the shift from independence, careers, and fulfillment of special capacities to an emphasis on femininity. What has been suggested is that the highest and the only commitment for women is the fulfillment of their own femininity within the context of domesticity. We are not suggesting that every woman must be creative outside the home to realize herself —this can be as confining and tension-producing as any other mold—but the absence of a collective ideology prevents women from mitigating their conflict on a structural level. Opposition to the formulation of an ideology comes from women as well as men. To cite Helen M. Hacker's often quoted paper, "Women as a Minority Group" (Social Forces, October 1951), *women themselves incorporate the prevailing attitudes toward women. Like other minority groups, their self-castigation can exceed that inflicted by the dominant group. Because our culture stresses achievement as forming the cornerstone of one's identity, it is also inevitable that women who achieve professional recognition like to think of themselves as exceptional and view their success as a reflection of their own special talents.*

If women find it difficult to accord other women the right to professional status, then surely the division of labor so evident in the professions must function to ensure men that their numerical predominance is a mark of their right to be there. Men suffer a blow to their egos when they see that some women, in their multi-faceted roles, can accomplish as much as men, whose sole role is that of breadwinner. But the structure of our society offers very few men the luxury of high ascribed status, and men whose ascendancy drives exceed their talents will, of necessity, protect themselves by making equality inaccessible to women. The sources of masculine defensiveness and women's conflicts are not viewed as structural problems. Because social change does not occur apart from proclamations of aims and expressions of will of particular groups, the absence of an ideology precludes change on the level at which it should occur. Ardent feminism may seem as quaint as the linen dusters and high button shoes of an earlier period, but it was the force of its ideology that precipitated change in women's traditional roles.

Both authors support the thesis that any change in normative behavior is contingent upon more substantive changes. As we have pointed out, Rossi stresses structural changes, whereas Degler points to the need for ideological change. Our feeling is that to suggest one apart from the other is, at best, an oversimplification of the problem.

13

SEX ON THE CAMPUS

ROBERT VEIT SHERWIN
AND GEORGE C. KELLER

Everyone knows that America, especially its college youth, is going through a "sexual revolution." Right?

There has been a tremendous increase in premarital sex; an abandonment of old reticences to talk about and explore the subject and a new frankness and openness; and a marked change in the laws about pornography, nudity, and sex in books, movies, colleges, and public life. Right?

Wrong!

Well, almost wrong. It's true that there have been changes in a few areas, but there is no hard evidence whatsoever that there has been anything amounting to a revolution in American sexual practices, attitudes, or legal codes in the past several decades.

Since few persons will believe this assertion, let us explain precisely what we mean.

Before we begin, it is necessary to point out that there is pitifully little information about human sexual behavior. Reliable data is scarce and conceptual schemes are scarcer. Thought about the *social* roots and consequences of sexual behavior is almost nonexistent, despite the fact that sexual behavior is one of the impor-

Reprinted with permission. Robert Veit Sherwin and George C. Keller, "Sex on the Campus," Columbia College Today, *Vol. 15 (Fall, 1967), pp. 24–34.*

tant causative factors in history—the establishment of the Church of England, for example, is to some extent the result of Henry VIII's case of syphilis—and is one of the key functions that determine the quality and tone of life in any society.

The taboos against the study of sex and against the open, objective discussion of the subject are so enormously powerful that even physicians and professors steer clear of the subject. Virtually nothing is taught about sex in U. S. medical schools; and many scholars, including the most daring ones, regard human sexual relations as forbidden territory. They, like many other persons, tend frequently to snicker like adolescents or frown like orthodox clergymen when the subject arises. (Of note is that many of the key studies of sexual behavior are not in the Columbia University libraries, the nation's third greatest university collection. Some have never been ordered, most are listed as missing).

All that we possess in the way of systematic research is contained in a dozen books and several dozen monographs and articles. As sociologist Winston Ehrmann of Iowa's Cornell College, one of the few serious scholars in this field, has written, "The amount of research is absurdly, ridiculously, and pitifully small. It is an interesting commentary on our value system to note that far more time and effort go into . . . the life cycle of a rare moth, the archaeological distributions of the potsherds of an Indian tribe, the possible influence of one minor English poet upon another, or the proper cultivation of the mango . . . than into the systematic research of human sex behavior, something that profoundly affects us all." Dr. John Gagnon of Indiana University's Institute for Sex Research adds, "It is as if all of the discussion about sexuality were really organized as a form of entertainment rather than as a serious consideration of the kinds of processes that are central to the human condition and the possibilities of human experience."

Therefore, our description here is admittedly based on fairly slender evidence. We simply do not yet know for certain many things about sexual behavior. For instance, we have had no *national* study of American sex habits and attitudes since that of Dr. Alfred Kinsey and his staff in 1953—14 years ago. There have been, however, several local studies, mostly with college students, and we have incorporated tentatively their findings.

Also, the language of sexual behavior is tricky. It is astonishing to report that despite the fact that there may be over 50 million acts of sexual intercourse in the world daily, the English language possesses no socially acceptable verb for the act of coitus. The verb "copulate" comes close but it does not necessarily imply vaginal penetration, only a union or coupling *with* someone. (One British writer has tried to revive the old English active verb "swive," as in "He swived her"; but has had no luck so far.) Other portions of sexual behavior are also very awkward to describe. The difficulty of description in this neglected field, therefore, is another hindering factor.

Then too, what constitutes a sexual act? Agreement is far from unanimous. Who is more sexually experienced, who is the real virgin: a popular, lively girl who has had numerous intense encounters of heavy petting with males, including several to orgasm, but no vaginal penetration, or the quiet lonely girl who has had one furtive encounter of actual intercourse, without pleasure or satisfaction? This problem is now further compounded by the fine physiological study of William Masters and Virginia Johnson, *Human Sexual Response* (1966), which reveals that female orgasm is largely a matter of clitoral, not vaginal, stimulation.

Despite these, and other, difficulties though, it is important to explain what we do know, however inconclusively, about sexual behavior—for several reasons. The concern about the population explosion, the new drive for sex education (which curiously has very little hard data to educate about), the prurient, misleading, and occasionally salacious attention of the mass media, and, most important of all perhaps, the increasingly serious and searching approach of America's young people, especially college youths, toward intrapersonal behavior seem to require it.

First, sexual behavior. All the evidence we have points to the fact that there has been no radical change in the incidence of premarital behavior in America in this century.

The closest thing to a "revolution" is the substantial rise in *female* involvement that occurred in the 1920's. While male participation has apparently climbed slowly from roughly 55 percent at the turn of the century to over 65 percent in the 1960's, female premarital activity was a relatively low 30 percent or so around 1900 but jumped to over 50 percent in the 1920's, where it has remained approximately to this day. [See graph.] The strong feminist feelings of the 1920's were apparently expressed in sexual terms by many women.

This greater willingness of women to indulge in premarital intercourse during the past four decades has brought about a sharp

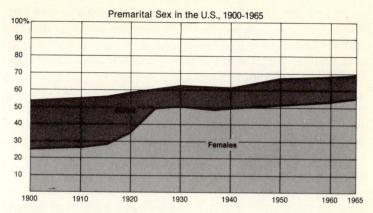

Premarital Sex in the U.S., 1900-1965

decline in prostitution in the United States, a development that the feminists vigorously fought for. Currently, there is relatively little prostitution in the nation; fewer than two percent of the college men, according to one survey, have ever visited a prostitute. Whatever prostitution still exists seems to be largely an activity of the fairly poor and the quite rich.

Inside marriage there have been two noteworthy changes in sexual behavior since 1900: a slight increase in extramarital intercourse and a marked increase in the quality of marital sexual life. About 35 percent of American married males have had an adulterous encounter, compared with perhaps 25 percent in the 1920's. Less than 10 percent are *regularly* adulterous though. Among married women the figures are still lower: around 15 percent have had coitus outside their marriage, and very few of them regularly. Adultery is not widespread in America, or increasing rapidly. Both men and women have more premarital intercourse in the few years prior to marriage than they have extramarital intercourse in the 40 years after.

As for the quality of sexual life inside marriage, there seems to be a change toward much less frigidity and impotence. The satisfaction of females especially has increased substantially. Female orgasm was an unusual thing in the first quarter of this century. Women were not supposed to enjoy sex; even a goodly portion of the women themselves thought so. As late as 1948, according to Kinsey's figures, 10 per cent of American married women had *never* had an orgasm. This percentage is probably lower now because the feeling that women have a right to satisfaction is spreading, partly as a result of higher education levels.

Nearly all young males masturbate, most of them to orgasm,

before they are 20, but only 60 percent of the females ever masturbate, and less than 40 percent of the girls under 20 do. This
represents no appreciable change from previous practices, though
as we shall see later, the *attitudes* toward this form of sexual activity have changed considerably.

Heavy petting, or the direct handling of either partner's genitals
or the female breast without intercourse, has seemingly increased
considerably during the century. Light petting, or "spooning" or
"necking" (kissing and hugging), was as far as most females who
desired to abstain from coitus would traditionally go, but now
many are willing to go further.

As part of our preparation for this article we held two-hour detailed interviews with several dozen college women from Barnard
and four other leading Eastern institutions. All but one of them
said that they had engaged in heavy petting, and many of those
who were still virgins said that they had allowed heavy petting on
either "two to five" or "five or more" occasions.

Of great importance is that a major portion of premarital sex,
particularly among college students, occurs among *engaged* couples intending to marry. For example, nearly half of all women
who have premarital intercourse do so *only with their fiances* or
persons they eventually marry. Almost one fourth of the males
also have their only experience with partners they subsequently
marry. This represents a crucial change. It means that an increasing number of premarital liaisons are being carried on with *affection,* by couples in some respects already married.

The engagement period has become, in effect, a trial marriage
among a greater number of people. The celebrated "honeymoon"
is more and more taking place *before* marriage. The nature of
courtship is being altered; instead of a courtship of romanticism
and play at some distance, young people are tending toward one
of shared work, leisure, and sex approximating married life. Sex is
being used more and more as an additional means of exploring a
potential partner's capacity to relate and degree of maturity. This,
incidentally, has been the pattern in Scandinavian countries for
some time.

Also of importance is the evidence that only two-thirds of the
males and one half of the females who engage in premarital coitus
are under 20 years of age, or teenagers. A high proportion of premarital sex is done, therefore, by *consenting adults,* not just by
experimenting college students and adolescents. Contrary to popular beliefs, about 40 percent of all American male college stu-

dents and over 55 percent of the coeds still graduate as virgins, according to most indications.

Very little sex in America, both in or out of marriage, has anything to do with reproduction. Roughly, only one copulation in 1,000 results in a pregnancy. The evidence is not in yet, but the supposedly revolutionary introduction of "the pill" seems to have little bearing on this fact, which has apparently been the case for some time. For example, Katherine Davis' study in 1929, *Factors in the Sex Life of 2,200 Women*, found that of the women having intercourse, 64 percent who had a grade school education were using contraception, 71 percent of the female high school graduates were, and 76 percent of the college women. This has led one commentator, Nelson Foote, to claim that sex is "the favorite form of *play* for millions of Americans . . . as our advertisers imply daily."

Still, of the females who have premarital coitus, nearly one out of five becomes pregnant. Since about half of the American women have premarital sex, it appears that about 10 percent of all the women in the United States have a premarital pregnancy. (The percentage of *college* women who get pregnant, however, is appreciably lower.) This fact may come as a surprise to some, but apparently it has been the situation for a long time. What may seem like a new and, to some, alarming trend is merely the uncovering of a long-time sexual pattern that had been masked and kept silent.

How do Americans handle premarital pregnancies? Three ways: they get married, they have the baby illegitimately, or they have an abortion.

The figures are far from firm, of course, but there are probably at least two million premarital pregnancies a year. By far the most usual consequence is marriage, and over one million couples annually take that course. One-sixth of all U. S. brides are pregnant on their wedding day.

This seems to be the choice of many people at all levels, but especially lower middle-class whites of average educational background. One recent study of Minnesota high school girls, for example, found that of those who married before graduation 69 percent were pregnant at marriage. Marriages of this kind are, of course, not unusual in other countries or throughout history. Of note is that they have been found in recent U. S. studies to be only slightly less stable than other marriages.

In 1964 there were reported to be 275,700 illicit births, though the figure may be a bit low since 15 states, including New York, do not record illegitimate births and the statistics for those states are estimated. This pattern is largely a lower class one, particularly a Negro lower class one. Non-whites account for about 60 percent of American illegitimacy; roughly 25 percent of all U. S. non-whites are currently born out of wedlock, as compared with 3.4 percent of the whites.

Illegitimacy in the United States is actually rather comparable with other countries. It is only half the illegitimacy of Austria, and less than that of Portugal, Sweden, France, and Germany. There has been a slight increase in American illegitimacy in the past half century, but nothing that would justify the word "revolution." Surprisingly, the rate of illegitimacy (illicit births per 1,000 unmarried females) has had its greatest recent growth among women between 20 and 40. Women between 15 and 19 years of age actually had a *decrease* between 1957 and 1963. It is females over 20 who account for two-thirds of U. S. illegitimacy.

The upper and middle class couples prefer abortions to illegitimate births, and this is what an increasing number of college women do with premarital pregnancies instead of having the child and putting it up for adoption or getting married. The study of Gebhard, Pomeroy, Martin and Christenson, *Pregnancy, Birth and Abortion* (1958), disclosed that perhaps 85 percent of all white, upper middle-class premarital pregnancies end in abortions.

Because they are illegal, abortions are expensive, but so widespread is the protest becoming against their illegality, that abortions are getting cheaper, more available to all social classes, and more professional. Over 75 percent of America's abortions—estimated at a million annually—are now performed by licensed physicians. Self-styled abortionists, who used to attempt, sometimes barbarously, half of all induced abortions several decades ago, now do less than 20 percent of them, while nearly 5 percent are done by friends, relatives, or the pregnant women themselves. We found that female students at five leading Eastern colleges had lists of available doctors, with their prices for abortions, in the dorms. Nearly 400,000 premarital pregnancies, perhaps, are annually taken care of in this fashion.

A sidelight on abortions. The number of *married* women who have abortions is greater than the number of unmarried women. Gottfried Newman in the *Encyclopedia of Sexual Behavior* estimates that 10 per cent of *all* pregnancies in America terminate in abortion, either spontaneous ("miscarriages") or induced. The percentage would undoubtedly be higher if the United States, like Japan, Russia, Sweden, and Denmark, allowed abortions to those who desired them.

Behaviorally, there are three fascinating pieces of information about human sex that have come to light in recent years, thanks largely to the scholarly researches of men like Kinsey, Burgess and Wallin, Erhmann, and Masters.

The first is that far from being a simple natural drive in all human beings, the sexual urge is a complex yearning capable of enormous cultural and educational manipulation, including virtual extinction, as in the case of many Roman Catholic clergymen. Clelland Ford and Frank Beach in their physiological-anthropological study, *Patterns of Sexual Behavior* (1951), assert that among the primates there is a "greater importance of the role of the cerebral cortex in the direction and control of sexual behavior" than among the lower mammals. "Particularly in the case of man, the role of learning is paramount," they say. Their book describes the amazing array of sexual patterns practised by different societies, an array that is as diverse as mankind's political or status patterns.

That human sexual behavior is primarily a *learned* activity, not an uncomplicated natural drive practised similarly around the world, or even uniformly in any society, was one of the basic demonstrations of Alfred Kinsey in his pioneering researches, published in 1948 and 1953. He found that within each society there are numerous patterns of sexual courtship and intercourse. In Kinsey's words, "There is no American pattern of sexual behavior, but scores of patterns, each of which is confined to a particular segment of our society." Sex, Kinsey and his associates showed, is a function of social class, education, religion, and geographic background.

Thus, males and females of different educational backgrounds engage in premarital sexual behavior to different degrees (approximate percentages):

	Males	Females
Grade school education	95%	50%
High school education	80%	55%
College education	65%	60%

And, persons of different religions with different frequencies of worship seem to have different practices:

Premarital Sexual Activity
(*in order of descending incidence*)
Jews, inactive
Protestants, inactive
Catholics, inactive
Catholics, devout
Protestants, devout
Jews, devout

Not religion or geography, however, but education and socio-economic position are the major determinants in American sexual behavior. And, those in the upper socio-educational level are astonishingly different—one might say almost a world apart—in their sexual practices from those in the lower socio-educational level.

Upper level young people are much less sexually active, but they pet more. They tend to reserve sex for someone for whom they feel affection. Their sexual play usually has more prolonged foreplay, a greater readiness to use a variety of coital positions, a higher incidence of oral-genital contact. The males tend to treat women more as equals, and women tend to take a more active role, with the result that females at this level have a greater frequency of orgasms. Possibly because of the greater number of sexual postponements, masturbation is higher; college men masturbate about twice as often as those with only a grade school education. Persons at this upper level, though, have a low incidence of homosexuality. For the upper socio-educational group, sexual activity is less frequent but more variegated, more artful.

Persons at the lower socio-educational levels have a radically different style. The frequency of male premarital sex is much higher; nearly one half of the boys who do not go to college have intercourse by the age of 15. Many fewer females participate, but those who do, do so with greater frequency. Persons at the lower level, especially the males, tend not to see sex as having a close relationship with affection or love. They are usually impatient with mere petting. Among this group sexual play has greater simplicity and directness; there is less foreplay, less variety, greater speed. It tends to be male-oriented, and women at this level experience fewer orgasms and less emotional satisfaction. Masturbation is lower, but homosexuality, especially among high school graduates without college education, is higher. At the lower socio-educational level, sex is more frequent, more restricted in formal maneuver, and more slam-bang in approach.

In an instructive monograph called "The Influence of Comparative Social Class of Companion Upon Premarital Heterosexual Behavior" (*Marriage and Family Living*, February, 1955), Winston Ehrmann pointed out that sex may be a major factor in social class mixing in the United States. His study revealed that American females tend to have the most premarital sex with males in the same social class, a considerable amount with those in a higher social class, and least with those of a lower social class. Males, on the other hand, had premarital intercourse most frequently with girls in a lower social class, some with those in the same class, and least with those of higher standing. That is, U. S. men tend to *descend* the social ladder for sexual partners while women tend to *ascend* the ladder. Ehrmann deduces, "Men raise their social class status by economic or professional endeavors, and women by marriage."

The second major finding of recent scientific studies of sex is that males and females appear to be significantly different creatures, sexually speaking. Kinsey, who was a biologist, found that, "The peak of sexual capacity comes, on the average, between 16 and 18 in men, but not until the later 20's or early 30's in women." Male capacity and probably desire drops from the late teens on, while female ability and interest rises toward a peak at 30 or so, and *stays* high until 50. This suggests some neat questions about mating and sexual patterns.

A few other studies have pointed to what seems to be a crucial difference in male and female biological urges that may cut across cultural lines. Males are apparently stimulated sexually much more rapidly and much more frequently; they seem to be more promiscuous by *nature*. Women seem to have no equivalent capacity for rapid excitation or powerful need for regular sexual activity. Ehrmann, in his book *Premarital Dating Behavior* (1959), cites as his "most important empirical finding" the likely fact that, "There are distinct male and female subcultures" in the United States. On careful examination he discovered that males are stimulated easily and quickly by numerous female parts, gestures, contacts, and so forth, and almost as easily by vicarious erotic symbols such as photographs, stockings, and the like. But female sexual arousal, he learned, is chiefly related to a whole romantic experience—a lovely, long walk on a beach, going steady, being deeply in love—and, to a lesser extent, to direct tactile pressures.

Thus, male sexuality is fairly easily awakened and is connected principally with suggestions of *physicality*, but female sexuality depends mainly on the symbols of *love*. Exactly how much of the differences between the sexes is owed to biology and how much to cultural factors is still an open question. But there does seem to be some concrete foundation for the often-criticized "double standard" in American and other societies. As one writer, James Collier, recently put it, "The double standard written into the law of many, many societies may be a true reflection of what . . . we must call human nature."

The third finding presents sex research with a baffling mystery. Kinsey and his associates discovered that the sexual history of an individual accorded with the pattern of the socio-educational group into which he *ultimately* moved as often as with the pattern of the group into which he was born and raised. That is, the pattern of a person's sexual behavior seems, in very many cases, to be established by the age of 16—and established according to the behavior patterns of his *future* socio-economic peers. How on earth does a young person escape from the sexual patterns to which he is exposed and instead take on patterns that will later be part of his environment—by his 16th birthday?

Erich Fromm, agreeing with Harry Stack Sullivan, contends, "It is not sexual behavior that determines character (as Freud argued), but character that determines sexual behavior." He admits that the sex instinct is "rooted in the chemistry of our body." He adds though, "This instinct is the root of *all* forms of sexual behavior," but "the particular way of satisfying it . . . is determined by the character structure."

This finding, which has been supported to some extent in one or two other studies, suggests that the influence of a person's *family* and/or his childhood experiences *outside* his particular social milieu, may be vitally determinative. Early learning may be crucial. This is, of course, what those who speak of the important early influences of family, school, church, television, and advertising contend.

What about sexual *attitudes?* Has there been as little change in people's outlook toward sex as there has been in actual behavior?

Here there have been some considerable changes. But there has been no "revolution" in attitudes.

The change has been chiefly in the willingness to talk about the subject, more openly and objectively, particularly among the young. Things that would seldom enter public conversation before World War II now frequently do. What used to be called "discretion" is disappearing slowly. College students particularly insist that sexual matters be treated as a normal, if somewhat more delicate, human activity. To them, it seems more "honest" that way. This change is evident in college literary magazines, English "creative writing" efforts, campus movies, and campus bull sessions. The change, however, is so far one that encompasses only the *personal,* Freudian aspects of sex; it has not been extended to the *social* implications of various kinds of sexual attitudes and behavior.

This new openness had some interesting consequences. Boys and girls in college, who used to refer to each other and their friends principally in terms of their geographical background, religion, color, nationality, career aim, character structure, or personality—"Californian," "Baptist," "Oriental," "Swede," "scientist," "square shooter," or "good-time Charlie"—now more frequently refer to each other in terms of their sexual attitudes and behavior —"livewire," "swinger," "gentleman," "slut," "cold fish," "Casanova," "tease," "animal," "wolf," "square," "sex fiend." Interviewers seeking information about sex no longer have the problem of an embarrassed interviewee hiding or omitting acts but the opposite danger of many interviewees nervously fabricating encounters to make it seem that he or she is "with it."

Also, as a result of the greater frankness of discussion there is a growing sense among parents, the press, and the students themselves that much more is happening than ever before. The change in *attitude* is mistaken for the change in *behavior.* Among the college girls we interviewed, two-thirds of whom were virgins, nearly all of them believed that "most" of the other college girls were engaging in intercourse and many of them guessed that between 10 and 20 percent of their college mates were promiscuous. (Less than two percent of the college students actually are promiscuous, even at the most notoriously "liberal" institutions.)

Theodore Newcomb reported in 1937 that in the 1930's only 25 percent of all young people in the U. S. thought it was all right for both parties to have sexual relations before marriage. "Even among college students the percentage was only 38 percent," he wrote. Today, 30 years later, the indications are that these percentages may have almost doubled, particularly among college males, including, incidentally, considerable numbers who decline to engage in premarital sex. "It's O.K. if it's a strictly personal matter and nobody gets hurt," we have been told over and over again by students. Or, "I don't believe in it myself, but I can't condemn anyone who does."

But among those who accept premarital intercourse, fully a majority, especially among females and among college students, accept it only if it is done with "love," "affection," or at least "consideration." Sociologist Ira Reiss of the University of Iowa has said that Americans are moving from their former standards to a new one, which he calls premarital "permissiveness with affection." He believes it will continue because of the greater leisure, higher education, and growing pragmatism of most Americans.

This shift is due, say researchers Burgess and Wallin in *Courtship, Engagement, and Marriage* (1953), to a great change in the objectives of the institution of marriage in America in this century. At the turn of the century, persons often married for social position, wealth, protection, religious reasons, or political advancement, and the parents frequently played a major role in arranging the marriage. But today persons more often marry for "fun," "happiness," or "companionship," with scarcely any intervention from parents. Young people thus often feel they need some sort of deep trial encounter to test—on their own—a mate's compatibility of temperament, interests, ideals, and values. Sex more and more is serving that function.

This new form of U. S. marriages is almost unique in the world, although other advanced societies are moving in this direction too. The idea that two young persons should marry for companionship and love alone, as they themselves define that, represents a triumph of the theory of self-determined fulfillment for each individual, even immature ones, over the social theories that emphasize goals such as class stability, economic growth, political harmony, family unity, and religious strength.

What the U. S. has done is enter a new period, possibly, that has as its implicit underlying assumption a neo-Adam Smith theory of social harmony. Each person by pursuing his own self-fulfillment contributes, as if by some hidden hand, to the social harmony and happiness of all. *Laissez-faire* economics is being replaced by *laissez-faire* morality.

In this emerging scheme, novel sexual attitudes play a central role. As one Smith College student told us, "Even most of the Goldwater Republican girls feel that personally and sexually they must be liberals in attitude."

Will the changes in *attitude* bring about a radical change in *behavior?* "This is the big question," according to Wardell Pomeroy, Kinsey's chief interviewer and now a psychologist in Manhattan. All one can answer now is that *so far* it apparently has not done so. There has only been an increase in heavy petting.

If some attitudes toward sex are changing, however, others are not, or are changing more slowly. On the question of *extramarital* sexual relations, for example, there has been almost no change in moral position. Americans (like people in nearly every other culture, by the way) disapproved strongly of extramarital sex several decades ago, and disapprove just as strongly now. Ira Reiss found that, "The same people who strongly favor being allowed to engage in premarital coitus will argue strongly against extramarital coitus." In our interviews we were struck by the number of college women who said that premarital intercourse was definitely not "wrong" but that extramarital sex definitely was. (Incidentally, America's divorce rate—the highest in the world after Egypt—has changed very little in the past 20 years. There was a significant increase during World War I and the 1920's and another small increase during World War II, but the rate—25 percent of all marriages—has remained constant since then.)

Likewise with attitudes toward masturbation and homosexuality. Most people no longer believe masturbation is "bad" either physically, morally, or psychologically, as 47 percent of America's women, according to Katherine Davis' study, did in 1929. It is more accepted now. But it is still a subject of embarrassment and silence among even the most emancipated young people. In our interviews, several girls, (including one who dressed and spoke like a Carnaby Street swinger) *blushed* or stammered when we asked about their masturbatory habits.

And homosexuality, currently a subject of discussion in the British House of Commons, which hopes to liberalize English laws against the practice, is still regarded by most Americans as something repulsive, unspeakable, or laughable.

As for attitudes on abortions, there seem to be many currents of opinion running. Certainly an increasing number of persons seek abortions annually, and almost as certainly a growing number accept it as a perfectly normal, simple medical procedure, like a tonsillectomy—which, medically speaking, it now almost is if done in the first three months. But a minority of those couples who have an abortion still feel that it is "necessary but somehow wrong," as one young graduate student's wife told us.

Hence, there have been some changes in some portions of the American public's *attitude* toward sexual behavior, but no radical overturning or abandonment of former standards.

As for the laws governing sexual behavior, a rapid survey of the hundreds of statutes governing sex in the 50 states of the United States could easily give a person the sense that sex is not legal in America.

Very little except face to face coitus, done in complete privacy by a man and woman legally married to each other, is permitted. The laws—each state has its own code, and many cities have additional regulations—are amazingly detailed in their stern prohibitions against fornication, adultery, animal contacts, prostitution, interracial intercourse, and homosexuality. Even for married persons, such omnibus words as "carnal abuse" or "sodomy" make it a criminal offense to indulge in fellatio, cunnilinctus, or other variations of lovemaking.

Actually, very few of these laws are ever enforced. For example, in New York State there have been fewer than five convictions for adultery in the 67 years of this century. If the laws were inforced systematically, approximately 90 percent of America's adults would be convicted as sex criminals.

Most of these laws were written one or two centuries ago. Unlike nearly every other kind of laws, which are constantly being rewritten, amended, or repealed, laws concerning sex have gone virtually unchanged. The fact that laws regarding sex can be, and are, largely ignored because of their non-enforcement makes it extremely difficult to arouse any interest or enthusiasm for their updating or repeal.

However, strong public protest does seem to be mounting against the tight restrictions on abortions and divorces; and there is growing concern about the strictures on homosexuality, so-called obscenity and pornography, and fornication (the voluntary, private act of sexual intercourse by two unmarried adults, usually defined as those over 18)—laws all written in an earlier day when religion played a prominent part in controlling the communities.

Recently, the American Law Institute in its Model Penal Code proposed that each state only include in its criminal laws sexual practices involving force (rape), adult corruption of minors, and public sex offenses. (Judge Learned Hand argued for this view consistently during his lifetime). The legal experts pointed out that most current laws are not enforced anyway; that whatever little enforcement is done is limited to the three areas that the code proposes be retained; that the present laws permit capricious prosecution by ambitious politicans and police figures and use by blackmailers; and that the failure to revise any group of non-enforced laws weakens respect for, allegiance to, and the power of enforcement of *all* American laws. Of note is that the model code is very conservative on the matter of abortions.

To its credit, the State of Illinois quietly and skillfully did revise its sex laws on January 1, 1962 to conform almost exactly to the Law Institute's proposals. All laws prohibiting sexual acts between consenting adults in privacy were eliminated from the criminal code. So far, however, Illinois is the only state to modernize the archaic legal regulations of sexual practices.

Illinois, following the Law Institute, made no change concerning the crime of abortion. Yet here is exactly where the present laws may be most cruel and close-eyed, and most in need of reform. At least, many persons think so, including an increasing number of the nation's skillful and respectable doctors, many of whom now give abortions illegally.

The area of sex law that most people think has changed radically is that of obscenity and pornography. They point to the wide circulation of books like *Fanny Hill,* the blatant new nudity and sexual episodes in movies, and the increased distribution of magazines aimed at sexual arousal or titillation. The fact is that whatever changes have occurred in this are principally further relaxations in enforcement, not changes in the laws, although such decisions as that of Judge Frederick van Pelt Bryan '25, who declared D. H. Lawrence's *Lady Chatterley's Lover* as art and not obscenity, do indicate a slight modification in the interpretation of some existing laws. But these recent interpretations may reflect, not a new sexual revolution, but an old American antipathy to censorship.

Actually the laws against pornography are as firm as ever, and their interpretations by some zealous officials are almost as censorious as in the past. For example, scientific material on a study of sex, destined for a world-renowned scientist, was held up by the U. S. Customs authorities for three years. However, some slight changes have occurred, and artful descriptions of sexual life or the human form are now easier to distribute.

Nonetheless, whatever slim evidence there is for believing that a sexual "revolution" is underway, such evidence is least observable in the area of legal administration of human sexual expressions.

It is difficult—extremely difficult—to discuss the subject of human sexual behavior. The topic is surrounded by such taboos, fears, commercialism, religious injunctions, public shame, and profound personal feelings. While Americans have achieved a marvelous cultural perspective on such matters as politics, status systems, and eating habits, we scarcely realize how particular American sexual practices, attitudes, and laws are. While we have gained a commendable historical perspective on such things as our economic system, our art forms, and our clothing, we have little sense of how historically rooted our sexual procedures and norms are.

Take the matter of language. Gordon Rattray Taylor in his book *Sex in History* (1954) reported that, "As late as 1790, the [London] *Times* could print the word 'piss'—a thing which would have been unthinkable in 1825." He also describes how 19th century Evangelism, political conservatism, and bourgeois propriety combined to completely alter spoken and written English: whore became "fast woman," pregnant became "with child," breast became "bosom," sweat became "perspiration," spit became "expectorate," and so forth. A hyperdelicacy about the ordinaries of life was imposed on our language which is with us to this day.

One of the most curious of phenomena is that America's colleges and universities, usually the pioneers in extending the nation's realm of information and rational thought, have on the matter of sex been, with few exceptions, more conservative than some U. S. clergymen. Even many of the nation's greatest scholars steer clear of sex the way they might of, say, astrology. For scientists, humanists, and historians this is a puzzling circumvention. For social and behavioral scientists it is a crippling and inexcusable omission. Indiana's John Gagnon says:

> There have been fewer than 100 pieces of adequate research that focus on sexuality in the behavioral science area. When this is compared with the volume of work on political sociology, perceptual defense, anomic scales, sensory deprivation, and the manifold other areas that are now generating their own journals as part of the information explosion, one can only be distressed with how little is known about the interactions of sexuality with socialization, family life, creativity, and all the rest of human behavior.

Sexual behavior, however one regards it, is one of the central functions and preoccupations of mankind. It deserves to be treated as such, without fear, titters, or commercialization.

What little the world has in the way of sex research is of recent origin. The first studies were done in Germany and Austria in the late 19th century. Krafft-Ebbing's noted *Psychopathologia Sexualis* (Psychopathology of Sex) was published in 1886, and Freud's investigations were done shortly after. The first organization for the scholarly study of sex was the *Institut für Sexual Wissenschaft* at Berlin in 1911.

However, as Winston Ehrmann has said, "Systematic sex research . . . is essentially an American development." It began with a 39-page study by Dr. Max Exner (1871–1943) for the Y.M.C.A. called *Problems and Principles of Sex Education: a Study of 948 College Men,* in 1915. In 1921 a small group of scientists, physicians, and philanthropists organized "The Committee for Research in Problems of Sex" as a branch of the National Research Council. It was supported chiefly by John D. Rockefeller, Jr. and the Rockefeller Foundation who gave over $1.5 million for research between 1922 and 1947.

It was this Committee that substantially backed the work of Indiana University's biologist Alfred Kinsey and his associates, who produced their studies on the *Sexual Behavior of the Human Male* in 1948 and the *Sexual Behavior of the Human Female* in 1953. Despite their flaws, the Kinsey studies are now regarded as the starting point in what is hopefully described as a new era in the scientific study of human sexual behavior. Freud is properly credited with pointing world attention to the centrality of sex in human nature, but his work was often conjectural and chiefly individual in focus. What Kinsey did was point to the *social* aspects of sex and ground his views better in biological and sociological research.

Recently, such organizations as the Society for the Scientific Study of Sex and the Sex Information and Education Council of the U. S. (SIECUS) have been formed to gather more data and provide better factual information. And, the National Institute of Child Health and Human Development in February, 1967, authorized a two-year study of American youth, with emphasis on sex habits and attitudes, at Indiana's Institute for Sex Research. Last year the *Journal for Sexual Research,* sponsored by the Scientific Study of Sex, began publication.

College students are often at the center of notoriety when the churches or the mass media depict what they feel is the new American sexual rampage. College students, including most Columbia College men, *are* advocates of revised sexual codes and laws. In this capacity their pressure to correct adult foot-dragging, fear, avoidance, and hypocrisy is a welcome effort.

The students' effort is marred too often by transparent self-serving and hedonism, their narrowly individualistic approach, and their occasional unnecessary rudeness, exhibitionism, or anti-social behavior. But the value of the college students' thrust should not be discounted because of their occasional lapses, lapses that the press and media are quick to emphasize because of their color and journalism's own commercialized prurience.

The dating patterns of college students, and indeed of nearly all young persons in the United States, is something that has changed substantially in this country. Prior to 1900 or so young people "kept company," or travelled in mixed groups, frequently with their parents. Children of upper class or religious families especially were usually chaperoned; care was taken to see that couples were not left alone prior to marriage. The prevalence of small town life with its moral consensus helped parents enforce these procedures. A kiss from a female often literally had to be "stolen." Male premarital sexual satisfaction, as is the case in Latin America today, where chaperonage is still the rule, was achieved heavily through prostitutes.

In the 1920's, the custom of "dating" began. That is, young couples were allowed to make a date and go somewhere together *alone,* without friends, parents, relatives, or nurses present. The causes of the new pattern are many: the rise of city life which smashed group activities and neighborhood surveillance; the spread of the automobile; the introduction of motion pictures which taught young people the art of courting; the spread of co-education; the feminist movement which urged girls to be more independent and break out of old patterns; industrialism, which did not separate male and female work as much as previous economic forms; the decline of religious adherence; and increased schooling for all.

In dating, the idea was to date as many boys and girls as possible. At dances, for instance, "cutting in" was not only accepted but encouraged. The pattern led to increased flirtation and greater petting, and even intercourse (the 1920's were the years of the large increase in *female* premarital sex). It also provided a fairly rational means of selecting a mate. The number of dates, too, protected young people from great intimacies and early marriages. The custom of dating maximized sampling and minimized emotional commitment prior to marriage.

Until the late 1940's it was mainly the "wallflowers" who "went steady." They couldn't flirt, or were not attractive, or psychologically needed just one boy or girl to lean on. But in the late 1940's "going steady" became more widespread. Young people dated many fewer members of the opposite sex and instead selected a succession of only a few mates, with each of whom they would have more prolonged, more intimate, more "steady" associations. This early pairing off encouraged the rise of heavy petting, or the "everything but" sexual pattern—the new compromise between more intense relationships and the still strong taboos against premarital sex. Flirtation became almost vestigial, cutting in at dances all but disappeared, and more and more young people had "their" girls or boys, with whom they "broke off" only after a fairly stormy brouhaha. The informal, the cool, strong personal allegiance, and much more subtle emotional maneuvering became the style. Premarital pregnancies rose slightly and earlier marriages increased sharply.

The new pattern of sexual courtship places a great emotional strain on the young people, especially since parents and other adults are almost totally absent and non-interfering in these trial meetings. Choosing a "steady" is a serious matter and "breaking off" can result in a physical or mental breakdown. Dr. Seymour Halleck, director of student psychiatry at the University of Wisconsin, has found a high correlation between students—particularly *female* students, who must often personally act as the sexual policeman in the absence of parental or community restraints, without losing their marital prospect—who are having affairs and heavy romances and psychological difficulty and mental illness.

The changes, which do not, in our opinion, amount to a revolution but do follow other historical developments, need to be observed more objectively and closely, analyzed, and understood. The present description of sexual behavior in this country is a national scandal in its impressionism, moralism, sensationalism, inaccuracy, and ignorance. It leads to erroneous characterizations and frequently weird social and political decisions and regulations. It is time to stop clucking and start studying.

If we take seriously the platonic prescription to "know thyself" or St. John's thought "The truth shall make you free," we cannot live with myths, gossip, "news," and loose conjectures about the so-called "sexual revolution." We should not close our scholarly minds to any area of human endeavor, including sexual behavior, which from all indications is a vitally important constituent of human nature and social life.

Commentary: *College Students and Sex—A Study in Paradox*

Before any plausible generalization can be made on a topic so laden with emotion, moralism, and ideological bias, certain basic premises have to be made explicit. In one traditional view, the college student is regarded as a cloistered scholar, unworldly, academic, and shunning sexual involvement lest he imperil his professional future. At the opposite pole, his image is one of a roistering, irresponsible, sexually free person, oblivious to the cares that will follow graduation from college. Neither of these extremes can be validated and must yield, therefore, to a consideration of those overall institutional factors that have a special impact upon college populations. The impressions which follow are in the nature of a series of interdependent assertions intended to provoke thought and discussion along more realistic lines.

To begin with, man is a social animal whose behavior is structured by his culture. For him, therefore, sex is not to be understood merely in terms of biological drives but, rather, as the cultural conditioning of attitudes toward sex. These attitudes in turn reflect social norms, the values of the group. To ascertain and isolate these values, the history of marriage and the family, particularly in western civilization, must be examined. These values include monogamy and a patriarchal structure reinforced by a double standard of morality. As a result of the Industrial Revolution, urbanization, and social crises, new standards of a more egalitarian and democratic character have emerged. These have modified but not superseded the traditional, patriarchal norms.

Where is the college student in relation to all this? That depends upon the social situation in which he finds himself vis-à-vis the social background factors that produced him. City, country, or suburb, social class, religion, and economic status, campus-type or commuter college—these are some of the variables involved. In a mobile, competitive society, where traditional cultural expectations are in conflict with newer modes of adaptation, the college student is especially vulnerable to role confusion.

For example, the traditional definition of the male sex role involves connotations of aggression, initiative, and dominance. By contrast, the female plays a passive and subordinate role in which the double standard places more restrictions upon her than upon the male. However, the increasing integration of the sexes (coeducation and emancipation of women from the home are prime illustrations) creates dilemmas that the college student recognizes. If the male espouses an egalitarian single-standard relationship in dating and courtship, will the female accept this as liberalism or as weakness? If the female assumes an egalitarian role in violating the taboo against premarital sex experience, will the male accept this in the interest of consistency or stigmatize her in traditional terms? As long as these questions remain even partially unanswered, the sex behavior of college students must be seen as, in effect, an etiquette of mate selection in which the rules of dating and courtship are guided by considerations of tactics and strategy rather than principle. The language is that of romantic love, but the behavior involves rational calculation and utilitarian factors related to maximum eligibility for marriage.

Nevertheless, the literature increasingly refers to the sexual problems and adjustments of college students, which is an indication that the present college generation may be less inclined than earlier generations to inhibit present satisfactions in accord with cultural expectations. To the extent that this is so, there are alternate levels of sociological explanation. When traditional norms are challenged, when social crisis is no longer the exception but the rule, when war leads not to peace but to cold war and the threat of thermonuclear annihilation, it may become easier to rationalize a hedonistic attitude toward sex. Where individuation is threatened by automation, bureaucracy, and the diffusion of mass culture, alienation from the dominant culture may result. For the college student, this may take the form of culture conflict with the parental culture because parents are not presumed to have faced the same problems. Under such circumstances, deviation from the norms may be an effort to communicate, a way to resolve the existentialist dilemma, which is the failure of communication.

Sex, for a significant number of college students, whether it takes the form of promiscuity or early marriage (one out of every four undergraduates is married), may be an effort to communicate, to find positive, albeit inarticulate, affirmation in lieu of alienation, to find response in place of rejection. In short, these students are hoping that sex will turn out to be the puberty rite that will compel a reluctant society to confer the accolade of adulthood upon them. Whatever approbation the older generation withholds, the peer group is exhorted to provide. A sexual relationship may therefore be one more effort to find order in chaos.

Once the attempt to find order in chaos is abandoned, then alienation and withdrawal may become the order of the day. Some members of the cohort may ask this question: Whose order are we looking for? If order is identified with the middle-class establishment then retreatism becomes the norm, and drugs or diggers may serve today as the equivalent for the rebellion expressed in sexual terms yesterday. The causes of disenchantment, withdrawal, or rebellion remain the same, but the particular manifestations differ in a rapidly changing and mobile society from year to year. These points are treated more comprehensively and in depth in the commentary entitled "The Hippies: A Wider Scene."

14

SOCIAL CHANGE
AND YOUTH
IN AMERICA

KENNETH KENISTON

Every society tends to ignore its most troublesome characteristics.[1] Usually these remain unfathomed precisely because they are taken for granted, because life would be inconceivable without these traits. And most often they are taken for granted because their recognition would be painful to those concerned or disruptive to the society. Active awareness would at times involve confronting an embarrassing gap between social creed and social fact; at other times, the society chooses to ignore those of its qualities which subject its citizens to the greatest psychological strain. Such pluralistic ignorance is usually guaranteed and disguised by a kind of rhetoric of pseudo-awareness, which, by appearing to talk about the characteristic and even to praise it, prevents real understanding far more effectively than could an easily broken conspiracy of silence.

Such is often the case with discussions of social change in America. From hundreds of platforms on Commencement Day, young men and women are told that they go out into a rapidly changing world, that they live amidst unprecedented new opportunities, that they must continue the innovations which have made and

From Youth: Change and Challenge, *edited by Erik H. Erikson,* © *1961 by the American Academy of Arts and Sciences,* © *1963 by Basic Books, Inc., Publishers, New York.*

will continue to produce an ever-improving society in an ever-improving world. Not only is social change here portrayed as inevitable and good, but, the acoustics of the audience being what it is, no one really hears, and all leave with the illusory conviction that they have understood something about their society. But it occurs to none of the graduating class that their deepest anxieties and most confused moments might be a consequence of this "rapidly changing world."

More academic discussions of social change often fail similarly to clarify its meaning in our society. Most scholarly discussions of innovation concentrate either on the primitive world or on some relatively small segment of modern society. No conference is complete without panels and papers on "New Trends in X," "Recent Developments in Y," and "The New American Z." But commentators on American society are usually so preoccupied with specific changes—in markets, population patterns, styles of life—that they rarely if ever consider the over-all impact of the very fact that our entire society is in flux. And however important it may be to understand these specific changes in society, their chief importance for the individual is in that they are merely part of the broader picture of social change in all areas.

Even when we do reflect on the meaning of change in our own society, we are usually led to minimize its effects by the myth that familiarity breeds disappearance—that is, by the belief that because as individuals and as a society we have made an accommodation to social change, its effects have therefore vanished. It is of course true that the vast majority of Americans have made a kind of adaptation to social change. Most would feel lost without the technological innovations with which industrial managers and advertising men annually supply us: late-model cars, TV sets, refrigerators, women's fashions, and home furnishings. And, more important, we have made a kind of peace with far more profound nontechnological changes; new conceptions of the family, of sex roles, of work and play cease to shock or even to surprise us. But such an adaptation, even when it involves the expectation of and the need for continuing innovation, does not mean that change has ceased to affect us. It would be as true to say that because the American Indian has found in defeat, resentment, and apathy an adaptation of the social changes which destroyed his tribal life, he has ceased to be affected by these changes. Indeed, the acceptance and anticipation of social change by most Americans is itself one of the best indications of how profoundly it has altered our outlooks.

Thus, though barraged with discussions of "our rapidly changing world" and "recent developments," we too easily can remain incognizant of the enormous significance, and in many ways the historical uniqueness, of social change in our society. Rapid changes in all aspects of life mean that little can be counted on to endure from generation to generation, that all technologies, all institutions, and all values are open to revision and obsolescence. Continual innovation as we experience it in this country profoundly affects our conceptions of ourselves, our visions of the future, the quality of our attachment to the present, and the myths we construct of the past. It constitutes one of the deepest sources of strain in American life,[2] and many characteristically "American" outlooks, values, and institutions can be interpreted as attempts to adapt to the stress of continual change.

Social Change in America

Many of the outlooks and values of American youth can be seen as responses to the social changes which confront this generation.[3] But merely to point out that society is changing and that youth must cope with the strains thus created is to state a truth so universal as to be almost tautological. Social change is the rule in history: past ages which at first glance appear to have been static usually turn out on closer study to have been merely those in which conflicting pressures for change were temporarily canceled out. Indeed, the very concept of a static society is usually a mistake of the short-sighted, a hypothetical construct which facilitates the analysis of change, or a myth created by those who dislike innovation.[4] All new generations must accommodate themselves to social change; indeed, one of youth's historic roles has been to provide the enthusiasm—if not the leadership—for still further changes.

And even if we add the qualifier "rapid" to "social change," there is still little distinctive about the problems of American youth. For though most historical changes have been slow and have involved little marked generational discontinuity, in our own century at least most of the world is in the midst of rapid, massive, and often disruptive changes, and these may create even greater problems for the youth of the underdeveloped countries than they do for Americans. Thus, to understand the responses of American youth to the problems of social change, we must first characterize, however tentatively and impressionistically, the most striking features of social change in this country.

Social change in America is by no means *sui generis;* in particular, it has much in common with the process of innovation in other industrialized countries. In all industrially advanced nations, the primary motor of social change is technological innovation: changes in nontechnological areas of society usually follow the needs and effects of technological and scientific advances. But though our own country is not unique in the role technology plays, it is distinguished by the intensity of and the relative absence of restraint on technological change. Probably more than any other society, we revere technological innovation, we seldom seek to limit its effects on other areas of society, and we have developed complex institutions to assure its persistence and acceleration. And, most important, because of the almost unchallenged role of technology in our society, our attitudes toward it spread into other areas of life, coloring our views on change in whatever area it occurs. This country closely approximates the ideal type of unrestrained and undirected technological change which pervades all areas of life; and in so far as other nations wish to or are in fact becoming more like us, the adaptations of American youth may augur similar trends elsewhere.

Our almost unqualified acceptance of technological innovation is historically unusual. To be sure, given a broad definition of technology, most major social and cultural changes have been accompanied, if not produced, by technological advances. The control of fire, the domestication of animals, the development of irrigation, the discovery of the compass—each innovation has been followed by profound changes in the constitution of society. But until recently technological innovation has been largely accidental and usually bitterly resisted by the order it threatened to supplant. Indeed, if there has been any one historical attitude toward change, it has been to deplore it. Most cultures have assumed that change was for the worse; most individuals have felt that the old ways were the best ways. There is a certain wisdom behind this assumption, for it is indeed true that technological change and its inevitable social and psychological accompaniments produce strains, conflicts, and imbalances among societies as among individuals. Were it not for our own and other modern societies, we might ascribe to human nature and social organization a deep conservatism which dictates that changes shall be made only when absolutely necessary and after a last-ditch stand by what is being replaced.

But in our own society in particular, this attitude no longer holds. We value scientific innovation and technological change almost without conscious reservation.[5] Even when scientific discoveries make possible the total destruction of the world, we do not seriously question the value of such discoveries. Those rare voices who may ask whether a new bomb, a new tail fin, a new shampoo, or a new superhighway might not be better left unproduced are almost invariably suppressed before the overwhelming conviction that "you can't stop the clock." And these attitudes extend beyond science and technology, affecting our opinions of every kind of change—as indeed they must if unwillingness to bear the non-technological side effects of technological innovation is not to impede the latter. Whether in social institutions, in ideology, or even in individual character, change is more often than not considered self-justifying. Our words of highest praise stress transformation— dynamic, expanding, new, modern, recent, growing, current, youthful, and so on. And our words of condemnation equally deplore the static and unchanging—old-fashioned, outmoded, antiquated, obsolete, stagnating, stand-still. We desire change not only when we have clear evidence that the status quo is inadequate, but often regardless of whether what we have from the past still serves us. The assumption that the new will be better than the old goes very deep in our culture; and even when we explicitly reject such notions as that of Progress, we often retain the implicit assumption that change *per se* is desirable.

Given this assumption that change is good, it is inevitable that institutions should have developed which would guarantee change and seek to accelerate it. Here as in other areas, technology leads the way. Probably the most potent innovating institution in our society is pure science, which provides an ever-increasing repertoire of techniques for altering the environment. An even greater investment of time and money goes into applied science and technology, into converting abstract scientific principles into concrete innovations relevant to our industrialized society. The elevation of technological innovation into a profession, research and development, is the high point of institutionalized technological change in this country and probably in the world. And along with the institutionalized change increasingly goes planned obsolescence, to assure that even if the motivation to discard the out-moded should flag, the consumer will have no choice but to buy the newest and latest, since the old will have ceased to function.

But the most drastic strains occur only at the peripheries of purely technological innovation, because of changes in other social institutions which follow in the wake of new commodities and technologies. Consider the effects of the automobile, which has changed patterns of work and residence, transformed the country-side with turnpikes and freeways, all but destroyed public trans-portation, been instrumental in producing urban blight and the flight to the suburbs, and even changed techniques of courtship in America. Further examples could be adduced, but the point is clear: unrestrained technological change guarantees the continual transformation of other sectors of society to accommodate the effects and requirements of technology. And here, too, our society abounds with planning groups, special legislative committees, cit-izens' movements, research organizations and community workers and consultants of every variety whose chief task is, as it were, to clean up after technologically induced changes, though rarely if ever to plan or coordinate major social innovations in the first place. Thus, citizens' committees usually worry more about how to relocate the families dispossessed by new roadways than about whether new roads are a definite social asset. But by mitigating some of the more acute stresses indirectly created by technolog-ical change, such organizations add to social stability.

One of the principal consequences of our high regard for change and of the institutionalization of innovation is that we have virtually assured not only that change will continue, but that its pace will accelerate. Since scientific knowledge is growing at a logarithmic rate, each decade sees still more, and more revolutionary, scientific discoveries made available to industry for translation into new commodities and techniques of production.[6] And while social change undoubtedly lags behind technological change, the pace of social innovation has also increased. An Amer-ican born at the turn of the century has witnessed in his lifetime social transformations unequaled in any other comparable period in history: the introduction of electricity, radio, television, the au-tomobile, the airplane, atomic bombs and power, rocketry, the automation of industry in the technological area, and equally un-precedented changes in society and ideology: new conceptions of the family, of the relations between the sexes, of work, residence, leisure, of the role of government, of the place of America in world affairs. We correctly characterize the rate of change in terms of self-stimulating chain reactions—the "exploding" metropolis, the "upward spiral" of living standards, the "rocketing" demands for goods and services. And unlike drastic social changes in the past (which have usually resulted from pestilence, war, military conquest, or contact with a superior culture), these have taken place "in the natural course of events." In our society at present, "the natural course of events" is precisely that the rate of change should continue to accelerate up to the as-yet-unreached limits of human and institutional adaptability.

The effects of this kind of valued, institutionalized, and accelerating social change are augmented in American society by two factors. The first is the relative absence of traditional institutions or values opposed to change. In most other industrialized nations, the impact of technology on the society at large has been limited by pre-existing social forces—aristocratic interests, class cleavages, or religious values—opposed to unrestrained technological change. Or, as in the case of Japan, technological changes were introduced by semi-feudal groups determined to preserve their hegemony in the new power structure. Technologically induced changes have thus often been curbed or stopped when they conflicted with older institutions and values, or these pretechnological forces have continued to exist side by side with technological changes. The result has been some mitigation of the effects of technological innovation, a greater channeling of these changes into pre-existing institutions, and the persistence within the society of enclaves relatively unaffected by the values of a technological era.[7] But America has few such antitechnological forces. Lacking a feudal past, our values were from the first those most congenial to technology—a strong emphasis on getting things done, on practicality, on efficiency, on hard work, on rewards for achievement, not birth, and on treating all men according to the same universal rules.

A second factor which increases the effect of technological change is our unusual unwillingness to control, limit, or guide directions of industrial and social change—an unwillingness related to the absence of institutions opposing innovation. Most rapid changes in the world today involve far more central planning or foreknowledge of goal than we are willing to allow in America. At one extreme are countries like China and Russia, which attempt the total planning of all technological, industrial, and social change. While unplanned changes inevitably occur, central planning means that the major directions of change are outlined in advance and that unplanned changes can frequently be redirected according to central objectives. Furthermore, most underdeveloped nations are aiming at developing a highly technological society; in so far as they succeed, the direction of their changes is given by the model they seek to emulate. Given three abstract types of change—planned, imitative, and unguided—our own society most closely approximates the unguided type. We do little to limit the effects of change in one area of life on other aspects of society, and prefer to let social transformations occur in what we consider a "free" or "natural" way, that is, to be determined by technological innovations. As a result, we virtually guarantee our inability to anticipate or predict the future directions of social change. The Russian knows at least that his society is committed to increasing production and expansion; the Nigerian knows that his nation aims at increasing Westernization; but partly by our refusal to guide the course of our society, we have no way of knowing where we are headed.

The Phenomenology of Unrestrained Technological Change

Man's individual life has always been uncertain: no man could ever predict the precise events which would befall him and his children. In many ways we have decreased existential uncertainty in our society by reducing the possibilities of premature death and diminishing the hazards of natural disaster. But at the same time, a society changing in the way ours is greatly increases the unpredictability and uncertainty of the life situation shared by all the members of any generation. In almost every other time and place, a man could be reasonably certain that essentially the same technologies, social institutions, outlooks on life, and types of people would surround his children in their maturity as surrounded him in his. Today, we can no longer expect this. Instead, our chief certainty about the life situation of our descendants is that it will be drastically and unpredictably different from our own.

Few Americans consciously reflect on the significance of social change; as I have argued earlier, the rhetoric with which we conventionally discuss our changing society usually conceals a recognition of how deeply the pace, the pervasiveness, and the lack of over-all direction of change in our society affect our outlooks. But nonetheless, the very fact of living amidst this kind of social transformation produces a characteristic point of view about the past and future, a new emphasis on the present, and above all an altered relationship between the generations which we can call the phenomenology of unrestrained technological change.[8]

The major components of this world view follow from the characteristics of change in this country. First, the past grows increasingly distant from the present. The differences between the America of 1950 and that of 1960 are greater than those between 1900 and 1910; because of the accelerating rate of innovation, more things change, and more rapidly, in each successive decade. Social changes that once would have taken a century now occur in less than a generation. As a result, the past grows progressively more different from the present in fact, and seems more remote and irrelevant psychologically. Second, the future, too, grows more remote and uncertain. Because the future directions of social change are virtually unpredictable, today's young men and women are growing into a world that is more unknowable than that confronted by any previous generation. The kind of society today's students will confront as mature adults is almost impossible for them or anyone else to anticipate. Third, the present assumes a new significance as the one time in which the environment is relevant, immediate, and knowable. The past's solution to life's problems are not necessarily relevant to the here-and-now, and no one can know whether what is decided today will remain valid in tomorrow's world; hence, the present assumes an autonomy unknown in more static societies. Finally, and perhaps of greatest psychological importance, the relations between the generations are weakened as the rate of social innovation increases. The wisdom and skills of fathers can no longer be transmitted to sons with any assurance that they will be appropriate for them; truth must as often be created by children as learned from parents.

This mentality by no means characterizes all Americans to the same degree. The impact of social change is always very uneven, affecting some social strata more than others, and influencing some age groups more than others. The groups most affected are usually in elite or vanguard positions: those in roles of intellectual leadership usually initiate innovations and make the first psychological adaptations to them, integrating novelty with older values and institutions and providing in their persons models which exemplify techniques of adaptation to the new social order. Similarly, social change subjects different age groups to differing amounts of stress. Those least affected are those most outside the society, the very young and the very old; most affected are youths in the process of making a lifelong commitment to the future. The young, who have outlived the social definitions of childhood and are not yet fully located in the world of adult commitments and roles, are most immediately torn between the pulls of the past and the future. Reared by elders who were formed in a previous version of the society, and anticipating a life in a still different society, they must somehow choose between competing versions of past and future. Thus, it is youth that must chiefly cope with the strains of social change, and among youth, it is "elite" youth who feel these most acutely.

Accordingly, in the following comments on the outlooks of American youth, I will emphasize those views which seem most directly related to the world view created by unrestrained change,[9] and will base my statements primarily on my observations over the past decade of a number of able students in an "elite" college. While these young men are undoubtedly more articulate and reflective than most of their contemporaries, I suspect they voice attitudes common to many of their age mates.

Outlooks of Elite Youth

One of the most outstanding (and to many members of the older generation, most puzzling) characteristics of young people today is their apparent *lack of deep commitments to adult values and roles.* An increasing number of young people—students, teen-agers, juvenile delinquents, and beats—are alienated from their parents' conceptions of adulthood, disaffected from the main streams of traditional public life, and disaffiliated from many of the historical institutions of our society. This alienation is of course one of the cardinal tenets of the Beat Generation; but it more subtly characterizes a great many other young people, even those who appear at first glance to be chiefly concerned with getting ahead and making a place for themselves. A surprising number of these young men and women, despite their efforts to get good scholarships and good grades so that they can get into a good medical school and have a good practice, nonetheless view the world they are entering with a deep mistrust. Paul Goodman aptly describes their view of society as "an apparently closed room with a rat race going on in the middle." [10] Whether they call it a rat race or not is immaterial (though many do): a surprising number of apparently ambitious young people see it as that. The adult world into which they are headed is seen as a cold, mechanical, abstract, specialized, and emotionally meaningless place in which one simply goes through the motions, but without conviction that the motions are worthy, humane, dignified, relevant, or exciting. Thus, for many young people, it is essential to stay "cool"; and "coolness" involves detachment, lack of commitment, never being enthusiastic or going overboard about anything.

This is a bleak picture, and it must be partially qualified. For few young people are deliberately cynical or calculating; rather, many feel forced into detachment and premature cynicism because society seems to offer them so little that is relevant, stable, and meaningful. They wish there were values, goals, or institutions to which they could be genuinely committed; they continue to search for them; and, given something like the Peace Corps, which promises challenge and a genuine expression of idealism, an extraordinary number of young people are prepared to drop everything to join. But when society as a whole appears to offer them few challenging or exciting opportunities—few of what Erikson would call objects of "fidelity"—"playing it cool" seems to many the only way to avoid damaging commitment to false life styles or goals.

To many older people, this attitude seems to smack of ingratitude and irresponsibility. In an earlier age, most men would have been grateful for the opportunities offered these contemporary young. Enormous possibilities are open to students with a college education, and yet many have little enthusiasm for these opportunities. If they are enthusiastic at all, it is about their steady girl friend, about their role in the college drama society, about writing poetry, or about a weekend with their buddies. Yet, at the same time, the members of this apparently irresponsible generation are surprisingly sane, realistic, and level-headed. They may not be given to vast enthusiasms, but neither are they given to fanaticism. They have a great, even an excessive, awareness of the complexities of the world around them; they are well-read and well-informed; they are kind and decent and moderate in their personal relations.

Part of the contrast between the apparent maturity and the alienation of the young is understandable in terms of the phenomenology of unrestrained change. For the sanity of young people today is partly manifest in their awareness that their world is very different from that of their parents. They know that rash commitments may prove outmoded tomorrow; they know that most viewpoints are rapidly shifting; they therefore find it difficult to locate a fixed position on which to stand. Furthermore, many young men and women sense that their parents are poor models for the kinds of lives they themselves will lead in their mature years, that is, poor exemplars for what they should and should not be. Or perhaps it would be more accurate to say, not that their parents are poor models (for a poor model is still a model of what not to be), but that parents are increasingly irrelevant as models for their children. Many young people are at a real loss as to what they should seek to become: no valid models exist for the as-yet-to-be-imagined world in which they will live. Not surprisingly, their very sanity and realism sometimes leads them to be disaffected from the values of their elders.

Another salient fact about young people today is their relative *lack of rebelliousness* against their parents or their parents' generation. Given their unwillingness to make commitments to the "adult world" in general, their lack of rebellion seems surprising, for we are accustomed to think that if a young man does not accept his parents' values, he must be actively rejecting them. And when the generations face similar life situations, emulation and rejection are indeed the two main possibilities. But rebellion, after all, presupposes that the target of one's hostility is an active threat: in classical stories of filial rebellion, the son is in real danger of being forced to become like his father, and he rebels rather than accept this definition of himself. But when a young man simply sees no possibility of becoming like his parents, then their world is so remote that it neither tempts nor threatens him. Indeed, many a youth is so distant from his parents, in generational terms if not in affection, that he can afford to "understand" them, and often to show a touching sympathy for their hesitant efforts to guide and advise him. Parents, too, often sense that they appear dated or "square" to their children; and this knowledge makes them the more unwilling to try to impose their own values or preferences. The result is frequently an unstated "gentleman's agreement" between the generations that neither will interfere with the other. This understanding acknowledges a real fact of existence today; but just as often, it creates new problems.

One of these problems appears very vividly in the *absence of paternal exemplars* in many contemporary plays, novels, and films. One of the characteristic facts about most of our modern heroes is that they have no fathers—or, when they do have fathers, these are portrayed as inadequate or in some other way as psychologically absent. Take Augie March or Holden Caulfield, take the heroes of Arthur Miller's and Tennessee Williams' plays, or consider the leading character in a film like *Rebel Without A Cause*. None of them has a father who can act as a model or for that matter as a target of overt rebellion. The same is true, though less dramatically, for a great many young people today. One sometimes even hears students in private conversations deplore the tolerance and permissiveness of their exemplary parents: "If only, just once, they would tell me what *they* think I should do." Young people want and need models and guardians of their development; and they usually feel cheated if they are not available. The gentleman's agreement seldom works.

It would be wrong, however, to infer that parents have suddenly become incompetent. On the contrary, most American parents are genuinely interested in their children, they try hard to understand and sympathize with them, they continually think and worry about how to guide their development. In other, more stable times, these same parents would have been excellent models for their children, nourishing their growth while recognizing their individuality. But today they often leave their children with a feeling of never really having had parents, of being somehow cheated of their birthright. The explanation is not hard to find; even the most well-intentioned parent cannot now hope to be a complete exemplar for his children's future. A man born in the 1910's or 1920's and formed during the Depression already finds himself in a world that was inconceivable then; his children will live in a world still more inconceivable. It would be unrealistic to hope that they would model their lives on his.

Another aspect of the psychology of rapid change is the *widespread feeling of powerlessness*—social, political, and personal—of many young people today. In the 1930's, there was a vocal minority which believed that society should and, most important, *could* be radically transformed; and there were more who were at least convinced that their efforts mattered and might make a difference in politics and the organization of society. Today the feeling of powerlessness extends even beyond matters of political and social interest; many young people see themselves as unable to influence any but the most personal spheres of their lives. The world is seen as fluid and chaotic, individuals as victims of impersonal forces which they can seldom understand and never control.

Students, for example, tend not only to have a highly negative view of the work of the average American adult, seeing it as sterile, empty, and unrewarding, but to feel themselves caught up in a system which they can neither change nor escape. They are pessimistic about their own chances of affecting or altering the great corporations, bureaucracies, and academies for which most of them will work, and equally pessimistic about the possibility of finding work outside the system that might be more meaningful.

Such feelings of powerlessness of course tend to be self-fulfilling. The young man who believes himself incapable of finding a job outside the bureaucratic system and, once in a job, unable to shape it so that it becomes more meaningful will usually end up exactly where he fears to be—in a meaningless job. Or, a generation which believes that it cannot influence social development will, by its consequent lack of involvement with social issues, in fact end up powerless before other forces, personal or impersonal, which *can* affect social change. In a generation as in individuals, the conviction of powerlessness begets the fact of powerlessness.[11] But, however incorrect, this conviction is easy to comprehend. The world has always been amazingly complex, and with our widening understanding comes a sometimes paralyzing awareness of its complexity. Furthermore, when one's vantage point is continually shifting, when the future is in fact more changeable than ever before, when the past can provide all too few hints as to how to lead a meaningful life in a shifting society—then it is very difficult to sustain a conviction that one can master the environment.

The most common response to this feeling of helplessness is what David Riesman has called *privatism*. Younger people increasingly emphasize and value precisely those areas of their lives which are least involved in the wider society, and which therefore seem most manageable and controllable. Young men and women today want large families, they are prepared to work hard to make them good families, they often value family closeness above meaningful work, many expect that family life will be the most important aspect of their lives. Within one's own family one seems able to control the present and, within limits, to shape the future. Leisure, too, is far more under the individual's personal control than his public life is; a man may feel obliged to do empty work to earn a living, but he can spend his leisure as he likes. Many young people expect to find in leisure a measure of stability, enjoyment, and control which they would otherwise lack. Hence their emphasis on assuring leisure time, on spending their leisure to good advantage, on getting jobs with long vacations, and on living in areas where leisure can be well enjoyed. Indeed, some anticipate working at their leisure with a dedication that will be totally lacking in their work itself. In leisure, as in the family, young people hope to find some of the predictability and control that seem to them so absent in the wider society.

Closely related to the emphasis on the private spheres of life is the *foreshortening of time span*. Long-range endeavors and commitments seem increasingly problematical, for even if one could be sure there will be no world holocaust, the future direction of society seems almost equally uncertain. Similarly, as the past becomes more remote, in psychological terms if not in actual chronology, there is a greater tendency to disregard it altogether. The extreme form of this trend is found in the "beat" emphasis on present satisfactions, with an almost total refusal to consider future consequences or past commitments. Here the future and the past disappear completely, and the greatest possible intensification of the present is sought. In less psychopathic form, the same emphasis on pursuits which can be realized in the present for their own sake and not for some future reward is found in many young people. The promise of continuing inflation makes the concept of a nest egg obsolete, the guarantee of changing job markets makes commitment to a specialized skill problematical, the possibility of a war, if seriously entertained, makes all future planning ridiculous. The consequence is that only the rare young man has life goals that extend more than five or ten years ahead; most can see only as far as graduate school, and many simply drift into, rather than choose, their future careers. The long-range goals, postponed satisfactions, and indefinitely deferred rewards of the Protestant Ethic are being replaced by an often reluctant hedonism of the moment.

A corollary of the emphasis on the private and the present is the *decline in political involvement* among college youth. To be sure, American students have never evinced the intense political concerns of their Continental contemporaries, and admittedly, there are exceptions, especially in the "direct-action" movements centered around desegregation. But the general pattern of political disengagement remains relatively unchanged, or if anything has become more marked. Those familiar with elite college students in the 1930's and in the late 1950's contrast the political activity of a noisy minority then with the general apathy now before world problems of greater magnitude. Instead of political action, we have a burgeoning of the arts on many campuses, with hundreds of plays, operas, poems, and short stories produced annually by college students. Underlying this preference of aesthetic to political commitment are many of the outlooks I have mentioned: the feeling of public powerlessness, the emphasis on the private and immediate aspects of life, the feeling of disengagement from the values of the parental generation. But most important is the real anxiety that overtakes many thoughtful young people when they contemplate their own helplessness in the face of social and historical forces which may be taking the world to destruction. It is perhaps significant that Harvard students began rioting about Latin diplomas the evening of a relatively underattended rally to protest American intervention in Cuba, a protest to which most students would have subscribed. So high a level of anxiety is generated by any discussion of complex international relations, the possibilities of nuclear war, or even the complicated issues of American domestic policies, that all but the extraordinarily honest or the extraordinarily masochistic prefer to release their tensions in other ways than in political activity. And in this disinvolvement they are of course supported by the traditional American myth of youth, which makes it a time for panty raids but not for politics.

In general, then, many college students have a kind of *cult of experience,* which stresses, in the words of one student, "the maximum possible number of sense experiences." Part of the fascination which the beat generation holds for college students lies in its quest for "kicks," for an intensification of present, private experiences without reference to other people, to social norms, to the past or the future. Few college students go this far, even in the small group that dresses "beat," rides motorcycles, and supports the espresso bars; for most, experience is sought in ways less asocial than sex, speed, and stimulants. But travel, artistic and expressive experience, the enjoyment of nature, the privacy of erotic love, or the company of friends occupy a similar place in the hierarchy of values. Parallel with this goes the search for self within the self rather than in society, activity or commitment, and a belief that truth can be uncovered by burrowing within the psyche. The experience sought is private, even solipsistic; it involves an indifference to the beckonings of the wider society. To be sure, Teddy Roosevelt, too, was in his way a seeker after experience; but unlike most contemporary American youths, he sought it in frantic extroversion, in bravado and heroic action; and its rewards were eventual public acclaim. But for most college students today, T.R. and the values of his era have become merely comic.

Youth Culture and Identity

Many of these outlooks of youth can be summed up as a sophisticated version of the almost unique American phenomenon of the "youth culture," [12] that is, the special culture of those who are between childhood and adulthood, a culture which differs from both that of the child and that of the adult. To understand the youth culture, we must consider not only the increasing gap between the generations but the discontinuity between childhood and adulthood.[13] Generational discontinuities are gaps in time, between one *mature* generation and the next; but age group discontinuities are gaps between different age groups at the *same* time. The transition from childhood to adulthood is never, in any society, completely continuous; but in some societies like our own there are radical discontinuities between the culturally given definitions of the child and of the adult. The child is seen as irresponsible, the adult responsible; the child is dependent, the adult is independent; the child is supposedly unsexual, the adult is interested in sex; the child plays, the adult works, etc. In societies where these age-group discontinuities are sharpest, there is usually some form of initiation rite to guarantee that everyone grows up, that the transition be clearly marked, and that there be no backsliding to childish ways.

But in our society we lack formalized rites of initiation into adulthood; the wan vestiges of such rites, like bar mitzvah, confirmation, or graduation-day exercises, have lost most of their former significance. Instead, we have a youth culture, not so obviously transitional, but more like a waiting period, in which the youth is ostensibly preparing himself for adult responsibilities, but in which to adults he often seems to be armoring himself against them. Of course, the years of the youth culture are usually spent in acquiring an education, in high school, college, vocational or professional training. But it would be wrong to think of the youth culture as merely an apprenticeship, a way of teaching the young the technical skills of adulthood. For the essence of the youth culture is that it is not a rational transitional period—were it one, it would simply combine the values of both childhood and adulthood. Instead, it has roles, values, and ways of behaving all its own; it emphasizes disengagement from adult values, sexual attractiveness, daring, immediate pleasure, and comradeship in a way that is true neither of childhood nor of adulthood. The youth culture is not always or explicitly anti-adult, but it is belligerently *non*-adult. The rock'n'roller, the Joe College student, the juvenile delinquent, and the beatnik, whatever their important differences, all form part of this general youth culture.

To understand this subculture we must consider its relation to both the discontinuities between age groups and the discontinuities between generations. I have noted that young people frequently view the more public aspects of adult life as empty, meaningless, a rat race, a futile treadmill; only in private areas can meaning and warmth be found. Childhood contrasts sharply with this image: childhood is seen as (and often really is) a time for the full employment of one's talents and interest, a time when work, love, and play are integrally related, when imagination is given free play, and life has spontaneity, freedom, and warmth. Adulthood obviously suffers by comparison, and it is understandable that those who are being rushed to maturity should drag their feet if this is what they foresee. The youth culture provides a kind of way-station, a temporary stopover in which one can muster strength for the next harrowing stage of the trip. And for many, the youth culture is not merely one of the stops, but the last stop they will really enjoy or feel commitment to. Thus, the youth culture is partially a consequence of the discontinuity of age groups, an expression of the reluctance of many young men and women to face the unknown perils of adulthood.

But the gap between childhood and adulthood will not explain why in our society at present the youth culture is becoming more and more important, why it involves a greater and greater part of young men and women's lives, or why it seems so tempting, compared with adulthood, that some young people increasingly refuse to make the transition at all. Rock'n'roll, for example, is probably the first music that has appealed almost exclusively to the youth culture; catering to the teenage market has become one of the nation's major industries. And, as Riesman has noted, the very word "teenager" has few of the connotations of transition and growing up of words like "youth" and "adolescent," which "teenager" is gradually replacing.[14]

The youth culture not only expresses youth's unwillingness to grow up, but serves a more positive function in resolving generational discontinuities. Erik H. Erikson would characterize our youth culture as a psychosocial moratorium on adulthood, which provides young people with an opportunity to develop their identity as adults.[15] One of the main psychological functions of a sense of identity is to provide a sense of inner self-sameness and continuity, to bind together the past, the present, and the future into a coherent whole; and the first task of adolescence and early adulthood is the achievement of identity. The word "achieve" is crucial here, for identity is not simply given by the society in which the adolescent lives; in many cases and in varying degrees, he must make his own unique synthesis of the often incompatible models, identifications, and ideals offered by society. The more incompatible the components from which the sense of identity must be built and the more uncertain the future for which one attempts to achieve identity, the more difficult the task becomes. If growing up were merely a matter of becoming "socialized," that is, of learning how to "fit into" society, it is hard to see how anyone could grow up at all in modern America, for the society into which young people will some day "fit" remains to be developed or even imagined. Oversimplifying, we might say that socialization is the main problem in a society where there are known and stable roles for children to fit into; but in a rapidly changing society like ours, identity formation increasingly replaces socialization in importance.

Even the achievement of identity, however, becomes more difficult in a time of rapid change. For, recall that one of the chief tasks of identity formation is the creation of a sense of self that will link the past, the present, and the future. When the generational past becomes ever more distant, and when the future is more and more unpredictable, such continuity requires more work, more creative effort. Furthermore, as Erikson emphasizes, another of the chief tasks of identity formation is the development of an "ideology," that is, of a philosophy of life, a basic outlook on the world which can orient one's actions in adult life. In a time of rapid ideological change, it seldom suffices for a young man or woman simply to accept some ideology from the past. The task is more difficult; it involves selecting from many ideologies those essential elements which are most relevant and most enduring. Such an achievement takes time and sometimes the longest time for the most talented, who usually take the job most seriously.

The youth culture, then, provides not only an opportunity to postpone adulthood, but also a more positive chance to develop a sense of identity which will resolve the discontinuity between childhood and adulthood on the one hand, and bridge the gap between the generations on the other. Of course, a few young men and women attempt to find an alternative to identify in other-direction. Unable to discover or create any solid internal basis for their lives, they become hyperadaptable; they develop extraordinary sensitivity to the wishes and expectations of others; in a real sense, they let themselves be defined by the demands of their environment. Thus, they are safe from disappointment, for having made no bets on the future at all, they never have put their money on the wrong horse. But this alternative is an evasion, not a solution, of the problem of identity. The other-directed man is left internally empty; he has settled for playing the roles that others demand of him. And role-playing does not satisfy or fulfill; letting the environment call the shots means having nothing of one's own. Most young people see this very clearly, and only a few are tempted to give up the struggle.

There is another small group, the so-called beats and their close fellow-travelers, who choose the other alternative, to opt out of the System altogether and to try to remain permanently within the youth culture. In so doing, some young people are able to create for themselves a world of immediate, private and simple enjoyment. But leaving the System also has its problems. The search for self which runs through the youth culture and the beat world is not the whole of life, and to continue it indefinitely means usually renouncing attainments which have been traditionally part of the definition of a man or a woman: intimacy and love for others; personal creativity in work, ideas, and children; and that fullness and roundedness of life which is ideally the reward of old age. So, though many young people are tempted and fascinated by the beat alternative, few actually choose it.

The vast majority of young people today accept neither the other-directed nor the beat evasion of the problem of identity. In many ways uncommitted to the public aspects of adult life, they are willing nonetheless to go through the motions without complete commitment. They have a kind of "double consciousness," one part oriented to the adult world which they will soon enter, the other part geared to their version of the youth culture. They are not rebellious (in fact they like their parents), but they feel estranged and distant from what their elders represent. They often wish they could model themselves after (or against) what their parents stand for, but they are sensible enough to see that older people are often genuinely confused themselves. They feel relatively powerless to control or to influence the personal world around them, but they try to make up for this feeling by emphasizing those private aspects of life in which some measure of predictability and warmth can be made to obtain. They often take enthusiastic part in the youth culture, but most of them are nonetheless attempting to "graduate" into adulthood. And though many hesitate on the threshold of adulthood, they do so not simply from antagonism or fear, but often from awareness that they have yet to develop a viable identity which will provide continuity both within their lives and between their own, their parents', and their future children's generations. And in each of these complex and ambivalent reactions young people are in part responding to the very process of unrestrained change in which they, like all of us, are involved.

Evaluations and Prospects

In these comments so far I have emphasized those attitudes which seem most directly related to the stresses of unrestrained change, neglecting other causal factors and painting a somewhat dark picture. I have done this partly because the more sanguine view of youth—which stresses the emancipations, the sociological understandability of youth's behavior, the stability of our society despite unprecedented changes, and the "adaptive" nature of youth's behavior—this more encouraging view has already been well presented.[16] But furthermore, if we shift from a sociological to a psychological perspective and ask how young people themselves experience growing up in this changing society, a less hopeful picture emerges. Rightly or wrongly, many young people experience emancipations as alienations; they find their many freedoms burdensome without criteria by which to choose among equally attractive alternatives; they resent being "understood" either sociologically or psychologically; and they often find the impressive stability of our society either oppressive or uninteresting. Furthermore, what may constitute an "adaptation" from one sociological point of view (e.g., the American Indian's regression in the face of American core culture) may be not only painful to the individual but disastrous to the society in the long run. A sociological and a psychological account of youth thus give different though perhaps complementary pictures, and lead to different evaluations of the outlook of American youth. Despite the stability of American society and the undeniable surfeit of opportunities and freedoms available to young people today, many of youth's attitudes seem to me to offer little ground for optimism.

The drift of American youth, I have argued, is away from public involvements and social responsibilities and toward a world of private and personal satisfactions. Almost all young people will eventually be *in* the system—that is, they will occupy occupational and other roles within the social structure—but a relatively large number of them will never be *for* the system. Like the stereotypical Madison Avenue ad-man who works to make money so that he can nourish his private (and forever unrealized) dream of writing a novel, their work and their participation in public life will always have a somewhat half-hearted quality, for their enthusiasms will be elsewhere—with the family, the home workshop, the forthcoming vacation, or the unpainted paintings. Their vision and their consciousness will be split, with one eye on the main chance and the other eye (the better one) on some private utopia. This will make them good organizational workers, who labor with detachment and correctness but without the intensity or involvement which might upset bureaucratic applecarts. And they will assure a highly stable political and social order, for few of them will be enough committed to politics to consider revolution, subversion, or even radical change. This orientation also has much to commend it to the individual: the private and immediate is indeed that sphere subject to the greatest personal control, and great satisfaction can be found in it. The "rich full life" has many virtues, especially when contrasted with the puritanical and future-oriented acquisitiveness of earlier American generations. And I doubt if commitment and "fidelity" will disappear; rather, they will simply be transferred to the aesthetic, the sensual, and the experiential, a transfer which would bode well for the future of the arts.

Yet the difficulties in this split consciousness seem to me overwhelming, both for the individual and for the society. For one, few individuals can successfully maintain such an outlook. The man who spends his working day at a job whose primary meaning is merely to earn enough money to enable him to enjoy the rest of his time can seldom really enjoy his leisure, his family, or his avocations. Life is of a piece, and if work is empty or routine, the rest will inevitably become contaminated as well, becoming a compulsive escape or a driven effort to compensate for the absent satisfactions that should inhere in work. Similarly, to try to avoid social and political problems by cultivating one's garden can at best be only partly successful. When the effects of government and society are so ubiquitous, one can escape them only in the backwaters, and then only for a short while. Putting work, society, and politics into one pigeonhole, and family, leisure and enjoyment into another creates a compartmentalization which is in continual danger of collapsing. Or, put more precisely, such a division of life into nonoverlapping spheres merely creates a new psychological strain, the almost impossible strain of artificially maintaining a continually split outlook.

Also on the demerit side, psychologically, is the willful limitation of vision which privatism involves, the motivated denial of the reality or importance of the nonprivate world. Given the unabating impact of social forces on every individual, to pretend that these do not exist (or that, if they do exist, have no effect on one) qualifies as a gross distortion of reality. Such blindness is of course understandable: given the anxiety one must inevitably feel before a volatile world situation, coupled with the felt inability to affect world events, blinders seem in the short run the best way to avoid constant uneasiness. Or similarly, given the widespread belief that work is simply a way of earning a living, refusal to admit the real importance to one's psychic life of the way one spends one's working days may be a kind of pseudo-solution. But a pseudo-solution it is, for the ability to acknowledge unpleasant reality and live with the attendant anxiety is one of the criteria of psychological health. From a psychological point of view, alienation and privatism can hardly be considered ideal responses to social change.

From a social point of view, the long-range limitations of these "adaptations" seem equally great. Indeed, it may be that, through withdrawal from concern with the general shape of society, we obtain short-run social stability at the price of long-run stagnation and inability to adapt. Young people, by exaggerating their own powerlessness, see the "system," whether at work, in politics, or in international affairs, as far more inexorable and unmalleable than it really is. Consider, for example, the attitude of most American youth (and most older people as well) toward efforts to direct or restrain the effects of social change. Partly by a false equation of Stalinism with social planning, partly on the assumption that unrestrained social change is "natural," and partly from a conviction that social planning is in any case impossible, young people usually declare their lack of interest. Apart from the incorrectness of such beliefs, their difficulty is that they tend to be self-confirming in practice. Given a generation with such assumptions, social changes will inevitably continue to occur in their present haphazard and unguided way, often regardless of the needs of the public. Or again, it seems likely that if any considerable proportion of American students were to demand that their future work be personally challenging and socially useful, they would be able to create or find such work and would revolutionize the quality of work for their fellows in the process. But few make such demands. Or, most ominous of all, if the future leaders of public opinion decide that they can leave the planning of foreign policy to weapons experts and military specialists, there is an all too great chance that the tough-minded "realism" of the experts will remain unmitigated by the public's wish to survive.

In short, an alienated generation seems too great a luxury in the 1960's. To cultivate one's garden is a stance most appropriate to times of peace and calm, and least apposite to an era of desperate international crisis. It would be a happier world than this in which men could devote themselves to personal allegiances and private utopias. But it is not this world. International problems alone are so pressing that for any proportion of the ablest college students to take an apolitical stance seems almost suicidal. And even if world problems were less horrendous, there is a great deal to be done in our own society, which to many, young and old, still seems corrupt, unjust, ugly, and inhuman. But to the extent that the younger generation loses interest in these public tasks, remaining content with private virtue, the public tasks will remain undone. Only a utopia can afford alienation.

In so far as alienation and privatism are dominant responses of the current college generation to the stresses of unrestrained change, the prospects are not bright. But for several reasons, I think this prognosis needs qualification. For one, I have obviously omitted the many exceptions to the picture I have sketched—the young men and women who have the courage to confront the problems of their society and the world, who have achieved a sense of identity which enables them to remain involved in and committed to the solution of these problems. Furthermore, for most students alienation is a kind of *faute de mieux* response, which they would readily abandon, could they find styles of life more deserving of allegiance. Indeed, I think most thoughtful students agree with my strictures against privatism, and accept withdrawal only as a last resort when other options have failed. But, most important, I have omitted from my account so far any discussion of those forces which do or might provide a greater sense of continuity, despite rapid change. Discussion of these forces may correct this perhaps unnecessarily discouraged picture.

Throughout this account, I have suggested that Americans are unwilling to plan, guide, restrain, or coordinate social change for the public good. While this is true when America is compared with other industrialized nations, it is less true than in the past, and there are signs that many Americans are increasingly skeptical of the notion that unrestrained change is somehow more "free" or more "natural" than social planning. We may be beginning to realize that the decision not to plan social changes is really a decision to allow forces and pressures other than the public interest to plot the course of change. For example, it is surely not more natural to allow our cities to be overrun and destroyed by the technological requirements of automobiles than to ask whether humane and social considerations might not require the banning or limiting of cars in major cities. Or to allow television and radio programming to be controlled by the decisions of sponsors and networks seems to many less "free" than to control them by public agencies. If we are prepared to guide and limit the course of social change, giving a push here and a pull there when the "natural" changes in our society conflict with the needs of the public, then the future may be a less uncertain prospect for our children. Indeed, if but a small proportion of the energy we now spend in trying to second-guess the future were channelled into efforts to shape it, we and our children might have an easier task in discovering how to make sense in, and of, our changing society.

I have also neglected the role that an understanding of their situation might play for the younger generation. Here I obviously do not mean that students should be moralistically lectured about the need for social responsibility and the perversity of withdrawal into private life. Such sermonizing would clearly have the opposite effect, if only because most young people are already perfectly willing to abandon privatism if they can find something better. But I do mean that thoughtful students should be encouraged to understand the meaning and importance of their own stage in life and of the problems which affect them as a generation. The emphasis on individual psychological understanding which characterizes many "progressive" colleges can provide only a part of the needed insight. The rest must come from an effort to end the pluralistic ignorance of the stresses confronting all members of the current younger generation. Here colleges do far too little, for courses dealing with the broad social pressures that impinge on the individual often deliberately attempt to prevent that personal involvement which alone gives insight. But one can imagine that a concrete understanding of the psychosocial forces that affect a generation might have some of the same therapeutic effects on the more reflective members of the generation that insight into psychodynamic forces can give the thoughtful individual.

And finally, I have underplayed the importance that values and principles can and do play in providing continuity amid rapid change. If one is convinced that there are guiding principles which will remain constant—and if one can find these enduring values—life can be meaningful and livable despite rapid change. But here we need to proceed cautiously. Technologies, institutions, ideologies, and people—all react by extremes when faced with the fear of obsolescence. Either they firmly insist that *nothing* has changed and that they are as integrally valid as ever before or—and this is equally disastrous—they become so eager to abandon the outmoded that they abandon essential principles along with the irrelevant. Thus, parents who dimly fear that they may appear "square" to their children can react either by a complete refusal to admit that anything has changed since their early days or (more often) by suppressing any expression of moral concern. The second alternative seems to me the more prevalent and dangerous. An antiquated outlook is usually simply ignored by the young. But person or institution that abandons its essential principles indirectly communicates that there are no principles which can withstand the test of time, and thus makes the task of the young more difficult.

Yet the bases for the continuity of the generations must of necessity shift. Parents can no longer hope to be literal models for their children; institutions cannot hope to persist without change in rite, practice, and custom. And, although many of the essential principles of parents, elders, and traditional institutions can persist, even those who seek to maintain the continuity of a tradition must, paradoxically, assume a creative and innovating role. We need not only a rediscovery of the vital ideals of the past, but a willingness to create new ideals—new values, new myths, and new utopias—which will help us to adapt creatively to a world undergoing continual and sweeping transformations. It is for such ideals that young people are searching: they need foundations for their lives which will link them to their personal and communal pasts and to their present society but which at the same time will provide a trustworthy basis for their futures. The total emulation or total rejection of the older generation by the young must be replaced by a recreation in each generation of the living and relevant aspects of the past, and by the creation of new images of life which will provide points of constancy in a time of rapid change.

Notes

1. An earlier version of parts of this paper was presented at the Annual Conference of Jewish Communal Services, May 1961, and was published in *The Journal of Jewish Communal Services* (Fall 1961).

2. It need hardly be added that our society's capacity for innovation and change is also one of its greatest strengths.

3. Among the other major factors creating stresses for American youth are (1) the discontinuities between childhood and adulthood, especially in the areas of sex, work, and dependency; (2) the great rise in the aspirations and standards of youth, which create new dissatisfactions; and (3) the general intellectual climate of skepticism and debunking, which makes "ideological" commitment difficult. In this essay, however, I will concentrate on the stresses created by social change.

4. One should not confuse static with stable societies. American society is extremely stable internally despite rapid rates of change. Similarly, other societies, though relatively static, are unstable internally.

5. Unconsciously, however, most Americans have highly ambivalent feelings about science and technology, usually expressed in the myth of the (mad) scientist whose creation eventually destroys him.

6. See Walter Rosenblith, "On Some Social Consequences of Scientific and Technological Change," *Dædalus* (Summer 1961), pp. 498–513.

7. Obviously, the existence of institutions and values opposed to technological change in a technological society is itself a major source of social and individual tension.

8. Other types of social change also have their own characteristic world views. In particular, the mentality of elite youth in underdeveloped countries now beginning industrialization differs from that in transitional countries like Japan, where technological and pretechnological elements coexist. American society probably

comes closest to a "pure" type of exclusively technological change.

9. Once again I omit any discussion of other sources of strain on youth (see [note] 3). Furthermore, I do not mean to suggest that these outlooks are the only possible responses to unrestrained change, or that they are unaffected by other historical and social forces in American life.

10. Paul Goodman, *Growing Up Absurd.* New York: Random House, 1960.

11. It is ironic that this generation, which is better prepared than any before it, which knows more about itself and the world and is thus in a better position to find those points of leverage from which things can be changed, should feel unable to shape its own destiny in any public respect.

12. Talcott Parsons, "Age and Sex Grading in the United States," reprinted in Parsons, *Essays in Sociological Theory, Pure and Applied* (Glencoe, Illinois: The Free Press, 1949). The beginnings of a youth culture are appearing in other highly industrialized countries, which suggests that this institution is characteristic of a high degree of industrialization.

13. Ruth Benedict, "Continuities and Discontinuities in Cultural Conditioning," in Clyde Kluckhohn and Henry A. Murray (eds.), *Personality in Nature, Society, and Culture.* New York: Norton, 1948.

14. David Riesman, "Where is the College Generation Headed?" *Harper's Magazine,* April 1961.

15. Erik H. Erikson, "The Problem of Ego Identity," in *Identity and the Life Cycle,* published as vol. I, no. 1 of *Psychological Issues* (1959). See also his "Youth: Fidelity and Diversity."

16. Talcott Parsons, "Youth in the Context of American Society."

Commentary: *Alienated Youth*

Kenneth Keniston and Erik H. Erikson have been viewed as the gurus of that portion of youth that feels alienated from dominant familial norms (at least this has been our impression on college campuses in recent years). Yet, Keniston's discussion on social change and youth in America does raise some important questions concerning social causation, assessment of current youth movements, and cross-cultural comparisons. In his search for explanations of youth's current predicament, he has perhaps overemphasized technology as a variable. Despite the fact that such overemphasis has long been present in American social theory (witness Thorstein Veblen, The Theory of the Leisure Class, *1899; William F. Ogburn,* Social Change, *1922; and Leslie White,* The Science of Culture, *1949), the interactionist position regarding the reciprocal influences of technology and social institutions can still have value.*

Specifically, Keniston's concept of "unrestrained technological change" may be a contradiction in terms, because analysis may prove that ideology and social institutions always restrain or structure technological change. When Keniston states that the Nigerian "knows that his nation aims at increasing westernization," this belies the implications of what is currently happening in Nigeria, namely a state involved in a civil war. The situation in Nigeria is quite complex, and we cannot pretend to supply a complete explanation. However, to avoid oversimplification, we should note that in Nigeria there are conflicts between tribalism and nationalism, between Islam and traditional indigenous religions, and between advocates of westernization and native nationalists who decry such advocacy as neocolonialism. In Nigeria, just as in Ghana, it would be a mistake to assume that there is any necessary cultural continuity in family systems or any other parts of the social structure, especially in view of recent events.

To avoid ambiguity in the preceding commentaries, we specified for whom and for what behavior was functional or dysfunctional and for whom and for what behavior connoted social acceptance or rejection. In evaluating Keniston's essay, we have to engage in comparable semantic analysis with regard to such terms as "alienation" and "commitment." If not all youth is alienated from dominant middle-class norms and if, verifiably, we are dealing only with college youth (and even in this category, an articulate minority), then the title "Social Change and Youth in America" may be too inclusive. Similarly, the question, Who are the uncommitted? may be asked. Are they, whoever they are, equally uncommitted in all institutional sectors and with regard to all social issues? Vietnam, both pro and con, gets a rise out of some, but those concerned with civil rights and the Negro may not be equally sensitive to Vietnam. Some who are uncommitted merely focus upon rejection of parental middle-class norms without a concern for what this conflict symbolizes within the larger social structure. If the opposite of uncommitted is committed, then the issue of commitment by whom and to what is a crucial question.

Therefore, alienation may be interpreted as a form of deviant behavior to be remedied by a wide variety of family and social therapies. At the same time it may also be interpreted as a form of liberation that is a prerequisite for creativity and sensitivity to the directions of necessary social change within the larger society. In reading Keniston, Erikson, Erich Fromm, David Riesman, and others in this tradition of sociological analysis, all these problems, semantic and sociological, must be remembered. Regardless of the current opinion, it is our view that the problems of youth are not qualitatively distinct from the larger society. This point is given further cogency in the concluding commentary.

It is probably the case that the percentage of today's youth that can be characterized by such phrases as "rebellious" has either increased or at the very least become more conspicuous. However, it is our view that the "decline" in political involvement is still characteristic of the majority of college youth. Commitment makes headlines, apathy does not.

15

THE INTELLIGENT SQUARE'S
GUIDE TO
HIPPIELAND

JUNE BINGHAM

No generation, it is said, can predict the weapons that the next one will use against it. Surely few Americans who grew up during the Depression and struggled to win middle- or upper-middle-class privileges for their family would have dreamed that, by 1967, some of their most gifted sons and daughters would purposely be hurrying from riches to rags.

Today, these visible, audible and sometimes smellable young rebels are loosely called hippies. Constituting a tiny minority, they are mostly white, carefully nurtured and educated beyond the average; some were former leaders of their class in school. Their young Negro counterpart is trying to achieve, rather than "drop out" of, higher education and professional status; or, if he is trapped in the slums, he may turn to addictive drugs, such as heroin, which are scorned by the hippies, or to violence, which is abhorred by them.

Within the hippie subculture—mostly urban—not all are intelligent and promising. Some are mentally ill or not very bright; some are merely unformed and seduced by the gross simplifications and absolute certainties that seem to result from even a rare use of LSD or a heavy use of marijuana. Mental hospitals throughout the United States report a startling drop in admissions

© 1967 by The New York Times Company. Reprinted by permission.

of the two kinds of schizophrenics whose symptoms are similar to those of someone on an LSD trip: the young inappropriately laughing hebephrenics and frozenly posturing catatonics have gone to live among the hippies who tolerate them, thus discouraging their seeking psychiatric treatment.

But partly because many hippies are imaginative, articulate and artistic, their world-view has spread to the far larger number of their well-shod and well-shorn contemporaries, especially to those appalled by the American involvement in Vietnam. Hippiedom, in one sense, is part of the Vietnam fallout.

But this is not all that it is. For there are hippies in England and Canada, Denmark and France, countries not involved in Vietnam or in the credibility gap.

The hippies are in rebellion also against nuclear fission, automation, and bigness in industry, labor and government—in sum, against everything that diminishes the importance of the individual. Their slogan is, "I am a human being: Do not fold, spindle or mutilate." And their value system is the mirror-opposite of the middle-class or square system (while the hippie terms himself a "human being," he terms the square "subhuman" or "humanoid").

If one imagines the questions that a suburban father would ask of a future son-in-law, about family background and religious affiliation, academic degrees and career prospects, previous record and future plans, the hippies would say that None of These Matter (they always seem to talk in capital letters). What matters, they say, is not what a person *does* but what he is, not outer forms or "games," but "Being At One With Yourself."

The hippie phenomenon, once thought to be only a passing phase, is probably more dangerous to its conforming nonconformists than to society as a whole. For the hippie minority, though revolutionary, is neither subversive nor violent. There has been a recent divorce between the hippies and the New Left. While the hippies reject the capitalist emphasis on "mine," whether my house, my money, my gadgets, my child or my work of art, they also reject the Communist practice of job assignment and restriction of the arts and individual freedom. The love ins, while sometimes unattractive, are an improvement over the deafening silence of the "cool" young of the McCarthy period, or the destructiveness of some beatniks, beats and hipsters, those immediate predecessors of the hippies. There is no hippie leader like Norman Mailer, who tried to link the hipster to Black Power.

The squares who wish to alert a hippie—or demihippie—to the hidden dangers to which he is exposed will find disgust less helpful than an attempt to understand the hippie "transvaluation of values." Though the hippies' positive program comprises little that is new or practical, their negative strictures may well be a judgment upon the squares' value system.

There is nothing new, for instance, in the hippies' privatism (the solipsists long ago took it to the end of the line), nor in their hedonism (ancient Greece coined the word for it), nor in their reversion to the Natural (Rousseau promoted the "Noble Savage" whether with hair on his face, like the hippie boys, or under the arms, like the hippie girls). Similarly, there is nothing new in the hippies' passivity and pipe dreaming (hashish—a stronger variety of pot—has been used for millennia).

The following hippie judgments, however, are worth square consideration:

At a time when sexual excitement by way of the media has reached laughable, if not obscene, proportions, these boys and girls in identical tight pants and shoulder-length hair are signaling that the male and female secondary sexual characteristics are not that important: their form of address for one another is "Man."

At a time when racial antagonisms erupt on the street, these boys and girls appear relaxedly integrated. The problems of poverty and the ghetto—together with those of leisure—are no problems to the hippies who embrace all three. In their own sections of cities there is little serious crime and no prostitution.

At a time when national and ideological rivalry may lead to nuclear apocalypse, the hippies preach, "Make love, not war," and refuse to offer themselves for service to their country if this means that they may have to kill or be killed.

At a time when Organization Man and his wife have been clutching material possessions not only for health and comfort but for prestige and a kind of security, the hippies share their food, their pad, their guitars, and such cash as they earn or are given. They would agree with Joseph Wood Krutch that true security depends upon how much one can do *without*, and they are proud of their own instantaneous mobility. Some move onto the land in small rural kibbutzlike settlements reminiscent of Brook Farm and other 19th-century idealistic experiments. Their guru, Allen

Ginsberg, notes that the only technologically complicated item they wish to own is a stereo phonograph.

At a time when some churches have been exposed as slumlords and some church membership stems from other than religious reasons, the hippies stretch for spiritual meaning beyond the Judeo-Christian tradition. This has led some to study Hinduism and Buddhism, ancient philosophies too long spurned by the West.

At a time when planning—by government, by business, by individuals—is still highly touted, the hippies do not bother to turn the leaves of the calendar, or look at their watches (if they own any), or read or listen to the news. They wish to live by whim, by spontaneity, by the non-rules of Now. They are not interested in what someone else has said is right or has planned for them. If they feel in the mood they will neglect all appointments to marvel at the sight of an onion: intricacy and beauty enclosing the purity of the Void. In reacting against pressures of home and school that may have started in kindergarten, many are taking what Erik Erikson has called a "psychological moratorium." Said a male 26-year-old demihippie: "We don't know what we'll be when we're 40; we'll have to wait and see."

At a time of Hidden Persuaders, when politics and advertising are frankly based on image-making, on fooling as many of the people as much of the time as possible, the hippies cry, "Hypocrisy!" As for the politeness and self-restraint that grease the social, as well as business and political, wheels, the hippies prefer discussion of Birth and Death, Creation and Destruction, to small talk. Say the Diggers, a leading subgroup in San Francisco's Haight-Ashbury section, " 'Normal' citizens with store-dummy smiles stand apart from each other like cotton-packed capsules in bottles."

At a time when the American divorce rate is one out of four marriages (in California, one out of two), the hippies point to square hypocrisy in the sphere of sex. Many adults who have preached virginity before marriage and fidelity after it have practiced neither, the hippies say, and many who have practiced these have done so out of fear rather than love—out of, if you will, a form of biological capitalism.

Says a girl hippie: "What's the big deal when a girl hoards a bit of skin just so she can exchange it for a gold ring or a ranch house in the suburbs?"

Says a boy: "In the days before the Pill, people made a virtue of necessity and praised virginity; well the necessity is gone."

A physical factor in this new equation, in addition to the Pill, is that the average age for the onset of menstruation is 12, whereas a hundred years ago it was 17; while our female forebears—who usually married young—had only a year or two between menstruation and marriage, a girl today may have, because of the length and expense of education, more than a decade.

At a time when the "nuclear family," just two parents and their children, often must, because of the father's job, move away from grandparents, uncles and aunts and cousins, the hippies have established a form of the "extended family" in their pads. Unwittingly they may dilute the intensity of Oedipal conflicts that once were lessened by buffers such as relatives and, you should excuse the expression, servants. This would be "unwittingly," because most hippies, in their sentimental or drug-flattened view of human nature, deny that there is such a thing as primal aggression and possessiveness. They choose to think of the child as born "beautiful" and they blame any subsequent destructive behavior on the society or the parents that warped him (this view includes Hitler).

Their intention, therefore, cannot be to dilute what they deny exists, a denial that persists despite the rather stunning evidence to the contrary provided by the Bible and Sophocles, Shakespeare and Freud, by the ethologists who have added "territoriality" as a newly observed category of the power drive, and by lovingly nurtured 2-year-olds themselves.

At a time when many squares assume that there has been no historic mutation, that nuclear warheads differ merely in quantity, but not in quality, from the fire raids of World War II, the hippies insist on historic discontinuity. They believe both in the infinite plasticity of human nature and also in themselves as "a new kind of human being."

In a limited sense perhaps they are right, since theirs is the first post-nuclear generation: their impressionable earliest years were spent with parents who, for the first time, had to face the fact that the future of human civilization and of all life on earth had been thrown into question.

Underneath the hippie refusal to sacrifice the present on the altar of the future is often a black despair which is sometimes relieved and sometimes accentuated by the drugs they take. Basically they seem to be saying that only what they have already enjoyed cannot be taken from them. Perhaps, indeed, a hippie who faces up to the depth of his despair is more realistic than the square who blocks it out, who meticulously plans his life as if his personal future—and that of mankind—were any longer more than a good bet. In a time of rapid change, the radical may turn out to be more solidly grounded than the stand-patter.

The hippies are hipped on the value of the individual and the disvalue of the state. Thoreau is one of their gods. They speak, therefore, less about some crazy state in the future causing the annihilation of the world than of the crazy individual who caused the annihilation of one man, a President in his prime (it was less Kennedy's program than his style that appealed to them).

Their philosophy of "eat, drink and be merry, for tomorrow we die" is not irrational if, in fact, tomorrow we all do die. It is uncreative, however, if we and they do not die—if, in fact, as seems to be the prospect, we live even beyond the age when we can contribute to our society or enjoy ourselves.

The questions raised by the hippies are thus often profound ones; but their solutions, being neither well-thought-out nor realistic, are of value mostly when they raise other questions. Their greatest contribution may turn out to be "set-breaking," the "put-on," which, though initiated by the "mind-expanding" drugs, can be followed without these. Primarily this involves an exploding of old mental associations, such as, "Love leads to marriage; marriage leads to children." Why? What if they don't? Certainly in some hippie pads—though not in all—sex has been broken out from the old privacy, the old heterosexual one-to-one, the old erogenous zones.

What will the hippie experimentation lead to? No one, psychiatrist or layman, can say for sure. The old and middle-aged take the dimmest of views. Often the demisquare young, like the psychiatrists, say let's wait and see; neither wishes to be caught voicing an automatic disapproval of something yet unproved.

The chief—and by now fairly well-proved—danger to the hippies comes from LSD. The person who takes it as rarely as once or twice, in moderate dosages, may have suffered a chromosome "breakage" comparable to that caused by radiation and perhaps equally inexpungeable. In the East Village, New York City's ["Haight-Ashbury"], there has been for sale, among other psychedelia, a campaign button with a one-word slogan, "Mutate." If the mutated babies of today's acidheads, babies reminiscent of the deformed creatures produced in Hiroshima and Nagasaki after 1945, begin appearing in sizable numbers, the irony will be almost unbearable: that the very people who most fear and hate the nuclear bomb should be the ones to perpetuate one of its direst by-products.

Many a hippie, as a result of learning about the chromosome breakage, has renounced LSD. But some continue taking large doses of marijuana, which has been found to reactivate the effects of LSD previously ingested. LSD, like malaria, can remain in the bloodstream or the brain (no one yet knows where) and after a week or a month (the longest period on record is two years)—with or without pot—can cause a freak-out. This may happen without warning, as when a person is driving a car, and in parts of the U.S. acidheads are having their driver's licenses revoked. Dr. Dana Farnsworth of Harvard suggests that no one make any major decision for three months after an LSD trip.

Another danger from LSD or heavy use of pot is that its host may become a psychological Typhoid Mary, spreading infection through word and example to the tender young. Says Dr. Woodrow W. Burgess, a psychiatrist at the University of California at Davis, these hippies "are untreatable because they are so subjectively convinced of a better way of living."

Their subjective conviction is so unshakable ("I know more about me than those doctors do") that some of them, consciously or unconsciously are self-appointed missionaries for their "better way" of living. Their negative bait to the adolescent is "Don't be chicken," their positive bait is, "LSD is the only way really to find yourself."

An adult who, for better or worse, has "found himself" sufficiently to know the areas wherein he is, and is not, chicken, may not be seriously tempted. But the adventurous young person naturally is tempted. No one, particularly when young, enjoys missing out on something good, even though, or especially because, it involves a mild amount of danger. The psychedelic "pusher"—not motivated by money like the narcotics pusher, but still "a clear and present danger" to those younger than himself—must be kept from long unchaperoned periods with baby-sitters or smaller siblings, lest he do them the "favor" of starting them at least on pot (hard-core hippies, such as Timothy Leary, give their own children LSD).

Certainly, to "find oneself" is a lofty—and ancient—goal. Unfortunately, however, it seems to involve arduous effort over an extended period of time. It can be done, but not on an "add water and mix" basis. The Lord Buddha, who left his affluent home 2,500 years ago to wander barefoot and long-haired in search of the answer to human suffering, spent 14 years in rigorous meditation before attaining the state of mind-expansion he called Nirvana and that others have termed "the peace that passeth understanding."

The Lord Buddha, also in contrast to the hippie, was tolerant of all kinds of people, princes as well as paupers, old as well as young, from every caste and no-caste; he did not consider the squares as untouchable, nor did he recline all day watching color-ama behind his eyelids; he constantly checked his ideas against reality. ("The chief advantage of the uninterrupted daydream," says Dr. Fritz Redlich, dean of the Yale Medical School, "is its absence of risk.")

While LSD can shake people loose from old rigidities, and has some value as a psychotherapeutic tool, the "instant psychoanalysis" that some hippies claim for it appears to be mainly a reduction of physical aggression. Unfortunately there is no comparable reduction of verbal aggression (Leary's speeches are rife with it). The hippie who claims to have "found himself" has thus found only a part of himself, a part he wishes to find. While the hippie validly condemns some conscious hypocrisies of the squares, he often expresses, unconscious hypocrisies or rationalizations that are damaging to other people—and ultimately to himself.

These rationalizations of the hippie may derive from carrying over into consciousness the both-and (as against either-or) thinking that is typical of the unconscious. In dreams we can all be both child and adult simultaneously, but in reality *either* we must prepare ourselves in youth for a career *or* we find ourselves unprepared in middle age. (The hippie answer: "It does not matter if an artist never produces a work of art, as long as he sees with the eyes of an artist." The hippie thus spares himself the need to choose one art form and master it.)

These rationalizations of his may derive from his preference for subjective feeling as against objective evidence ("There is no such a thing as objective truth"). Science, of course, is disparaged ("The truth has never been found under the microscope"), and so is cause-and-effect reasoning when inconvenient (a hippie may reject the advice of a doctor who himself has not taken LSD, but accept, in time of pregnancy, the advice of a male obstetrician, who has obviously not given birth).

These rationalizations of the hippie may derive from his paucity of mental furniture. Though bright, he is likely to be a drop-out who has studied little, and that little confined mostly to the recent past.

Society, moreover, is a subject he knows even less about than he does about the individual. For example, more than 30 years ago Reinhold Niebuhr showed that, while the individual can hold self-sacrificial love, *agape*, as his highest goal (and may indeed sacrifice himself for a national aim such as democracy), a state, because of its internal dynamics and the built-in responsibilities of its leaders, cannot. Sometimes, indeed, the very idealism and selflessness with which the citizen devotes himself to his society becomes a power factor in the injustice perpetrated by this society on other societies. The highest goal for international affairs, therefore, cannot be love, but justice, and the idealists who refuse to face the difference between "Moral Man and Immoral Society"* may muddy the issues and thus perhaps abet the forces of ruthlessness.

Admittedly terrible as are some aspects of the current American scene, the anthill society of China is no improvement. And when even a small section of America's greatest natural resource—namely, her young people—absent themselves from social responsibility, one is reminded that ancient Rome fell less because of the hammering outside of the gate than of the listlessness within.

The hippie, however, cares little for history or for Santayana's dictum that those who do not study history are doomed to repeat it. "Who cares what those old writers had to say?" He refuses to admit that patterns may exist in history, just as he refuses to admit that patterns may exist in hippie behavior. He views himself as freely choosing each step he takes, while to the outsider he appears to be riding an escalator in a clump with his peer group. A hippie on a "high" will paint a picture he is certain is original; a psychiatrist can spot it at once as drug-influenced: It has no integral unity, merely repetitive motifs embellished with tiny—and often merry—detail.

All in all, the hippie, despite his high potential, often ends up with less self-knowledge than his square contemporary. Trying directly to "find oneself" seems paradoxically less effective than first becoming the kind of person upon whom others can rely and then learning existentially from this revealing experience.

* Niebuhr today says ruefully that he should have named his seminal book "*Im*moral Man and *Even More* Immoral Society."

The hippie honestly believes that he is practicing Love, but if you shut your eyes while he discusses suburbanites, you would think he was a bigoted white talking about Negroes.

The hippie honestly believes that he is achieving Freedom, but in fact he is slamming doors on himself, now as in the future. Because he operates on whim ("if it feels good, I'll do it,") he cannot be relied on in momentous times such as birth or death, family celebrations or crises. While dropping out he may have made himself worth dropping, by the very people who are nearest, if not dearest, to him.

The hippie honestly believes that he is honest. *He* has nothing to hide—nothing, that is, except the curved knife that he refuses to admit generically rests in the human hand. When the person the hippie cuts by way of his "honesty" cries out in pain, the hippie's first reaction is genuine surprise. His second is, "Well, that's your problem." Since, as he believes, there was, in his own purity, no wish to hurt, then the victim must surely be at fault, must have some hidden weakness that he would do well to explore.

And if the victim, in his freedom, has no wish thus to explore? Then the hippie may turn visibly hostile: "You are jealous, you wish you could live the way I do." If the older person responds that his concern is not about his own life at the moment but about the hippie's, the pat answer is that older people often use their worry as a means of subjugating the young. For the hippie, therefore, to avoid hurting his elders would be an unthinkable caving-in to pressure, a loss of his own integrity.

A clear difference between the hippies of today and their parents-when-young is that the parents handled their not so uncolorful rebellion discreetly and in the fear, if not of God, then of their parents. The hippies, on the other hand, through their ambivalent behavior—pregnancies out of wedlock, diaries left open to shocking pages—or their unambivalent appearance, trumpet their rebellion and thus challenge their parents, if not God, to smite them down.

A clear difference between the parents of today and their parents is the reluctance to smite the young down. Rarely is the cry "Never darken my doorstep" heard in the land; infrequently are the old expletives "impertinence" or "insolence" dusted off.

Instead, many concerned squares, either to keep open the paths of communication, or to help their almost-grown child, under whose truculence they think they hear a muted cry for help, or simply in the generic American willingness to admit that oneself may have goofed, are making the supreme effort to dissolve their own crystallized hierarchy of values into liquidity again. Is it possible, these parents ask themselves (or their spouse), that their dismay at their hippie is, in part, based on their own fear of loss of job, or of respect by their neighbors, or of approval by relatives?

In any event, some men and women in their 40's and 50's are putting themselves through, for a second time, the anxieties, even the agonies, of what is now called the "identity crisis"—it used to be called "growing pains." (One frantic parent in an attempt to save a hard-core hippie's marriage took LSD with the couple; the marriage did not survive, and the parent barely so.)

While the lucky parents can dissolve their value-system and re-establish one that does not make their whole past life seem futile, the unlucky ones may look back on the various crossroads of life and think, too late, that they took the wrong turn. The young person, through his unintentionally cruel questioning, may be toppling Humpty Dumpty at a time in life when all the king's horses and all the psychiatrists cannot put Humpty Dumpty together again.

Those now over 40 were often burdened by their late-Victorian and pre-Freudian parents with a harsh conscience, a tendency to overblame themselves. They are sandwiched between a generation that questioned too little and a generation that questions too much. They themselves never had the white meat of the turkey. When they were children, the best parts were saved, as a matter of course, for the adults; by the time they grew up, the best parts were being saved, as a matter of course, for the children.

Having been children in an adult-centered world, they are now adults in a child-centered world. And how do they react to finding themselves in this historic tide rip of values? By feeling guilty.

How can parents live through the period when their hippie or demihippie is testing every parental value; when he is busily devaluing the sacrifices they have made; when, in an odd reverse of the historic wheel, his brooding presence is reminiscent of nothing so much as that of a Victorian chaperone as he counts each parental drink, each cigarette, each tranquilizer, each white lie, each hour "wasted" in front of television or in talk about nonultimate matters, each mile above the speed limit (if the parents break the law by way of a car, the hippie argues he can break it by way of drugs)?

Here are five main survival suggestions for square parents:

(1) To fight guilt and despair, since these are likely to be both inappropriate and counterproductive. The hippiedemic is in the air, whetted by the media, and it affects young people from united as well as disrupted homes, from permissive and strict ones. Just as parents cannot predict the form of rebellion chosen by the next generation, so they are not individually responsible for it.

(2) To rely on that tough, effective teacher, the parents' ally, Experience. The young person who refuses to learn the easy way will simply have to learn the hard way. But the gnarled old teacher has tended over the generations to keep to the same lesson plan: that the work one loves can be more fun than fun, and that permanent relationships grounded in loyalty are vastly preferable to ephemeral ones.

(3) To distinguish between parental affection and approval: affection is built in, approval must be earned. Though the parents may never fully approve of their grown child—or vice versa—a family, like a nation and a world, can, with effort, make room for diversity.

(4) To try to give an object lesson in tolerance and humor, cheerfully and admittedly borrowing those hippie attitudes that will come in handy for the time of retirement. Whereas the hippie has much to learn about work, the square may have much to learn about leisure, especially in appreciation of the arts and nature. Even before retirement the square may wish to shed some encrusted bugaboos, such as compulsive punctuality or servitude to already announced plans. Indeed, his health may benefit if he learns, as the young say, to "hang easy."

(5) To have hope that within the two years it usually takes for diminishing returns to set in, the hippie will emerge from the dangerous Children's Crusade of his time, the better prepared to cope in middle age with the gyrations of his and his children's century, the twenty-first.

Commentary: *The Hippies: A Wider Scene*

There is justification for including the hippie phenomenon in an anthology on the family, for it reflects the overt and covert values that have been transmitted to the young vis-à-vis the family.

The sociology of the hippies has not been sufficiently investi-

gated. Our knowledge about them derives for the most part from journalistic reporting and essays published in a variety of journals. Despite the absence of "hard data," we feel that the existing literature is consistent enough to yield some general comments and interpretation.

The hippies arrived on the large cultural scene several years ago and constitute a prototype ushered in by an era of affluence and technology. Their ties to the Puritan ethic are less than nebulous. From a structural point of view, the hippies can be viewed as an extension of the larger culture. For the fact is that automation and the computer have been steadily eliminating jobs, thus promising a future in which the term "worker" as we now know it will become obsolete. The hippies represent a prototype of future nonworkers in our society. Ambition, success, and college, along with other comforting shibboleths of our culture, are all meaningless categories. Their rejection of traditional definitions of work and of the customary division between work and play are the consequences of increased leisure as well as a reaction to the meaningless jobs marshaled in by cybernetics.

Another force contributing to the emergence of the hippies is that, demographically speaking, over half the population in the United States consists of those who are under twenty-five, and there are more middle-class young people than ever before. It is from this cohort that hippies are recruited. Education has played a viable role in the lives of most of these youngsters in providing a measure of sophistication and training in the nuances of adult behavior. For structural reasons, therefore, they are better able to perceive the inconsistencies and contradictions of the adult world with sharp acumen. The dissension of the country over Vietnam, the moral issue of segregation, and the poverty found in an otherwise affluent society have led the young to question the sanity and logic expounded by educational institutions. Where is the answer to be found? Or, where is it to be asked? Can it be said that the university will provide the context for this pursuit? The hippies' answer is a categorical "No." The manifest unrest taking place on campuses throughout the nation indicates that youth views adult leadership as ineffectual.

What motivates individuals to retreat, to turn off middle-class values? The façade of unconventional dress, the unruly hair, and the painted bodies all tell us little that is really significant about the ideas lying behind their pattern of living. Consider for a moment that the hippies recoil from the moral and intellectual mal-

aise of the culture at large. They argue that the pretenses and false fronts of the straight world are illusory, that if one were to open the hood of this seemingly shiny car one would find it rusty and full of grime and muck. The straight man is viewed as a slave in the human market. He functions as a machine, producing without creating. His individuality and dignity are submerged into the mass as thoroughly as metal is submerged in an alloy. As the hippie sees it, man's energies are so dominated and enslaved by the ideal of success that he is stripped of a passion for qualities. Young people, therefore, are bereft of enthusiasm, and old age is devoid of wisdom. Because of the dichotomy between thought and action, there is no way for man to channel the diffused drift of his life. If man is unable to integrate the fragments of his life, he takes refuge in shibboleths. Therefore, the hippies argue further, the ascendancy of reason over feeling, of quantity over quality, has only served to emphasize the irrelevance of the individual.

But obviously the hippies are not unique in their indictment of contemporary society. Others who have paused long enough to ponder the relevancy of their own life style have made similar observations. In fact, their stance transcends the categories of class or age. The generation gap, which is so often used to explain the lack of dialogue between youth and adults, seems largely mythical. An inestimable number, both young and old, never pause to reflect on the forces pulling them in diverse directions. Can the hippie scene be explained as something new, or is it an old pattern of rebellion of the young against the older generation repeating itself? In a sense it is both; it is the old theme of the young replacing the old, but its form differs from any other historical period.

The differences between young people of the twenties and those of the sixties are found in the current concern with unconscious processes, LSD, spirituality, antireason, and antitechnology. And yet, one can argue that drugs may play the same role that alcohol did for the workers of the industrial period. Indeed, alcohol and various euphoria-producing drugs provide continuous retreats in the middle-class milieu. The greater deleteriousness or effect of one drug over another is not being debated here. What is being suggested is that the hippies' form of adaptation to diverse pressures and strains has literally been set by conventional society. Viewed from this perspective, the hippies are apt to invoke great hostility and resentment from conventional society because they touch at so many points. It may be, as some observers have noted, that the hippies reactivate latent anxiety in members of the straight world because they awaken the gypsy in all. To be sure, even where generational continuity is assured because of the slow-changing pace of a society, the rebellion of youth still occurs. But it occurs against exemplars, as Kenneth Keniston puts it, who have some relevance for them. In a rapidly changing society, the models a youth chooses are derived from various sources, so that a process of selectivity and synthesis is required of him. This is a particularly stressful experience.

To complicate the picture further, recent research on family roles indicates that parents often subtly ascribe the role of scapegoat to a particular son or daughter. This child's function is to bear the brunt of the anxieties and conflicts of the parents. The scapegoating is rarely intentional or malevolent—no parent sets out to make his son or daughter a hippie. But the secret admiration and psychic sanction of rebellious behavior may far outweigh verbal recriminations. On all levels of adult-youth relationships, the exchanges carry a residue of covert sanctions and overt disapproval. The interaction of adults with young people permits the former to be distracted from the central core of their own problems by treating the young as "the problem."

For structural reasons, parents are limited in their ability to advise and guide the lives of their own children. This stems not only from their context of experience, which is different from their children's at any point in time, but also from a basic ambivalence to values that are continuously subjected to change in an urbanized society. Their basic inability to act as mentors is clearly seen when an attempt is made to draw parallels between the parents of the adult generation and themselves. The immigrants, or inner directed parents, may have confronted difficulties in trying to master the external world, but they had very strong values, which they imposed upon their children. Contemporary parents run the risk of experiencing the repeated obsolescence of their own values. If change remains a constant in our society, and knowledge continues to accrue to the specialist at a rapid pace, then the child will increasingly seek guidance to relevant values outside the family context. Parents find difficulty in guiding their children with any wisdom when they have to struggle perennially with choosing values relevant to their children's lives as well as their own. To some extent their ambivalence is expressed through the prescription and proscription of deviant behavior previously alluded to.

When the parent is confronted with an instance of such deviation by his child he is apt to react not only by scapegoating but also by guilt feelings verbalized in such questions as, "What did I do that was wrong?" In either case, he ignores social causation and acts as if the family existed within a vacuum and all problems involving failure of communication and alienation were internally generated.

Although all hippies are virtually in collision with the inconsistencies between practiced and professed values of American life, not all of them become totally disillusioned with ideologies. There are, after all, different kinds of hippies ranging from high school dropouts and teen-agers to aging hangers-on from the beat generation. Some are talented, some are pathetic, and some are human vegetables. The hippies' emphasis on love, total freedom, and a turning inward to experience an inner world spiraling about in unconscious reverie symbolizes the meaningless experience of conscious life. For if society is fragmented, if it is empty, and if its goals are futile, then one's perspective can only have relevance to a world other than this one. If this world is dehumanizing, then one tries to find a humanizing one.

Parenthetically speaking, one thought may help to bridge the so-called generation gap. Within the subculture of youth, as well as the hippie contraculture, there are individuals and groups who are political activists, just as in the older generation there are political activists with a heritage from the thirties and forties. However, one more arch is needed for this bridge to be constructed semantically as well as substantively. The commentators on the present generation regard political activism (for example, within the civil rights movement or the peace movement) as nonideological, whereas the older generation's activism was always ideological. Once this issue is faced, all talk of a generation gap will possibly be recognized for the oversimplification that it is.

June Bingham is not alone in regarding the hippie contraculture as a revolutionary or social movement. Yet it must be remembered that social movements exist on a continuum of collective behavior that includes a large number of phenomena, and these phenomena share some of the characteristics of a social movement but do not have the characteristic of being vehicles for dramatic lasting social change. Fads, fashions, and related types of activity *are all included in this category. Theodore Abel wrote many years ago that a social movement is more than a protest against the status quo, more than tactics and strategy, more than even charismatic leadership* (Why Hitler Came to Power, 1938). *It also has to be structured in terms of an ideology. We question whether hippies are united by an ideology or even for that matter a centralized leadership. At best, they may be defined as a protomovement or a quasi-movement. Only time can tell which direction hippies will take, or for that matter, whether or not they, like the beat generation before them, will be succeeded by some new as yet undiscernible manifestation.*

APPENDIX

APPENDIX I

SUPPLEMENTARY
BIBLIOGRAPHY

This Bibliography has been selected with several criteria in mind. First, to assist the teacher in making additional assignments as well as to orient the student and general reader in the direction of our point of view, it is necessary to provide a listing that is not as specific as the books and articles cited in some of the selections. We have been guided in our compilation by such criteria as cross-cultural relevance, currency of publication, implications for the patriarchal-equalitarian continuum of ideology, representativeness of various social science approaches and institutional stresses rather than a problems approach only.

The titles of the individual items are descriptive enough to require no individual annotation. Most of the items are original contributions to the literature and are not general or textual in scope. They may well serve as bases for term reports as well as more extensive research. Every entry is comprehensible to the undergraduate reader and, at the same time, avoids any implication of condescension or popularization. It is selective as well as timely, and it is crucial for the understanding of family systems. However, we have not attempted to include a comprehensive listing here.

Bell, Robert R. *Premarital Sex in a Changing Society*. Englewood Cliffs, N. J.: Prentice-Hall, 1966.

Bernard, Jessie. *Marriage and Family Among Negroes.* Englewood Cliffs, N. J.: Prentice-Hall, 1966.

————. *Academic Women.* University Park, Pa.: Pennsylvania State University Press, 1964.

Blood, Robert O., Jr. *Love Match and Arranged Marriage: A Tokyo–Detroit Comparison.* New York: Free Press, 1967.

Cassara, Beverly B. (ed.). *American Women: The Changing Image.* Boston: Beacon Press, 1962.

Cuber, John F., and Peggy Harroff. *The Significant Americans: A Study of Sexual Behavior Among the Affluent.* New York: Appleton-Century-Crofts, 1966.

Desai, I. *Some Aspects of Family Life in Mahuva.* New York: Asia Publishing, 1964.

Ehrenwald, Jan. *Neurosis in the Family.* New York: Harper & Row, 1963.

Elkholy, Abdo A. *The Arab Moslems in the United States.* New Haven, Conn.: College and University Press, 1966.

Erlich, Vera St. *Family in Transition: A Study of 300 Yugoslav Villages.* Princeton, N. J.: Princeton University Press, 1966.

Farber, Seymour M., Piero Mustacchi, and Roger H. L. Wilson (eds.). *Man and Civilization: The Family's Search for Survival, 1965.* New York: McGraw-Hill, 1965.

————, and Roger H. L. Wilson (eds.). *The Potential of Women.* New York: McGraw-Hill, 1963.

Ginsberg, Eli. *Life Styles of Educated Women.* New York: Columbia University Press, 1967.

Goode, William J. *World Revolution and Family Patterns.* New York: Free Press, 1963.

Greenfield, Sidney M. *English Rustics in Black Skin: A Study of Modern Family Forms in a Pre-Industrial Society.* New Haven, Conn.: College and University Press, 1966.

Klein, Viola. *The Feminine Character: History of an Ideology.* London: Kegan Paul, Trench, Trubner, 1964.

Lopreato, Joseph. *Peasants No More: Social Class and Social Change in Southern Italy.* San Francisco: Chandler, 1967.

Mace, David, and Vera Mace. *The Soviet Family.* Garden City, N. Y.: Doubleday, 1963.

McKinley, Donald. *Social Class and Family Life.* New York: Free Press, 1964.

Mead, Margaret, and Frances Kaplan (eds.). *American Women: The Report of the President's Commission on the Status of Women and Other Publications of the Commission.* New York: Scribner, 1965.

Musgrove, Frank. *Youth and the Social Order.* Bloomington: Indiana University Press, 1964.

Nye, Ivan F., and Felix Berardo (eds.). *Emerging Conceptual Frameworks in Family Analysis.* New York: Macmillan, 1966.

Rainwater, Lee. *Family Design, Marital Sexuality and Family Size.* Chicago: Aldine, 1965.

Reiss, Ira L. *Premarital Sexual Standards in America.* New York: Free Press, 1960.

Rosenberg, Morris. *Society and the Adolescent Self-Image.* Princeton, N. J.: Princeton University Press, 1965.

Rosow, Irving. *Social Integration of the Aged.* New York: Free Press, 1967.

Singer, Irving. *The Nature of Love: Plato to Luther.* New York: Random House, 1966.

Smith, Michael G. *West Indian Family Structure.* Seattle: University of Washington Press, 1962.

Stolz, Lois M. *Influences on Parent Behavior.* Stanford, Calif.: Stanford University Press, 1967.

Suggs, Robert C. *Marquesan Sexual Behavior.* New York: Harcourt, Brace & World, 1966.

Udry, Richard J. *The Social Context of Marriage.* Philadelphia: Lippincott, 1966.

Wakin, Edward. *Portrait of a Middle-Class Negro Family at the Edge of Harlem.* New York: William Morrow, 1965.

Whitten, Norman E., Jr. *Class, Kinship and Power in an Ecuadorian Town: The Negroes of San Lorenzo.* Stanford, Calif.: Stanford University Press, 1965.

Wittenberg, Rudolph M. *The Troubled Generation.* New York: Association Press, 1967.

APPENDIX II

ANNOTATED LIST OF
DOCUMENTARY FILMS

There are many documentary films in the area of marriage and the family that have been used as teaching aids. Most of them, however, suffer in varying degrees from ethnocentrism in that they elaborate on a spectrum from soap opera to bathos, the pseudoproblems of the American middle-class family in a Hollywood version. In the list that follows we have tried to avoid this trap by stressing the cross-cultural approach so that the student and general reader may see themselves and their family problems in a more realistic sociocultural perspective.

In addition, an effort has been made to refute the view that the sociological and the artistic levels must be inherently incompatible. Each of the films listed has validity not only as sociology but also as art. This is attested to by the festival awards and other critical acclaim accompanying their public release. (All of these films are available in 16 mm. prints in order to facilitate college and university utilization.)

Come Back, Africa. 1959. Produced by Lionel Rogosin. Distributed by Contemporary Films, 267 West 25th Street, New York.

This film depicts what it is like to be a native in Johannesburg today. Made in secret (the South African police were told a musical travelogue was being filmed) with a nonprofessional cast, the thread of the story grew from actual experiences of the collaborators.

Children Adrift. 1958. Produced by Henri Diamant-Berger. Distributed by Contemporary Films, 267 West 25th Street, New York.

This film is "A compassionate study of a lonely boy in a foreign-refugee camp outside Paris." It is a poetic document concerned with the upheaval suffered by one boy as a result of World War II.

Phoebe—Story of Premarital Pregnancy. 1965. Produced by the National Film Board of Canada. Distributed by McGraw-Hill Text-Films, 330 West 42nd Street, New York.

This film deals with the mental and emotional reactions of Phoebe, a teenager, when she discovers that she is pregnant. It reveals her thoughts about telling her parents, her boyfriend, and school authorities, and it dramatizes their various possible reactions to her.

The Neglected. 1965. Produced by the Mental Health Film Board. Distributed by Contemporary Films, 267 West 25th Street, New York.

This film deals with the impact of poverty on the mental health of families. It shows how the professional staff of child protective services can change the pattern of family relationships that have threatened the health and emotional well-being of the children.

Four Families. 1960. Produced by the National Film Board of Canada. Distributed by McGraw-Hill Book Co., 330 West 42nd Street, New York.

This film depicts family life in India, Japan, France, and Canada, with a commentary by Margaret Mead. It focuses on the care and attention accorded a one-year-old baby in each of these cultures. Miss Mead's contention is that different patterns of socialization determine the social character of each nation.

Apu Trilogy: The World of Apu. 1959. Distributed by Audio Film Center, 10 Fiske Place, Mount Vernon, New York.

Apu Trilogy by Satyajit Ray, as well as his more recent films *Devi, Nayak,* and *Mahanagar* dramatize for the Bengali region of India what has been man's fate in the West much earlier, namely the transitions and culture conflicts involved between rural and urban life, villages and cities, traditional religion and modern science, and patriarchal and equalitarian norms. In addition, it also shows the changes in roles of husband and wife and parents and children.

5½—Reflection on an Age. 1966. Produced by Robert Newman. Distributed by United Church Board for Homeland Ministries, 287 Park Avenue South, New York.

This film deals with a five-and-one-half-year-old Negro boy's anxieties regarding his marginality in American society. It depicts the external pressures of his environment and then goes on to show how these become internalized and are subsequently expressed in the form of self-rejection.

Faces in the Shadows. 1953. Distributed by Cinema 16 Film Library, 80 University Place, New York.

This is an impressionistic film made by Peter Weiss which dramatizes the loneliness and sense of futility of the aged in urban Sweden. It shows that their behavior is characterized by the same sense of despair as that of the aged in any society in which the older generation has become dysfunctional.

Day Shall Dawn. 1959. Produced by Asejay Kardar. Distributed by Contemporary Films, 267 West 25th Street, New York.

This film is a dramatization of Bengal village life, with a good eye for the material details. The story involves the clash between rich and poor and traditional and modern patterns.

INDEX

June Bingham is the biographer of Rheinhold Niebuhr and U Thant and the coauthor, with Dr. Fritz Redlich, of "The Inside Story: Psychiatry in Everyday Life."

Carl N. Degler is a professor of history at Vassar College, Poughkeepsie, New York.

Francis X. Femminella is an assistant professor of sociology at the State University of New York at Albany.

Sidney M. Greenfield is in the Department of Anthropology at the University of Wisconsin, Milwaukee.

Alexander J. Humphreys is an associate professor at Loyola University, Los Angeles, California.

George C. Keller of Columbia University, is the editor of *Columbia College Today*.

Kenneth Keniston is an assistant professor of psychology in the Department of Psychiatry at the Yale Medical School, New Haven, Connecticut.

Robert A. LeVine is an associate professor of anthropology in The Committee of Human Development at the University of Chicago, Illinois.

Talcott Parsons is a professor of sociology at Harvard University, Cambridge, Massachusetts.

Ping-ti Ho is a professor of Chinese history at The University of Chicago, Illinois.

Lee Rainwater is a professor of sociology and anthropology at Washington University, St. Louis, Missouri, and a research associate in the university's Social Science Institute.

Aileen D. Ross is a professor of sociology at McGill University, Montreal, Canada.

Alice S. Rossi is a research associate in the Department of Sociology at the University of Chicago, Illinois.

Robert Veit Sherwin is an attorney, author, and national authority on laws relating to sex. He is also Administrative Director of the Society for the Scientific Study of Sex.

Jan Stehouwer is a lecturer at the University of Åarhus, Denmark.

Ezra F. Vogel is Associate Director, East Asian Research Center of Harvard University, Cambridge, Massachusetts.

37   196PT   **6204**
05/96   03-204-00   GBC